Presidential Primaries and the Dynamics of Public Choice

LARRY M. BARTELS

Presidential Primaries and the Dynamics of Public Choice

Princeton University Press
Princeton, New Jersey

Published by Princeton University Press, 41 William Street,
Princeton, New Jersey 08540
In the United Kingdom: Princeton University Press, Guildford, Surrey

Library of Congress Cataloging-in-Publication Data will be
found on the last printed page of this book

ISBN 0–691–07765–7
02283–6 (pbk.)

This book has been composed in Linotron Baskerville

Clothbound editions of Princeton University Press books
are printed on acid-free paper, and binding materials are
chosen for strength and durability. Paperbacks, although satisfactory
for personal collections, are not usually suitable for library rebinding

Printed in the United States of America by Princeton University Press,
Princeton, New Jersey

To Elizabeth Murphy Bartels—
my dynamic phenomenon of choice

CONTENTS

LIST OF ILLUSTRATIONS

LIST OF TABLES

PREFACE

The idea of writing this book goes back at least to 1976, when I began both to study the presidential nominating process under the tutelage of F. Christopher Arterton and observe the dynamics of the process at work in the triumph of Jimmy Carter. I put the idea aside for several years, believing that the process was too complex and historical experience too limited for an analysis of the sort I envisioned to be feasible.

By 1980 I was ready to begin again, and I remember being delighted as well as provoked when three different friends—all reasonably sophisticated liberal Democrats—began to talk enthusiastically about George Bush in the weeks following his dramatic emergence in the 1980 Iowa Republican caucuses. Their enthusiasm for Bush soon faded, but my own fascination with a process that could produce such enthusiasm continued to grow. In the spring of 1980 I produced a preliminary statistical analysis of the year's primary outcomes in an effort to sort out the role of momentum in the presidential nominating process.

During the next few years I expanded and refined my analysis of primary outcomes, eventually producing a dissertation with the same title as this book but corresponding roughly in focus to the current Chapters 2, 8, 9, 10, and 12. I wrote that dissertation for the department of political science at the University of California, Berkeley, and I must continue to thank my teachers and fellow students there for advice and encouragement.

The main weaknesses of my dissertation, in my own estimation, were its lack of grounding in the actual psychology of individual primary voters and its lack of a general organizing principle for the very different experiences of recent primary campaigns. However, the additional material in this book is intended to remedy those two weaknesses: I provide both a detailed analysis of individual attitudes and perceptions in a nominating campaign (Chapters 3 through 6) and an explicit connection between individual-level political behavior and the variations observable across campaigns at the aggregate level (most explicitly in Chapter 7, but also in the revised analysis presented in Chapters 8, 9, and 10).

A detailed analysis of individual attitudes and perceptions in the preconvention period became possible when the National Election

Studies (NES) began to conduct extensive, high-quality opinion surveys at the right times. My first individual-level analysis of preferences and expectations in a nominating campaign (Bartels 1985) was based on data gathered by the NES in spring 1980. The analysis reported in a subsequent article (Bartels 1987) used 1984 NES data, as does much analysis in this book. Like all scholars interested in elections and political behavior, I am indebted to the National Science Foundation for its support of these and other NES data collection efforts.

During the past few summers my own research has also been supported directly by the National Science Foundation, allowing me to proceed with my work much more quickly and efficiently than I might otherwise have done. I owe this good fortune, and much else, to my friend, teacher, and collaborator, Henry Brady. As a member of my dissertation committee at Berkeley he was sufficiently provoked by the limitations of my work to want to do better. But in the process of doing better he has continued to carry me along, serving as a collaborator in an intellectual as well as an administrative sense. His series of papers on the primary process has been a source of considerable insight and inspiration, particularly as I wrestled with the large issues of institutional evaluation and design addressed in Chapter 11. His forthcoming book comparing the primary and convention systems will be of considerable interest to anyone wanting to pursue the political and institutional questions raised by my analysis.

During the course of my research and writing I have incurred intellectual debts to many other friends and colleagues, at the University of Rochester and elsewhere. Nelson Polsby, another member of my dissertation committee at Berkeley, allowed me to draw on his considerable insight into the origins and political implications of the contemporary presidential nominating process. Two fellow students of that process, John Geer and Elaine Kamarck, shared their own unpublished dissertations with me; Geer also provided helpful comments on my manuscript. Doug Rivers at Cal Tech and Merrill Shanks at Berkeley each gave me an opportunity in a very pleasant setting to try out an early version of my argument at a key stage in its development.

Two of my students at Rochester, Larry Evans and Paul Janaskie, provided very capable research assistance. The University of Rochester itself and my department chairmen, Bruce Bueno de Mesquita and Bing Powell, have been eminently supportive. My colleague Ted Bluhm served as a kindred soul and sounding board for my struggles, reflected in Chapter 12, with the philosophical limitations of the classical theory of public choice. And Dick Fenno has helped impress upon me the importance and feasibility of writing a book addressing the central political issues at stake in the presidential nominating process, not just the more parochial concerns of the existing academic literature.

I also owe a special debt of gratitude to my principal dissertation adviser, Christopher Achen. His prompt and patient assistance while I was writing the dissertation led to numerous specific improvements that survive in the following pages; and his more recent reading of the revised manuscript led to additional improvements. But more importantly, the spirit and basic thrust of my work owe much to his instruction and example.

Several other friends read and commented on the manuscript in various stages of completion. I am particularly grateful for the detailed suggestions about style and substance provided by John Zaller (for Part II) and Harold Stanley. I am also very grateful to Stanley Kelley and Steven Rosenstone for providing remarkably wise, thorough, and constructive reviews of the entire manuscript on behalf of Princeton University Press, to John Sheedy for drawing the numerous illustrations, and to Sandy Thatcher, Lydia Jeanne Duncan, Lisa Nowak Jerry, Charles Ault, and the staff of the Press for turning the manuscript into a real book.

Finally, I want to thank my family for their love and support. My parents provided my first education and paid for a second, expecting nothing more in return for either than the pleasure of seeing me become wise and happy. At least I am happy. That fact I owe largely to them, and to my best friend Denise. Unlike most wives in prefaces, she did no typing, read no drafts, and made no suggestions. Her interests lie elsewhere. For the sake of my sanity and perspective I wouldn't have it any other way.

All of the above-named persons will, I trust, pardon the dedication of this book to someone who made no direct contribution at all to its completion—my first child. She did at least provide a powerful incentive for closure, arriving three weeks after the finished manuscript. Perhaps for that reason, I think of them as a pair. Both were fun to make. But now the book is finished. With Elizabeth the real fun is just beginning.

Rochester, New York
May 1987

PART I

The Notion of Momentum

CHAPTER ONE

The Nominating Process

AT THE BEGINNING OF 1976, Jimmy Carter was a relatively unknown one-term exgovernor of a medium-sized southern state. Although he had been running for president full-time for more than a year, he had failed to attract the public support of any major national political figure. A Gallup poll indicated that fewer than 5 percent of the Democratic party rank and file considered him their first choice for the party's nomination.

Five months later, Carter was quite clearly about to become his party's nominee. The last primaries in California, New Jersey, and Ohio had left him with more than 70 percent of the delegates he needed to win; most of his major opponents had dropped out of the race; and Chicago's Mayor Daley had, in effect, announced that the party's remaining unaligned politicians considered Carter unstoppable. Among the public, Carter was the first choice of an absolute majority of Democrats—leading his nearest rival by a margin of almost forty percentage points—and a winner by almost twenty percentage points in trial heats against the incumbent Republican president.

The events that transformed the Carter of January into the Carter of June seemed to have little to do with politics in the traditional sense—ideologies, interests, or public policies. Carter proposed no innovative solutions to the major problems facing the country, nor did he mobilize any new and potent combination of powerful social groups. What he did manage, it seems clear in retrospect, was to exploit more successfully than anyone else before or since the strategic possibilities inherent in the contemporary presidential nominating process. Beginning with intensive personal campaigning in Iowa and New Hampshire, he parlayed early victories into media attention, resources, and popular support sufficient to produce later victories and eventual nomination. The key to success, it appeared, was not to enter the campaign with a broad coalition of political support, but to rely on the dynamics of the campaign itself, particularly its earliest public phases, to generate that support.

A plaintive but largely accurate account of Carter's success was offered after the fact by one of his chief rivals, Morris Udall (quoted by Witcover 1977: 692–93).

> We had thirty primaries, presumably all of them equal. After three of those primaries, I'm convinced, it was all over. The die was cast. Just imagine the whole process being completed by Carter who wins New Hampshire by twenty-nine to my twenty-four, he comes in fourth in Massachusetts, and then he beats Wallace by three percentage points in Florida. In the ensuing two weeks he shot up twenty-five points in the Gallup Poll, almost without precedent, by winning two primaries and coming in fourth in another one.
>
> If there was a state in America where I was entitled to relax and feel confident, it was Wisconsin. I'd been there thirty times and I had organization, newspaper endorsements, and all the congressmen and state legislators. Well, I take a poll two weeks before the primary and he's ahead of me, two to one, and has never been in the state except for a few quick visits. That was purely and solely and only the product of that narrow win in New Hampshire and the startling win in Florida. And he won there only because everybody wanted to get rid of George Wallace.
>
> It's like a football game, in which you say to the first team that makes a first down with ten yards, "Hereafter your team has a special rule. Your first downs are five yards. And if you make three of those you get a two-yard first down. And we're going to let your first touchdown count twenty-one points. Now the rest of you bastards play catch-up under the regular rules."

Although Carter has been the most dramatic beneficiary of Udall's "special rules," he has by no means been the only candidate hoping to play the game on such favorable terms. George McGovern, George Bush, John Anderson, Gary Hart, and others have all followed, or tried to follow, similar paths in recent campaigns. None has succeeded to the same degree, but all have adapted their strategies to the possibility that they too might break out of the pack, leaving others to "play catch-up." That possibility is at the heart of the phenomenon campaign observers have come to call "momentum."

Despite its recognized political importance, momentum has a certain ineffable quality about it. Experts claim to know it when they see it, but they are not very good at either defining or describing it. Thus, Arterton (1978a: 10) wrote that "journalists and campaigners speak of the importance of 'momentum,' a vague conception that the campaign is expanding, gaining new supporters, and meeting (or, if possible, overachieving) its goals." Aldrich (1980a: 100) argued that "momentum and related dynamic concepts . . . are important (if often difficult to observe) aspects of all campaigns." And Reeves (1977: 180), with journalistic succinctness, called momentum "the political cliché used to describe what is happening when no one is sure."

My aim in this book is to explore more systematically the nature and impact of momentum in the contemporary presidential nominating process. I focus on the complex interconnections among initial primary results, expectations, and subsequent primary results that make it possible for a candidate like Carter, Bush, or Hart to emerge from relative obscurity into political prominence in a matter of days or weeks—and on the individual political behavior that produces those interconnections. My hope is that momentum may come to be viewed as something more concrete and more significant than a vacuous journalistic cliché.

1.1 The Process in Outline

Presidential elections are relatively uncomplicated. There are always two major candidates, one representing the incumbent party and the other an established opposition party. Elections are decided primarily by relatively stable partisan loyalties and by the incumbent party's recent success (or lack of success) in managing the economy. As a result, although much of the psychology and sociology of the individual voter's choice remains mysterious, election outcomes can be predicted in advance with considerable accuracy (for example, by Rosenstone 1983).

The process by which each party chooses its candidate for the presidency presents quite another picture. Instead of two contenders there may be half a dozen or more. Some candidates may be well-known political figures; others may be virtually unknown to the electorate. The issues dividing them may have little to do with the issues on which the winner will eventually wage the general election campaign. And they compete in fifty separate state-level delegate selection processes governed by a bizarre assortment of complex rules.

In addition, and perhaps most importantly, the modern presidential nominating process has a dynamic aspect unmatched by any other electoral process. Its key institutional feature is that individual state primaries are spread over a period of three and a half months. As the focus of attention moves around the country from week to week, politicians, journalists, and the public use the results in each state to adjust their own expectations and behavior at subsequent stages in the process. One week's outcome becomes an important part of the political context shaping the following week's choices. Thus, each primary must be interpreted not as a final result but as a single episode in the series of interrelated political events that together determine the nominee.

In view of these complicating features, it should not be surprising that analysts, observers, and pundits courageous enough to predict the outcomes of recent nominating campaigns have routinely been embarrassed. In 1972 they settled on Edmund Muskie as the Democratic nominee; in the event, Muskie faded early, and the nomination was actually won by a relative unknown named George McGovern. For 1976 the standard scenario had a deadlocked Democratic convention turning to Hubert Humphrey; but Carter's early blitzkrieg kept Humphrey out of the race, and the party's would-be power brokers spent the month between the end of the primary season and the opening of the convention making well-publicized pilgrimages to Carter's front porch in Plains. On the Republican side, Ronald Reagan was counted out after a series of early primary defeats, but he came back to force a see-saw contest all the way to the convention. Reagan in 1980 and Walter Mondale in 1984 were supposed to win their parties' nominations with little difficulty, but nobody told George Bush and Gary Hart.

In addition to producing some surprising results, campaigns since 1972 have reflected some important shifts in the traditional balance of power among the various participants in the presidential nominating process. Most obviously, the proliferation of primaries has increased the power of the active segment of the voting public that participates in primaries, at the expense of professional party elites. But there have been other winners and losers as well. Convention delegates, their deliberative role having largely disappeared with the advent of mass public choice, have become increasingly subservient to the candidate organizations they are elected to support. And the media—particularly the elite segment of the press licensed to analyze national electoral politics—has gained an important long-running story, complete with a cavalcade of varied and colorful weekly contests to be previewed, reported, and interpreted. Indeed, the attention of the media is an essential element in the dynamics of momentum, injecting the workways of journalists into the electoral process in an important new way.

Finally, the importance of early results in generating momentum has given disproportional influence to states whose primaries or caucuses happen to occur early in the nominating season. New Hampshire has jealously guarded its traditional first-in-the-nation primary, and Iowa has done likewise with its more recent monopoly of the opening caucuses. The jealousy is hardly suprising: the tremendous concentration of the attention of politicians, the press, and the public on these states for two weeks every four years would be good for the hotel business, even if it had no impact at all on who gets nominated. Of course, it does have an important impact on who gets nominated—an impact no candidate can afford to ignore.

1.2 Some Basic Issues

Political observers have debated the pros and cons of nearly every aspect of the contemporary presidential nominating process—the role of the media, the role of money, the openness of the process, its complexity, and even its efficacy as a vehicle for mass political education. But the most heated debates have focused on the most central question of all—the quality of nominees produced by the process. One side argues that nominees are now less indebted to party bosses, more representative of the party rank and file, and more extensively tested than ever before. The other side argues that they are warped by the experience of spending months, sometimes years, building intense factional support among minorities of the minority of the public who participate in presidential primaries and caucuses.

Some of the heat on both sides of these debates is attributable to the widespread perception that the process has not yet reached a stable institutional equilibrium and that opportunities still exist to shape it to any of a variety of political ends. As we shall see in Chapter 2, today's process arose from a quite remarkable episode of political reform. Continued tinkering with less central aspects of the system every four years since has accustomed political activists and political scientists alike to think of every imperfection of the system as a reason to propose some further institutional reform. For some, the heartfelt, if somewhat unrealistic, ideal is a return to the good old days of strong national conventions dominated by party elites. Others want and expect a national presidential primary as the logical conclusion to the historical pattern of increasing public participation in the nominating process. Still others have different goals and correspondingly different plans.

The extent to which all of these various debates and plans for reform flourish in the absence of any sophisticated understanding of how the modern presidential nominating process actually works, or of how it would work differently if the rules were changed, is striking. What would happen if the recent trend toward "front-loading" of primaries early in the campaign season was accelerated and formalized? What is the optimal length of time between primaries? How many candidates are too many? The answers to interesting practical questions like these depend on the answers to more basic empirical and theoretical questions—questions that debaters interested in reform have seldom bothered to examine in any serious way. For example, how do fundamental political predispositions influence the behavior of primary voters? How quickly does the public learn about new candidates? Under what circumstances will primary success itself generate subsequent primary success? And what are the psychological processes underlying this dynamic tendency? Any evaluation of the nominating process that is more than disguised prejudice and any reform that is more than accidentally successful in promoting the values of its proponents will have to be built on some systematic answers to questions like these.

A sophisticated evaluation of the nominating process must also deal with some basic issues at a higher and more abstract level. Given the dynamic nature of the nominating process, what does it mean to say that a candidate is "representative" of the party's primary voters? Is the point of the process to represent individual voters' preferences at the moment they happen to cast their ballots? Or the preferences they might have at some later point when more fully informed? How do we count preferences that might have been, preferences for candidates who have dropped out of the race, or, for that matter, for candidates who never got into the race in the first place? Statements of abstract principle that may seem unproblematic in less complex settings tend to unravel when applied to processes of public choice in which there are strong and salient dynamic elements.

The complexity of the contemporary presidential nominating process and its tendency to produce varied and unexpected results has led some observers to discount the possibility of explaining primary outcomes in any systematic way. This pessimistic view has

presidents faced serious opposition, two in which larger and more fragmented fields of candidates included a single more or less dominant figure, and one in which there was a large field with no clear preprimary favorite.

The analyses of primary outcomes in these chapters provide considerable additional support for the proposition that momentum is an important factor in the contemporary nominating process. Although the results vary considerably from race to race, in at least two instances the impact of momentum appears to have been decisive in the choice of a nominee. To the extent that such things can be demonstrated in retrospect, it seems likely that both Jimmy Carter and Gerald Ford owed their nominations in 1976 to the political benefits they derived from momentum. In a system without the dynamic forces operating in the contemporary nominating process—for example, in a one-day national primary system—neither candidate would have been nominated.

Despite the tendency of some political observers to belittle the impact of election outcomes on the wider political system, I believe that Carter's performance in the White House was sufficiently distinctive to make reasonable people care that he was the Democratic nominee rather than, say, Henry Jackson or Morris Udall. Similarly, the significance of Ford's nomination on the Republican side has been reinforced by the performance in office of the man who would have won the Republican nomination in 1976 if Ford had not, Ronald Reagan.

In addition to demonstrating the decisive importance of momentum under specific political circumstances, my analysis goes some way toward providing the systematic theory of primary voting across campaign settings which Ceaser considered so unlikely. I show that the marked differences in the manifest effect of momentum from one campaign to another can be accounted for by the same basic explanatory factors and interactions among those explanatory factors addressed in Part II. In particular, the same fundamental political effects of uncertainty described in Part II can be shown to produce the general pattern of aggregate results described in Part III. Finally, at the aggregate level as at the individual level, my analysis provides evidence regarding the impact of factors other than momentum on primary voting. Indeed, the analysis as a whole amounts to a reasonably complete picture of the ideological, regional, demographic, and other factors that shape primary outcomes across the range of primary states.

Part IV offers some perspective regarding the implications of my empirical analysis for broad political and theoretical questions of the sort raised in Section 1.2. In Chapter 11 the emphasis is on political institutions. Who wins and who loses in the contemporary nominating process? To what extent does the process facilitate the parties' efforts to deal with fundamental political issues? What are the prospects for, and the likely consequences of, further reform of the nominating process?

Chapter 12 serves as a kind of epilogue to the main body of the book. It addresses, although it certainly does not resolve, fundamental questions of abstract theory having to do with the nature and logic of public choice. What basic principles should an electoral system satisfy? Are those principles compatible with the peculiar demands of a process in which political issues are relatively unstructured, uncertainty is rampant, and change is endemic? Can a theory of democracy based on an essentially static view of human preferences be adapted to a dynamic world? If not, how might a more adequate theory accommodate and reflect the inherent dynamics of public choice?

Much of my analysis throughout this book is based on the application, both to data from public opinion surveys and to actual primary outcomes, of statistical models that can only be described precisely in the relatively arcane and technical terms familiar to specialists. In the body of the book I have attempted, as much as possible, to avoid the language of statistics and speak in the more familiar language of politics. I hope that general readers interested in following the substance of the argument—the basic outlines and political implications of the statistical results—will be able to do so without undue difficulty. Those wanting more detailed technical descriptions of the data, models, and parameter estimates on which my analysis is based will find them in the appendixes at the end of the book.

CHAPTER TWO

From Back Rooms to "Big Mo"

THE NOMINATING PROCESS described in Chapter 1 and analyzed throughout the remainder of this book is radically different from the process that existed a hundred, or fifty, or even twenty years ago. The new system is dominated by candidates and by the news media; the old system was dominated by professional party politicians. The central decision-making mechanism in the new system is mass voting; the central mechanism in the old system was face-to-face bargaining. The locus of choice in the new system is the primary ballot box; the locus of choice in the old system was the convention backroom. Every important feature of the contemporary nominating process was far less prominent in the process that gave us Franklin D. Roosevelt, Dwight D. Eisenhower, and (lest we forget) John W. Davis and Warren G. Harding.

Looking back, it is natural to ask whether the dramatic changes of recent years have been good or bad for the American political system. Many political analysts have attempted to answer that question; the answers, not surprisingly, have been as varied as the values and experiences of the analysts themselves.[1] My goal here is less ambitious. Rather than attempting to produce any systematic evaluation of the old and new nominating systems, I simply attempt to describe how the old system worked and how we got from there to here. The story, sketchy as it is, provides some historical perspective on the process that exists today.

2.1 The Old System

The first effective presidential nominations were made by congressional caucuses—groups of party elites conveniently gathered to-

[1] Major works addressing the political merits of the contemporary nominating process include Polsby's *Consequences of Party Reform* (1983), Ceaser's *Presidential Selection* (1979) and *Reforming the Reforms* (1982), and Crotty's *Decision for the Democrats* (1978) and *Party Reform* (1983). Both Polsby and Ceaser are critical of the current system. Ceaser's perspective is primarily historical; Polsby's is wider ranging, relating the structure of the contemporary nominating process to the institutional decline of parties, the nature of candidate appeals, and the governing styles of the

gether in Washington, yet, at least loosely and indirectly, "representing" their constituents in the country. Before long, however, the looseness and indirectness of the relationship—for example, some districts were shut out of a given party's congressional caucus—generated complaints that "King Caucus" was insufficiently responsive to public opinion in the country as a whole. As a result, during a period of twenty years or so centered around the presidencies of Andrew Jackson and his political lieutenant Martin Van Buren, the parties gradually developed a system of national conventions whose major function was to nominate candidates for the presidency.

For many years these conventions were attended exclusively by delegates chosen at state and local party conventions. But the wave of progressive reforms at the beginning of the twentieth century initiated an important modification of the convention system: the direct election or instruction of some delegates by party "masses" in state-level presidential primaries. Use of the primary system reached an early peak in 1916, when twenty states held primaries, but declined somewhat thereafter. From 1920 to 1968, an average of fifteen states held primaries before each convention, and about 40 percent of all delegates were chosen or bound by primary voting (Arterton 1978a: 7).

The resulting system, in which limited primary voting was overlayed on the nineteenth century's boss-dominated, convention-centered process, has been referred to by Polsby and Wildavsky (1976: 225), Ceaser (1979), and others as a "mixed system." But the mix was far from being an equal one, as Ceaser has pointed out (1979: 228–30). During the fifty years or so that the "mixed system" remained virtually unchanged, several candidates successfully employed "inside strategies," relying primarily on private appeals to party leaders. Herbert Hoover and Al Smith in 1928, Franklin Roosevelt in 1932, Adlai Stevenson in 1952, and Hubert Humphrey in 1968 are all examples of successful "inside" candidates. By contrast, no candidate (with the possible exception of Dwight Eisenhower in 1952) ever succeeded with an "outside strategy," based on aggressive appeals to the party rank and file. Some—for example, Harold Stassen in 1948 and Estes Kefauver in 1952 and 1956—failed in spite of their demonstrated considerable popular appeal during the primary season.

---

presidents who survive the process. Crotty's treatment is more sympathetic to the work of the reformers and more sceptical about the virtues of the older elite-dominated system.

Although a large number of convention delegates were formally selected in presidential primaries, a variety of institutional barriers faced candidates trying to run successful primary-centered campaigns. Some primaries were mere "beauty contests," with no direct bearing on delegate selection. In several states where delegates were directly elected, their election was insulated from national political currents by legal means, including prohibitions on the identification of prospective delegates' candidate preferences on the primary ballot. In other states, most notably California and Ohio, a tradition of "favorite son" candidacies often effectively barred outsiders from competing in the primaries. The result, as Ceaser (1979: 227) noted, was that "while somewhere between forty and fifty percent of the delegates in each party were chosen in primaries, the actual percentage that any national candidate could hope to win was considerably less."

As a result, the main function of primaries during this period, from the candidates' viewpoints, was to provide a public arena for tests of electoral strength. Often the real goal was not to win the delegates directly at stake in a primary but to demonstrate the candidate's popularity to the party leaders who actually controlled the convention. The classic example is John Kennedy in 1960, whose victory in the West Virginia primary was crucial not because it brought a handful of West Virginia delegates but because it convinced powerful party leaders in other states that Kennedy could win Protestant votes in a general election.

Obviously, the best of both worlds was a candidate with broad support from both the party bosses and the general public. But in the absence of such an ideal solution, it was clear whose preferences would prove decisive. From the perspective of the present, this is the most striking feature of the old nominating process: if push came to shove, power rested in the hands of the party leaders.

The goals of those party leaders were concisely characterized by Polsby and Wildavsky (1964: 64): "to gain power, to nominate a man who can win the election, to unify the party, to obtain some claim on the nominee, to protect their central core of policy preferences, and to strengthen their state party organizations." To a considerable extent, these goals were reflected in the actual selection of nominees under the old system. Most, though far from all, nominations by both parties followed a common political pattern identified by David, Goldman, and Bain (1960: 93–95): the nominees were men of basically moderate political views, between fifty and fifty-five years of age, incumbent governors or cabinet members of proven executive ability and proven electoral appeal, from populous, competitive states.[2]

The basic mechanism by which party leaders attempted to achieve their goals was face-to-face political bargaining, with each other and with the candidates. Hence the "smoke-filled rooms" of political lore, in which party bosses, prominent elected officials, and candidates and their managers wheeled and dealed, exchanging blocs of delegate support for policy concessions, patronage, and other plums up to and including the vice presidency. Backroom deals were facilitated by the fact that a relatively small number of major party figures (governors, big city mayors, and state party chairmen) often controlled substantial blocs of delegates. In most states party leaders simply selected members of their organizations to serve as national convention delegates; elsewhere primary voters chose delegates, also likely to be party officials or workers.

A survey of convention delegates in 1948 found that four-fifths "regularly attended state and county party organization meetings," and that three-fifths "either were or had been state party officers" (David, Goldman, and Bain 1960: 181). These delegates could never afford to forget that, as Polsby and Wildavsky (1964: 62) put it, they spent "1400 days every four years as members of their state parties and less than a week at the national convention." The most important consequence of their party ties was that many were, for practical purposes, bound to follow the lead of the state party leaders to whom they owed their positions at the convention and at home. In the words of David, Goldman, and Bain (1960: 188),

> Although the individual delegate is the essential building block in the convention voting structure, the actual working unit for most purposes is the state delegation as a whole. In the process of its selection, by whatever method, a whole series of express or implied commitments has accumulated in regard to candidates, issues, and its relationship to state and national party organizations.

[2] Recent books on the nominating process often provide little more than caricatures of the pre-1968 system. For more detailed and balanced descriptions I referred to books written while the system itself was still alive and well. I have found the two works cited in this paragraph—David, Goldman, and Bain's *The Politics of National Party Conventions* (1960) and Polsby and Wildavsky's first edition of *Presidential Elections* (1964)—to be the best of the genre.

This network of commitments facilitated the main business of the convention, arriving at an agreement about who would be the party's candidate for the presidency. In a system with fewer primaries, less publicity, and more latitude for dealing than is available now, it was relatively common for a number of factional candidates to arrive at the convention with none commanding sufficient delegate strength to be nominated. Of the thirty-six party conventions between 1900 and 1968, roughly one-third involved significant factional conflict. Because the bargaining and consensus-building central to the process actually occurred at the convention, several ballots were sometimes required before any candidate emerged with majority support. The most colorful (and often cited) example of a multiballot convention came in 1924, when the Democrats needed 103 ballots over a ten-day period to settle on John W. Davis.[3]

The normative underpinning for this elite-dominated bargaining process was the notion that party competition could be counted upon to make politicians act in the public interest. According to an apt analogy proposed by E. E. Schattschneider (1942: 60),

> The parties do not need laws to make them sensitive to the wishes of the voters any more than we need laws compelling merchants to please their customers. The sovereignty of the voter consists in his freedom of choice just as the sovereignty of the consumer in the economic system consists in his freedom to trade in a competitive market.

Nominations were thus declared to be the business of the party regulars, and any question about the internal democracy of the process by which the parties nominated their candidates was ruled irrelevant. Characteristically for Schattschneider, all this was done with a well-turned aphorism (1942: 60): "Democracy is not to be found *in* the parties but *between* the parties."

2.2 Upheaval and Reform

The old system of presidential nominations was never as monolithic in practice as in the descriptions of some simplifiers and nos-

[3] The convention that nominated Davis, like all Democratic conventions until 1936, operated under a rule requiring a two-thirds majority for the winning candidate. Obviously, one effect of the two-thirds rule was to make it even less likely that any single candidate would enter the convention with sufficient support to win the nomination.

talgics. Most conventions were always single-ballot affairs; most delegates in both parties, as early as 1952, were first-timers; and the nominees they selected included such uncharacteristic characters as Wendell Wilkie, a business executive with no prior political experience.

In any event, by the late 1950s and early 1960s perceptive observers had noticed important changes in the nominating process. Convention stalemates were already becoming a thing of the past. Bloc voting by state delegations was on the decline.[4] And most importantly, the media and the public were becoming more important actors in the nominating process. "Since the early 1940's," David, Goldman, and Bain wrote (1960: 146),

> presidential nominating campaigns have been subject to real and significant changes, for which the combined impacts of the primaries, the public opinion polls, and the mass media of communication seem to be mainly responsible. The effect can be seen in many elements of the campaigns—in the augmented efforts of candidates (and their managers) to prove that they have popular support; in the marked rise of voter participation; and in the number of candidates already billed as popular national favorites that the conventions increasingly find at their doors on opening day.

In view of these trends, it seems clear that the old nominating process was doomed to extinction; some perceptive analysts even claimed it was already dead. Writing in the mid-1960s, James W. Davis (1967: 2) announced "a remarkable transformation in the process of nominating presidential candidates." This transformation of twenty years' duration flowed from precisely the trends noted by David and his colleagues: the increasing importance of the news media, the public, and especially primary voters. These changes point squarely in the direction of the modern nominating process. Nevertheless, the transformation announced by Davis—if it had stopped in 1967—would have left us with a very different process than the one we have today. The political events of the following year highlight the extent of the differences and go a long way toward explaining the specific institutional changes that followed.

[4] Documentation for these trends and for the characteristics of the old system referred to in the previous paragraph was presented by David, Goldman, and Bain (1960: 214–16, 185, 95, 243, 191).

At this crucial turning point, 1968, an already nearly obsolete process was buffeted by an incredible series of political shocks.[5] In January the Viet Cong and North Vietnamese regulars launched a major offensive against U. S. troops in South Vietnam. In March an unheralded antiwar maverick, Senator Eugene McCarthy, challenged incumbent president Lyndon Johnson in New Hampshire and won 42 percent of the primary vote. A Johnson write-in effort won 48 percent of the vote, but the results were widely interpreted as a "moral victory" for McCarthy and a major embarrassment for the president. Four days later Senator Robert Kennedy—heir to the president whose assassination had put Johnson in the White House in the first place—hastily entered the race in time to compete in the later primaries. Two weeks later Johnson appeared in a dramatic national television broadcast to announce the beginning of a long search for peace in Vietnam and his own shocking decision not to seek reelection. Johnson's vice president, Hubert Humphrey, threw his hat into the ring within a month, but he decided that it was too late and too politically dangerous to compete in the primaries. In April the assassination of civil rights leader Martin Luther King, Jr., set off rioting in the nation's black ghettos. Then in June, on the final night of a bitter primary season, Robert Kennedy, too, was shot and killed.

In August the party regulars, many of whom were already selected as delegates before any of these events occurred, succeeded in nominating Humphrey at the Democratic convention in Chicago. To this extent the backroom system triumphed one last time; however, by then the party was hopelessly divided. The final disaster came on the very night of Humphrey's triumph, as the television cameras cut from the convention hall to show Mayor Daley's Chicago police battling with young anti-Humphrey demonstrators in the streets outside. Humphrey's nomination—and the nominating process itself—had been "stained with blood."[6]

Even before the Chicago convention, demands for reform had been coming from the left wing of the Democratic party. Supporters of McCarthy and Kennedy believed their candidates were being robbed of the nomination by a system rigged in favor of the established party leaders. Certainly procedural irregularities, such

[5] My account of the events of 1968 and their effect on the subsequent shape of the nominating process follows closely that of Polsby (1980; 1983: chap. 1). The best book-length historical account was written by three British journalists (Chester, Hodgson, and Page 1969).

[6] The phrase is Theodore White's (1969: 301).

as unpublicized "public" caucuses, were not hard to find. Humphrey, himself an inveterate reformer in a somewhat older style, supported the creation of a party commission to make the nominating process fairer and more open.

After Chicago, and Humphrey's subsequent defeat in the general election, the impetus for change was, if anything, stronger and broader based. The most important of a quadrennial series of Democratic party reform efforts was launched with the creation of a commission initially chaired by Senator George McGovern, a leading figure in the party's liberal wing. The McGovern–Fraser commission, as it came to be called, set itself the task of rewriting party rules so as to give all rank-and-file Democrats the opportunity for "full, meaningful, and timely" participation in the nominating process.[7]

The normative basis for the McGovern–Fraser reforms included an explicit rejection of the claim that nominations are the business of party leaders. A generation earlier Schattschneider may have been correct in believing that "the ordinary partisan . . . has rarely exhibited a strong desire to run the party, any more than the ordinary baseball fan really wants to manage the club" (1942: 56). But by the late 1960s at least some of the fans were getting distinctly restless. The demand for greater public participation in the nominating process was one aspect of a broader political agenda centered in the left wing of the Democratic party and focusing on the role of ordinary citizens in the political system. As a tract of the period put it, "the choice facing the American people [is] whether or not they will demand a greater voice in decisions affecting the world in which they live or whether they will leave such decisions to professional party elites, officeholders, bureaucrats, or others" (Saloma and Sontag 1972: 352).

Such demands for participation provided the guiding impetus for the party's reform efforts. According to one academic activist, "The reformers want[ed] a direct correspondence between the individual party member and national-level decisions, a relationship that deemphasizes the role and contributions of any intermediate agencies" (Crotty 1978: 269). And the McGovern–Fraser commission itself defended its recommendations in similar terms. "We believe," it announced in its report (Democratic Party 1970: 49), "that popular participation is more than a proud heritage of our party,

[7] The best and most detailed study of the actual process of reform is Byron Shafer's *Quiet Revolution* (1984).

more even than a first principle. We believe that popular control of the Democratic Party is necessary for its survival." Schattschneider notwithstanding, the real or imagined desire of ordinary partisans to run the party had become a considerable force for change in the political system.

The specific guidelines produced by the McGovern–Fraser commission required five important changes in the Democratic party's procedures for delegate selection. Each change sought quite directly to address a major complaint of the insurgent factions in the 1968 campaign. First, to prevent the selection of delegates before the campaign was even underway, the commission interpreted "timeliness" to require that delegate selection procedures in each state begin during the calendar year of the convention. Second, to open the delegate selection process to rank-and-file party members, the commission required "adequate public notice" for every step in that process. Third, the common practice of providing delegate positions automatically to certain party or public officials was prohibited as being inconsistent with the demands of "full, meaningful, and timely" participation by the "party rank and file."[8] Fourth, opportunities for participation by certain minorities (blacks, women, and people under thirty years of age) "in reasonable relationship to their presence in the population" were to be guaranteed by "affirmative steps." In 1972 these "affirmative steps" included actual quotas, but the controversy surrounding the quota system led to its subsequent abandonment in favor of a somewhat looser affirmative action standard. Finally, fair representation of rank-and-file candidate preferences was held to prohibit the use of the unit rule, which allocated all of a state's delegates to the candidate receiving a plurality of votes in the state. The commission encouraged the adoption of proportional representation systems in which any candidate receiving at least 15 percent of the primary vote in a state would get some delegates; however, the so-called "loophole" system in which the unit rule is applied at the congressional district level was still allowed.

2.3 The Emergence of Momentum

Taken collectively, the institutional reforms triggered by the Democratic debacle of 1968 transformed the presidential nominating

[8] This provision was weakened by subsequent reform commissions. In 1984, almost 15 percent of the seats at the Democratic convention were set aside for representatives of the party's congressional delegation.

process. The old system, dominated by party regulars meeting in national conventions, was gone for good. In its place emerged—almost immediately in its essentials, but with marginal adjustments still to come—the nominating process as we know it today. One of the most significant consequences of the reforms was a rapid growth in the number of presidential primaries, first among Democrats but, with a slight lag, on the Republican side as well.[9] As a result, as Figure 2.1 makes clear, the number of delegates selected in primaries also increased precipitously—from 40 percent in 1968 to about 60 percent in 1972 and more than 70 percent in 1976.

Ironically, this consequence seems not to have been intended, or even foreseen, by the reformers themselves. According to Austin Ranney (1975: 205–6), a political scientist and member of the McGovern–Fraser commission,

> most of the commissioners strongly preferred a reformed national convention to a national presidential primary or a major increase in the number of state presidential primaries. And we believed that if we made the party's nonprimary delegate selection processes more open and fair, participation in them would increase greatly and consequently the demand for more primaries would fade away. But quite the opposite happened. Since 1969 no fewer than eight states have newly adopted primaries, and in 1976 nearly 70 percent of all the delegates will be chosen or bound by them, as compared with less than half in 1968 and before. . . . In a majority of the eight states the state Democratic parties, who controlled the governorships and both houses of the legislatures, decided that rather than radically revising their accustomed ways of conducting caucuses and conventions for other party matters it would be better to split off the process for selecting national convention delegates and let it be conducted by a state-administered primary which the national party would have to accept.

In fewer words, party regulars unenthusiastic about the possible effects of public participation in matters of central (local) party

[9] Not all observers agree that the boom in primaries was actually precipitated by the reforms. For alternative explanations see Bode and Casey (1980). Recent changes in the rules governing the Republican nominating process have tended, in general, to follow the initiatives of the Democrats. Although no major internal struggle in the Republican party paralleled the Democrats', there have been significant institutional changes (Crotty and Jackson 1985: 44–49). These changes seem to have been spurred by both simple emulation and the need to adjust to changes in state primary laws promulgated by Democratic legislatures.

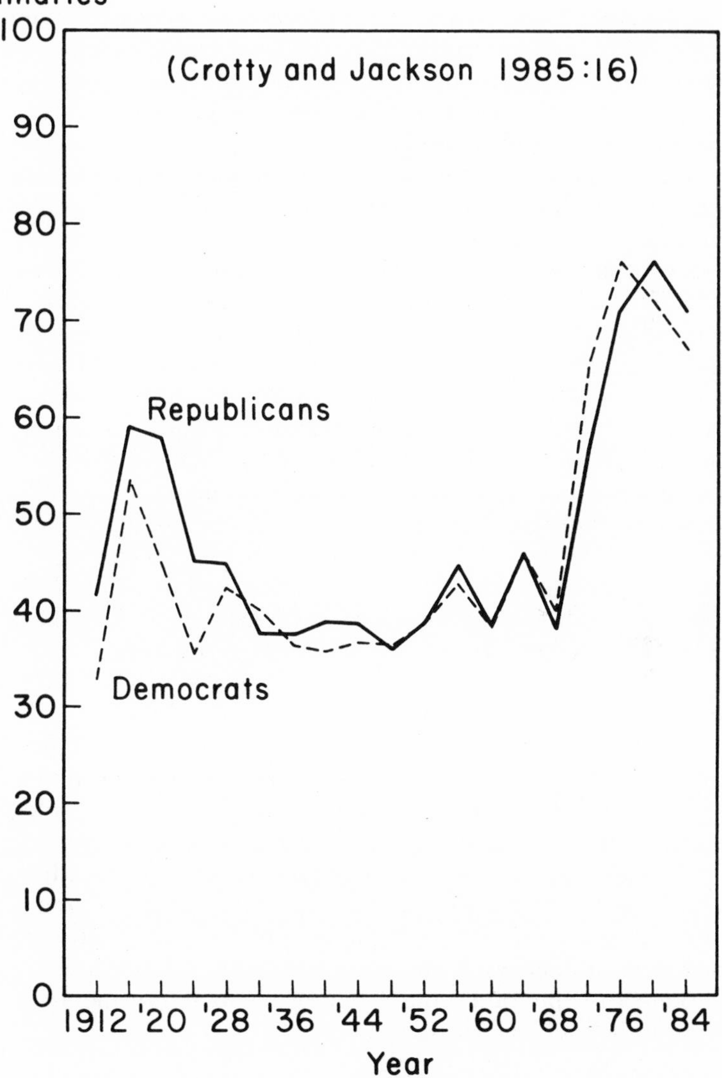

FIGURE 2.1 Delegates Selected in Presidential Primaries, 1912–1984.

concern found it more convenient to keep their caucuses to themselves by adopting primaries at the presidential level.

In addition to encouraging politicians to create more primaries, the new rules encouraged more candidates to enter those primaries. The Democratic party's abolition of the unit rule made it possible for minor candidates to finish well back in a state's primary voting and still win convention delegates. This effect of the rules was magnified a few years later, when the uncovering of Watergate abuses inspired major changes in the laws regulating campaign finance. These changes improved the relative financial positions of minor candidates by prohibiting large contributions and matching small ones with public funds.

The final major feature of the contemporary nominating process—the central importance of the news media—originated when institutional reform converged with a major social trend and a literary inspiration. The major social trend was the long-term growth in importance and activism of the news media, and particularly television, in American society and in the American political system. The literary inspiration was Theodore White's. The phenomenal success of White's "Making of the President" books gave journalists vivid examples of the historical drama and human interest to be found in presidential politics. When White began to cover presidential primaries in 1956 he was all alone, figuratively and sometimes literally. But the mainstream press caught on to the formula of early, detailed, and colorful reporting of campaign events and personalities. By 1972 the managing editor of the *New York Times* probably spoke for many of his colleagues around the country when he told his reporters, "We aren't going to wait until a year after the election to read in Teddy White's book what we should have reported ourselves" (quoted by Crouse 1973: 36).

For reporters intent on covering the presidential campaign in unprecedented detail, the reforms were a definite boon. The reformers' emphasis on "openness," "timeliness," and "adequate public notice" helped ensure not only that prospective participants could participate in the selection process but also that the press could observe and report on that process. Even the forging of political alliances became more public under the new rules; prominent officeholders were virtually forced to make early public commitments to specific candidates in order to assure themselves of seats at the national convention.

Candidates were faced with the task of discovering the strategic possibilities inherent in the new media-oriented, primary-dominated system. With more primaries, and tighter connections between primary results and actual delegate selection, it became increasingly difficult for candidates to pick and choose which primaries they would enter. But at the same time, spending restrictions made it impossible to build full-scale campaign organizations in every primary state. The only way out of this double bind was to exploit the increasingly public nature of the nominating process, in particular the increasingly active role of the news media, to generate the support formerly fueled by grass-roots campaigning. Given the interest of the news media in simple, dramatic stories, the best way to attract the sort of attention that might lead to widespread public support was to win primaries. Candidates who did win primaries—the earlier and oftener the better—found that these primary successes, magnified by the news media, sometimes generated more new support than any amount of money could buy.

As one strategist put it, "All of the past rules about how quickly and suddenly and massively the electorate moves had to be put on the shelf quickly" (Reagan pollster Richard Wirthlin, in Moore 1981: 109). Not surprisingly, the most successful candidates were those who both unlearned the past rules most quickly and saw that the electorate could be moved dramatically in systematic ways connected with the inherent dynamics of the new system.

The first and best of these quick learners was Jimmy Carter. Carter in 1976 deliberately concentrated his resources in a few early states, hoping that victories in those states would help him attract the additional attention and money necessary to run a real national campaign. As campaign strategist Hamilton Jordan wrote some eighteen months before the primary season began (quoted in Schram 1977: 379, 378),

> The press shows an exaggerated interest in the early primaries as they represent the first confrontation between candidates, their contrasting strategies and styles, which the press has been writing and speculating about for two years. Good or poor showings can have a profound and irrevocable impact on succeeding primaries and a campaign's ability to raise funds and recruit workers.

Carter's success in 1976 must be attributed, in part, to this strategic insight. But Carter was not alone in noting that primary victories could have crucial indirect benefits. "In 1976," Arterton (1978a: 7) observed, "most presidential candidates built their political strategy upon the demonstration effect of important primary victories."

By 1980 the concept of momentum—a neat encapsulization of "the demonstration effect of important primary victories"—was virtually institutionalized. Political reporters and pundits adopted it as a standard part of their analytical repertoire. Textbooks, even those with their roots in the old system, recognized it.[10] Politicians in Iowa and New Hampshire, cognizant of their states' critical importance to candidates and the media in a momentum-driven system (and the consequent increases in local morale and hotel bookings) fought to preserve their first-in-the-nation status. And the Carter White House engineered a rearrangement of the primary calendar in an attempt to minimize the potential adverse impact of momentum on the president's chances for reelection.[11]

[10] An interesting barometer of academic recognition can be constructed by comparing successive editions of Polsby and Wildavsky's standard text, *Presidential Elections*, on the role of primaries in the nominating process:

> Primaries are important largely because the results represent an ostensibly objective indication of whether a candidate can win the election. The contestants stand to gain or lose far more than the small number of delegate votes which may be at stake. Thus a man situated as was Richard Nixon in 1960 . . . (1964: 72).
>
> Primaries are important largely because the results represent an ostensibly objective indication of whether a candidate can win the election. The contestants stand to gain or lose far more than the growing number of delegate votes which may be at stake. Thus a man situated as was Richard Nixon in 1960 . . . (1971: 131).
>
> Primaries are important largely because most of the delegates are selected in them and also because the results represent an ostensibly objective indication of whether a candidate can win the election. The contestants stand to gain or lose far more than the growing number of delegate votes that may be at stake. A man situated as was Richard Nixon in 1960 . . . (1976: 108).
>
> Primaries are important largely because most of the delegates are selected in them and also because the results represent an ostensibly objective indication of whether a candidate can win the election. The contestants stand to gain or lose far more than the growing number of delegate votes that may be involved. Success in early primaries—even those, like New Hampshire, where there are only a handful of delegates at stake—takes on enormous importance because the mass media focus on front-runners, giving them a great advantage in publicity. This makes front-runners' appeals through the mails for money more successful, brings advantages in the later primaries, where name recognition is a significant determinant of the vote, and greatly reduces the capabilities of lagging candidates to catch up.
>
> This means that early and vigorous participation in primaries is now the only strategy available to serious presidential aspirants. It was not always thus. It made no sense for a man situated as Richard Nixon was in 1960 . . . (1980: 84).

[11] One key Carter political operative who also happens to be a political scientist

A new high (or low) was reached early in the 1980 campaign when candidate George Bush began referring gleefully to "Big Mo" after his upset victory in the Iowa caucuses. Since Bush's campaign was directly modelled on Carter's four years earlier, success in Iowa's "functional equivalent of a primary"[12] was the crucial selling point for the primaries to come—a fact Bush himself took no pains to conceal. The public debut of "Big Mo" in a Bush appearance with Bob Schieffer on the CBS "Morning" show has been preserved for history by Greenfield (1982: 39–40). Looking forward to New Hampshire, Bush announced,

> "What we'll have, you see, is momentum. We will have forward 'Big Mo' on our side, as they say in athletics."
> " 'Big Mo'?," Schieffer asked.
> "Yeah," Bush replied, " 'Mo,' momentum."

Having invented "forward 'Big Mo' " after Iowa, Bush went on to discover backward "Big Mo" a few weeks later in New Hampshire. He quickly dropped the whole idea, but the press transferred it intact to other candidates, in 1980 and every four years thereafter.

(Kamarck 1986) has described in detail how recent institutional reforms in both parties have been shaped by the maneuverings of the competing candidates for short-term political advantage. "The most dramatic change in the strategic requirements of the post reform nominating system has been to narrow dramatically the range of strategic options open to presidential candidates," Kamarck wrote (1986: 23). "The cultivation of momentum became the only real strategy available. . . . This has lead to presidential candidates adopting, as part of their strategies, the manipulation of the underlying rules of the game in order to enhance their chances at creating or sustaining momentum" (1986: 23, abstract). Kamarck went on to argue that the Democratic party's reform efforts from 1976 onward "have been more dominated by [these] candidate inspired concerns than by traditional reform concerns" (1986: 21).

[12] This apt description was offered by one of Bush's chief rivals, Howard Baker.

PART II

The Nature of Momentum

CHAPTER THREE

The Campaign as Horse Race

EVERY ELECTION CAMPAIGN is an amalgam of personalities and incidents, part high drama and part farce, political history masquerading as a street brawl disguised as a democratic ritual. A journalist sent to report on such an event could legitimately return with anything from a comic strip to a sociological treatise. Some have. But the bulk of campaign coverage reproduces over and over again a surprisingly small number of standardized story-types, evolved over many years in the twin crucibles of professionalism and competition for an audience.

Observers of campaign coverage—people who report on the media reporting on the political process—have identified several specific story types: the candidate profile, the whistle-stop report, and the charge and countercharge. But these same observers have repeatedly noted the predominance of a single story-type, a genre now referred to almost universally as "horse race" coverage. As the label suggests, "horse race" reporting focuses on who's ahead, who's gaining ground, and who will be first across the finish line. The horse race only incidentally touches on matters of political substance; instead, the emphasis is on competition for competition's sake.

The exact share of coverage devoted to the horse race obviously varies somewhat with the campaign setting, the specific news medium, and who is counting. But the general pattern is clear enough. In covering a presidential campaign, the media tell us more about who is winning and who is losing than they do about who is fit to be president. For example, Robinson and Sheehan measured the amount of "candidate information," "policy issues," and "horse race" coverage on the "CBS Evening News" during the 1980 presidential campaign. The results are shown in Figure 3.1, with separate monthly readings for horse race coverage on one hand and candidate and issue coverage on the other. In January, while CBS was running its introductory features on several of the candidates, candidates and issues together received about as much coverage as the horse race. In every other month of the primary campaign, horse race coverage dominated. In March, April, and

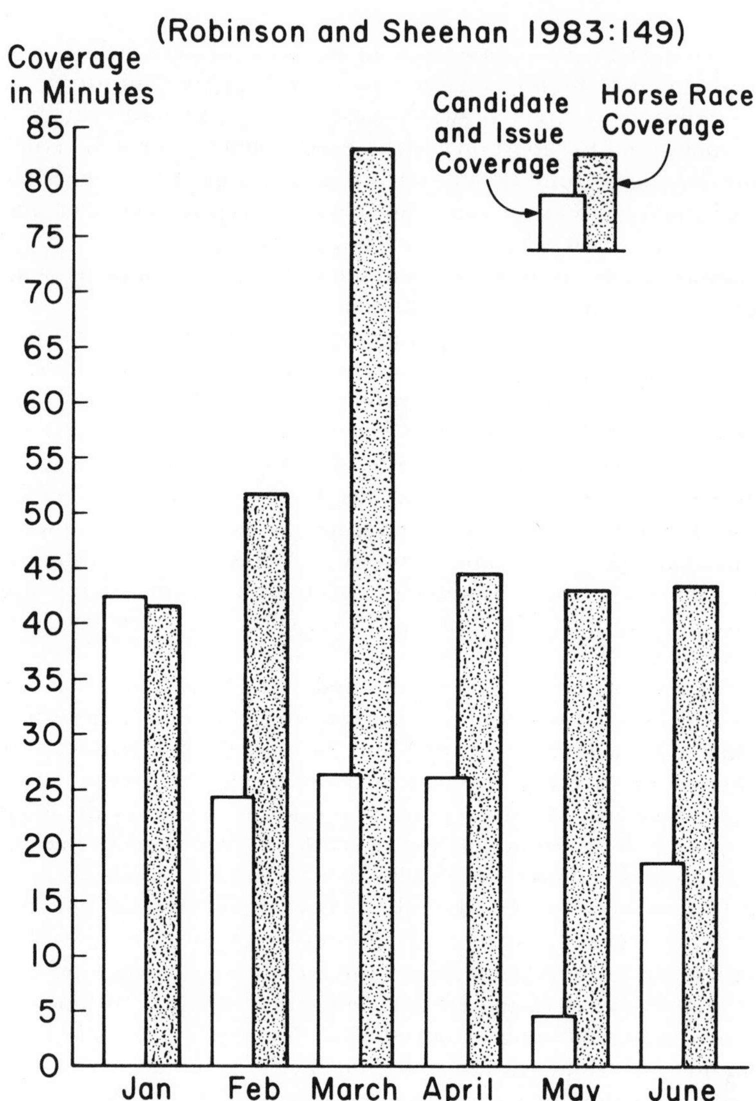

FIGURE 3.1 Nature and Quantity of Campaign Coverage, CBS Evening News, 1980.

May—the heart of the primary season—the horse race got three times as much play as the substance of the campaign. Overall, a regular viewer of the "CBS Evening News" would have been exposed to seven and a half hours of campaign coverage during the first six months of 1980; of that seven and a half hours, a little more than five hours would have been devoted to what Robinson and Sheehan categorized as "horse race" coverage, with less than two and a half hours devoted to "candidate information" and "policy issues" coverage.[1]

Summarizing these data and others from their study, Robinson and Sheehan (1983: 148) wrote, "At every level, in every phase, during each and every month, CBS and UPI allocated more newsspace to competition between candidates than to any other aspect of the campaign. Horse race permeates almost everything the press does in covering elections and candidates." This chapter considers the nature and impact of horse race coverage. We shall see that the horse race permeates not only what the media do in covering primary campaigns but also the public's perceptions of the candidates and the process. Prospective primary voters, it turns out, learn much about those specific features of both the candidates and the process that happen to be central to the media's horse race story. In later chapters we shall see that the resulting perceptions, especially those about who is winning and who is losing, impinge on prospective voters' substantive political judgments and behavior in important ways.

3.1 Patterns of Horse Race Coverage

The media's fascination with the horse race accounts for several interesting regularities in press coverage of presidential nominating campaigns. Most obviously, the emphasis on winning central to horse race reporting ensures that candidates who do win receive the lion's share of media coverage. Thomas Patterson's data on the relationship between success in the 1976 Democratic primaries and media coverage, shown in Figure 3.2, provide the clearest evidence on this point. In each week of the primary season, Patterson (1980: 45) found, about 60 percent of all campaign coverage went to the week's primary winner; the losing candidates, and there were several, divided the remaining 40 percent. As Figure 3.2 makes clear,

[1] By comparison, coverage of the conventions and general election (July through October) amounted to a bit less than five hours of "horse race" and a little more than three hours of "substance."

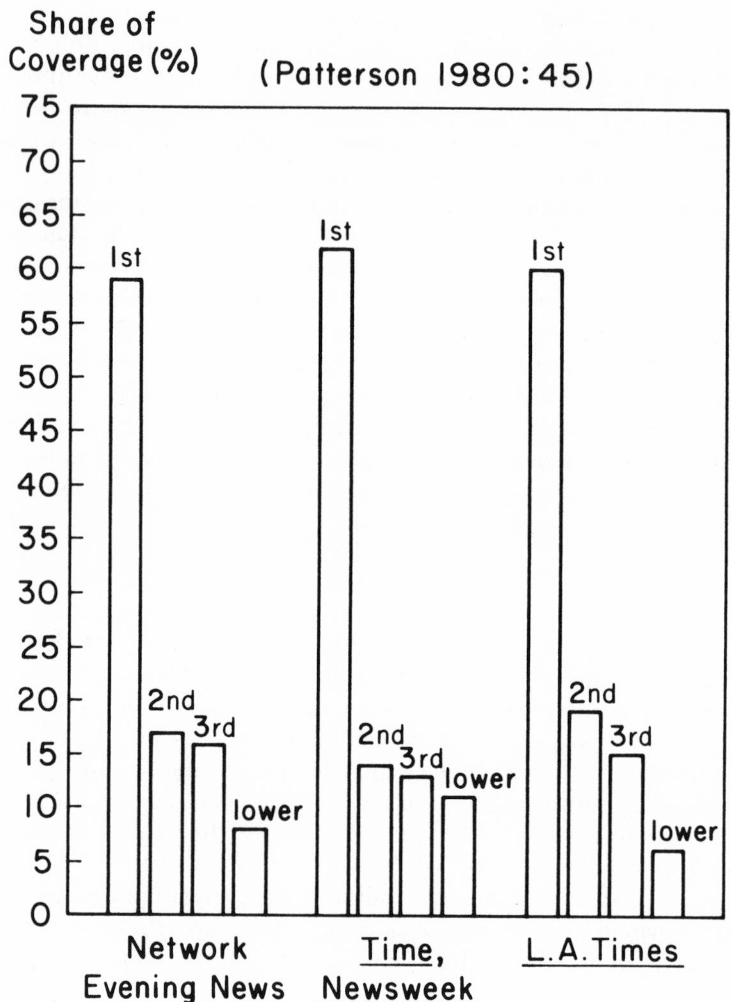

FIGURE 3.2 Weekly News Share of Democratic Candidates by Order of Finish in Week's Primary, 1976.

this pattern was repeated almost identically in a variety of media—network newscasts, major news magazines, and a prestigious big city newspaper.[2]

In addition to covering primary winners, the media tend to give substantial attention to some candidates who do "better than expected." As with any horse race, prerace handicapping, a source of interest in its own right, serves as a bench mark against which actual results are measured. The history of primary campaigns is dotted with famous examples of losers treated like winners (Eugene McCarthy in New Hampshire in 1968) and winners treated like losers (Edmund Muskie in New Hampshire in 1972).

The media are most likely to get carried away covering unexpected "winners" they find personally and politically attractive. The best example is John Anderson, whose second-place showings in the 1980 Republican primaries in Massachusetts and Vermont translated into almost twenty minutes of mostly flattering coverage on the "CBS Evening News" in the subsequent month—more than Ronald Reagan, who was busy getting himself nominated, and more than George Bush, Howard Baker, John Connally, Phil Crane, and Robert Dole put together (Robinson and Sheehan 1983: 81). This coverage occurred in spite of the fact that CBS's own correspondent, Bruce Morton, admitted on the air—correctly, as it turned out—that he could not see Anderson doing even that well again, anywhere in the country, in the remaining three months of the Republican primary season (Greenfield 1982: 51).

The other notable example of the media lavishing coverage on a surprising nonwinner was that of Gary Hart in Iowa in 1984. In keeping with their recent tendency to avoid declaring "moral victories," the media made it clear that Walter Mondale won big in the Iowa caucuses, just as expected. Morton on CBS (quoted by Adams 1985: 12) said of Hart, "when you lose three-to-one, you've lost." All the same, Hart got more coverage than Mondale in the subsequent week. As Robinson and Sheehan (1983: 80) wrote of the 1980 campaign, "access belongs to those who beat the political odds."

Both Anderson in 1980 and Hart in 1984 were especially fortunate in having "beat the political odds" early in the primary season. The newsworthiness of early surprises is magnified by their possi-

[2] The same pattern also held in two smaller newspapers studied by Patterson—the Erie, Pennsylvania, *Times* and *News*.

ble implications for the horse race writ large—the quest for the nomination itself. As the primary season proceeds, the weight of the delegate count bears down more and more heavily on the media's latitude for interpreting an unexpected victory as a major change in the candidates' relative standings. With attention focusing increasingly on the candidates' (perhaps a single candidate's) efforts to assemble a convention majority, the accumulation of delegates becomes the main bench mark for assessing the significance of day-to-day campaign events.

Robinson and Sheehan (1983: 80–82) found a similar pattern in media coverage: a decline during the 1980 primary season in what they called "the elasticity of the newshole for primary surprises." According to Robinson and Sheehan, the first two big surprises of the 1980 campaign, George Bush's upset win in the Iowa caucuses in January and John Anderson's second-place showings in Massachusetts and Vermont at the beginning of March, each roughly quadrupled the candidate's coverage from one month to the next. Edward Kennedy's victories in New York and Connecticut in late March nearly doubled his coverage, but Bush's late win in Michigan in May had virtually no effect.[3]

In addition to reflecting the changing focus of media interest, this pattern of coverage reflects the more obvious fact that the media simply pay less attention to later contests than to earlier ones. The media's disproportionate emphasis on New Hampshire's first-in-the-nation primary has been noted by press-watchers in every recent campaign, and since 1976 New Hampshire has had to share star billing with Iowa's first-in-the-nation caucuses. In 1980, Robinson and Sheehan found (1983: 176), Iowa and New Hampshire each received more than 45 minutes of coverage on the "CBS Evening News," plus more than six hundred column inches on the UPI wire. In each medium, Iowa and New Hampshire together accounted for 28 percent of all primary-season coverage.

A similar tendency toward media "front-loading" is evident in Figure 3.3, which compares the timing of newspaper coverage and primary voting in the 1984 primary season.[4] About 30 percent of

[3] Robinson and Sheehan's estimate of the effect of New York and Connecticut on Kennedy's coverage is based on a comparison between February and March, but the primaries occurred on 22 March, and much of the difference in total coverage for the two months is probably due to other factors. The estimates for Bush and Anderson seem more reliable.

[4] For my purposes, the 1984 primary season ran from mid-January (six weeks before the first caucuses in Iowa) through mid-June (two weeks after the last pri-

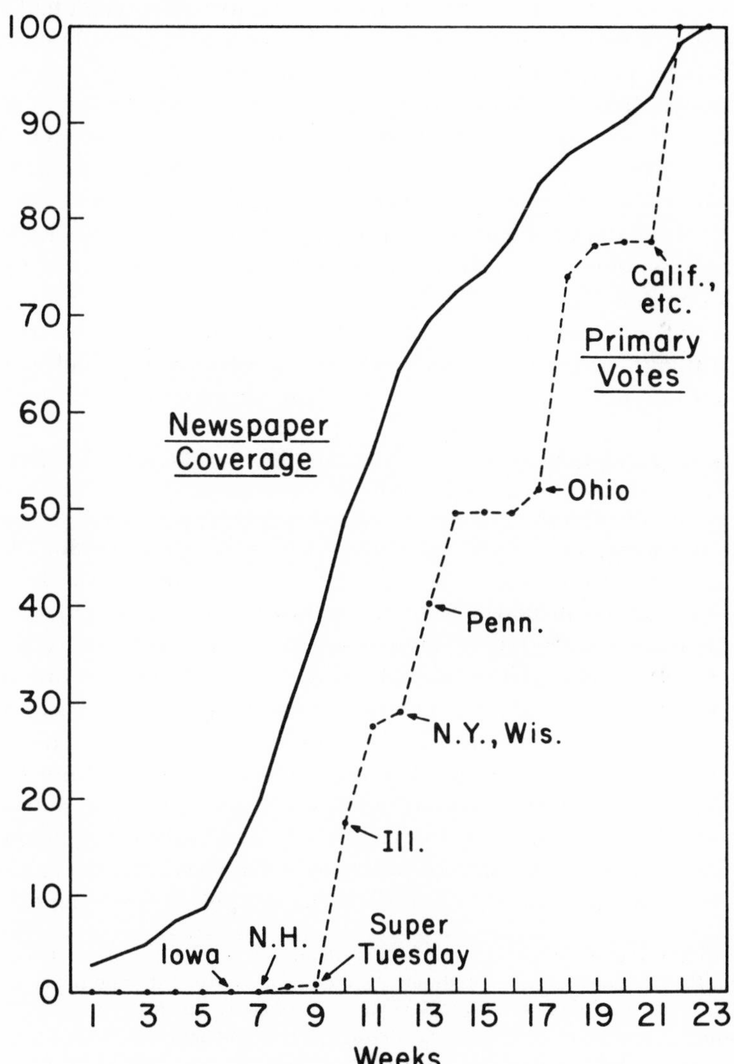

FIGURE 3.3 Newspaper Coverage and Primary Votes, 1984.

the total newspaper coverage in 1984 came in the first eight weeks of the campaign, a period ending one week after Hart's New Hampshire upset. During the same period less than 1 percent of the season's primary votes were cast. Coverage and Hart's fortunes began to decline after "Super Tuesday"—the important grouping of primaries in five states, including Florida and Massachusetts, two weeks later. By the beginning of May, with more than half the year's primary votes still to be cast, the media had already said almost 80 percent of what they had to say about the 1984 primary process. The four million votes cast on June 5, the last big day of the primary season, generated about half as much coverage in the subsequent week as had the 100,000 votes cast in New Hampshire more than three months earlier.

The media's fascination with the horse race helps to account for the phenomenon of "front-loading," as for much else about the timing and focus of campaign coverage. But the horse race is not merely a matter of timing and focus; it also permeates the tone of campaign coverage. Candidates who are winning, especially those winning unexpectedly, tend to get relatively good press; those who are losing appear in a less appealing light. Patterson provided a good description of the sort of shading involved. Carter's 1976 primary successes, he wrote (1980: 48),

> provided him with news coverage that was more favorable than that received by his opponents. Evaluations of the candidates were keyed primarily to their success. A winning candidate was said to be an effective campaigner and organizer while a loser was normally presented as lacking in these talents. Moreover, since popular support is considered a *sine qua non* of success, a winning candidate usually was described by such adjectives as likeable and appealing. Although a losing candidate normally was not described in opposing terms, it was often stated or implied that voters were not particularly attracted by his personality and style. During the primaries Carter received more than two favorable news mentions about his performance and per-

maries in California and elsewhere). This definition conforms with the design of the 1984 National Election Study survey, the major source of data on public opinion during the 1984 campaign. Newspaper coverage is measured by the average proportion of each day's front page devoted to the campaign by four newspapers: the *New York Times, Washington Post, Houston Chronicle,* and *Rochester Democrat and Chronicle.* Appendix A.1 contains details regarding these measurements, together with coverage data for other recent campaigns.

sonality for each unfavorable one. No other candidate received even a favorable balance of coverage.

Carter's run of good press in early 1976 created something of a media backlash against front-runners in subsequent primary campaigns. As Michael J. Robinson commented (1981: 207),

> The major change in media coverage in 1980 . . . was the increasing speed at which the national media moved to minimize their own bandwagon effects. After the Iowa caucuses in 1976, the media gave Carter almost three months of comparatively easy riding. It was not until Pennsylvania that the media went after Carter, using his "ethnic purity" remark as their justification. The "ethnic purity" episode indicates the extent to which the media had, by 1976, understood their new mission: removing the wheels from bandwagons that they had helped to create. (Who else could remove them?) In 1980, however, national media simply got better and quicker at dewheeling.

A new pattern emerged: unknown candidates who broke out of the pack received very favorable coverage until they showed signs of becoming front-runners; then they were scrutinized much more carefully. George Bush in 1980 got good press for a month after his upset victory in the Iowa caucuses, but the honeymoon ended before the New Hampshire primary (Robinson and Sheehan 1983: 100–101).[5] Gary Hart in 1984 was a little, but only a little, luckier. According to Adams (1985: 12), "Hart's coverage was virtually free of any harsh criticism, unflattering issues, or cynical commentary" in the week between his surprising second-place showing in Iowa and the crucial first primary in New Hampshire. But only two days after his New Hampshire triumph made him the media's new front-runner, the "first sustained criticisms" of Hart began to appear. During the subsequent two weeks, leading up to the crucial "Super Tuesday" primaries, Hart was accused of "exploiting" the memory of John F. Kennedy and of "courting" George Wallace; he was described as an ineffective senator and a man "driven" by ambition; his former boss, George McGovern, was said to have "deep reservations" about him; and embarrassing controversies

[5] The incident that precipitated the turnaround was Bush's handling of a debate hall controversy in Nashua, New Hampshire. Bush's effort to keep several of his rivals out of the debate was widely viewed as an embarrassing blunder. The network news shows gave the story a total of thirteen minutes the next night, and continued to refer to it for several more days (Robinson and Sheehan 1983: 105–6).

were raised regarding his correct age and the circumstances surrounding the change of his family name. The night before the Super Tuesday primaries, NBC featured attacks against Hart by Walter Mondale, John Glenn, Claude Pepper, and Richard Viguerie; Hart himself "was not once shown defending himself or uttering a single word" (Adams 1985: 13–14). This was dewheeling with a vengeance.

While recent bandwagon candidates have walked a thin line between canonization and vilification, losing candidates have suffered even harsher treatment: silence and "the deathwatch." "The deathwatch," according to Robinson and Sheehan (1983: 78), "generally begins with a reference to the candidate's low standing in the polls, moves on to mention financial or scheduling problems, and ends with coverage of the final press conference, in which the candidate withdraws." This striking example of deathwatch coverage illustrates the point: during the first ten weeks of 1980, former vice-presidential nominee Robert Dole got a dozen mentions on the "CBS Evening News"; of these, nine had to do with his failing prospects ("signs of pulling out," "wondered how much farther he could go," "about sounded taps for his campaign"). "None of the comments were explicitly critical of Dole" in any substantive sense, Robinson and Sheehan reported (1983: 79); "three-fourths, however, declared Dole's campaign dead or dying."

This relentless "winnowing" of losing candidates (Matthews 1978) reflects both the literary and the organizational needs of the news media. It is virtually impossible to tell a coherent continuing story about a political struggle involving half a dozen major characters. And even if such a story could work as literature, it could not work for long as a logistical reality. The latter fact is evident in the reaction of David Broder, dean of national political reporters, to predictions that the grouping of eighteen separate state primaries and caucuses in a Super Tuesday showdown a few weeks into the 1988 primary season might keep several candidates in each party alive until that point. "The existing communications system can deal with seven or eight candidates in each party," Broder wrote (*Washington Post National Weekly Edition,* 13 April 1987, p. 7),

> as long as they are concentrated in one or two places. But once the campaign explodes to 18 states, as it will the day after New Hampshire, when the focus shifts to a super-primary across the nation, the existing communications system simply will not accommodate more than two or three candidates in each party.

> Neither the television networks, nor newspapers nor magazines, have the resources of people, space and time to describe and analyze the dynamics of two simultaneous half-national elections among Republicans and Democrats. That task is simply beyond us. Since we cannot reduce the number of states voting on Super Tuesday, we have to reduce the number of candidates treated as serious contenders. Those news judgments will be arbitrary—but not subject to appeal. Those who finish first or second in Iowa and New Hampshire will get tickets from the mass media to play in the next big round. Those who don't, won't. A minor exception may be made for the two reverends, Jesse L. Jackson and Marion G. (Pat) Robertson, who have their own church-based communications and support networks and are less dependent on mass-media attention. But for no one else.

As Broder himself noted, these considerations "are not complex, but they are rarely described, for journalists find them embarrassing. They spotlight the uncomfortable role the mass media play in presidential politics."

3.2 The Audience Reaction

It is always dangerous to assume that what appears in newspapers and on television thereby enters the public consciousness. In describing the results of a 1984 survey of news coverage and public awareness or unawareness, Robinson and Clancey (1985: 60) wrote, "We found public memory about news and world affairs short enough to qualify as mass amnesia." Attorney General-designate Edwin Meese provided a typical example (1985: 61):

> Meese made the network news forty-three times in just thirty-one days, and he was the lead story on at least eight separate occasions—total news time: 5,100 seconds. But despite Meese's ongoing status as a lead story on network news during the month before our survey, the Meese mess, no matter how generously defined, failed to penetrate the cognitive map of even four Americans out of ten.

However, Robinson and Clancey did find one sort of news for which the public's level of information "went way beyond statistical chance" (1985: 61)—the primary horse race. More than six weeks after the fact, a majority of Robinson and Clancey's respondents recalled correctly that Gary Hart had won the 1984 New Hampshire primary. And 65 percent "knew (without prompting) that Walter Mondale had won the [current] week's big primary in Pennsylvania. The media, then, do provide a 'primary education' in an election year. Our people knew more about winners and losers in primaries than they knew about anything else."

In addition to knowing about winners and losers in specific primaries, people know, or at least believe they know, about the state of the overall race for the nomination. This fact is reflected in their almost universal willingness to estimate the various candidates' chances, as in the 1984 National Election Study survey. Of the 583 Democrats in the NES survey who were asked to estimate Gary Hart's chances (those interviewed after New Hampshire who recognized Hart's name), exactly *two* refused to do so. (By way of comparison, 8 of these respondents refused to rate Hart on a "feeling thermometer," and 149 refused to guess where he stood on the issue of cutting government services.)

The most obvious explanation for the salience of candidates' chances in the public consciousness is the media's emphasis on the horse race. One reason for the tremendous volume of horse race reporting in nominating campaigns is that campaign events provide a steady stream of convenient "news hooks" for stories about how a candidate is doing; by contrast, issue positions are seldom timely unless they have changed, been misstated, or led to dramatic conflict between candidates. Given a weekly parade of primary outcomes and the patterns of coverage documented in Figures 3.1 and 3.2, it is hardly surprising that information about winners and losers filters through to even mildly attentive media consumers.

But there appears to be more to it than that. Noting that even heavily covered campaign issues (for example, Gary Hart's name change) elicited meager public recognition, Robinson and Clancey argued that "news focus doesn't explain fully why winners and losers stick better in the national memory than other day-to-day news events" (1985: 62). Patterson also pointed out that the game aspects of the campaign (winning and losing, strategy and logistics, appearances and hoopla) loomed even larger in the public's recollections of campaign news than in the campaign news itself. In the 1976 primaries, Patterson found (1980: 29, 86), the game accounted for about 60 percent of media coverage but 80 percent of the stories spontaneously recalled by survey respondents.

My own guess is that the public absorbs more of the horse race than of other campaign news in part because the horse race has simple evaluative content. As part of their study of objectivity in media coverage, Robinson and Sheehan (1983: 42) coded every explicit evaluation of the candidates' "competence," "integrity," "consistency," and "successfulness" on the "CBS Evening News" and the UPI wire during the 1980 campaign. They found that about 30 percent of all stories contained explicit evaluations of "successfulness." By contrast, only a few percent contained explicit evaluations on *any* of the substantive dimensions of "competence," "integrity," or "consistency"; reporters find it very difficult to offer these sorts of substantive judgments about a candidate without transgressing the conventional boundaries of objective journalism. Thus, as Robinson and Sheehan wrote (1983: 41), "journalists made precious few explicit comments concerning any personal qualities of the candidates, other than about their prospects for winning or losing." Prospective voters wanting straightforward advice about the good guys and the bad guys in the primary season drama have little choice but to infer what they can from reports of who is winning and who is losing.

Then, too, the simplicity of the relevant message in horse race stories makes them particularly suited to an audience whose attention to and interest in political news is sporadic. When the details of an issue story fade from memory, often within minutes, there is probably little left, but when the details of a horse race story fade from memory the residual evaluative content may remain. One respondent in Patterson's 1976 survey, asked to recall the content of the previous day's most memorable news story, replied (1980: 62): "Can't pinpoint it exactly. Carter is coming up so fast was the main point though." The substantive political significance of this "main point" may be obscure, but its potential relevance for a voter faced with a choice between Carter and some less fortunate candidate is not.

Another explanation for the public salience of the horse race is its dramatic unity, lacking in most campaign news. Issue flaps come and go, but the horse race continues from week to week. A passing fact ("Carter is coming up so fast") can be connected with past and future facts in a simple yet significant way. A perceptive analysis of the public appeal of primary coverage by newspaper-turned-television journalist Christopher Lydon focused precisely on the parallels between a good primary season horse race and any other good continuing drama. Television, Lydon said (Foley, Britton, and Everett 1980: 60), is now the medium of politics as entertainment series, as a sort of real-life thriller series that in 1976 dramatically took place. It was a 10 o'clock Tuesday night series. That was when Cronkite and the others came in and gave us essentially what became the adventures of little Jimmy Carter—watch Jimmy run, watch Jimmy improve, watch Jimmy surprise us again. You introduce a character. You hope to have your man in that spot in this conflict series, this real-life public conflict, in which the public and the political world will say, hey, that's good, strengthen that character, double his part, bring him forward, make him a star.

Of course, even a star needs good material. For most of the primary season Carter had it: the untraditional background, the colorful family, the primary upsets, and Hubert Humphrey lurking just offstage. The resulting jealousy and frustration among Carter's opponents is evident in the complaint of an adviser to Henry Jackson's campaign, Ben Wattenberg (quoted in Moore and Fraser 1977: 92–93).

> After the Massachusetts primary, Jackson, unlike Carter, was not on the cover of *Time*. He was not on the cover of *Newsweek*. We did not get articles about his cousin who has a worm farm. And that was the story of the Jackson campaign for the next six weeks, and that was what I think killed that campaign. Jackson had won a totally unanticipated victory, beyond what the press had expected, in a state with ten times as many delegates as New Hampshire, and the effect was barely visible. We were dismayed.

Jackson simply did not—perhaps he could not—adjust his strategy to the dynamics of the modern nominating process. Carter could and did.

But late in the primary season even the Carter story began to wear thin. Fortunately for the media, two new characters came along in May—Jerry Brown and Frank Church. As Matthews (1978: 71) described it, this "second wave" of primary competition "saved the story by providing an element of uncertainty and suspense in the Democrats' nominating picture. A suspension of disbelief is helpful in enjoying most theatrical productions; it was essential in order to take the second wave seriously. But most of the media did." Brown and Church did not go far, but they helped get Carter through the dull period between the early primaries and the convention. And, although he still faced more than his share of low ratings, he was not finally cancelled for another four and a half years.[6]

3.3 Horse Race Perceptions and Reality

We have seen that, at least in its broad outlines, the horse race penetrates the public consciousness. But how does it shape specific public perceptions about the candidates' chances of winning the nomination? My analysis of those perceptions is based on two broad categories of explanatory factors. Factors in the first category are objective in character: they reflect concrete campaign events and the translation of those events by the media into shared perceptions of the various candidates' chances of being nominated. Thus, they are primarily suited to explaining changes over time or differences among candidates in horse race perceptions at the aggregate level. Factors in the second category are subjective in character: they reflect both individual differences in political predispositions and media use and the translation of those differences into differing perceptions of the candidates' chances. Thus, they are primarily suited to explaining the substantial individual-level variation in perceptions of chances observable for a given candidate in a given objective political situation.

An obvious place to begin in attempting to specify the connection between concrete campaign events and public perceptions of the candidates' chances is with the mediating role of the press, particularly the standard patterns of horse race coverage described in Section 3.1. We have seen that the media pay considerable attention to primary results, to unexpected primary successes and failures, and to the overall race as reflected in the delegate count. It should not be surprising to find that these same features of the campaign tend to shape public perceptions of who is likely to win and who is likely to lose.

Relating these campaign events to public perceptions of the candidates' prospects requires survey data on perceptions of the candidates' chances for survey respondents in a variety of objective campaign circumstances. Such data are unavailable in most election surveys, which interview large numbers of respondents at a

[6] A year into the Carter presidency, Russell Baker wrote a column claiming that if Jimmy Carter was a television series, he would be canceled. But as Lydon pointed out (Foley, Britton, and Everett 1980: 67), subsequent events provided the opportunity for some dramatic rewriting (less "Green Acres," more "A-Team"), keeping the series alive through most of 1980.

single point in time, thus failing to capture any natural temporal variation in campaign circumstances over a primary season. In contrast, the 1984 NES included interviews conducted during every week of the campaign, from mid-January through the end of the primary season. As a result, considerable variation exists in the objective campaign circumstances prevailing at the time the respondents were interviewed; some were contacted before Gary Hart's first big victory in New Hampshire, some at the height of his post-New Hampshire surge, some after his subsequent primary defeats in Illinois, New York, and Pennsylvania, and so on. This feature of the 1984 NES survey makes it possible to analyze in some detail the effect of campaign events on public perceptions of the candidates' chances.

To capture the effects of campaign events on public perceptions of the candidates' chances, I rely here on three specific measures of candidate success in each week of the 1984 primary season. These three indicators are intended to reflect various aspects of campaign success or failure that might be expected to shape public perceptions of the candidates' chances.[7]

Cumulative Primary Vote Shares. It seems reasonable to expect that public perceptions of the candidates' chances reflect, in part, their overall success, or lack thereof, in attracting primary support. For each week of the primary season my measure of each candidate's overall success in attracting primary support is that candidate's share of the total primary vote to date, with performance each week weighted by the amount of newspaper coverage given to that week's results and gradually discounted over time.[8] Hart's share of the cumulative primary vote, measured in this way, ranged from about 15 percent just after the Iowa caucuses to 45 percent just

[7] Details regarding the construction of these measures appear in Appendix A.3.

[8] The amount of media coverage given to each week's primary results seems likely on theoretical grounds to be a better predictor of the impact of those results than the mere number of votes cast in each week's primaries. Some discounting of past results seems reasonable, and in the absence of sufficiently detailed data to estimate an appropriate discount rate I have simply assumed arbitrarily that the impact of each week's primary results decays by 10 percent in each subsequent week of the primary season. The corresponding "half-life" attributed to primary results is about six and a half weeks; in 1984, for example, primary voters in Pennsylvania are presumed to weigh the results from the previous week's New York primary about twice as heavily as the results from the Iowa caucuses seven weeks earlier, disregarding the difference in media coverage of the events in New York and Iowa.

before Super Tuesday and stabilized at about 40 percent after Super Tuesday.

"Objective" Probabilities of Nomination. For a variety of reasons, cumulative primary vote shares may not provide an accurate reflection of the candidates' objective chances of winning the nomination. A small lead in the overall primary vote is obviously less significant in early March, when most primaries have not yet been held, than at the end of the primary season in June. And in any event, the nomination is determined, in the end, on the basis of delegate totals, only imperfectly related to primary vote totals. Thus, I have tried to construct a measure of the various candidates' objective standings in the overall race for the nomination, as determined not merely by their performance in newsworthy primaries but also by their success in accumulating enough caucus, convention, and uncommitted delegates to provide an eventual majority. The measure is based on weekly delegate counts published by *Congressional Quarterly Weekly Report* and other media sources, updated each week and translated into objective probabilities of nomination.[9] The weekly trends in objective chances for Hart and Mondale in the 1984 campaign are shown in Figure 10.4.

Previous Week's Vote Shares. Strong primary showings are almost always interpreted as, at least potentially, significant political events, even if that interpretation has little basis in previous primary results or in any sober assessment of the candidates' objective chances of winning the nomination. To capture the possible impact of such interpretations on subjective public perceptions of the candidates' chances I measure each candidate's share of the primary vote not only for the primary season as a whole but also in the single most recent primary or set of primaries.[10] In effect, this

[9] The translation of weekly delegate counts into "objective" probabilities of nomination is described in Appendix A.3. In each week of the campaign, the translation is based on three factors: the proportion of delegates a candidate has won so far, the proportion of remaining delegates he would have to win in order to achieve a majority at the convention, and the likelihood (estimated on the basis of historical experience from several recent campaigns) that his subsequent performance will differ sufficiently from his past performance to push him over that critical delegate threshold.

[10] Since my interest here is less in chronological time than in what might be termed "campaign time," I make no distinction between situations in which the most recent primary occurred in the immediately previous week and situations in which the most recent primary occurred two or more weeks earlier. When there is

measure reflects the disproportionate news value of recent, as opposed to cumulative, primary successes.

To gauge the impact of these three distinct kinds of success on perceptions of the candidates' chances, I used data from the 1984 NES survey to analyze the statistical relationship between each respondent's perceptions of Hart's and Mondale's chances and the candidates' actual success as reflected by the values of these three indicators at the time the respondent was interviewed. The results of the analysis, shown in Table A.8 in Appendix C.1, show how public perceptions of the candidates' chances during the 1984 primary season actually responded to the three distinct types of candidate success. As a result, they allow us to judge both the overall correlation between public perceptions and campaign reality and the effects of specific campaign events on subjective estimates of the candidates' chances.

For example, the results shown in Table A.8 indicate that the three objective measures of candidate success taken together account for an increase in Hart's perceived chances of being nominated of sixteen percentage points in the week after his New Hampshire upset.[11] About half of this sixteen point increase reflected a jump of 13.4 percentage points in Hart's share of the cumulative primary vote after New Hampshire. Another 3.6 percentage points reflected the direct, short-term impact in the subsequent week of Hart's New Hampshire victory. And the remaining 4.4 percentage points reflected an increase of about 6.5 percentage points in Hart's objective probability of being nominated after his New Hampshire upset.

Primary results and delegate accumulations appear from this analysis to have influenced public perceptions in about the way that might be predicted given some knowledge of the media's coverage of nominating campaigns. Thus, we can account quite accurately, at least at the level of overall public perceptions, for changing expectations throughout the primary campaign. This fact is illustrated in Figure 3.4, which compares the average actual perceptions of Hart's chances for each week of the 1984 NES survey with estimates based on the objective factors considered here. The correspondence between actual and estimated perceptions is quite

---

more than one primary in the most recent set I average each candidate's vote share in each state, with states weighted by the number of delegates at stake in each.

[11] This total effect exactly matches the actual increase in Hart's perceived chances among NES survey respondents during the same period.

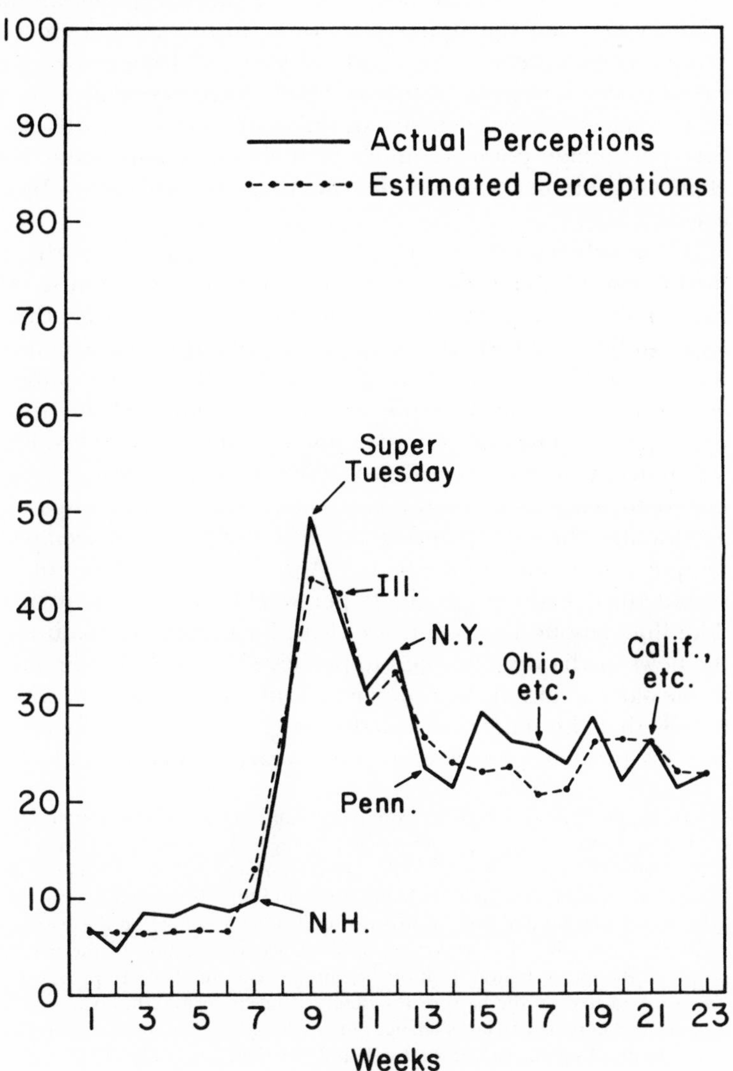

FIGURE 3.4 Actual and Estimated Perceptions of Hart's Chances, 1984.

close, deviating on average by about three percentage points per week.

It seems clear from these results that, in the aggregate, public expectations about the horse race respond in reasonable, predictable ways to actual campaign events. But the aggregate trend conceals considerable individual-level variation. That variation is evident in Figure 3.5, which shows the range in perceptions of Hart's chances between the upper and lower fifths of the Democratic sample in each week of the 1984 NES survey.[12] In any given week, the objective aspects of campaign reality were essentially constant. Nevertheless, sizable segments of the public frequently differed by fifty percentage points or more in their judgments about Hart's chances—judgments made on the basis of the same objective events.

People's differences in their exposure and attention to the mass media might explain these individual differences. Because information about campaign events (and their implications for the various candidates' prospects) is provided primarily by the media, we might expect media exposure and attention to heighten public reactions to these events. In the survey data from 1984 this appears to happen at some points in the campaign but not at others. Figure 3.6 shows average perceived probabilities that Hart would be nominated for each week of the campaign among two groups of respondents—the upper and lower fifths of the total Democratic sample in frequency of media use. Although the small sample sizes (about thirty-eight respondents per week) create substantial random fluctuations, two points are clear. First, those most attuned to the news media were quickest to perceive Hart's electoral potential in the early weeks of the campaign. This fact is consistent with the notion that the media provided enough information about Hart and his prospects to generate some reaction among avid media-

[12] Here and elsewhere I present the perceptions of the top and bottom fifths of the NES sample in order to provide an indication of the extent of variation among respondents. Because each week of the NES survey included only a small number of Democratic respondents, between twenty-four and fifty-three, I have simulated the behavior of the top and bottom fifths of each week's sample on the basis of the entire sample, rather than reporting only the actual responses of the five to ten people in the top or bottom fifth of the sample. The simulated responses in each case were created on the basis of the observed linear relationship between media use and perceptions of Hart's chances for each week's respondents, plus the observed levels of media use for the tenth and ninetieth percentiles of the sample as a whole. Throughout this book week-by-week comparisons of the top and bottom fifths of the survey sample are based on the same procedure.

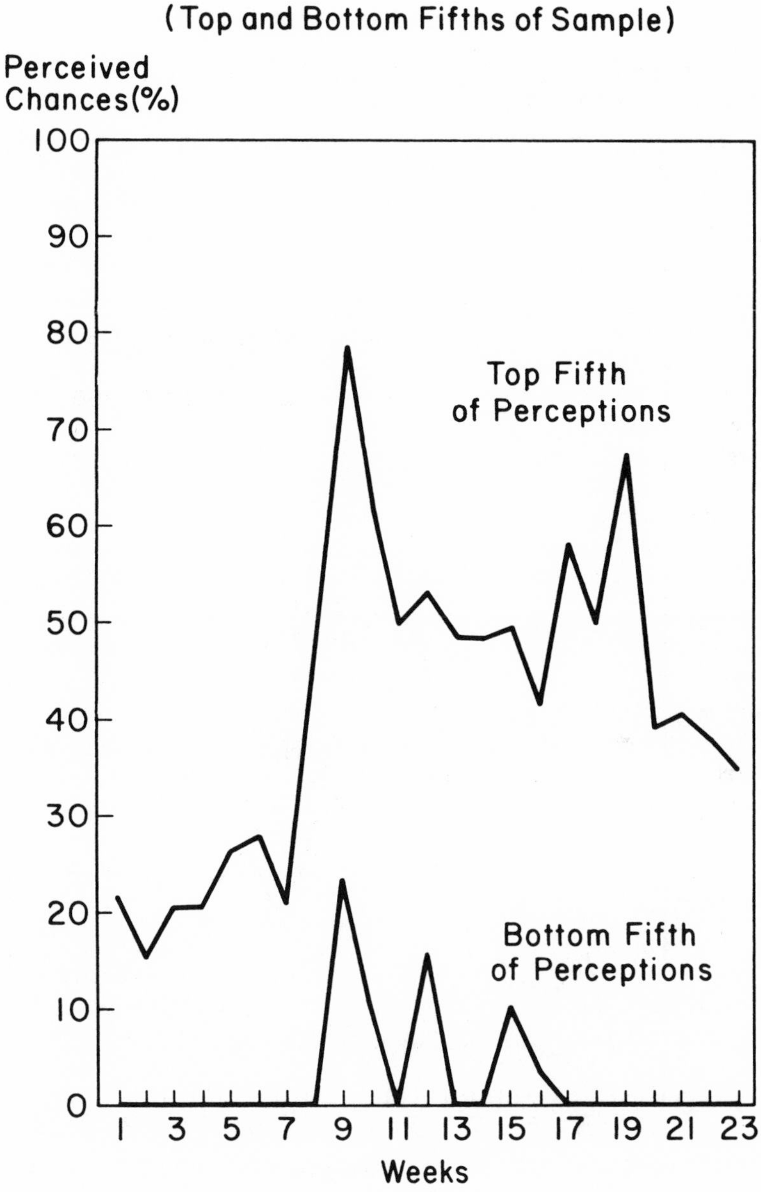

FIGURE 3.5 Range of Perceptions of Hart's Chances, 1984.

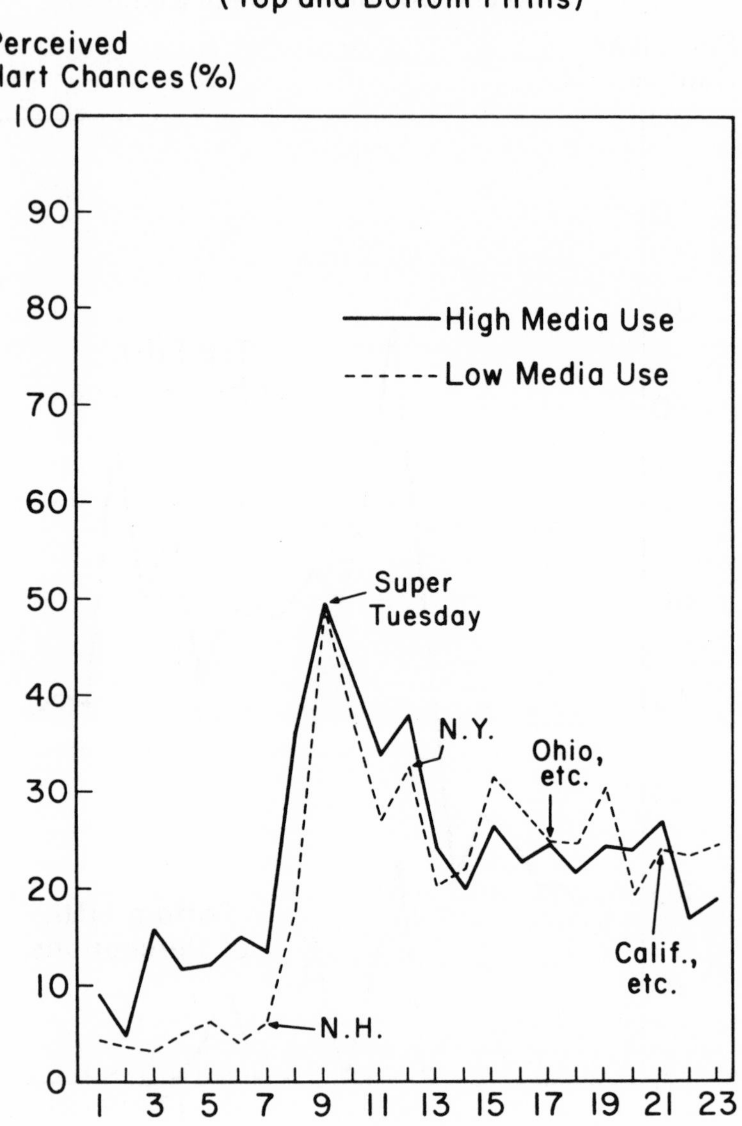

FIGURE 3.6 Media Use and Perceptions of Hart's Chances, 1984.

users, but not enough to make much of an impression on the least attentive portion of the audience. Second, the pattern changed after Hart moved from the political junkies' page of the *New York Times* to the cover of *Newsweek* and the top of the network news shows after New Hampshire. Although reaction was a little slower among those least attuned to the media, both groups shared essentially the same perception of Hart's chances within two weeks after the New Hampshire primary. Presumably by that point Hart was such a hot political topic that even those who followed the media least assiduously had been fairly bombarded with information about his prospects.

Media exposure and attention effects help to account for some of the wide differences in perceptions of Hart's chances among different respondents facing the same objective campaign circumstances, but they are insufficient to account for the bulk of those differences. A more powerful explanation for variations in perceptions revolves around the role of *projection* in respondents' perceptions of campaign events. It is a common finding in social psychology that people attempt to bring their beliefs into conformity with their evaluations not only by altering the latter to fit the former but also by altering the former to fit the latter. Social scientists have recognized for more than thirty years that this phenomenon of "projection" could play an important role in the development of political opinion—that beliefs about political reality (for example, whether the Soviets want war or peace, whether poor people are lazy or unlucky) could not only influence but also be influenced by positive or negative feelings toward the political objects involved.

The impact of projection on political expectations in a campaign setting was first examined by the authors of *Voting*. "Vote intentions," they wrote (Berelson, Lazarsfeld, and McPhee 1954: 289),

> are always very highly correlated with expectations as to who will win the election. Two interpretations of this result offer themselves. On the one hand, we might be dealing with a "bandwagon effect"; people may tend to vote for the man whom they expect to be the winner. On the other hand, it might be a matter of projection; people may expect that the candidate toward whom they (and their friends) feel favorably inclined will win. It is safe to assume that both of these interpretations are correct; but how can their relative importance be assessed?

The approach to this problem adopted by Berelson, Lazarsfeld, and McPhee was based on individual-level analysis of changes in expectations and preferences over time using data from repeated interviews with the same respondents. "When subjected to analysis of this kind," they reported (1954: 289), "data from the 1940 and 1948 elections suggest that the bandwagon effect and the projection effect are approximately equal in strength." My own analysis of expectations and preferences in the 1980 presidential nominating campaigns (Bartels 1985) was based on somewhat different methods, but it produced results similar to Berelson, Lazarsfeld, and McPhee's. A strong projection effect was present in every campaign setting for which data were available in 1980—among Democrats and Republicans, at the beginning and in the middle of the primary season, and regardless of the closeness of the race; in every instance, a change of ten percentage points in a respondent's probability of preferring a candidate increased by about six percentage points the respondent's probability of expecting the same candidate to win the nomination.[13]

Figure 3.7 demonstrates the impact of projection in another way, by relating horse race perceptions in 1984 not directly to preferences, but to preexisting political predispositions. Average weekly estimates of Hart's chances are charted in Figure 3.7 for the fifth of the sample most predisposed on the basis of social and political characteristics to support Mondale and also for the fifth of the sample least predisposed to support Mondale.[14] The differences are substantial. Those most predisposed to oppose Mondale were more willing to believe that Hart was a viable alternative, especially at the height of Hart's post–New Hampshire surge but also almost uniformly throughout the remainder of the primary season.[15] From New Hampshire to the end of the primary season,

[13] The "bandwagon" effect was also evident in 1980, but it varied markedly in strength across these different campaign settings. That side of the reciprocal relationship between expectations and preferences will be examined in greater detail in Chapter 6.

[14] Predispositions toward Mondale rather than Hart are used as the basis of distinction because Mondale was better known, particularly at the beginning of the primary season; thus, predispositions toward him were more important in conditioning reactions to the campaign. The nature and role of political predispositions is addressed in greater detail in Chapter 5.

[15] This projection effect need not be due entirely to active misinterpretation of campaign news. It may also stem, in part, simply from the natural inclination of casual campaign-watchers to pay particular attention to news involving their favorite candidates. Data generated by Patterson (1980: 78–79) indicate that survey respondents in the 1976 campaign were noticeably more likely to recall stories about their favorite candidates than about opposing candidates. For example, Ford supporters remembered mostly stories about Ford; Reagan supporters remembered

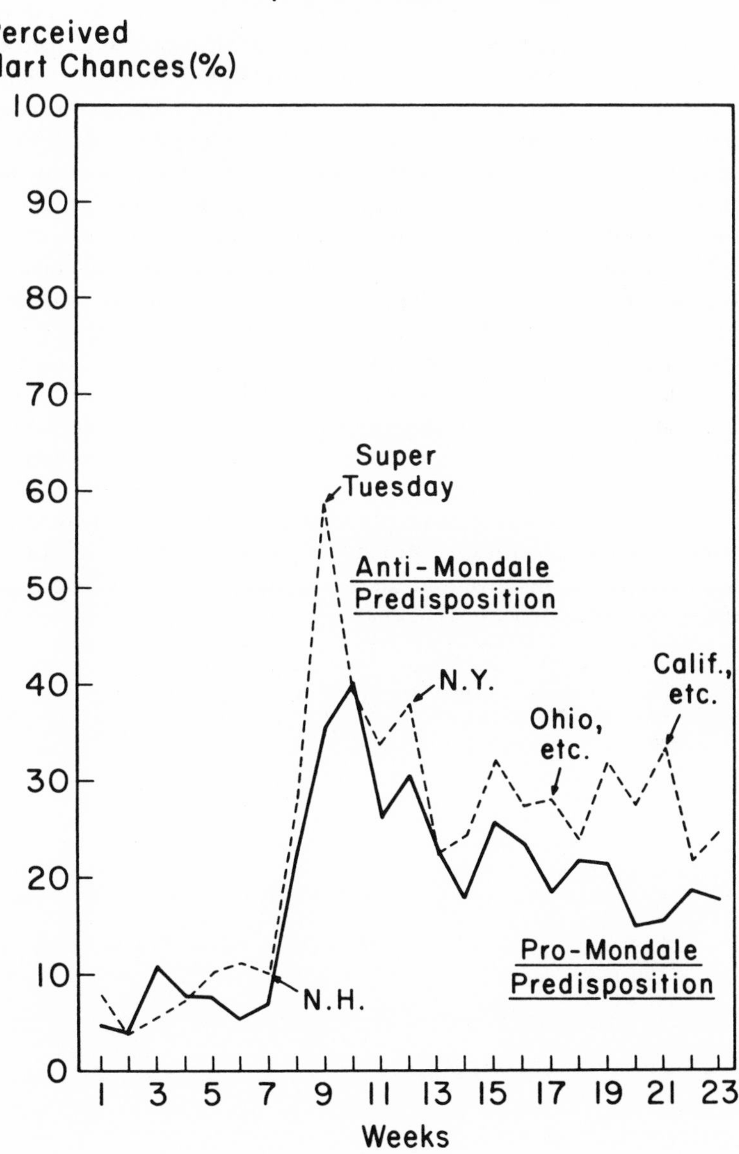

FIGURE 3.7 Mondale Predispositions and Perceptions of Hart's Chances, 1984.

those Democrats most predisposed to oppose Mondale rated Hart's chances substantially more favorably than did those most predisposed to support Mondale.

Clearly, given these results, respondents come to the campaign with different predispositions and perceive the same events in significantly different ways. At the same time, it is obvious from the figure that a shared reality informed perceptions at both extremes. That shared reality was the reality discerned, codified, and transmitted to the public by the news media. The very fact that respondents were sufficiently engaged by the horse race to project their own preferences onto campaign events provides indirect testimony to the power of the media's horse race fascination.

If the media audience was nothing more than an audience, the pattern of horse race coverage and audience reaction documented in this chapter would be merely an interesting sidelight on the nominating campaign. But, in fact, the media audience subsumes the primary electorate. As a result, the media's fascination with the horse race colors the "primary education" not only of passive campaign observers but also of active participants in the nominating process. The story of primary winners and losers is absorbed by the public, transmuted, and played back to the media by subsequent primary electorates. In Chapter 6 we return to the political implications of this give and take—the heart of modern presidential nominating process dynamics.

---

mostly stories about Reagan. Because these stories were predominantly favorable, the selectiveness of public retention helps account for the tendency of each camp to overrate its candidate's chances.

CHAPTER FOUR

Learning and Uncertainty

In ELECTORAL POLITICS mere public familiarity, although far from sufficient to ensure a candidate's success, does appear necessary. Voters do not cast their ballots for candidates they do not feel they know, at least superficially. In the 1984 NES survey, for example, 691 Democratic respondents were willing to choose a favorite candidate for the Democratic nomination. Of these 691 respondents, only 4—about half of 1 percent—chose a candidate they did not recognize or did not feel capable of rating on a general "feeling thermometer." Results like these identify the first hurdle facing anyone running for president as the hurdle of public familiarity. This fact is probably not surprising. But in view of the wide variation in levels of familiarity across the field of candidates in a nominating campaign, it *is* significant. Some candidates have already cleared this first hurdle before the campaign begins; others never clear it.

Table 4.1 shows the proportion of the public claiming some familiarity with each of the candidates in the early stages of recent presidential nominating campaigns.[1] The range of familiarity re-

[1] "Familiarity" is measured in a variety of ways in different surveys. Simple name recognition is probably the most common measure, but recognition, requiring little real familiarity, is subject to pervasive ceiling effects. Both Patterson's 1976 panel survey and the 1980 NES survey included slightly more stringent filtering questions, in which respondents were asked, for each of the candidates they had heard of, whether they felt they "knew something about" the candidate. Claiming to "know something about" a candidate is the measure of familiarity used in Table 4.1 and in Figure 4.1 for the 1976 and 1980 campaigns. The percentages in Table 4.1 are based on responses from party identifiers only, including 573 Democrats and 293 Republicans in Los Angeles and Erie, Pennsylvania, from the February wave of Patterson's 1976 survey and 504 Democrats and 339 Republicans nationwide from the January–February wave of the 1980 NES survey. There is no strictly comparable measure in the 1984 NES survey. However, respondents in both the 1980 and 1984 NES surveys were asked to rate the candidates they had heard of on a general "feeling thermometer." Most, though not all, did so. Willingness to rate a candidate is obviously not the same thing as claiming to know something about him, but the 1980 data suggest that the difference is of little practical importance. For eleven different candidates in each of two waves (one in February and one in April), the proportion of own-party respondents willing to rate each candidate was between 0.4 and 2.4 percentage points less than the proportion claiming to know something

flected in the table is striking. At one extreme, prospective candidates like Gerald Ford, Ronald Reagan, and Edward Kennedy entered campaigns already known to virtually the entire population. At the opposite extreme, candidates like Lloyd Bentsen, Fred Harris, and Philip Crane began with very low levels of public recognition. For these less fortunate candidates, running for president was merely a constant and ultimately unsuccessful struggle to put themselves before the public.

4.1 Learning, the Media, and the Horse Race

To put Table 4.1 in perspective, many of the men known to less than half of the public were, nevertheless, political figures of some significance. If we exclude Edward Kennedy and John Glenn as special cases, the nine other incumbent senators in the table were known, on average, by only 36 percent of the public. Obviously, being a senator—even being one of the large subset of senators sufficiently ambitious to run for the presidency—is simply not enough, by itself, to put a prospective candidate firmly in the public consciousness.

For those candidates who do not happen to be incumbent presidents or vice presidents, former presidential candidates, astronauts, or Kennedys, the first goal of the campaign is, therefore, to make themselves known to the public. And either directly or indirectly, that means getting media coverage. Unfortunately for the candidates, the networks do not lavish airtime on everyone who wants to be president. They parcel it out in seconds, like the precious commodity it is, in accordance with their own well-defined norms of newsworthiness. This presents the candidates with a real "Catch-22." The only way to become a somebody is to get media coverage, but the only way to get media coverage is to be a somebody.

Some of the force of this predicament is conveyed by Arterton's analysis (1978b: 31–32) of the various candidates' media strategies in the 1976 Democratic campaign.

---

about him; the average difference was 1.5 percentage points. Differences of this magnitude are insufficient to affect any of the arguments in the text. Therefore, willingness to rate each candidate is treated as an equivalent measure of familiarity for the 1984 campaign in Table 4.1 and elsewhere. The percentages for 1984 in Table 4.1 are based on responses from 188 Democrats interviewed before the Iowa caucuses in the 1984 NES rolling cross-section survey.

TABLE 4.1 Familiarity with Primary Candidates, 1976, 1980, and 1984

Democrats (%)		Republicans (%)	
	1976		
George Wallace	73.8	Gerald Ford	90.8
Sargent Shriver	44.3	Ronald Reagan	81.6
Henry Jackson	29.1		
Morris Udall	23.4		
Birch Bayh	22.2		
Jimmy Carter	21.5		
Frank Church	21.1		
Fred Harris	12.9		
Lloyd Bentsen	7.3		
	1980		
Jimmy Carter	98.4	Ronald Reagan	92.0
Edward Kennedy	94.8	John Connally	72.9
Jerry Brown	63.9	Howard Baker	53.4
		George Bush	46.6
		Robert Dole	41.9
		Philip Crane	7.7
	1984		
John Glenn	94.1		
Walter Mondale	93.6		
Jesse Jackson	93.6		
George McGovern	93.1		
Alan Cranston	63.8		
Gary Hart	46.3		
Reubin Askew	41.5		
Ernest Hollings	36.7		

Sources: Calculated from 1976 Patterson survey; 1980 and 1984 NES surveys.
Note: Percentages are based on the proportion of party identifiers "willing to rate" or "knowing something about" candidates at the beginning of the primary season. For more precise definitions of familiarity and descriptions of samples, see Chapter 4, fn. 1.

The initial position of a presidential campaign [organization] in its relations with media organizations depends heavily upon its political circumstances. To a limited degree, campaigns are able to exercise some choice in their news strategy; to a greater degree, their choices are constrained by their current nomination prospects. A number of the politicians who sought the Presidency in 1976 began their quest under conditions that demanded diligent efforts to achieve a meager amount of national coverage. With the exception of Wallace and Jackson, during the preprimary period all the Democratic candidates were basically

> in supplicant positions vis-à-vis the national news media. Two candidates, Carter and to a lesser extent, Harris, concluded, moreover, that their prospects were regarded as so low that seeking national media attention would not be even worth the effort involved.

These "supplicant" second- and third-tier candidates were, as Harris's own press secretary put it, "caught in a kind of vicious circle" (Arterton 1978a: 9).

One way for a candidate to break out of this vicious circle is to do something so dramatic that the media have to pay attention. Jesse Jackson's mission to Syria in December 1983 to negotiate the release of a captured U. S. airman is a case in point. During the first eight weeks of 1984, Jackson got more media coverage than all the other Democratic candidates combined—and more than Mondale got during the entire primary season (Brady 1985a: Tables 3 and 4). The payoff for Jackson in terms of public familiarity is reflected in Table 4.1.[2] But Jackson's strategy, although inspired, is also extremely risky.

Short of a dramatic political coup like Jackson's, the only sure way for relatively unknown candidates to overcome the hurdle of public awareness is to demonstrate their "seriousness" in the currency most valued by the press—electoral success. Before the first actual caucuses and primaries the candidates' opportunities to demonstrate electoral success are, of course, quite limited. That is why informal caucuses, straw polls, and the like are sometimes blown up to bizarre proportions. But these preliminary skirmishes are small potatoes compared to the first real political tests, in Iowa and New Hampshire. Candidates who do well in those states are vaulted into public prominence, those who do not are left behind, hardly heard from again except briefly when they formally withdraw from the race.

The effects of this "winnowing" process (Matthews 1978) are clearly evident in the candidates' subsequent public visibility. Figure 4.1 shows how the proportion of the public claiming to "know something about" some of the candidates changed during the 1976

[2] Of course, not all of Jackson's coverage or recognition was due to his Syrian trip. Jackson's very candidacy was newsworthy because his was the first major presidential campaign by a black candidate. Nevertheless, a detailed look at the media coverage data suggests that Jackson's mission to Syria was a genuine media bonanza, bringing him much more coverage than he would have received simply in his role as a black trailblazer.

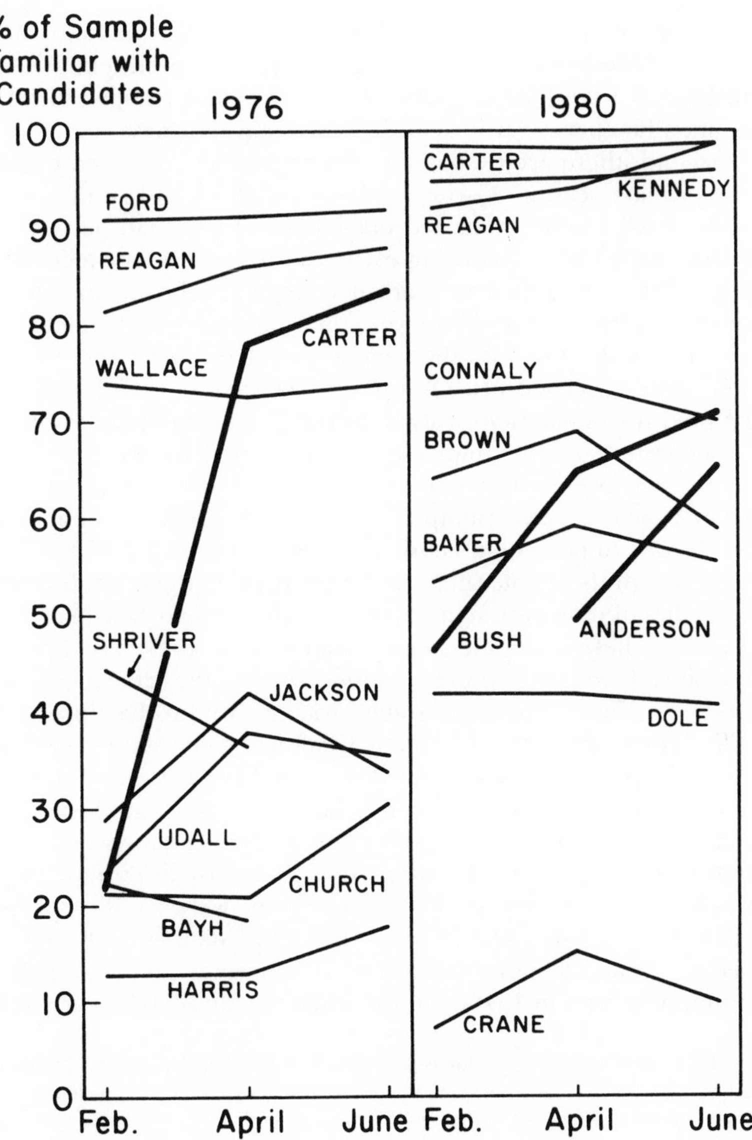

FIGURE 4.1 Changes in Public Familiarity with Primary Candidates, 1976 and 1980.

and 1980 primary campaigns. The various candidates' fortunes can be summarized in three distinct patterns.

First, some candidates were well known at the beginning of the campaign and remained well known. This group included Ford, Reagan, and Wallace in 1976, and Carter, Kennedy, Reagan, and—at a slightly lower level—Brown and Connally in 1980. Most of these candidates were veterans of previous presidential campaigns; all were familiar public figures. Not surprisingly, they remained familiar regardless of their electoral fortunes.

Second, there are candidates who successfully emerged during the primary season—Carter in 1976, and Bush and Anderson in 1980. Each candidate started out known to less than half of the public, each had a surprising early season primary or caucus success, and each gained substantial recognition during the subsequent several weeks. Moreover, the gains in recognition were roughly proportional to the magnitudes of the successes: Anderson's pair of second-place finishes in Massachusetts and Vermont boosted his familiarity by about fifteen percentage points; Bush's upset victory in the Iowa caucuses increased his familiarity by more than twenty-five percentage points; and Carter's string of primary and caucus triumphs in early 1976 drove his familiarity level from 20 percent in February to 80 percent in June.[3]

Although these emerging candidates provide the most dramatic examples of momentum in action, the third set may be equally significant. These candidates began with relatively low levels of public visibility, failed to capture attention during the campaign, and were winnowed. There are some variations within this third category: Henry Jackson and Morris Udall had some success early in the 1976 primary season, gained some visibility between February and April, but stalled (or worse) between April and June; and Frank Church had some success late in the primary season and only began to gain visibility after April. But, most important, these candidates failed to crack the big time. Some were significant players in the primary season drama (Jackson, Udall, and Church together garnered more than four million votes and won half a dozen primaries in 1976), but they failed to attract the nearly-uni-

[3] The payoff in familiarity for Bush's Iowa victory is underestimated in Figure 4.1 because the first (February) reading in the 1980 NES survey was taken after the Iowa caucuses. Gallup and other polls conducted earlier in the year suggest that Bush gained more in recognition before this first reading than after it. See, for example, Keeter and Zukin (1984: 72–73).

versal public recognition necessary to make them successful contenders.

To examine these same patterns of familiarity in more detail, it is helpful to turn to the weekly data generated by the 1984 NES survey. Figure 4.2 shows weekly trends in public familiarity during the 1984 primary season for three candidates—Walter Mondale, Gary Hart, and Ruebin Askew. (As in Figure 4.1, familiarity is measured by the proportion of survey respondents of the candidate's party who are willing to rate him at a given point in the campaign.) Mondale is typical of the candidates well known at the beginning of their campaigns. The proportion of Democratic survey respondents familiar with him in each week varied, for the most part, between 90 and 100 percent. Hart is the one contender, in 1984, who fit the second pattern of emergent candidates; although relatively unknown at the beginning of the campaign, he, too, had achieved nearly universal familiarity by the end of the primary season. Finally, Askew is representative of candidates who, like Hart, began the primary season relatively unknown but did not have the good luck to emerge into the forefront of public attention during the campaign; Askew ended the primary season about where he began it, known to roughly half of the Democratic respondents in the NES sample.

Figure 4.2 is more interesting than Figure 4.1 because it sheds light on the detailed dynamics of Hart's emergence. The connection between the horse race and public familiarity appears with striking clarity. Almost all manifest public learning about Hart occurred in precisely the three-week window beginning with his second-place finish in the Iowa caucuses, continuing with his dramatic primary victories in New Hampshire and Vermont, and ending with the Hart–Mondale standoff on Super Tuesday. Moreover, the rate at which the public learned about Hart during this period provides a remarkable example of the potential impact of electoral success and consequent media attention on the political consciousness of the public; in three weeks Hart more than doubled his level of public familiarity, becoming known, if we can extrapolate from these figures, to nearly four million people every day. As Hart himself put it (WGBH 1984), "You can get awful famous in this country in seven days."

So far I have dealt with familiarity only in the most basic sense of willingness to rate the candidates. But it seems reasonable to expect that the dynamics of learning about the candidates in this general sense would also apply to more specific perceptions about

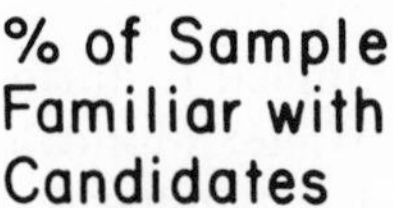

FIGURE 4.2 Familiarity with Mondale, Hart, and Askew, 1984.

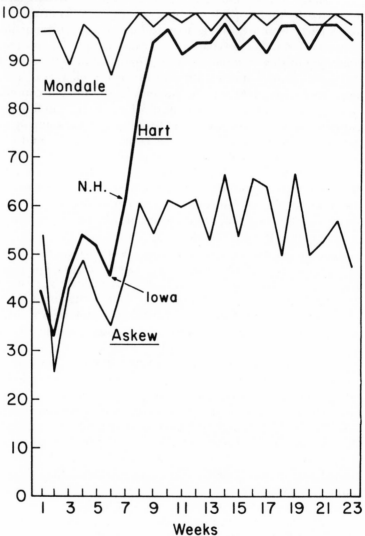

the candidates' political identities. Figure 4.3 shows how the trend in familiarity with Hart shown in Figure 4.2 compares with the corresponding trends in willingness to rate him on a battery of twelve character traits and place him on three issue scales.[4] Because these questions were not asked about Hart in the first seven weeks of the NES survey, it is impossible to make the relevant comparisons until after the New Hampshire primary. By that time a little less than half the sample was willing to place Hart on each of the issues, and a little more than half was willing to rate him on each of the character traits. Both these proportions thus lagged two weeks or so behind the corresponding proportion willing to provide an overall rating of Hart, although they increased even faster than overall ratings in the subsequent two weeks. After Super Tuesday all three trend lines were essentially flat, but it is worth noting that the ceiling for issue placements is somewhat lower than for overall ratings or traits.[5]

4.2 The Nature of Uncertainty

The notion of familiarity considered thus far is based on the manifest behavior of survey respondents—their willingness or unwillingness to rate or claim to "know something about" a candidate. But this manifest behavior reflects indirectly a psychological reality of more general importance for electoral behavior: the fact that every prospective voter is more or less uncertain about who the candidates are and how they measure up to the voter's own political standards. The nearly universal familiarity with some candidates evident in Table 4.1 should not be mistaken for the absence of uncertainty about the candidates' quality in this broader sense.

Uncertainty, as I use the term here, is uncertainty about a can-

[4] The character traits included "hard-working," "decent," "compassionate," "commands respect," "intelligent," "moral," "kind," "inspiring," "knowledgable," "sets a good example," "really cares about people like me," and "provides strong leadership." Survey respondents were asked how much they thought each of these traits fit their impression of each candidate. The issue scales included general ideology (liberal-conservative), government services, and defense spending. Respondents were asked if they usually thought of each candidate as a liberal, a conservative, or a moderate, whether they thought the candidate wanted to increase or decrease defense spending, and so on.

[5] This difference probably reflects, among other things, the fact that respondents who did not place themselves on a given issue were not asked to place Hart; thus, apparent familiarity with Hart's positions is limited by the respondents' unwillingness to place themselves.

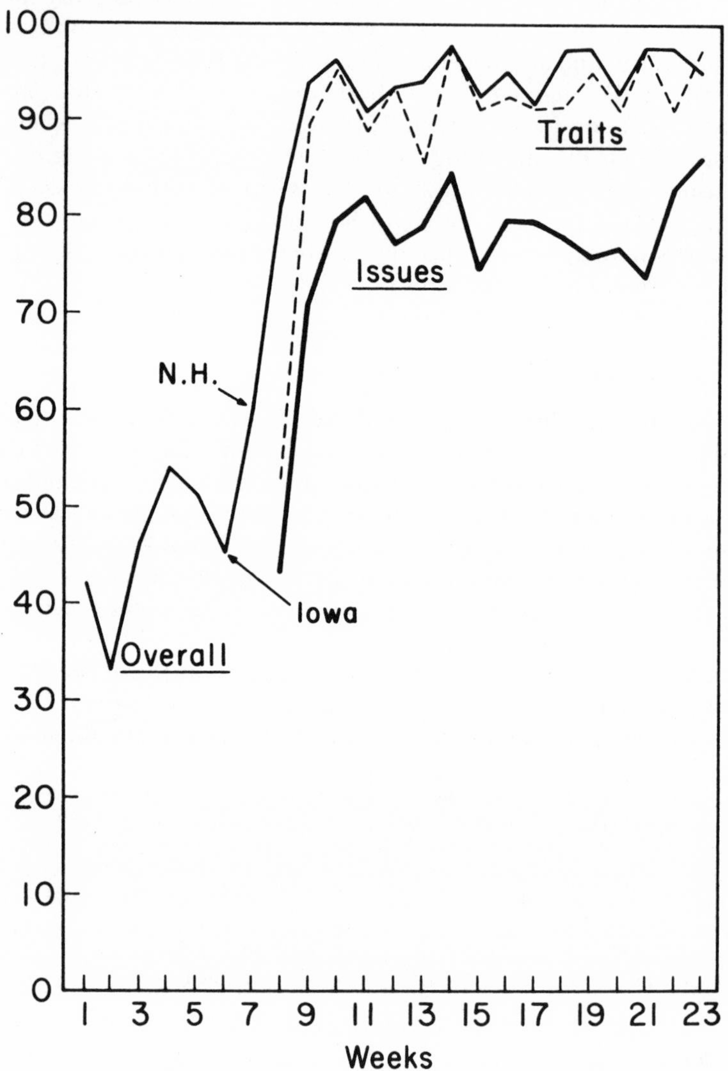

FIGURE 4.3 General and Specific Familiarity with Hart, 1984.

didate's "true" rating on some overall evaluative scale. For the sake of concreteness, it will be helpful to describe the specific evaluative scale used by survey respondents in the NES surveys, and then to define the concept of uncertainty in terms of the underlying attitudes which that evaluative scale is intended to tap. The mechanism used in NES surveys to elicit respondents' general evaluations of candidates is called a "feeling thermometer." Respondents are read an introductory statement along these lines:

> I'd like to get your feelings toward some of our political leaders and other people who are in the news these days. I'll read the name of a person, and I'd like you to rate that person using this feeling thermometer. You may use any number from 0 to 100 for rating. Ratings between 50 degrees and 100 degrees mean that you feel favorable and warm toward the person. Ratings between 0 degrees and 50 degrees mean that you don't feel too favorable toward the person. If you *don't feel particularly warm or cold* toward the person, you would rate the person at the 50 degree mark.

Then respondents are read the candidates' names and asked to supply a thermometer rating for each.

The simplest possible interpretation of these thermometer ratings is that they correspond directly to the evaluations respondents carry around in their heads. It is as if I had, tucked away in a corner of my brain, an index card reading: "Gary Hart: 63." When called upon by my friendly interviewer to evaluate Hart, I need simply rummage through my index cards, pull out Gary Hart's, and read off the rating. However, one of the difficulties with this simple interpretation is that real people may never bother to summarize their impressions of a candidate in anything like an overall evaluation until called upon by the interviewer to do so. Rather than simply reading off "Gary Hart: 63," I might have to gather together fugitive scraps of information from here and there: "Gary Hart (last week's debate): 75," "Gary Hart (yesterday's television ad): 41," "Gary Hart (views of coworkers): 55," and so on. I would then have to synthesize these varied scraps of information into an overall evaluation in which the debate, the television advertisement, and the coworkers each received their due weight—all on the spur of the moment and with a stranger waiting to record the result.[6]

[6] This view of public opinion as something constructed on the spot after sampling

Another difficulty with the simple view is that, even if I can accurately and reliably synthesize my various impressions of Hart on the spur of the moment, the resulting summary evaluation may still involve some substantial element of uncertainty. Gary Hart may be a "40" or he may be an "80"; short of devoting my life to a study of his character, capabilities, and career, and perhaps even then, how am I to know for sure? It is simply impossible to be entirely certain about such a matter.

Fortunately, it is possible to take account of this second difficulty in a natural way, simply by supposing that my summary evaluation takes the form not of a single rating like 63 but of a range of more or less likely possibilities. It is convenient to represent this range of possibilities as a *probability distribution* like the one pictured in Figure 4.4(a). The specific probability distribution illustrated in the figure represents one example of an uncertain evaluation. It suggests that my best estimate of Hart's quality is 63 (the *probability density* is greatest at this point), but that 50 and 80 are also fairly plausible possibilities (the probability density is less at these points than at 63, but still appreciably greater than zero). Some other possibilities are much less plausible. All the ratings below 30, for example, have very little probability density attached to them; this suggests that, although I am unsure about Hart, I do know enough about him to be confident that he is not an out-and-out disaster.

Probability distributions like the one shown in Figure 4.4(a) can take a wide variety of forms—flat or peaked, symmetric or skewed, and so on. But much of the flavor of any specific distribution can be summarized in two simple characteristics: where it is centered along the "thermometer," and how spread out it is around that central location. The first of these characteristics is called the *mean* of the distribution; the second is called the *variance* of the distribution. The probability distribution illustrated in Figure 4.4(a) has a mean of 63 and a variance of 144. For purposes of comparison, Figure 4.4(b) shows a distribution with a mean of 36 and a variance of 144, and Figure 4.4(c) shows a distribution with a mean of 63 and a variance of 576. The means and variances of these distributions have natural substantive interpretations. In each case, the mean reflects my average evaluation of Hart, weighing all the possibilities by their relative plausibility. When confronted by an interviewer wanting a single "thermometer rating" for Hart, this is the

from some collection of "considerations" or "schema" has been developed and defended by Zaller (1984) and Feldman (1985).

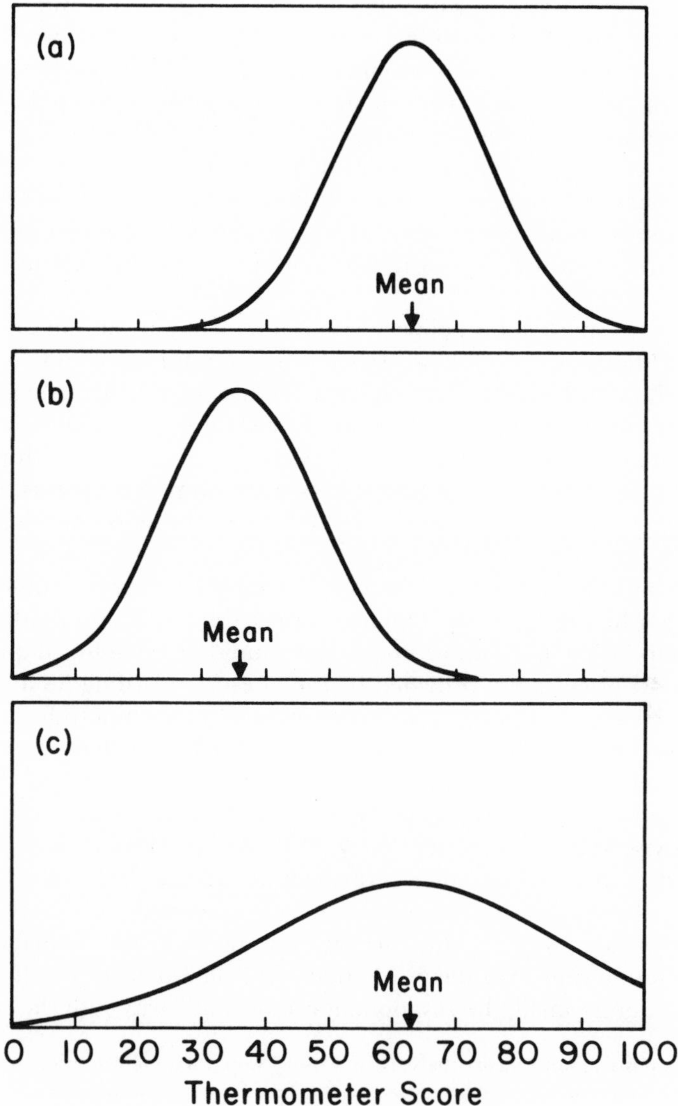

FIGURE 4.4 Hypothetical Uncertain Evaluations.

number I would want to report.[7] And in each case, the variance of the distribution reflects how *uncertain* I am about Hart: distributions with smaller variances (like the ones in Figure 4.4(a) and 4.4(b)) reflect less uncertainty about Hart than those with larger variances (like the one in Figure 4.4(c)).

All of this may seem somewhat abstract and pedantic. But it has the great virtue of providing a systematic logical framework in which to consider one of the most prevalent and important features of the political environment in actual primary campaigns—uncertainty about the candidates. If you are willing to imagine people carrying candidate evaluations around in their heads as probability distributions, it is no difficult matter to picture those probability distributions with bigger or smaller variances and to talk correspondingly about the evaluations as more or less uncertain.

This perspective on political uncertainty will play an important role in the analysis to follow, especially in Chapters 5, 6, and 7. For now, though, I want to put it to very limited use in addressing the subjects of familiarity and learning introduced in Section 4.1. In particular, I want to relate the survey data on familiarity with primary candidates from Section 4.1 to the survey respondents' underlying uncertainty about the candidates in the sense developed here.

My basic assumption is that, when faced with a survey question asking whether they are familiar with a candidate, respondents compare what they know about the candidate to some implicit standard of certainty provided by the question wording. (Thus, a question asking whether you "know enough about him to have an opinion" might invoke a higher standard of certainty than one asking whether you "have ever heard anything about him.") If they know enough about the candidate, respondents answer positively; otherwise they answer negatively. Because uncertainty is represented by the variance of a probability distribution, my interpretation of responses to survey questions dealing with candidate familiarity amounts to this: if the variance of the probability distribution reflecting the respondent's evaluation of the candidate is sufficiently small, the respondent claims familiarity with the can-

[7] It is possible to formalize the sense in which I would want to report the mean, using the criterion of average squared error. See, for example, Blackwell (1969: 36–38). For present purposes the point seems intuitively plausible enough to stand without explicit justification.

didate; if not, the respondent does not claim familiarity with the candidate.[8]

It should be obvious that a respondent's willingness or unwillingness to rate a candidate on the feeling thermometer provides a very indirect and imperfect indication of the respondent's underlying uncertainty. More direct, more sensitive indicators would obviously be preferable, but they do not exist. If we are to study uncertainty at all, we must make do, for the moment, with the data already at hand. At least the simple threshold model of response suggested here makes it possible to begin to get at underlying levels of uncertainty, if we have some ideas about how that uncertainty might be related to other characteristics of individual respondents and of the settings in which they respond. As in my analysis of perceptions of the candidates' chances in Chapter 3, I investigate here a combination of personal and environmental factors. Among the latter the most obvious predictor of public familiarity is the sheer quantity of coverage a candidate gets in the news media. Among the former the most obvious predictor of familiarity for a given individual is the extent to which that individual is exposed to and pays attention to the news media's campaign coverage.

Thus, I aim to relate observable patterns of familiarity in the survey data to media coverage and individual media use, using my notion of underlying uncertainty and the threshold model of survey responses. It is instructive to see how much can be accounted for using these simple ingredients. Even the dramatic growth of public familiarity with Gary Hart in 1984 can be readily and systematically accommodated by a threshold model driven by these explanatory factors. This fact is evident in Figure 4.5, which compares the aggregate trend in willingness to rate Hart from Figure 4.2 with predicted rates based on the threshold model.[9] Given the imperfections of the data on which the predictions are based, the correspondence is striking.

[8] This "threshold model" is described in more detail in Appendix B.1. It makes sense to suppose that respondents might gauge their own uncertainty, the standard of certainty invoked by the question, or both with some imprecision; I account for this possibility by supposing a random element also enters into the comparison.

[9] The statistical evidence relating familiarity with Hart to education, individual media use, and media coverage via the threshold model is reported in Table A.14 in Appendix C. The estimated levels of familiarity shown in Figure 4.5 for each week of the 1984 primary season were generated by applying the statistical relationships in Table A.14 to the observed characteristics of each week's respondents in the 1984 NES survey.

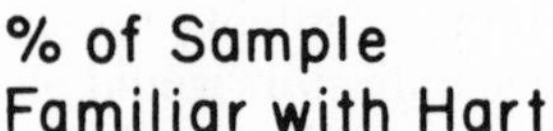

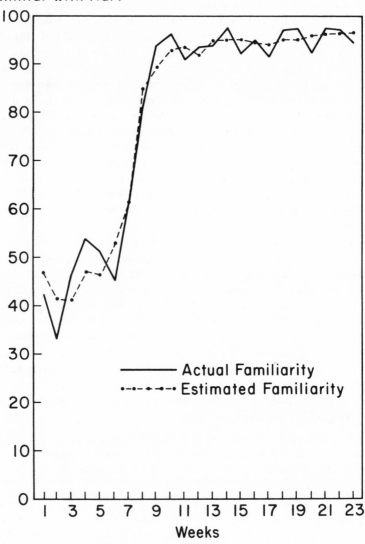

FIGURE 4.5 Actual and Estimated Familiarity with Hart, 1984.

In addition to capturing the overall trend in willingness to rate Hart, the threshold model accounts nicely for the distinctive reactions of those portions of the public most and least attentive to the news media. These reactions are shown in Figure 4.6.[10] It is clear from the figure that the fifth of the sample most attuned to the news media became familiar with Hart considerably earlier than the fifth least attuned to the news media. Virtually all of the most attuned segment of the public had crossed the threshold of familiarity even before Hart's New Hampshire victory; after that point there were only occasional exceptions to the pattern of universal familiarity. In contrast, only a third of those least attuned to the media were familiar with Hart before New Hampshire; the lion's share of the learning in this group occurred in the two weeks after New Hampshire, and the proportion of the group familiar with Hart continued to increase gradually throughout the primary season. It is reassuring to note that the relatively simple model of uncertainty employed here reproduces these patterns with substantial accuracy.

The results in Figures 4.5 and 4.6 provide some support for both the threshold model of survey response and the notion of underlying uncertainty adopted here. Because they relate observable survey responses to underlying uncertainty, the results also allow us to make some useful inferences about how much and how quickly individual respondents learned about the candidates, even though we cannot observe that learning directly. In particular, we can use the manifest changes in aggregate familiarity evident in the NES data (the increasing proportion of the sample willing to rate Hart in Figures 4.5 and 4.6) to infer corresponding changes in the relative uncertainty of respondents' underlying evaluations of Hart at various stages in the campaign.[11] For example, Figure

[10] The actual familiarity levels in Figure 4.6 were calculated by isolating the top and bottom fifths of the entire Democratic primary sample with respect to media use and plotting the proportion familiar with Hart in each group for each week of the primary season. The estimated familiarity levels were calculated by applying the statistical results from Table A.14 in Appendix C to the average media use values for the upper and lower fifths of the sample.

[11] The logic by which the relative uncertainty of unobserved latent evaluations can be deduced from observed survey responses is detailed in Appendix B.1. It is impossible, in this context, to learn anything about *absolute* levels of latent uncertainty. But by estimating latent uncertainty about each candidate for each respondent on the basis of both observed characteristics and observed connections between characteristics and willingness to rate the candidates, we can compare *relative* uncertainty among respondents, among candidates, and over time.

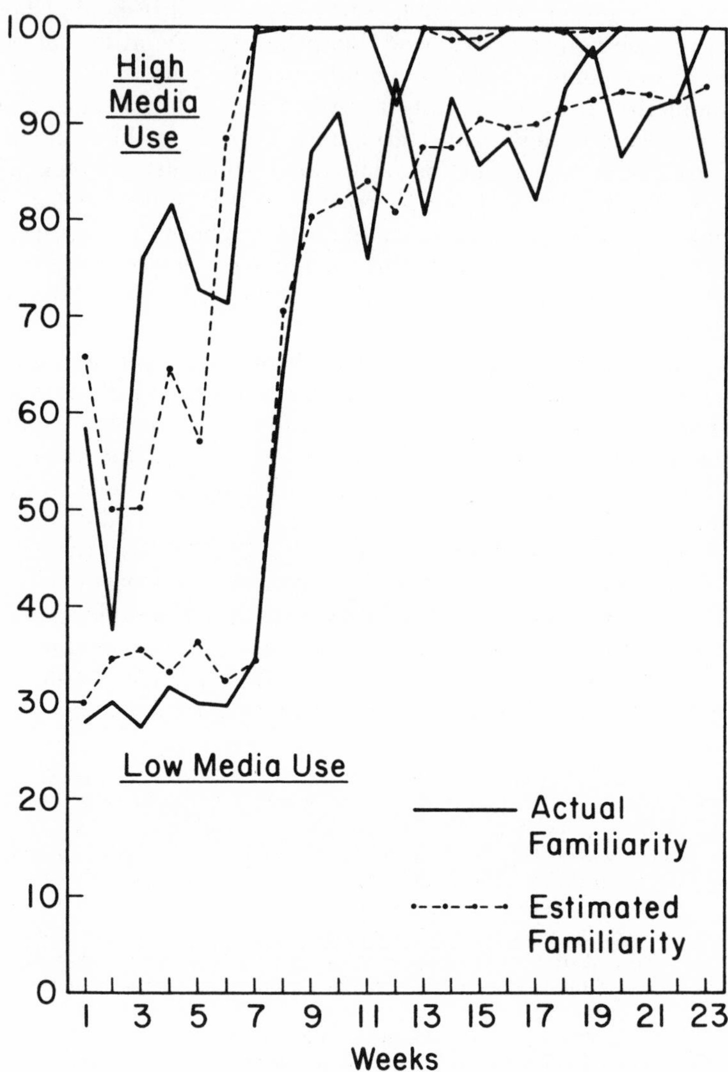

FIGURE 4.6 Media Use and Familiarity with Hart, 1984.

4.7 shows probability distributions representing uncertain evaluations of Hart among high and low media users at the beginning and end of the 1984 primary season. For each group, the probability distribution in Figure 4.7 illustrates the average variance (uncertainty) of Hart evaluations implied by the survey responses in Figure 4.6. The scale on which the distributions are shown is inherently arbitrary, but comparisons of the *relative* uncertainty implied by each of the four distributions are meaningful and politically significant. Comparing first the top and bottom panels on the left side of the figure, we see that respondents in the upper fifth of the sample in terms of media exposure and attention were less uncertain about Hart at the beginning of the campaign, on average, than those in the lower fifth. The variance of the distribution is perceptibly smaller for the high media use group. By comparing the left and right panels for each level of media use, we also see that those most attuned to the media learned more during the campaign (the reduction in variance from the left panel to the right panel was greater), although both groups were much more certain about Hart in June than they had been in January.

It is also possible to compare underlying uncertainty across candidates. Figure 4.8 shows average distributions of uncertain evaluations for both Hart and Mondale at the beginning of the campaign and again at the end of the campaign for the entire Democratic sample in the 1984 NES survey. A comparison of the top and bottom panels on the left side of the figure shows, not surprisingly, that respondents were considerably less uncertain about Mondale than about Hart at the beginning of the campaign. Moving from left to right, we see that they learned about both candidates during the subsequent five months, but particularly about Hart; thus, the difference in uncertainty between the two candidates was considerably less at the end of the campaign (the right side of Figure 4.8) than at the beginning (the left side of the figure).

The same pattern of learning is illustrated in another way in Figure 4.9, which shows average levels of information about Mondale and Hart for each week of the 1984 primary season. Information is, roughly speaking, the flip side of uncertainty: the *less* uncertain a respondent's evaluation of a candidate is, the *more* information she has about the candidate and, given the threshold model of the survey response, the more likely she is to be willing to rate the candidate on a "feeling thermometer."[12] The figure suggests that

[12] More technically, information is measured here by the *precision* of the average

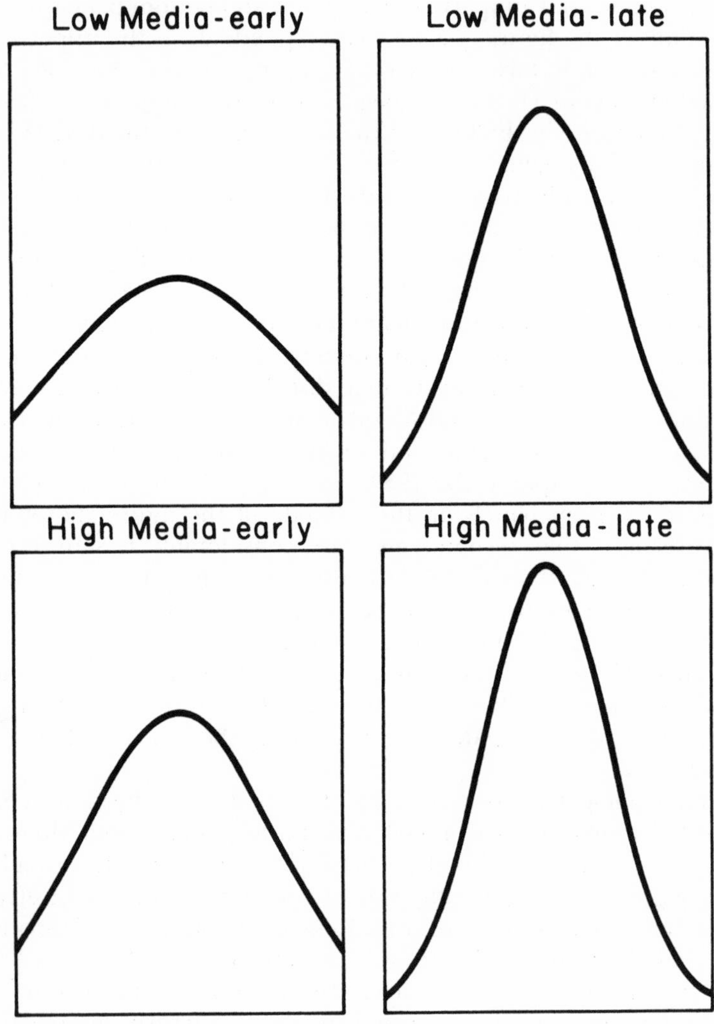

FIGURE 4.7 Media Use and Reduction in Uncertainty about Hart, 1984.

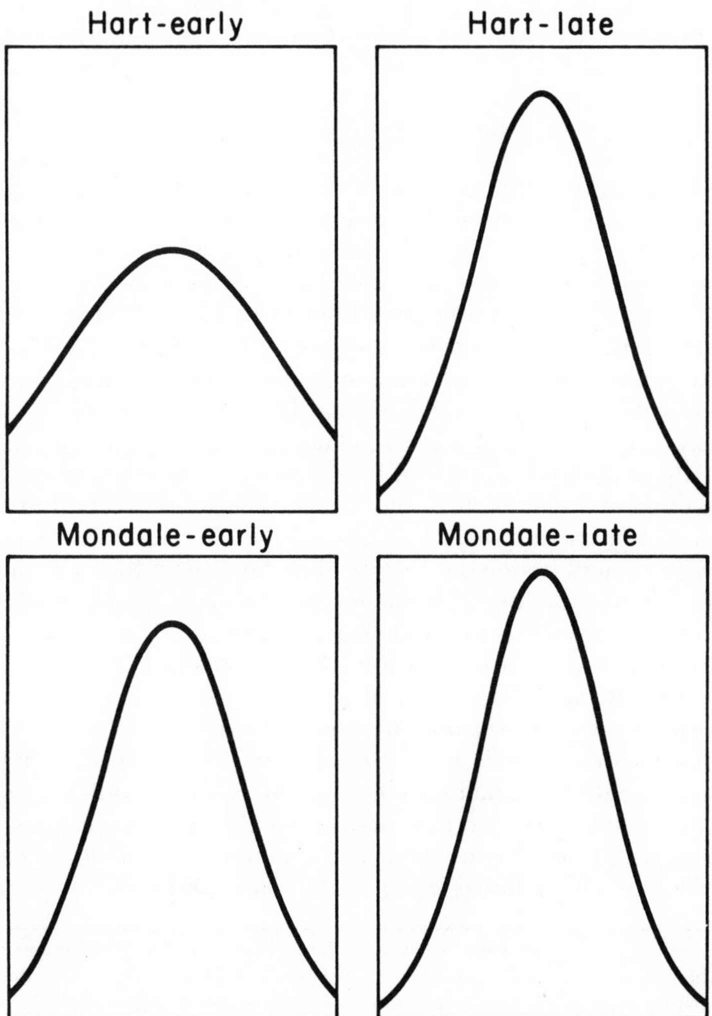

FIGURE 4.8 Relative Uncertainty about Hart and Mondale, 1984.

information about Mondale increased at a moderate, fairly steady rate once the public phase of the campaign began in Iowa. Information about Hart accumulated much more rapidly in the first month of the public campaign (the month of Iowa, New Hampshire, and Super Tuesday), but then it increased at a more moderate rate comparable to the corresponding rate for Mondale. Thus, the relative similarity of average levels of uncertainty for Mondale and Hart at the end of the campaign, shown in the right half of Figure 4.8, can be seen in Figure 4.9 to reflect a political reality already substantially established some three months earlier.

4.3 The Effects of Uncertainty

The patterns of uncertainty sketched out in Section 4.2 seem plausible in light of the particular circumstances of the 1984 campaign. Thus, they provide some additional support for the notions and indicators of information and uncertainty outlined here. But what do information and uncertainty thus defined have to do with primary voting? The key connections are of three distinct sorts.

First, I have shown that a minimal level of information, enough to be willing to rate a candidate on a "feeling thermometer," is virtually a necessary condition for political support. Thus, differences among candidates in levels of information (the sort illustrated for Hart and Mondale early in the 1984 campaign in Figure 4.9) can have considerable political significance, if they leave many prospective voters under the threshold of familiarity for one candidate but over the threshold for another. Similarly, major increases in information about a candidate over the course of a primary season (for example, those shown for Hart in Figure 4.9) can greatly expand the candidate's pool of potential supporters by moving prospective voters over the threshold of basic familiarity.

If this threshold effect was the only effect of information on the vote, it would be significant enough. But as it turns out, information is positively related to support even among those prospective voters who have already crossed the minimal threshold of basic familiarity. Other things being equal, voters prefer the devil they

---

respondent's evaluation, where precision is defined as the reciprocal of the variance of the evaluation. Like the probability distributions in Figures 4.7 and 4.8, the information levels in Figure 4.9 are meaningful only in relative terms. The absolute scale values from one to ten shown in the figure are arbitrary, although the zero point does have a substantive significance which will become clearer in Chapter 5.

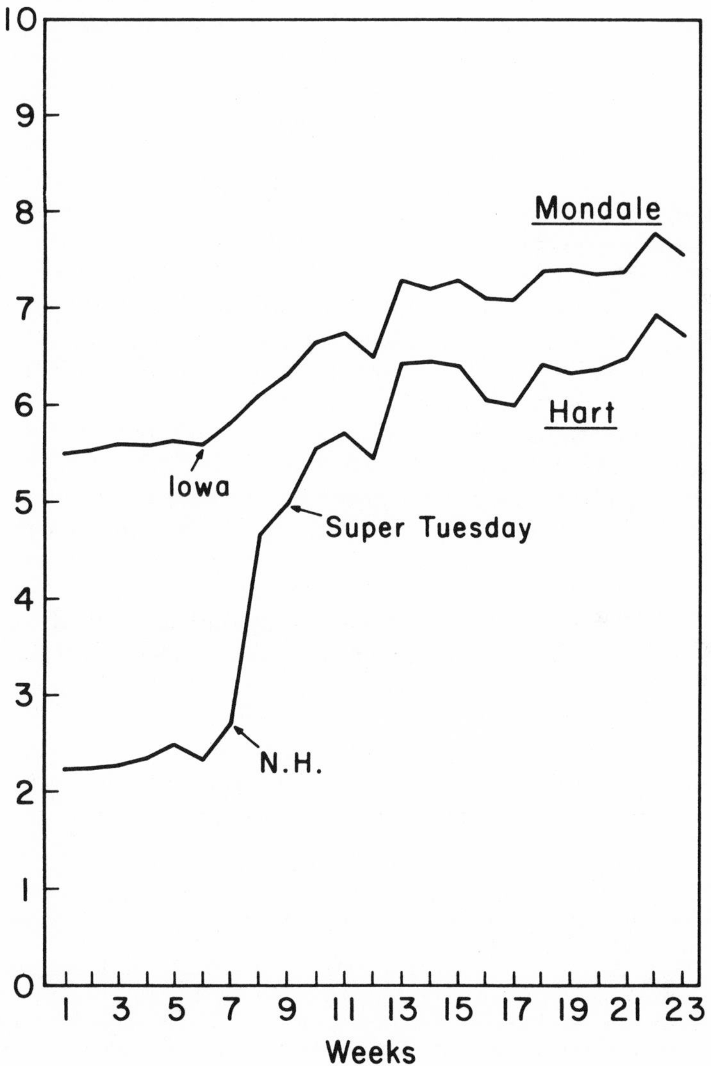

FIGURE 4.9 Average Levels of Information about Hart and Mondale, 1984.

know more about to the devil they know less about.[13] As a result, even differences in information levels well beyond the threshold level marked by the willingness to rate a candidate on the feeling thermometer may have significant political implications.

The combined impact of these two distinct information effects on choices between Mondale and Hart in the 1984 primary campaign is shown in Figure 4.10. For each of three hypothetical evaluations (thermometer ratings), the figure shows how the probability of supporting a candidate varied with information about the candidate (measured on the same arbitrary one-to-ten scale shown in Figure 4.9) because of the combined effects of the familiarity threshold and of more general "risk aversion."[14] For low levels of information—for example, the average level for Hart at the beginning of the 1984 campaign (marked by the "Early" point in the figure)—even those respondents who evaluated a candidate fairly favorably were very unlikely to support him. This portion of the figure merely reiterates the point that some minimal level of familiarity is virtually a necessary condition for supporting any candidate. The rest of the figure shows that support increased dramatically with increasing information, first among those respondents most favorably inclined toward the candidate on other grounds and eventually among those less favorably inclined as well. The total gains in support for Hart attributable directly to his emergence into the public consciousness between mid-January ("Early") and mid-June ("Late") ranged from more than sixty percentage points among respondents who viewed him very favorably to about fifteen percentage points even among respondents who were moderately unfavorable toward him on substantive grounds.

These results make it clear, from the candidate's viewpoint, why being well known is a very considerable political resource and why the amount of information prospective primary voters accumulated about Gary Hart during the 1984 campaign was of tremendous political significance. Candidates well known to the public at

[13] This is one of many situations in which people prove to be "risk averse"—that is, to prefer a relatively known quantity to an otherwise equally attractive but relatively unknown quantity. For some independent evidence that voters are risk averse, see Bartels (1986).

[14] The information effects shown in Figure 4.10 are based on the statistical result reported under the heading of "Information" in the first column of Table A.18 in Appendix C. Analysis there, based on the assumption of a two-candidate race, includes only those respondents in the 1984 NES survey who expressed support for Mondale or Hart as either their first or second choice for the Democratic nomination. A more detailed description of the analysis is presented in Appendix C.5.

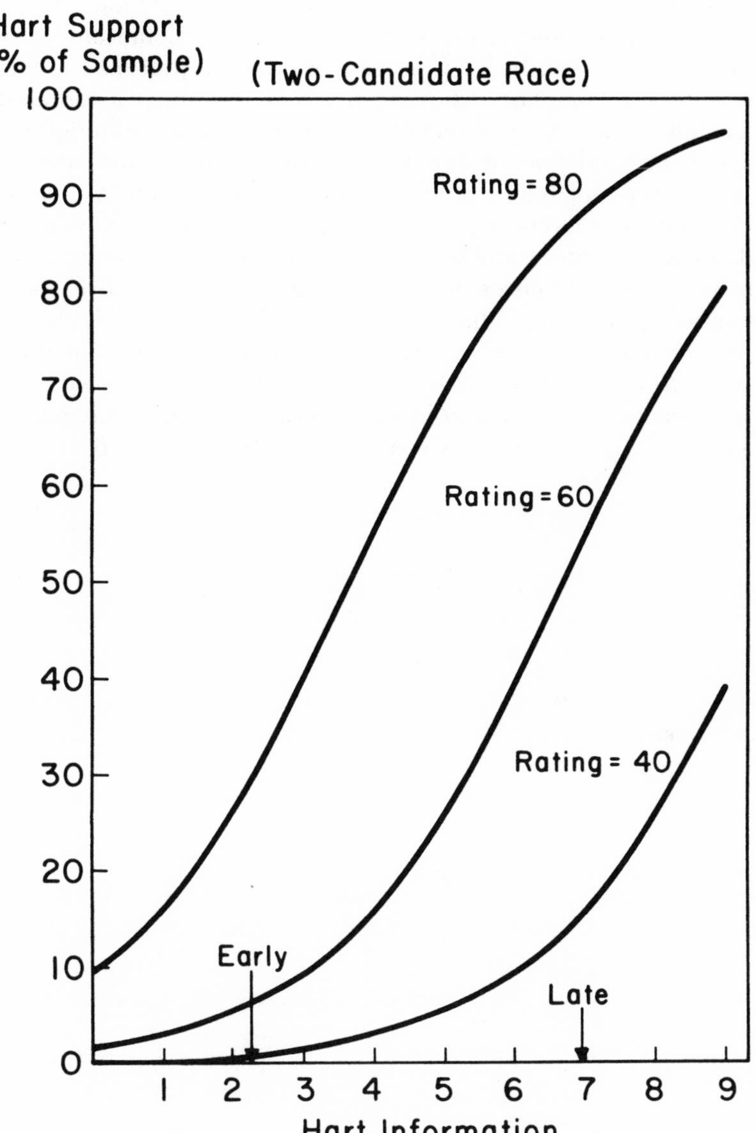

FIGURE 4.10 Direct Effect of Information on Support for Hart, 1984.

least have a chance to attract widespread political support; candidates who remain unknown do not. Candidates like Hart, who go from being unknown to being well known in a matter of days or weeks, go from certain defeat to potential victory.

The third important connection between information and primary voting is somewhat less obvious but equally significant: information may alter the very process by which a prospective voter evaluates a candidate. Knowing more or less about a candidate may allow the voter to make more or less sophisticated judgments about the candidate on substantive grounds, disregarding the fact that information is an absolute resource in and of itself. As a result, differences in levels of information and uncertainty across candidates, across voters, and over time provide a significant key to corresponding differences in the very nature of prospective voters' political evaluations. Thus, the patterns illustrated in this chapter provide some leverage for the systematic incorporation of information and uncertainty into a more general analysis of the dynamics of candidate evaluation in presidential nominating campaigns. That more general analysis is developed in Chapters 5, 6, and 7.

CHAPTER FIVE

Politics in the Campaign

So far I have described a strangely apolitical political world, in which the general public's prevailing perceptions of the campaign have more to do with the candidates' current standings in the horse race than with issue positions, group interests, or leadership capacities. This emphasis is not accidental. The horse race does color public reactions to the nominating campaign in pervasive and important ways. But political substance matters, too. Through the din of horse race coverage, the hoopla of rallies, and the frantic chasing after "Big Mo," the enduring political identities of candidates and citizens gradually shape the perceptions and evaluations on which primary votes are based.

Perhaps surprisingly, the contention that political issues matter in primary campaigns is at odds with the observations of some campaign analysts. An analysis of 1984 NES data by Shanks et al. (1985: 37) led them "to dismiss issue and ideological proximity as factors in the 1984 contest between Mondale and Hart." Bicker (1978: 108) commented on the 1976 Democratic campaign: "issues and attributes of candidates seemed to play little if any role in the voters' choice." And Gopoian (1982: 544), summarizing his analysis of primary voting among both Democrats and Republicans in 1976, concluded that "the 'indistinct mutterings' of candidates and voters alike precluded" the sort of policy accountability envisioned in democratic theory.

In this chapter I aim to provide a coherent account of when and how political substance does matter in primary campaigns. Part of the perception that issues are unimportant reflects the overly narrow conception of "issues" prevalent in mainstream voting research. If we focus more broadly on prospective voters' political predispositions—predispositions based on a wide variety of social characteristics, policy stands, and group attachments—the role of politics in the campaign looks more significant and more comprehensible. Even then, issues can sometimes appear unimportant in primary campaigns because the competing candidates project similar political appeals; under these circumstances a given issue stand or group attachment may be an important consideration in voters' evaluations of the candidates and still have no observable *net* impact on the voters' choices of one candidate or another. Finally, issues *are* less important in some campaigns than in others, for some candidates than for others, and for some voters than for others. By relating issue effects to key features of the campaign context, specifically, to prevailing levels of information about the candidates, the analysis presented here provides a systematic explanation for those variations.

5.1 Political Predispositions

Walter Mondale entered the 1984 Democratic campaign with a strongly developed political identity. Mondale began his political career as a protégé of Hubert Humphrey in Minnesota's traditional liberal school of New Deal Democratic party politics. Throughout his career the principles he learned in that school remained paramount: loyalty to the traditions of the Democratic party and to the variety of liberal causes and New Deal interest groups on which those traditions were built.

Given these facts about Mondale's basic political character, it should not be surprising to find that prospective voters tended to evaluate him, in part, on the basis of their own corresponding political predispositions. By *political predispositions* I mean the whole range of social characteristics, group loyalties, and basic issue stands that shape public attitudes about politics. These relatively permanent characteristics and loyalties constitute the landscape against which the highly dynamic events of a particular nominating campaign are played out. As a result, they provide our most important points of leverage for making political sense out of the specific events of any given campaign season.

The first column of Table 5.1 shows that evaluations of Mondale during the 1984 campaign *were* related to the social and political characteristics of the people doing the evaluating in systematic, comprehensible ways. Indeed, it is possible to read off from the table exactly the set of longstanding political loyalties I have ascribed to Mondale—loyalties to the traditional Democratic brand of New Deal liberalism central to Mondale's career for two decades or more. Mondale was viewed relatively favorably by those advocating liberal positions on domestic spending (for the environment and jobs) and foreign policy (cooperation with Russia, defense cuts); by the older, socially traditional wing of his party; by those with attachments to various New Deal interest groups (unions, the

TABLE 5.1 Political Predispositions, 1984

	Mondale	Hart
Liberalism		
Liberal ideology (0–1)	—	4.7
(−) Cut government spending (0–1)	7.6	10.4
Environmental spending (0–1)	7.2	9.4
Government jobs (0–1)	5.4	—
Cooperate with Russia (0–1)	4.3	—
(−) Defense spending (0–1)	3.8	—
New Deal		
Black	4.9	−8.9
Jewish	8.7	−6.6
Catholic	1.2	−3.1
Union household	3.8	−4.9
(−) Income (in $1,000s)	0.093	—
Traditionalism		
(−) Education (in years)	—	−1.04
Age (in years)	0.115	−0.048
(−) Residential mobility (0–1)	7.6	—
Church attendance (0–1)	2.7	—
Spending to fight crime (0–1)	4.1	—
(−) Worse off financially (0–1)	−1.8	−8.8
Partisanship		
Strong Democrat	8.9	—
Weak Democrat	3.3	—

Source: Calculated from 1984 NES data.
Note: Figures reflect the effects of political and social characteristics on overall 0–100 thermometer ratings.

poor, Jews, blacks, and Catholics); and by those with strong partisan Democratic loyalties.

The numbers in the table show the magnitude of the impact of each of these characteristics on respondents' average ratings of Mondale on the hundred-point thermometer scale.[1] For example, the entry of 3.8 for "Union household" indicates that—other things being equal—respondents in labor unions (or with family members in labor unions) rated Mondale a little less than four points more favorably than did respondents with no union attachments. Similarly, the entry of 0.093 for "(−) Income (in $1,000s)" indicates that, on average, respondents with family incomes of

[1] These results, and those in the second column for Hart, are based on the statistical analysis of predispositions reported in Table A.15 in Appendix C. Unless otherwise specified in Table 5.1, each characteristic is measured on a zero-to-one scale for comparability. Characteristics omitted for either candidate had no significant effect.

$10,000 rated Mondale a little less than four points more favorably than did those with family incomes of $50,000 (since a $40,000 difference in income multiplied by an effect of .093 points per $1,000 produces a net difference of 3.7 thermometer points)—again, other things being equal.[2]

The second column of Table 5.1 provides parallel results for evaluations of Gary Hart. Like Mondale, Hart was viewed more favorably by liberals than by moderates. But unlike Mondale, Hart received relatively unfavorable ratings from social traditionalists, especially those with little formal education, and from respondents with various New Deal attachments. These results, too, make considerable sense in light of Hart's political identity as a new-style liberal unwilling, as he once said disparagingly, to be a "little Hubert Humphrey."

The results in Table 5.1 demonstrate quite clearly that political predispositions played an important role in voters' evaluations of the candidates in the 1984 campaign. Somewhat paradoxically, they also suggest two explanations for the inability of some previous analysts to find significant political effects in this and other recent nominating campaigns. One explanation turns on the distinction between direct and net effects; the other turns on how narrowly or broadly we conceive of the political factors influencing electoral choice.

First, even when ideology and issues have a significant impact on reactions to each of the candidates, they may fail to have a significant net effect on the choice between candidates (see Table 5.1). In 1984, survey respondents with relatively liberal issue positions were significantly more favorably disposed toward Mondale than those with more moderate positions, but they were also more favorably disposed toward Hart and by about the same amount. Both Mondale and Hart appear in Table 5.1 as essentially liberal political figures.

The same point is made even more clearly in Figure 5.1, which shows average public perceptions of Mondale and Hart on three issues—liberal ideology, government services, and defense spending. The two candidates appear virtually indistinguishable on these

[2] For each characteristic, the implicit comparison is with respondents assigned a score of zero on that characteristic—extreme conservatives in the case of "Liberal ideology," nonblacks in the case of "Black," and so on. For the partisanship variables ("Strong Democrat" and "Weak Democrat") the implicit comparison is with respondents who profess no partisan attachment but say they "lean" more toward the Democrats than toward the Republicans.

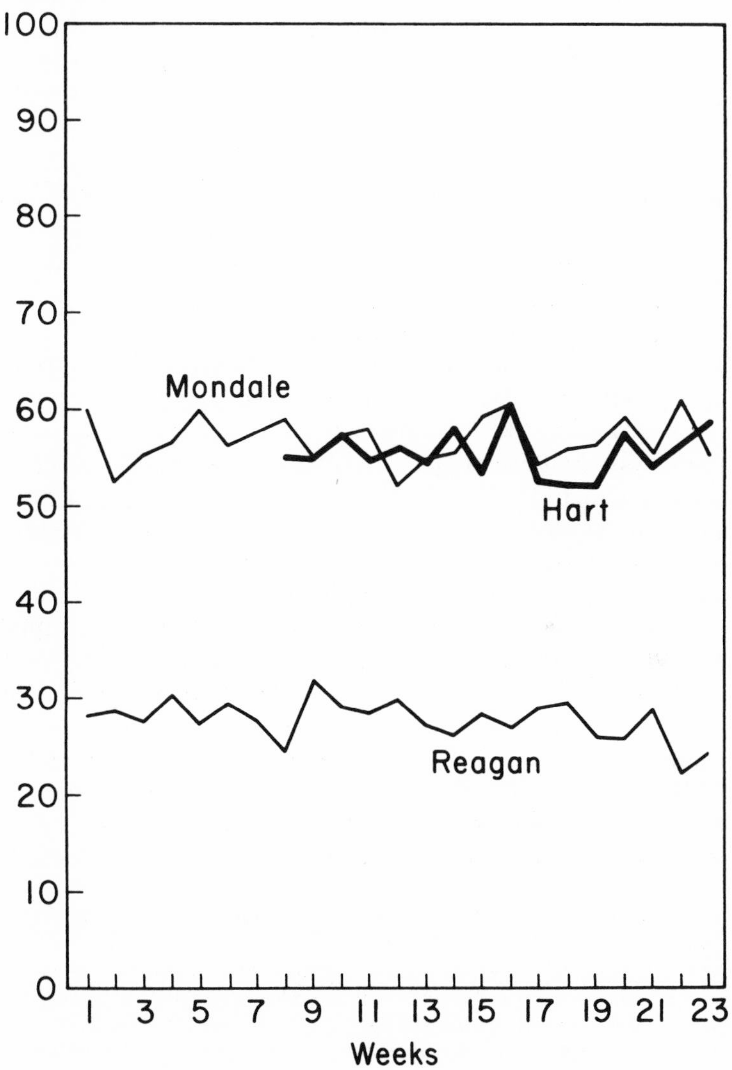

FIGURE 5.1 Perceived Liberalism of Mondale, Hart, and Reagan, 1984.

issues; both were viewed throughout the campaign as moderate liberals.[3] These public perceptions are consistent with Hart's own claim during the campaign that he and Mondale were "absolutely committed . . . to the same values and goals."[4] The insignificance of the differences between them is underlined by a further comparison, also shown in Figure 5.1, with a candidate who *was* politically distinct—Ronald Reagan.[5]

Given this pattern of issue positions, any effort to explain *choices between* Mondale and Hart on the basis of issues and ideology would be largely unsuccessful; the net effect of substantive political factors would be considered negligible. Such a conclusion might be justified in a strict descriptive sense, but it would provide a very misleading picture of the role of substantive political factors among the potential bases of choice in primary campaigns.

The Mondale–Hart campaign is only one of several in which the effects of ideology and issues may have been obscured by similarities in the positions of the competing candidates. The 1980 Republican campaign has been described as one in which all the candidates, with the sole exception of John Anderson, tried to look as much as possible like Ronald Reagan (Cannon and Peterson 1980): Crane was like Reagan but younger, Connally was like Reagan but more dynamic, Bush was like Reagan but with a better resumé, and so on. The 1976 Democratic campaign included a number of candidates who were similarly indistinguishable on ideological or policy grounds (Birch Bayh, Jimmy Carter, Henry Jackson, Sargent Shriver, and—waiting in the wings—Hubert Humphrey). There were, of course, important differences among these candidates, but they were mostly differences of nuance and style rather than of basic political values. Even the two campaigns involving major challenges of incumbent presidents (Reagan's in 1976 and Kennedy's in 1980) were fought on relatively narrow portions of the national political landscape. In each of these instances it seems likely that some effects of issues and ideology on evaluations of the

[3] The same similarity of perceptions is evident when the issues are considered one at a time rather than in the summary form shown in Figure 5.1.

[4] Hart's rejoinder to attacks on his credentials as a mainstream Democrat appeared in the *Washington Post National Weekly Edition*, 19 March 1984, page 6.

[5] The clear difference in perceived issue positions between Reagan on one hand and Mondale and Hart on the other provides some indication of why issue differences and "issue voting" have been easier to find in general elections than in primary campaigns.

candidates would cancel out in choices among candidates, in much the way that they do in Table 5.1.

Second, many political effects are unlikely to be captured by the survey analyst's usual array of issue and ideology questions (see Table 5.1). In 1984, a wide variety of political and social characteristics influenced survey respondents' reactions to Mondale and Hart. Clearly ideology and issues, the factors typically employed by survey analysts to account for electoral choice, are far from being the respondent's only politically relevant characteristics. Depending on the nature of the candidates and the campaign, other factors—such as social position and group interests—may be equally significant. The political effects of these predispositional factors reflect in part the role of "issues" not measured directly, since no survey is likely to include all, or even the few most relevant, campaign issues.[6] But even "complete" data on issues would probably not eliminate entirely the role of other factors. Many characteristics in Table 5.1 seem to matter not as proxies for unmeasured issue positions but as symbolic attachments. For example, even with ideal data it would be hard to point to a concrete "issue" capable of accounting for Hart's popularity among the young or for the antipathy toward him among blacks and Catholics. These reactions had more to do with style and rhetoric than with issue stands, but style and rhetoric are part of politics, too.

5.2 Political Activation

Thus far we have established that political predispositions are important in structuring public reactions to candidates during the primary season. In other settings that might be enough, but the nature of the nominating process demands a more dynamic view. In a world where learning plays the crucial and pervasive role described in Chapter 4, we must allow for the confusing and fascinating fact that, as David, Goldman, and Bain (1960: 249) put it, "the alternatives of choice must be discovered as part of the process."

This feature of the campaign is evident in Figure 5.2, which shows the changing relationship between political predispositions

[6] For example, critics have complained that the 1984 NES survey asked about the "wrong" issues: government services instead of trade policy, Russia instead of Jerusalem, defense spending instead of the nuclear freeze. Obviously, it is easier to select the "right" issues in retrospect than in prospect.

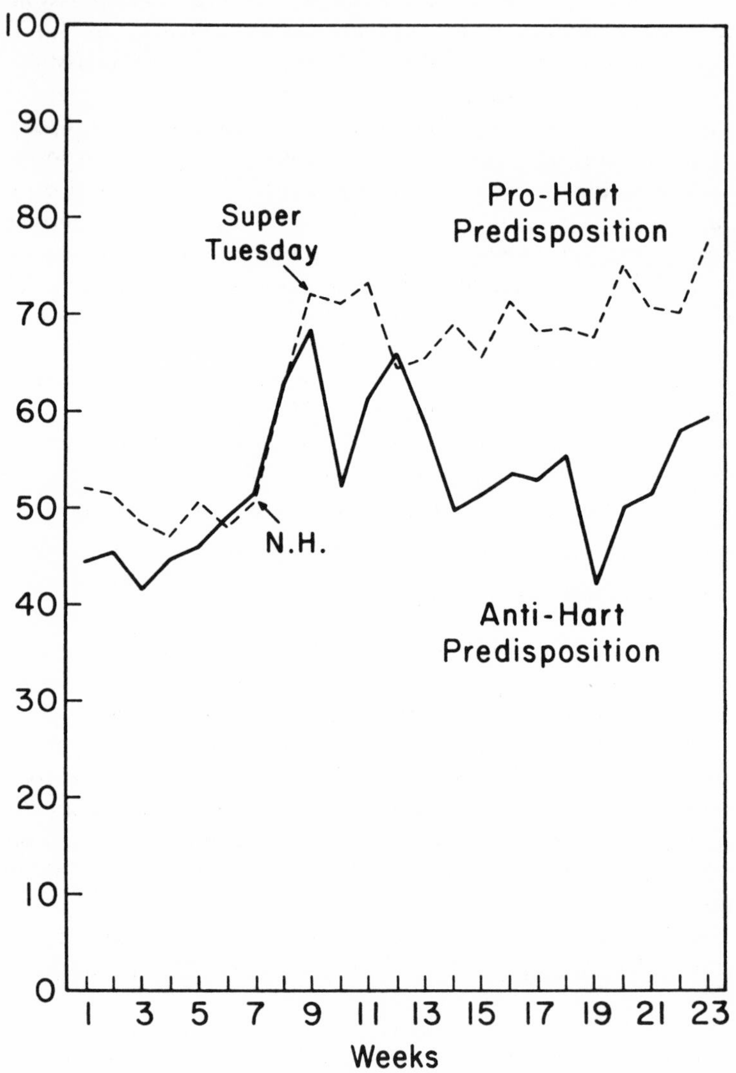

FIGURE 5.2 Predispositions and Evaluations of Hart, 1984.

and evaluations of Gary Hart during the 1984 primary season.[7] There are some inexplicable variations from week to week, but two facts stand out. First, respondents' evaluations of Hart before Super Tuesday bore little systematic relationship to their underlying political predispositions. The main trend in this early phase of the campaign was the increasingly favorable evaluation of Hart after Iowa and especially New Hampshire; this trend applied with equal force to respondents at both ends of the spectrum of political predispositions.

Second, the gap between respondents with pro-Hart predispositions and those with anti-Hart predispositions widened in the weeks after Super Tuesday. As information about Hart continued to accumulate, evaluations came more and more to reflect respondents' underlying predispositions. A similar trend appears in the evaluations of Mondale shown in Figure 5.3. At the beginning of the campaign, differences in evaluations of Mondale based on the preexisting political characteristics in Table 5.1 were relatively small; but as information about Mondale accumulated, underlying political values became an increasingly important determinant of public reactions to his candidacy. Finally, since Mondale was better known than Hart throughout the campaign (a point noted in Chapter 4), the generally greater role of predispositions in evaluations of Mondale in Figure 5.3 than in evaluations of Hart in Figure 5.2 is consistent with the notion that the role of substantive political judgments in the campaign increases systematically with increasing information about the candidates.

This process of *political activation* in the 1984 campaign appears in somewhat different form in Figure 5.4.[8] The figure shows the

[7] The effect of predispositions on evaluations of Hart shown in Figure 5.2 for each week of the 1984 campaign was calculated from the estimated relationship between Hart predispositions and thermometer scores in each week of the campaign, using the overall average predispositions of the most favorably and least favorably predisposed fifths of the NES primary season sample to represent pro-Hart and anti-Hart predispositions. A parallel procedure was used to illustrate the effect of Mondale predispositions on evaluations of Mondale in Figure 5.3.

[8] The term "activation" is suggested by Berelson, Lazarsfeld, and McPhee's related concept of "reactivation" (1954: 291–92): "In 1948 . . . the psychologically most interesting (and, at the same time, the politically most relevant) phenomenon was the last-minute return of many voters to an earlier disposition. These were persons who had voted for Roosevelt in 1944 and often had many demographic characteristics or past political allegiances which would predispose them to a Democratic vote. In June, 1948, however, they expressed little confidence in Truman and intended to vote for Dewey. Yet just before election day they changed in their

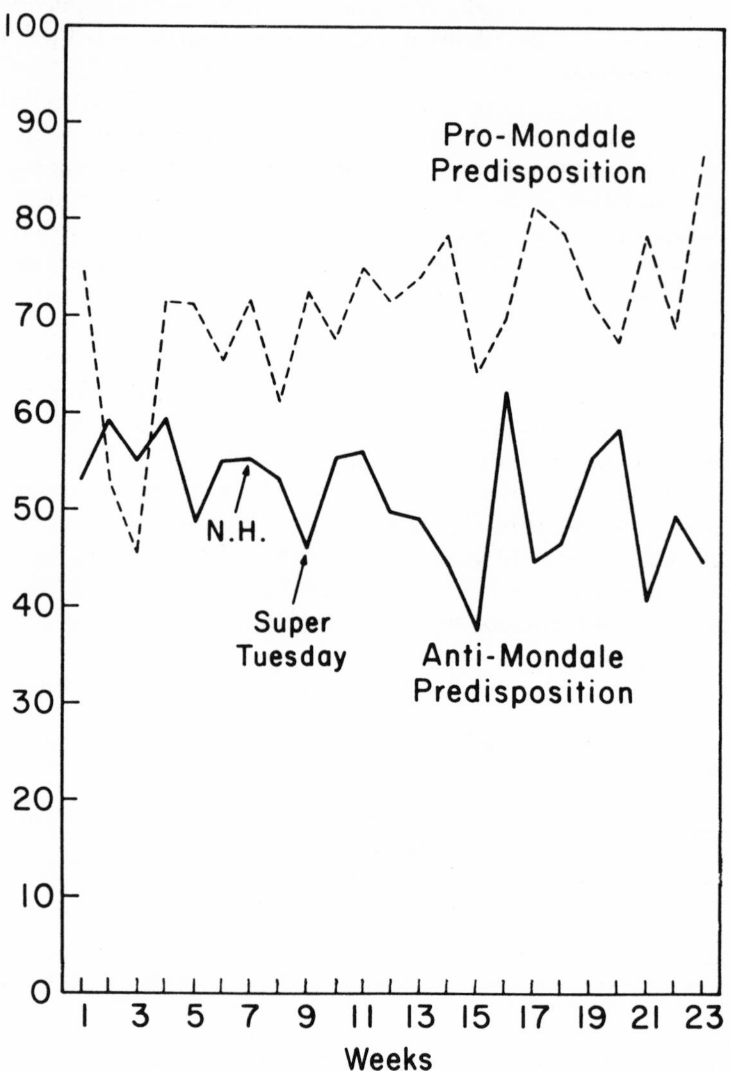

FIGURE 5.3 Predispositions and Evaluations of Mondale, 1984.

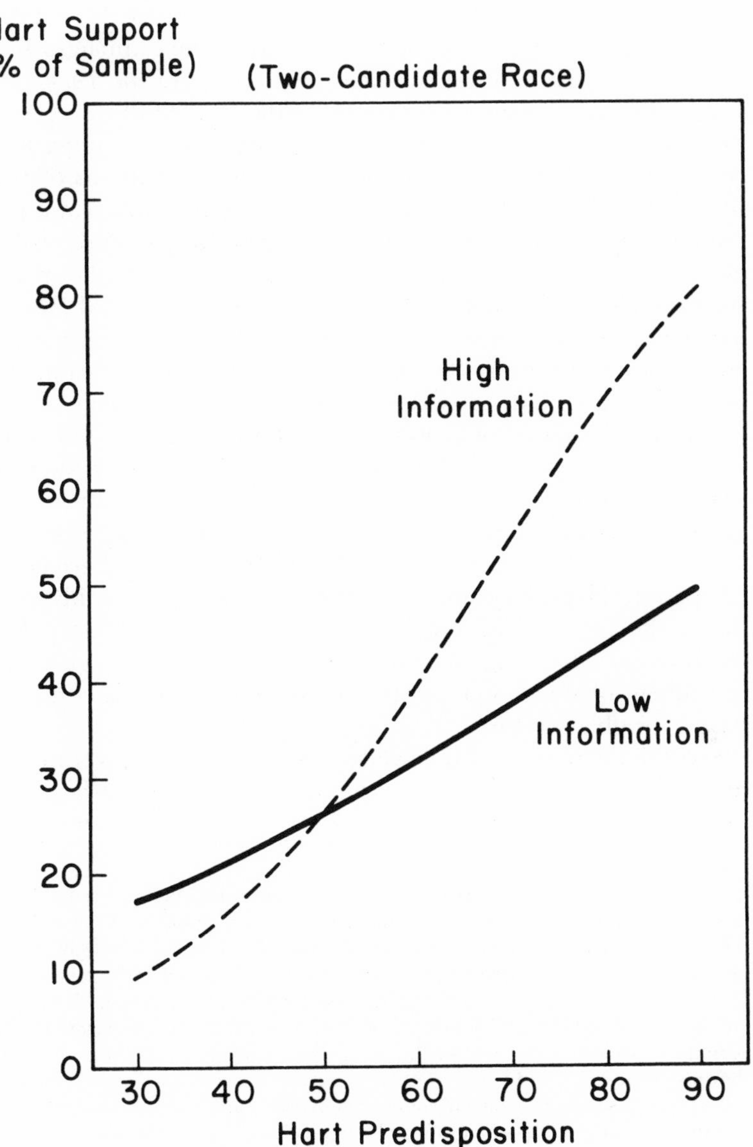

FIGURE 5.4 Political Predispositions and Hart Support, 1984.

estimated effects of predispositions toward Hart on survey respondents' choices between Hart and Mondale for two levels of information.[9] "Low information" represents the survey respondents' average level of uncertainty about Hart at the beginning of the 1984 campaign; "high information" represents the average level of uncertainty about Hart at the end of the campaign. Both effects show that political substance was crucial in the 1984 campaign. Political activation is reflected in the fact that differences in predispositions toward Hart had considerably less impact on choices between the two candidates under the conditions of relatively low information prevailing at the beginning of the campaign than under the conditions of relatively high information prevailing at the end of the campaign.[10] At the beginning of the campaign, for example, respondents with college degrees supported Hart by less than five percentage points more than those with eighth-grade educations, other things being equal; by the end of the campaign the corresponding difference was about twelve percentage points.

This phenomenon of political activation is important in two respects. First, it provides the best evidence we have seen thus far that learning in the campaign involves more than superficial familiarity with the candidates' names. As information increases and uncertainty decreases according to the dynamics described in Chapter 4, the public comes increasingly to evaluate candidates on their political merits, in accordance with longstanding political predispositions. This fact is of obvious significance for any normative assessment of the contemporary nominating process as a mechanism for public choice.

Second, the pattern of political activation that emerges from Figures 5.2, 5.3, and 5.4 is also an important key to the variations in

intentions. Their final Democratic vote was thus the reactivation of a previous tendency."

[9] The estimated effect of predispositions on choices in Figure 5.4 reflects both the estimated effect of predispositions on thermometer ratings from Table A.17 and the estimated effect of thermometer ratings on choices from Table A.18 in Appendix C. The difference evident in the figure between levels of information stems from the assumption, in the statistical analysis on which the results in Table A.17 are based, that the effect of predispositions varies directly with information. This assumption derives in turn from the more direct evidence of political activation shown in Figures 5.2 and 5.3.

[10] The analysis posits a similar connection between information about Mondale and the effect of predispositions toward him on choices. Since Mondale was better known than Hart throughout the campaign, the impact of predispositions toward him was greater than that pictured for Hart.

issue effects across candidates, voters, and campaigns noted at the beginning of this chapter. If information conditions the extent to which voters bring political predispositions to bear on their evaluations of the candidates, we can predict with some confidence that issue effects will be most pronounced for relatively well-known candidates and for relatively well-informed voters. Since we know much about learning and information and about how they vary across voters, across candidates, and over time, we can make considerable sense of otherwise unintelligible differences in the role of substantive political factors in different campaign settings. That is one basis for the typology of primary campaigns developed in Section 7.3.

5.3 Issue Perceptions and Reality

Before attempting to synthesize my analyses of politics, uncertainty, and the horse race in an overarching discussion of momentum and candidate choice, I turn in this section to a subsidiary question of considerable interest: how prospective voters develop their perceptions of the candidates' political identities. My treatment of this question focuses on one limited, albeit important, aspect of the candidates' political identities—their stands on the issues.

Early electoral analysts (most notably Berelson et al. 1954) focused much attention on precisely the sorts of social circumstances and group loyalties that make up what I call "political predispositions" and on the dynamic relationship between these fundamental political characteristics and actual electoral choices. But these aspects of the political world have been downplayed in more recent electoral research. First, the work of the so-called Michigan school (most notably Campbell et al. 1960) established party identification, issue positions, and candidate images as the central explanatory factors in voting research. This "holy trinity" of parties, issues, and candidate images has dominated the field, and most analysts have shown more interest in the relative effects of these factors on the vote than in their social and political origins. More recently, analysts interested in "rational choice" and the "spatial theory of voting" have narrowed the focus still further, concentrating almost entirely on the positions of candidates and voters in "issue space." In this view (see, for example, Enelow and Hinich 1984), campaigns are attempts by candidates to stake out winning positions on dimensions representing various policy alternatives, and vote choices reflect calculations by voters of how close they are to the various candidates' positions.

A view of the world in which candidates begin with recognized positions on major political issues may make sense in general election campaigns, where candidates are well-known political entities with substantial histories of public pronouncements on the issues. However, the same view makes less sense in a primary campaign where, as we have seen in Chapter 4, some candidates are virtually unknown to the public. In an environment of substantial uncertainty and fluidity, a question of considerable political interest is how prospective voters form precisely those perceptions of candidates' issue positions that the "spatial theory of voting" takes as given. Are voters' perceptions of where the candidates stand rooted in political reality? Do they reflect that reality more or less directly? What are the sources of misperception, and what are the political consequences of that misperception?

These questions arise with particular force for those candidates, like Carter, Bush, and Hart, who emerge from relative obscurity to become major political figures in a matter of days or weeks. What voters know about such candidates during their first weeks in the limelight may be crucial for interpreting and evaluating the dynamics of the nominating process. The data presented in Figure 4.3 make it clear that the public's willingness to place Hart on the issues changed only a little less quickly than their familiarity with him. By the second week after Hart's New Hampshire victory, Democrats were about as willing to place him on the issues as they were to place Mondale. But how did those perceptions relate to Hart's real political character?

A first approach to this question can be made simply by asking whether respondents agreed among themselves about Hart's issue positions. To a surprising extent, they did not. This fact is illustrated in Figure 5.5, which shows separate trends in perceptions for the top and bottom fifths of the NES sample—the 20 percent of the respondents in each week of the study who perceived Hart as being most liberal and the 20 percent who perceived him as being most conservative.[11] The gap between these two groups is substantial, suggesting that different respondents developed very different perceptions of where Hart stood on the campaign issues. It is

[11] As in Figure 5.1, perceptions of Hart's stands on three distinct issues—abstract ideology, government services, and defense spending—are summarized as a single overall perception in Figure 5.5.

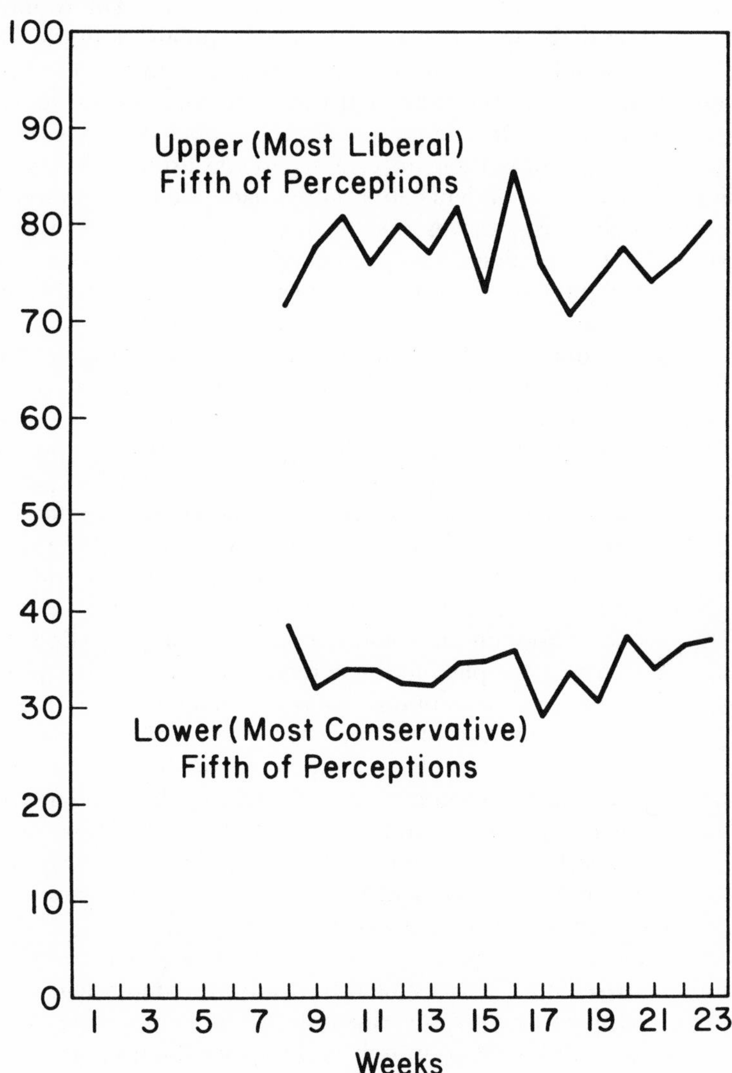

FIGURE 5.5 Range of Perceptions of Hart's Liberalism, 1984.

also worth noticing that this gap is virtually constant throughout the campaign; the accumulation of information about Hart did little or nothing to generate a consensus about his positions.

How are we to account for these substantial individual differences in perceptions of Hart's stands? The last few years have witnessed a small boom in research on public perceptions of what candidates, parties, and groups stand for in politics. For example, Conover and Feldman (1984) studied perceptions of Jimmy Carter's issue stands in 1976 in the Patterson panel survey. They concluded that during the campaign Carter became increasingly associated with the Democratic party's traditional positions on the issues. Facing considerable uncertainty about Carter's own true positions, survey respondents apparently made the quite reasonable inference that his positions must be in general congruence with his party's. Not surprisingly, this psychological connection became significantly tighter once Carter was formally chosen as the Democratic nominee.

Taking a somewhat different tack, Brady and Sniderman (1985) studied public perceptions of where politically salient groups (blacks and whites, liberals and conservatives, Democrats and Republicans) stand on the issues. Their work is particularly interesting because it was based on a specific, concrete model of perception in which survey respondents are presumed to minimize two kinds of incongruity: (1) between their perceptions and the candidates' actual positions and (2) between their perceptions and their overall positive or negative orientations toward the candidates. The second consideration is another form of the projection phenomenon, which I applied to horse race perceptions in Chapter 3. As with horse race perceptions, survey respondents may tend to place candidates on the issues not where the candidates really are but where the respondents want them to be. Therefore, other things being equal, respondents would tend to pull candidates they like on other grounds toward their own preferred positions on the issues and perhaps even push candidates they dislike away from their own positions. Brady and Sniderman's analysis suggests that, for political groups, this is precisely what happens.

My own analysis of perceptions of primary candidates' issue positions is based on a model similar to Brady and Sniderman's. Like them, I suppose that respondents must balance competing desires to place the candidates accurately and to place them where the respondents themselves would like them to be. But my model is more general than Brady and Sniderman's; it allows each tendency to be more powerful for some respondents than for others. In particular, I suppose both that the impact of reality increases with information about the candidates and that the impact of projection increases with interest in the campaign. The first supposition reflects the fairly obvious fact that respondents who know little or nothing about a candidate will have difficulty weighing the candidate's true positions on the issues even if they want to. The second supposition is based on the possibility that those respondents most interested in the campaign will feel the greatest psychological pressure to bring their perceptions of the candidates' stands into congruence with their overall evaluations.

Both phenomena are evident, albeit dimly, in respondents' placements of Mondale and Hart in the 1984 NES survey.[12] The statistical evidence is relatively weak; but if it is correct, it suggests that perceptions of where the candidates stood sometimes depended as much on where the person doing the judging wanted them to stand as on the candidates' actual positions.[13] As expected, this projection effect varied with general attitudes toward the candidates: the tendency to exaggerate how close each candidate was to one's own position was greatest for those most favorably disposed toward the candidate, present to a lesser extent even for those who were neutral in their overall evaluation, and actually reversed (distance from one's own position was exaggerated) for those who strongly disliked the candidate.[14]

This pattern is evident in Figure 5.6, which shows the effect of projection on perceived issue distances for Hart across the whole

[12] The statistical evidence for issue projection is reported in Table A.16 in Appendix C.4. The t-statistics for the four relevant parameter estimates range from 0.67 to 1.08.

[13] My model produces estimates of the candidates' actual positions in addition to estimates of the effect of projection. For 1984 these estimated true positions confirm my descriptions of the candidates' political views: both Mondale and Hart were somewhat to the left of center, with Mondale slightly more liberal overall. Both candidates were most clearly liberal on the issue of defense spending; Hart's positions on both government spending and the abstract ideology dimension fell almost exactly at the midpoint of the scale. There is no evidence, either for 1984 or in parallel analyses of Reagan and Bush's true positions in the 1980 Republican campaign, of systematic change in any candidate's true positions between the beginning and end of a primary season.

[14] The reverse projection effect set in when the candidates were rated below about thirty degrees on the zero-to-one hundred thermometer scale; the proportion of actual thermometer ratings that were that unfavorable ranged from about 6 percent for Mondale and Hart to about 20 percent for Jesse Jackson.

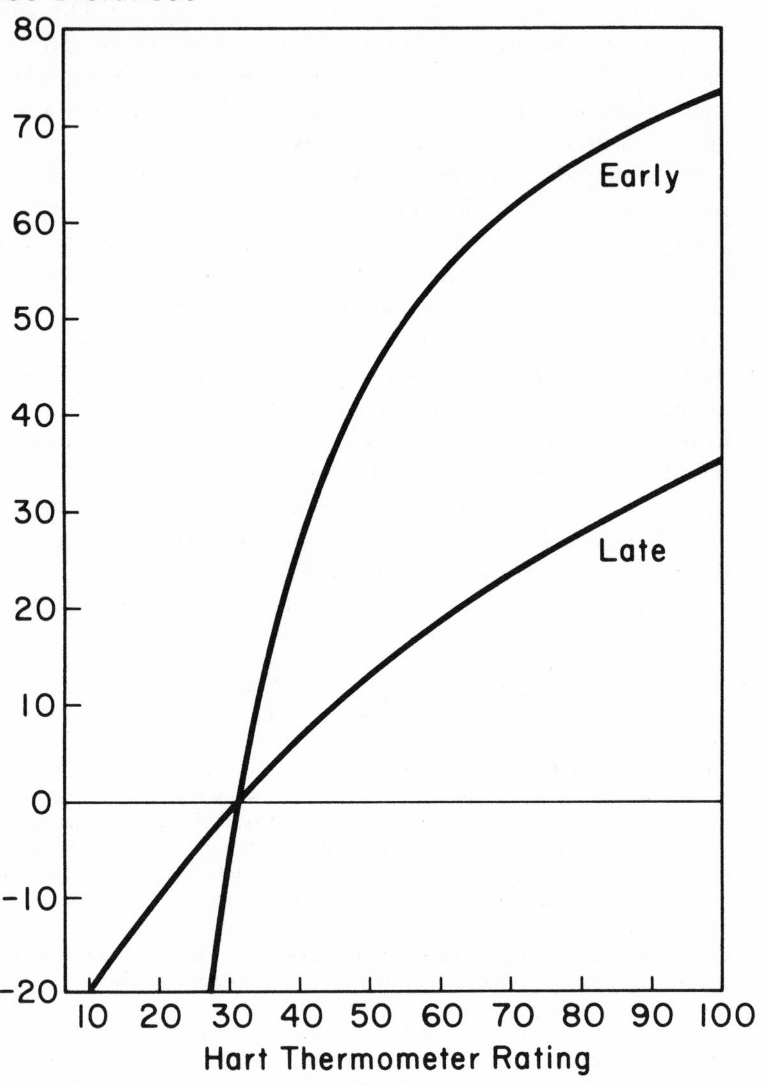

FIGURE 5.6 Hart Thermometer Ratings and Issue Projection, 1984.

range of possible thermometer evaluations.[15] The estimated relationship between thermometer ratings and projection is illustrated for two different levels of information—the average levels for Hart at the beginning and end of the primary season. As expected, the relationship appears to have been considerably stronger in the early stages of the campaign, when little was known about Hart's real issue stands, than at the end of the primary season, when information about his actual stands was relatively plentiful.[16]

These results help to account for a much-noted feature of political campaigns—the deliberate ambiguity of the candidates' issue appeals. At the same time, they indicate why some candidates have seemed more willing to resort to ambiguity than others. Three primary candidates have been specifically criticized by campaign observers for refusing to run issue-oriented campaigns. In 1976 Jimmy Carter was charged with "fuzziness" soon after his first dramatic primary victories. According to Patterson (1980: 38), "The claim that Carter was avoiding the issues . . . was voiced by a number of reporters very early in the primaries." The same claim also found its way into scholarly accounts of the campaign. For example, Ceaser (1982: 105) wrote that, "In 1976, Jimmy Carter won the nomination by blurring many of the issues and by emphasizing broad themes like efficiency and honesty in government." George Bush in 1980 was also criticized for his lack of political substance in the first few weeks after his dramatic Iowa triumph. Greenfield (1982: 43) cited attacks from several prestigious elements of the campaign press: *Newsweek* referred to Bush's "vague solutions" to policy problems, the *Washington Post* called him "ill-prepared to respond to simple questions about basic issues," the *Wall Street Journal* reported that his campaign was "short on detail," and so on. "At times," Greenfield himself wrote (1982: 44),

> Bush's reluctance to land firmly on a policy stand reached proportions bordering on the absurd. Once, asked whether he would support an embargo on the importing of Russian-made

[15] The pattern shown in Figure 5.6 is based on the analysis of issue perceptions described in Appendix C.4. The effect of evaluations on projection is reflected in the statistical results for "False consensus" and "Differential projection" in Table A.16.

[16] The model outlined in Appendix B.2 allows respondents with more information about a candidate to attach more weight to the candidates' actual issue stands; doing so reduces the relative impact of projection shown in Figure 5.6. The estimated effect of information in the 1984 data is shown in Table A.16 in Appendix C.

> Stolichnaya vodka, Bush said, "I've got to be careful. I'd have to know where it's bottled, and if it's bottled in the United States, how many people are employed doing it."

Finally, in 1984 Gary Hart's issue commitments were questioned not only by the press but also by Walter Mondale, whose "Where's the Beef?" jibe was the most memorable rhetorical event of the campaign season.

Why would these candidates—precisely those who succeeded in breaking out of the pack to become major contenders—be the three for whom vagueness and lack of substance became serious campaign issues? Political scientists' usual explanations for issue ambiguity provide no real clues. One explanation, first suggested by Shepsle (1972), is that voters like the risk of supporting a candidate whose positions they are unsure about and that candidates oblige such risk-seekers by keeping their issue pronouncements vague and ambiguous. However, I have provided evidence elsewhere that, on the contrary, voters actually dislike risk and indeed penalize candidates with uncertain issue positions (Bartels 1986). The effect of uncertainty described in Section 4.3 also suggests that risk aversion is more likely than risk seeking. But even without such evidence it is obvious that Shepsle's theory does little to explain the pattern identified here: if voters like risk, other candidates should have been as willing to accommodate them as Carter, Bush, and Hart apparently were.

Another explanation, first suggested by Page (1976; 1978: chap. 6) is that candidates take vague positions on losing issues to deemphasize those issues in the voters' minds. Here, too, the theory fails to explain the specific pattern of vagueness I have identified: if candidates merely avoided clear stands on losing issues, as Page argued, it is hard to account for the fact that, of all the successful candidates in recent nominating campaigns, Carter, Bush, and Hart alone apparently could not find many winning ones.

My analysis suggests two somewhat better explanations. First, it seems clear from the data for Hart in Figure 4.3 that issue stands take somewhat longer to communicate to the public than simple awareness. This fact implies that "new" candidates will inevitably go through a period in which they are well known but their issue positions are not; during this period they will be vulnerable to charges of vagueness from the press and from opposing candidates. *Time* magazine noted Hart's problem in this regard at the height of his surge (12 March 1984: 25): "Because campaign positions are inevitably reduced to sketchy impressions and shorthand phrases, Hart has been vulnerable to caricature as the candidate who merely espouses the *idea* of new ideas. In fact, he bristles with notions about how Government should be run." One of Bush's senior campaign officials made a similar complaint: "It doesn't matter how much or how long or how often a candidate talks about issues to small groups in Iowa, or answers issue-oriented questions, or talks in terms and substance [*sic*] of why he ought to be nominated, if the coverage is on the momentum and the horse race" (David Keene, quoted by Moore 1981: 96).

Of course, it is worth recalling that Bush *did not* spend most of his time talking about issues, or answering issue-oriented questions, or talking in terms of substance. He did not struggle valiantly against an uncooperative press corps to explain his position on either the importation of vodka or many of the more pressing issues of the campaign. Nor did Jimmy Carter; his issue positions were consciously and deliberately ambiguous. Patrick Caddell's campaign polls carefully tracked public perceptions of Carter's fuzziness,[17] and his conclusions about how to deal with the problem are evident in an internal strategy memorandum he wrote in late March (quoted by Schram 1977: 101–2): "We have passed the point when we can simply avoid at least the semblance of substance. This does not mean the need to outline minute, exact details. We all agree that such a course could be disastrous. However the appearance of substance does not require this. It requires a few broad, specific examples that support a point. . . ." The Carter strategists hit on an elegantly simple way to offer "the appearance of substance." According to chief media strategist Gerald Rafshoon (quoted by Moore and Fraser 1977: 99), "We ran the same type of advertising in Pennsylvania as we had earlier, but we labeled it as issues."

Bush in 1980 and Hart in 1984 similarly attempted to benefit from ambiguity at some points in the campaign and to project "at least the semblance of substance" at others. Bush, after several weeks of proclaiming himself the candidate of "Big Mo," simply and enthusiastically announced an about-face after losing in New Hampshire. "I'm the issues candidate now," he told the press (Greenfield 1982: 39, 52). "What I want to do is talk about issues." At the corresponding stage of the 1984 campaign, eerily similar pronouncements emanated from the Hart camp. "We will be very,

[17] On this point see, for example, Schram (1977: 120–21).

very message-oriented and issue-oriented," campaign manager Oliver (Pudge) Henkel told the *Washington Post.* "We want to get the campaign away from the ephemeral notion of momentum and back to the issues."[18]

Any complete accounting of the role of issues in the campaign must somehow explain why these candidates, more than others, found vagueness an attractive, although only temporarily attractive, campaign strategy. The most successful explanation seems to revolve around the influence of projection on public perceptions of the candidates' issue stands. The main implication of the evidence on issue projection is that, if allowed to do so, people will tend to perceive candidates' stands on the issues as similar to their own stands. But this is true, to some extent, for all candidates. Why would Carter, Bush, and Hart be particularly likely to benefit from projection? For one thing, although some projection occurs even for candidates who receive neutral thermometer evaluations, it is clear from Figure 5.6 that the projection effect is strongest when a candidate is already favorably perceived on other grounds. This is precisely the situation Carter, Bush, and Hart found themselves in after their first surprising primary victories. With momentum on your side and people willing to believe the best about your political stands, why go out of your way to rock the boat? All three candidates seemed to recognize this strategic imperative.

The other reason why Carter, Bush, and Hart may have been in particularly favorable positions to benefit from projection relates to the fact, evident in Figure 5.6, that the impact of projection seems to vary inversely with the amount of information prospective voters have about a candidate. Across the whole range of evaluations shown in the figure, respondents' perceptions of Hart's issue stands were significantly less restrained by reality early in the campaign than at the end of the primary season. Similarly, during most of the campaign perceptions of issue stands were less restrained by reality for Hart than for Mondale—again because Hart

[18] Reported in the *Washington Post National Weekly Edition,* 2 April 1984, page 11. For the benefit of the still-unconvinced, a Hart fundraiser echoed the same theme a few weeks later (23 April 1984, page 10): "A lot depends on whether we can get the discussion back on issues." The Hart organization's effort to "refocus" was actually its second of the campaign. Earlier (at the urging of Caddell, according to some reports) Hart had abandoned his "propensity to deal with complicated subjects at length" (13 February 1984, page 10) in favor of a new approach deemphasizing detailed positions and stressing the general theme of "new leadership." Hart denied that the shift was Caddell's idea. "It was planned all along," he said (19 March 1984, page 11). "I intended all along to shift to the theme."

was a relatively unknown quantity. As *Newsweek* magazine put it at the time (12 March 1984: 23), "The former vice president's image seems fixed, while the dynamic Hart can appear to be all things to all voters with his vague appeals for 'new leadership'."[19]

With projection most prevalent for relatively unknown candidates, it should not be surprising to find exactly those candidates most willing to soft-pedal their actual issue stands. But the pattern of results in Figure 5.6 also provides some indication of why ambiguity tends to be a temporary strategy, even for new candidates. Most obviously, new candidates do not remain new: by June of 1984 Hart was almost as well known as Mondale and thus not much better situated than Mondale to benefit from projection. In addition, the successful new candidate's favorable evaluations on nonissue grounds are unlikely to last through the entire campaign, and, as evaluations become less favorable, ambiguity becomes a correspondingly less attractive strategy. Finally, the tendency of prospective voters to project their own issue preferences onto the candidates seems to increase with interest in the campaign; this trend tends to peak fairly early, especially when a surprising new candidate with momentum breaks out of the pack, and then trail off as the primary season wears on.[20]

The implications of these various candidate- and time-related considerations for the extent of issue projection in the 1984 campaign are illustrated in Figure 5.7. The difference in the situations facing Hart and Mondale is particularly clear from the figure. For Hart the figure shows a fairly steady decline in the average amount by which respondents underestimated the actual distance between his issue stands and their own, from more than 40 percent of the actual distance at the beginning of the campaign to about 20 percent of the actual distance at the end of the primary season. This

[19] The contrast between *Newsweek*'s description of Hart's "vague appeals" and *Time*'s emphasis (already noted) on the "inevitability" of "sketchy impressions and shorthand phrases" highlights the conjunction of strategic and structural sources of ambiguity in the early stages of a successful new candidate's campaign. A Mondale adviser quoted in the same *Newsweek* article provided a useful reminder that the strategic opportunities inherent in such a situation are not entirely one-sided. "Gary Hart is a blank tablet," he said, "and we've got to write on it before he does." The result was an aggressive attack by Mondale on Hart's character and record.

[20] The estimated effect of political interest on the extent of projection in the 1984 NES data is reported in Table A.16 in Appendix C. The statistical result suggests that the magnitude of the projection effect for those survey respondents extremely interested in the campaign was more than twice that for respondents extremely uninterested.

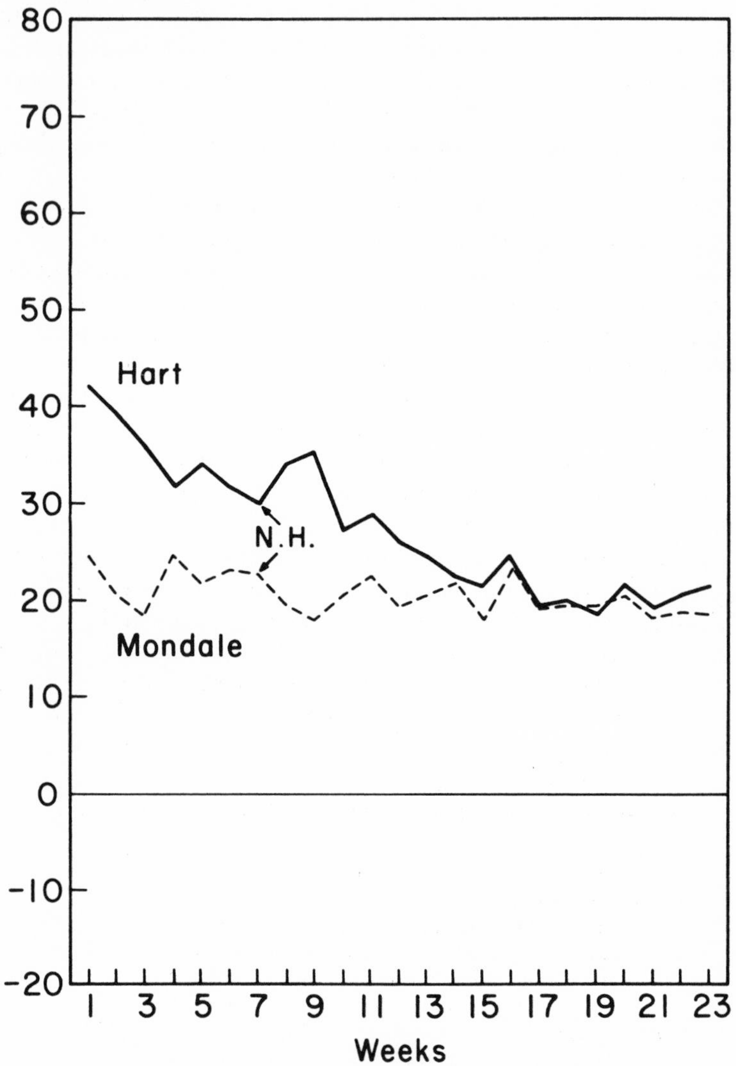

FIGURE 5.7 Average Levels of Issue Projection for Hart and Mondale, 1984.

secular decline reflects the effect of increasing information about Hart on the accuracy of prospective voters' perceptions of his issue stands. The only significant break in the downward trend occurred in the first two weeks after Hart's New Hampshire upset, when a jump in the favorability of Hart thermometer ratings and a temporary increase in respondents' interest in the campaign caused a temporary increase in the average magnitude of the projection effect. This temporary increase was washed out by additional information after Super Tuesday. By about mid-April, the fourteenth week of the campaign season, the average projection effect for Hart had reached a relatively steady state between 20 and 25 percent of actual issue distances. This steady state for Hart in the second half of the campaign corresponded closely to the average effect of issue projection for Mondale, which remained essentially constant throughout the primary season at the same relatively low level.

These results on the dynamics of issue projection provide one more indication of the fluidity of substantive political considerations in presidential nominating campaigns. Projection seems to distort public perceptions of the candidates' stands most powerfully for relatively unknown candidates in the early stages of a primary season. If an unknown contender is fortunate enough to emerge into public prominence on the strength of a "better than expected" showing in Iowa or New Hampshire he soon begins to pay a price for his new familiarity in the form of more critical, more realistic, scrutiny of his issue stands. This process fits the more general pattern of political activation described in this chapter. In each instance the candidates' real political identities may not always matter at the start, but they matter in the end. The danger, from an institutional standpoint, is that by then it may be too late.

CHAPTER SIX

Expectations and Choice

HAVING ANALYZED THE ROLE of learning and uncertainty in Chapter 4 and the role of political substance in Chapter 5, I return in this chapter to the role of expectations about the outcome of the nominating process. The analysis in Section 3.3 used campaign events and the reporting of those campaign events by the media to account for public perceptions of the candidates' chances. The analysis in this chapter treats those same perceptions as a key explanatory factor in attempting to account for actual electoral choices. The effect of expectations about the race on prospective voters' preferences and choices lies at the heart of any description of momentum as a dynamic political phenomenon. It completes the complex cycle involving candidates, journalists, and the public that links primary results at any given point in a campaign to subsequent campaign events. Thus, an attempt to explain how and why expectations influence electoral choices provides a fitting conclusion to my examination of the nature of momentum.

6.1 Varieties of Momentum

I touched in Chapter 1 on the vagueness of the notion of momentum in recent accounts of nominating campaigns. But if the notion is vague, it is also multifaceted. Analysts and observers have described a variety of very different psychological processes capable of accounting for the general fact that people's expectations about the campaign influence their own choices and consistent with the dynamic pattern of increasing support that characterizes momentum at the aggregate level.

In this section I survey some of these various psychological processes, emphasizing the logic of each process on its own terms. The problems involved in actually distinguishing among the various processes and in assessing their impact on observable electoral behavior are addressed in the remainder of this chapter.

Strategic Voting

Political analysts have identified two distinct species of strategic voting, each of which could play a role in primary campaigns.

First, because the nominating campaign is merely the first stage in a two-step choice process culminating in early November, the selection of a nominee must be viewed not as an end in itself but as a preliminary to the fall campaign. No matter how attractive a candidate may be to the party rank and file, it makes little sense to nominate him if he cannot win the general election.

This fact implies that a vote for any candidate in the nominating phase of the campaign is really a vote for the end result of a general election between that candidate and the nominee of the other major party.[1] Of course, that result may itself be quite uncertain, even when the identities of the candidates are known.[2] Nevertheless, a prospective voter who can guess the chances of his or her party's various candidates in the general election can maximize expected satisfaction by choosing one both attractive and electable.[3]

Second, the desire to avoid "wasting" a vote on a minor candidate in a multicandidate race is relevant in primary campaigns. The logic of the notion is that a voter should attempt to maximize favorable impact on the outcome of the election, rather than to simply express support for a favorite candidate. If the voter's favorite candidate has no chance to win, it may make sense to vote for a second-best candidate who does have some chance, forestalling the election of a still less attractive alternative.

There are two logical difficulties with this second notion of strategic voting. First, it requires that voters attach considerable importance to the fact that they are more likely to be able to swing the election in favor of a second-choice candidate than in favor of a first-choice candidate. But the actual probability of swinging a statewide election to *any* candidate is so infinitesimally small it is hard to see why anyone who bothered to calculate it would then bother to vote at all. Second, no one has been able to describe convincingly how the calculations necessary to vote strategically in this sense ought actually to be made in an election as complicated as a presidential primary. How should prospective voters calculate the likely impact of their choices on the end result of a process in

[1] I assume here that no third party or independent candidate has any real chance of winning the general election.

[2] There is also the difficulty of guessing who will be the other party's nominee; this additional uncertainty does nothing to alter the basic situation and will be ignored here.

[3] More precisely, the expected utility associated with each potential nominee is the product of his probability of winning the general election multiplied by his utility rating, where the utility ratings are scaled so that zero represents the nominee of the opposing party (or probability-weighted average of possible opponents).

which primary results are only loosely and somewhat mysteriously related to delegate selection, in which delegates' commitments to candidates may change with changes in political circumstances between the time the delegates are selected and the time of the convention, and in which these changes in political circumstances themselves depend, in part, on how political elites choose to interpret the choices of primary voters? Perhaps the best course is to ignore these complications and hope that prospective voters do the same.

Cue-Taking

We have seen that prospective voters in presidential nominating campaigns often face considerable uncertainty. In view of this uncertainty, it would not be surprising to find that prospective voters seek information relevant to evaluating the candidates. Such information is often readily available in the political environment in the form of endorsements of particular candidates by "cue-givers." If someone whose opinion I value tells me that I ought to support (say) Jimmy Carter, this endorsement will go some way toward reducing my own uncertainty about whether Carter is "right" for me. The fact that I consider the cue-giver a useful and trustworthy source of political information will be sufficient to make me revise my own opinion to a greater or lesser extent. I will still be uncertain about my choice, but I will consider it somewhat more likely than I did before that Carter is the candidate I ought to support.[4] There need not be any actual process of persuasion involving the transfer of specific substantive information about the candidate; the fact of the endorsement itself motivates me to change my substantive opinion about him.

An endorsement in this sense may be from a recognizable individual with some specific political status (Richard Daley, Coretta Scott King, Charleton Heston), or it may represent the more diffuse influence of perceived public opinion in the uncertain voter's decision calculus.[5] In the case of general public opinion, the operative logic is, roughly, that "25,000 solid New Hampshirites (prob-

[4] The exact amount by which my own opinion should change in response to a given cue can be calculated from the statistical formula known as Bayes' theorem. Essentially, Bayesian opinion change is a product of prior uncertainty multiplied by the "strength" of the cue in an evidential sense.

[5] In either case the influence of a cue-giver could actually be negative: an endorsement from Richard Daley could help to convince me that Jimmy Carter is *not* the candidate for me. I assume that negative influence may occur for some public figures but is unlikely for general public opinion.

ably) can't be too far wrong." For a prospective voter willing to be swayed by this sort of logic, the only institutional mechanism necessary to translate primary successes into momentum is some (possibly "neutral") channel through which the verdict of public opinion in each week's primaries can be transmitted to uncertain voters in subsequent primaries. As we have already seen in Chapter 3, the mass media perform this task very efficiently.

Contagion

The strategic voting and cue-taking models are both based on the assumption that prospective voters attempt to behave "rationally" within the complex political environment of a presidential nominating campaign. Voters attempt in the strategic voting model to calculate the potential impact of their support on the actual outcome of an election and in the cue-taking model to exploit information available in the environment to reduce uncertainty about their own preferences. But it may also be possible to account for the dynamics of nominating campaigns by supposing that prospective voters respond in less rational, calculating ways to the events of the campaign. For example, they might respond quite unthinkingly to changes in simple political stimuli, such as the frequency with which candidates' names appear on television and in the newspapers. Given the emphasis of the media on primary winners, such a response, in the absence of some counterbalancing force, would produce a powerful cycle of primary success, increasing support, further primary success, and so on—in a word, momentum.

In this view, momentum looks less like a political process than like a communicable disease. The exposed come down with "Big Mo" more or less regardless of their political instincts or interests. Or, to shift metaphors, the candidate with momentum plays essentially the same role as a moderately hot new rock star. Once the bandwagon begins to roll, people are swept away by the excitement, the new face, the surprising victories, the television interviews, the magazine covers. As with any other fad, their reactions are essentially automatic and uncritical. The only worrying aspect of this particular fad is that its object—unlike even a hot new rock star—may become president.

Supporting a Winner

One final possibility is that voters do respond favorably to a winning candidate, but not in the uncritical, elemental way envisioned in the contagion theory. Rather, they may simply enjoy the feeling of "going with a winner"—even a winner about whose substantive qualities they have no illusions. The gratification derived from such support would have little to do with rational political action, but neither would it reflect the irrational, automatic response of the contagion theory; rather, it would be the gratification of a rational, apolitical spectator enjoying vicarious involvement in the horse race for its own sake.

We have already seen that media coverage of the nominating process focuses on the dramatic continuing story of winners and losers; this story seems to interest even portions of the public with little interest or involvement in the political substance of the campaign. The status of the race in the minds of these casual observers must be similar to that of the Kentucky Derby in the minds of casual sports fans. And as with the Kentucky Derby, casual fans may find the race more fun to watch if they have at least a psychological investment in a contender. The investment need not be large or based on any complicated calculation about underlying qualities.

In many respects the dynamics implied by the desire to support a winner are similar to those implied by the contagion theory: a winning candidate will attract increasing public support under either theory. The important difference concerns how the psychological bases of that support influence our interpretations and evaluations of the process in each instance. In the case of the contagion theory, prospective voters delude themselves into believing that a winning candidate is a substantively attractive one. If the desire to support a winner is the operative motivation, political substance is irrelevant; the campaign is a game, and winning itself is what matters.

These theories of momentum share a common focus on the role of expectations in nominating campaigns and more particularly on the potential impact of expectations on evaluations and choices. To assess the empirical validity of the theories, we must examine the actual effect of expectations about the candidates' chances. Previous analyses have used a variety of data and models in attempting to demonstrate that expectations influence preferences. Patterson (1980: 129) showed that respondents' perceptions about some (but not all) candidates' chances in the February wave of his 1976 panel survey were positively correlated with changes between February and April in the favorability of the respondents' evaluations of those candidates. Shanks and others showed that evaluations were related to expectations in the 1980 and 1984 NES surveys

(Shanks and Palmquist 1981; Shanks et al. 1985). My own analysis of the same 1980 NES data (Bartels 1985) demonstrated that expectations influenced preferences even after controlling for the reciprocal "projection" effect of preferences on expectations. And Brady (1984b) found that experimental manipulations of college students' expectations through the presentation of simulated poll results produced systematic changes in the subjects' evaluations of the candidates.

From this accumulation of evidence, clearly expectations do matter. But how and why they matter is something else again. Each theory of momentum provides a plausible reason for expecting expectations to influence choices. But at the same time, each provides a very different picture of the psychology of momentum, with very different implications for any analysis of the nominating process as a mechanism for public choice. There is little or no strong evidence for or against any specific form of momentum—only for a general connection between expectations and choices.

Of course, no one variety of momentum precludes the others. Indeed, a preliminary consideration of the apparent role of momentum in the 1984 campaign suggests quite clearly that no single theory will entirely explain it. Consider, first, the time trend of support for Gary Hart during the 1984 campaign, shown in Figure 6.1. Support for Hart was minimal before his dramatic victory in New Hampshire, shot up to more than 50 percent in the two weeks after New Hampshire, and then gradually declined to less than 30 percent in the second half of the primary season. How much of this change can be accounted for by any one of the notions of momentum in Section 6.1?

Some analysts have thought of "thermometer scores" like those described in Chapter 4 as proximate causes of the vote, positing simply and naturally that prospective voters choose the candidate they evaluate most favorably.[6] Not surprisingly, these decision rules work quite well in empirical terms; the vast majority of respondents do report voting for the candidate they "like best" in this sense. For example, Page and Jones (1979: 1072) reported that more than 95 percent of the respondents in the 1972 and 1976 NES surveys who rated one presidential candidate higher than the other on the thermometer scale reported voting for that candidate.

[6] For example, Markus and Converse (1979) and Page and Jones (1979) built complicated statistical models in which comparative evaluations of general election candidates, measured by thermometer scores, were caused by partisan ties and issue evaluations and in turn led to consonant vote choices.

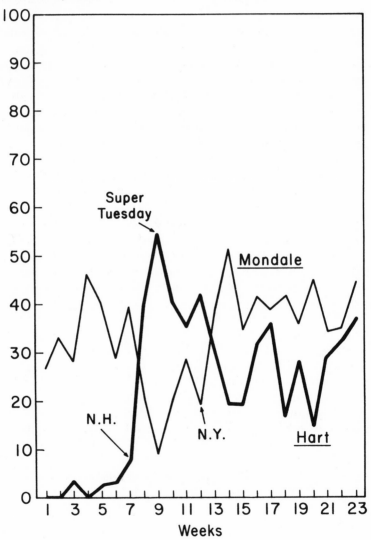

FIGURE 6.1 Support for Mondale and Hart in the 1984 NES Survey.

The problem with the analysis, of course, is that an "explanation" of voting decisions that *begins* with summary evaluations of the candidates does not really explain very much.[7] Indeed, it is hard to know what to make of cases in which the final vote is inconsistent with the general evaluation; my own guess is that these cases reflect errors in the measurement of evaluations or votes rather than any alternative calculus of choice.

The situation is different in nominating campaigns. For one thing, general evaluations in the form of thermometer scores do considerably less well as predictors of candidate preferences. In the 1984 NES survey, for example, Shanks et al. (1985: 21) found that "substantial numbers of respondents said they 'preferred' a candidate other than the one they liked best." Less than 62 percent of those who named Mondale as their first choice for the nomination also rated him above all the other candidates on the feeling thermometer, and the corresponding figure for Hart was about 74 percent (1985: table 8).

Some of the inconsistencies between evaluations and choices are certainly attributable to random error in one or the other measure, just as in general election campaigns. But the pattern of inconsistencies in the primary season data for 1984 makes it clear that more was happening than just measurement error. For example, *all* "first choices" that represented defections from "most liked" candidates before New Hampshire were defections away from other candidates and toward Mondale; by contrast, in the two weeks after New Hampshire 80 percent were defections toward Hart (Shanks et al. 1985: 23). Inconsistencies of this sort can only be explained by reference to the political context in which choices were being made at these two points in the campaign.

Clearly, choices cannot be entirely accounted for by any theory in which the effect of expectations is presumed to work solely through changes in the sorts of substantive evaluations of the candidates represented in the NES data by thermometer ratings. This fact seems to rule out both the cue-taking and the contagion models as satisfactory explanations for the dynamics of primary support because both models are based on the presumption that voters develop more favorable substantive impressions of candidates who are doing well in the horse race. It does not rule out the

[7] Obviously this criticism does not apply to works, including both of those cited in the previous footnote, in which general evaluations are themselves accounted for by less proximate political factors.

models based on either strategy or a simple desire to support a winner, since those models rely on mechanisms other than changes in substantive evaluations of the candidates to translate expectations into preferences. Thus, we need to look a bit further into the apparent bases of changing preferences in the 1984 campaign.

The notion that voters simply like to support winners suggests that a winning candidate's support should increase in every segment of the electorate, independent of particular voters' own political identities. A simple test of this view is presented in Figure 6.2, which shows separate time trends of support for Hart among the upper and lower fifths of the 1984 NES sample with respect to political predispositions toward Mondale.[8]

The obvious but important point to be gathered from Figure 6.2 is that the desire to support this particular winner was very unevenly distributed in the population. Respondents predisposed to look for an alternative to Mondale found one in the three weeks between the Iowa caucuses and Super Tuesday. Estimated Hart preferences for the anti-Mondale respondents jumped during this three-week period from about 5 percent before Iowa (when Hart was one of several minor candidates scrambling to avoid elimination) to over 70 percent just before Super Tuesday (by which time Hart had become the only viable alternative to Mondale). At the same time respondents predisposed to support Mondale reacted relatively calmly to the Hart bandwagon. Estimated Hart preferences for the pro-Mondale group started out at less than 2 percent before Iowa and never reached as much as a third of the group at the height of Hart's fortunes. On average, about 15 percent of those most favorably predisposed toward Mondale supported Hart in the weeks after Super Tuesday, compared to 40 percent of those least favorably predisposed toward Mondale. Although there is some room here for a momentum effect independent of real political content, it seems clear that no apolitical bandwagon explanation can fully account for the main patterns of response to Hart's emergence.

The pattern in Figure 6.2 appears to rule out pure excitement

[8] The levels of support for Hart shown in Figure 6.2 are based on separate estimates of the relationship between predispositions toward Mondale and choices between the two candidates for each week of the primary season. The levels of support for Hart among pro-Mondale and anti-Mondale respondents in each week were calculated by applying these weekly estimates of the relationship between predispositions and support to the average Mondale predisposition in the upper and lower fifths of the entire NES primary season sample.

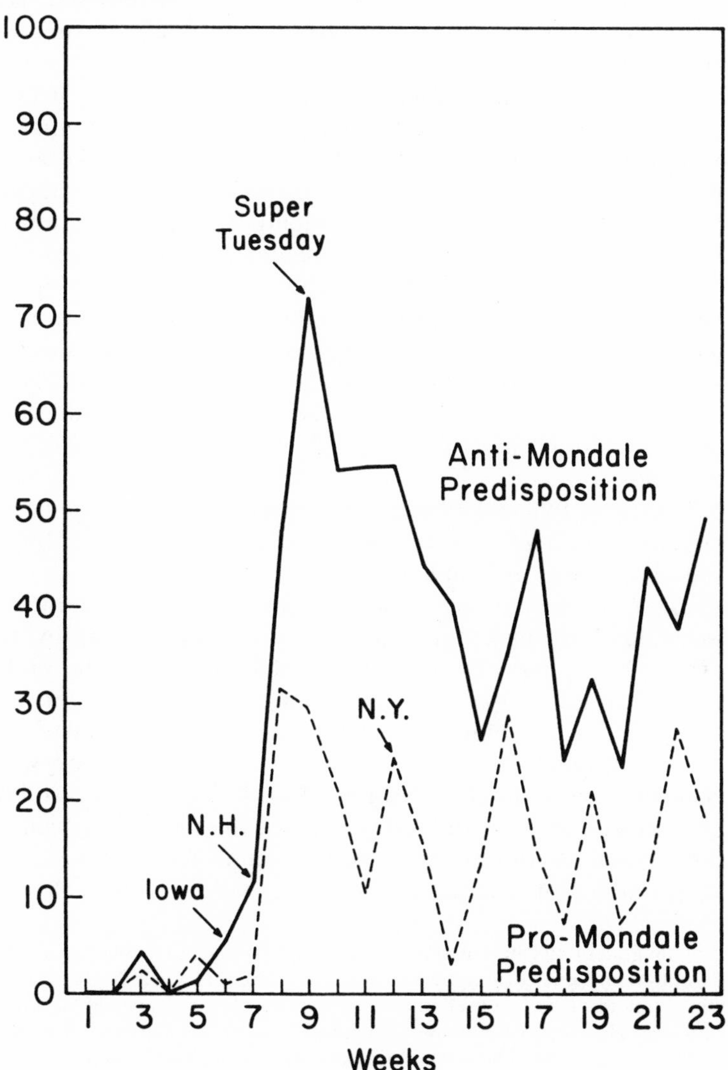

FIGURE 6.2 Political Predispositions and Hart Support, 1984.

or gamesmanship as a satisfactory explanation for the dynamics of Hart's support. People appear to have reacted to Hart's candidacy in ways that make considerable sense, given their underlying political predispositions. At the same time, we have seen that concrete perceptions concerning Hart's political and personal qualities, as summarized in thermometer ratings, are also insufficient to account for the dynamics of his support. One other possibility is that prospective voters' choices depended on strategic responses to Hart's candidacy.

The beauty of the strategic voting hypothesis is that it fits the broad outline of the facts so far described: it suggests that anti-Mondale respondents switched their support to Hart because he quickly became the one challenger on whom a vote would not be "wasted"; it also suggests that pro-Mondale respondents remained relatively unmoved because Mondale never fell so far behind that a vote for him would be "wasted." Unfortunately, the beauty of the hypothesis begins to fade when we focus our attention on the pattern of support for Hart in the six weeks after Super Tuesday. It is clear from Figure 6.2 that even those respondents least inclined to support Mondale began to abandon Hart in large numbers once his momentum began to ebb. And they had no "strategic" rationale for doing so.

This point follows from the logic of strategic voting applied to a two-candidate race. If your favorite candidate is ahead, obviously you should vote for him. But even if your favorite candidate is losing, you have nothing to gain by voting for his opponent; doing so would simply make the unhappy outcome (infinitesimally) more likely. Only if there is another candidate waiting in the wings, a third alternative capable of challenging your least-favorite candidate, does it make sense to consider abandoning your favorite. But for anti-Mondale Democrats after Super Tuesday, there was no viable alternative to Hart. In spite of his stumbles he was still their best, practically their only, hope. Thus, the rapid evaporation of Hart's support after Super Tuesday is simply inconsistent with any simple notion of strategic voting.[9]

[9] I am grateful to Paul Janaskie for this insight. It is worth noting that about half the anti-Mondale respondents who abandoned Hart after Super Tuesday moved to minor candidates or "no preference." Movements of this sort would be consistent with strategic voting if the minor candidates had better chances of winning than Hart's, but none did. The rest of those who abandoned Hart went to Mondale in spite of their anti-Mondale predispositions, a move with no apparent strategic rationale.

6.2 How Expectations Matter

The lesson to be drawn from Section 6.1 is that no one of the several distinct forms of momentum outlined there is sufficient to account for the dynamics of Hart's support. Thus, any comprehensive analysis of the politics and psychology of momentum must reflect the fact that the total effect of expectations on choices is complex, composed of several simultaneous currents involving different motivations and responses to the same campaign events and having different political implications. The problem is identifying these several simultaneous currents in the observable behavior of prospective voters and doing so with sufficient precision to estimate the magnitude and significance of each.

In this section I provide new, more specific evidence about how expectations matter. I distinguish three separate effects of expectations on preferences in the 1984 NES data and estimate the impact of each on choices between Walter Mondale and Gary Hart. In Section 6.3 I explore the distinct psychological and political implications of these separate effects, relating them to the varieties of momentum introduced in Section 6.1.

The first of these three distinct effects of expectations on preferences is an indirect effect mediated by prospective voters' evaluations of the candidates. In the survey data this appears as a direct effect of expectations on respondents' thermometer ratings of the candidates, which in turn determine the respondents' choices between candidates. Since the effect of perceived chances is reflected in the respondents' substantive evaluations of the candidates, I refer to this as the *internalized* effect of expectations.

This internalized effect of expectations on choice between Walter Mondale and Gary Hart in 1984 is shown in Figure 6.3.[10] The effect is illustrated for two different levels of information: "low information" represents the average level of uncertainty about Hart at the beginning of the 1984 campaign, and "high information" the average level of uncertainty about Hart at the end of the campaign.[11] Given what we have learned so far about the dynamics of the nominating process, it should not be surprising that the in-

[10] The estimated internalized effect of expectations in Figure 6.3 is based on the estimated effect of perceived chances on thermometer ratings in Table A.17 and on the estimated effects of thermometer ratings on candidate choice in Table A.18, both in Appendix C.5.

[11] Information levels were higher for Mondale than for Hart at both points; thus, the effect of expectations about Mondale was smaller than that shown for Hart at both points.

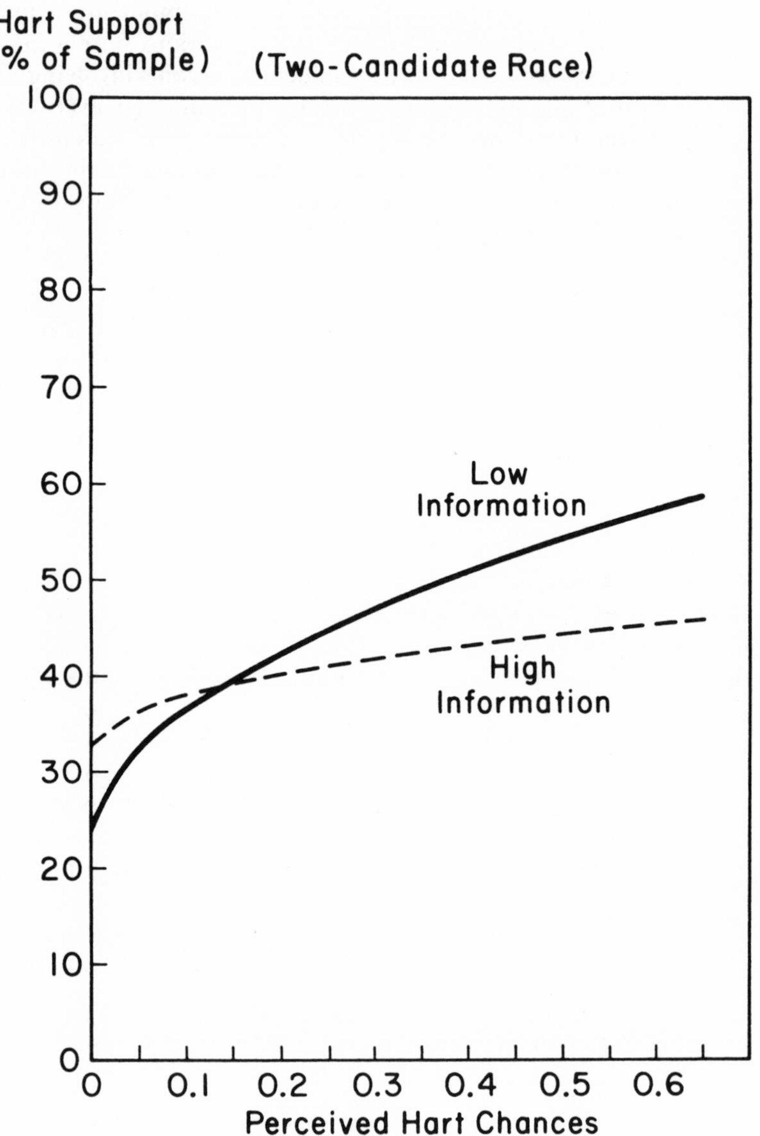

FIGURE 6.3 Internalized Effect of Expectatons on Hart Support, 1984.

ternalized effect of expectations decreased with information; that is, respondents were less open to suggestions about the candidates' qualities as they learned more about those candidates. For example, at the beginning of the campaign an increase in an average respondent's perception of Hart's chances from 10 percent to 20 percent would have improved Hart's rating by about three points on the hundred-point thermometer scale, thereby increasing the voter's probability of choosing him over Mondale by about six percentage points.[12] At the end of the campaign the same 10 percent increase in the same respondent's perception of Hart's chances would have improved the thermometer rating by about one and a half points and increased the voter's probability of choosing Hart by about two percentage points.

I conclude from these results that the internalized effect of expectations via thermometer ratings did have a discernible impact on choices between Mondale and Hart, particularly in the early stages of the 1984 campaign. But thermometer ratings are not the only possible determinants of choices among candidates in nominating campaigns. Indeed, we have already seen that in the 1984 campaign choices sometimes deviated significantly and systematically from thermometer ratings. There is considerable reason to suspect that these defections from thermometer ratings, as well as the thermometer ratings themselves, were influenced by changing perceptions of the candidates' chances.

The second distinct effect of expectations on preferences focuses on the fact that first Mondale and then Hart received more support than thermometer ratings alone would warrant. I presume they did so because of a *direct* effect of expectations on choices, over and above the internalized effect via thermometer ratings shown in Figure 6.3. The apparent impact of this direct effect on the choices of NES survey respondents in the 1984 campaign is shown in Figure 6.4.[13]

As in Figure 6.3, the effect of expectations is shown separately for two different levels of information—the average levels for Hart at the beginning and end of the campaign. As with the internalized effect of expectations in Figure 6.3, the direct effect of expecta-

[12] Of course, an average respondent would have been unlikely to perceive Hart's chances as being as high as 20 percent at the beginning of the 1984 race. The numbers in the example are chosen to facilitate meaningful comparisons between candidates and over time.

[13] The estimated direct effect of expectations in Figure 6.4 is based on the statistical results for perceived chances in Table A.18 in Appendix C.5.

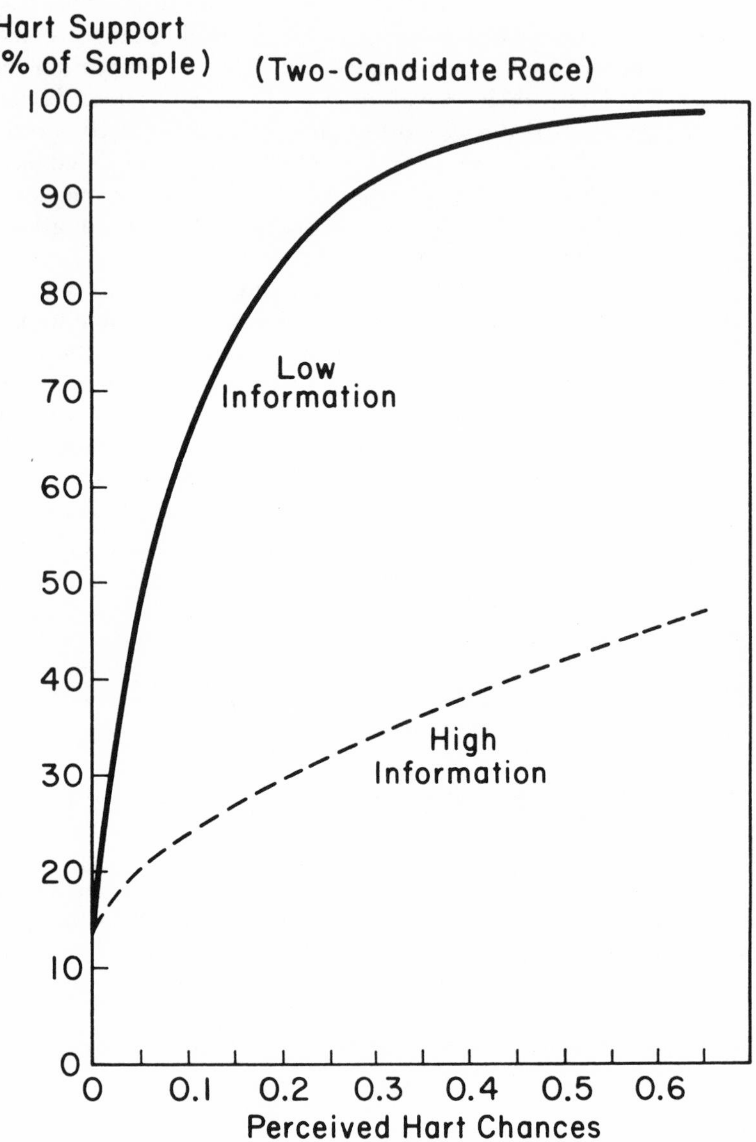

FIGURE 6.4 Direct Effect of Expectations on Hart Support, 1984.

tions on choice was greatest at the beginning of the campaign and declined with increasing information. But the difference in the magnitude of the effect with changes in information is much greater for the direct effect in Figure 6.4 than for the internalized effect in Figure 6.3. In addition, at each stage in the campaign the estimated direct effect of expectations was considerably greater than the estimated internalized effect. For example, the same early change in expectations that would have increased an average respondent's probability of supporting Hart by about six percentage points due to the internalized effect in Figure 6.3 would have increased it by more than three times that much due to the direct effect in Figure 6.4; and for less favorable expectations the corresponding differences are even greater. Given the amount of information available about Hart by the end of the primary season the differences in the magnitude of the direct and internalized effects of expectations are less dramatic but still substantial. From these differences it appears that, throughout the campaign, the bulk of the impact of expectations on choices was unmediated by changing substantive evaluations of the candidates as expressed by thermometer ratings.

The third and final effect of expectations on preferences considered here also focuses on discrepancies between thermometer ratings and choices. But it is based on the notion that expectations may affect choices not only directly, regardless of thermometer ratings, but also in combination with thermometer ratings. I refer to this as the *interactive* effect of expectations on choices. The nature of the interactive effect of expectations on choices is illustrated in Figure 6.5 for choices between Mondale and Hart in 1984.[14] The effect of perceptions of Hart's chances on the probability of supporting him is shown for three different levels of overall evaluations—moderately negative, moderately positive, and highly positive. It is not surprising that the probability of supporting Hart increased with the favorability of a respondent's overall evaluation of him. What is characteristic of the interactive effect of expectations is that the payoff from improving perceptions of Hart's chances was also greatest among respondents who already viewed him favorably on other grounds. For example, a perceived increase in Hart's chances from 10 percent to 20 percent increased

[14] The estimated interactive effect of expectations in Figure 6.5 is based on the statistical result for the "Thermometer-Expectations Interaction" in Table A.18 in Appendix C.5.

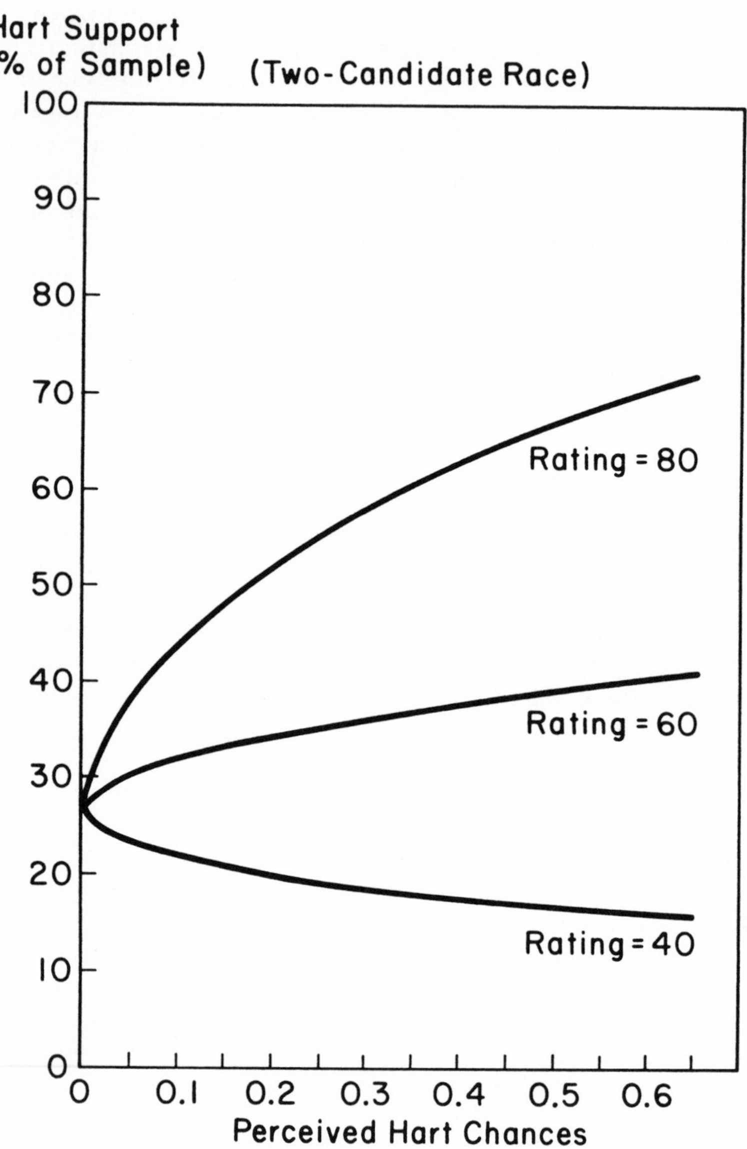

FIGURE 6.5 Interactive Effect of Expectations on Hart Support, 1984.

the probability of supporting him by less than three percentage points among respondents who rated him moderately favorably, but by about eight percentage points among those who rated him extremely favorably. The pattern of mobilization suggested by these results is a quite plausible one: as a candidate's chances improve he first attracts increasing support from those most favorably inclined toward him on other grounds, but his support also increases more gradually among those with less favorable but still positive evaluations. For respondents whose evaluations of a candidate are actively unfavorable this pattern is reversed: as the candidate's chances improve, those respondents who dislike him most are driven away most quickly.[15]

In summary, we have evidence in the 1984 NES data for three significant, distinct effects of expectations on preferences: (1) an internalized effect caused by increasingly favorable thermometer ratings; (2) a direct effect over and above the effect of thermometer ratings; and (3) an interactive effect involving the joint impact of expectations and thermometer ratings. The combined impact of these three distinct effects is illustrated in Figure 6.6.[16] As with the internalized and direct effects in Figures 6.3 and 6.4, I show the total effect of expectations separately for the average levels of information prevailing for Gary Hart at the beginning and end of the 1984 campaign. Each total effect is quite dramatic. The same prospective voter can be virtually certain to oppose a candidate or virtually certain to support a candidate, simply depending on voter perceptions of the candidate's chances. Even relatively small changes in expectations can have very substantial effects. For example, an increase in Hart's perceived chances from 10 to 20 percent would increase an average respondent's probability of supporting him by about twenty-five percentage points at the beginning of the campaign and by about eight percentage points at the end of the primary season.

The substantial difference in the effect of expectations between

[15] The latter pattern presumably reflects the fact that respondents are more willing to express support for a candidate they do not like very much if they believe he has no real chance to win than if they view him as a serious contender.

[16] The combined effect shown in Figure 6.6 is based on the statistical results in Table A.18 for expectations alone, in combination with thermometer ratings, and in combination with information. This combined effect is less than the sum of the separate effects illustrated in Figures 6.3, 6.4, and 6.5 because of the threshold feature of the model of choice on which the analysis is based. An average respondent will often quite likely support a candidate on the basis of any one of the effects considered singly, leaving little room for additional response to other effects.

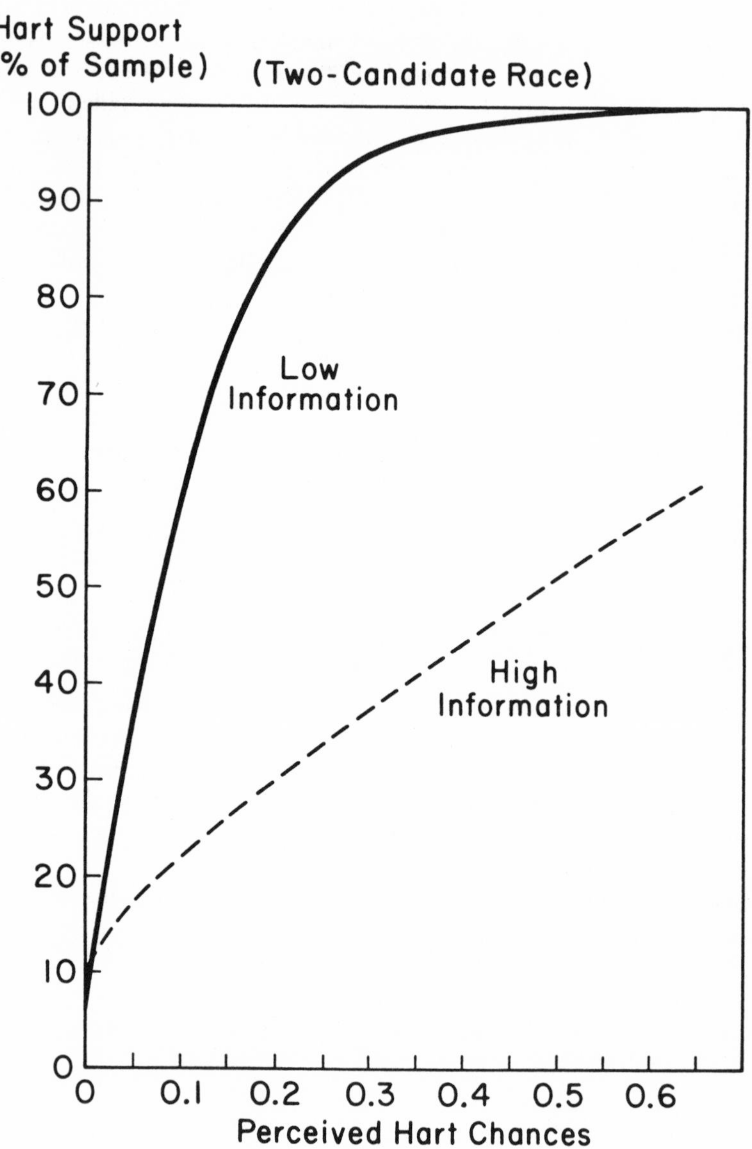

FIGURE 6.6 Total Effect of Expectations on Hart Support, 1984.

the beginning and end of the 1984 campaign highlights the role of information in muting momentum based on expectations. Thus, it helps explain why, although most formal models of the dynamics of momentum in the nominating process (for example, Aldrich 1980b) suggest that expectations and preferences should drive each other in a continuing upward spiral, the most notable bandwagons in recent campaigns have all appeared to slow by the end of the primary season. The connection between uncertainty and momentum evident in Figure 6.6 also provides a somewhat fuller explanation for the pattern of bandwagon effects evident in my own previous work on expectations and preferences in the 1980 nominating campaigns. Using data from the 1980 NES survey and a different model than the one developed here, I had concluded (Bartels 1985: 814) that

> although bandwagons were much in evidence immediately after the Iowa caucuses, particularly on the Republican side, they had all but disappeared by April. Only further investigation will make clear whether these results indicate a more general pattern. But if they do, they put the dynamics of the presidential nominating process in a new light. The bandwagon phenomenon focused on by earlier analysts, important as it obviously is, may not necessarily lead in the real world to the kinds of outcomes predicted by our simple models. Rather than doing better and better (or worse and worse) in an unbroken cycle, candidates may reach plateaus of support determined in part by their political skills and circumstances.

Now I might write, "plateaus of support determined by the underlying political predispositions of primary voters." Otherwise, the conclusion based on the 1980 data applies surprisingly well to this more elaborate analysis of 1984 data.

It is important to keep in mind that the estimated effects in Figure 6.6 apply only to an idealized average respondent in the 1984 NES survey. As a result, they tend to overstate the actual net effect of expectations in the sample as a whole. Another way to gauge the significance of expectations is to estimate their aggregate effect on each week's actual respondents, taken as they came, during the 1984 campaign. Although this sort of aggregate effect can obscure powerful influences on individual respondents' choices that happen to cancel out across a heterogenous collection of respondents in a given week and also confound changes in the effects of expectations during the campaign with changes in the expectations themselves, it has the great advantage of providing a picture of the concrete significance of expectations in an actual campaign setting.

The total aggregate effect of expectations on support for Hart in 1984 is shown in Figure 6.7.[17] The three main phases of the 1984 campaign are clearly evident in the figure. During the first seven weeks of the campaign season, before the New Hampshire primary, neither candidate gained any significant net support on the basis of expectations. Mondale dominated the horse race, but he was so well known that prospective voters were already deciding whether or not to support him primarily on other grounds.[18]

The relative unimportance of expectations in influencing support for a candidate as well known as Mondale was in early 1984 should not be surprising in view of the analysis already presented in this chapter. But it was surprising to Mondale's own advisers. Pollster Peter Hart recalled (in Moore 1986: 59)

> being with Mondale out in Des Moines right after the Iowa caucuses and his asking, "What kind of effect will this [Mondale's victory] have on New Hampshire?" And I said "dramatic," remembering Bob Teeter in 1980 telling me they'd gotten a tremendous roll with Bush. . . . Here we had just gotten 50 percent and beaten the rest of the field combined. We went out on Tuesday and Wednesday night and came back with data on Thursday morning. . . . Mondale's support in New Hampshire was basically at about 34 percent going into the Iowa caucuses. Coming out of the Iowa caucuses, we moved up to about 38 percent.

As a well-known front-runner, Mondale simply did not have the potential to benefit from momentum that the relatively unheralded Bush had had in early 1980. The candidate who did have that potential in 1984 was Gary Hart. In the second phase of the campaign, lasting for a month after his upset victory in New Hampshire, Hart gained considerable aggregate support due to the impact of expectations. This gain, amounting on average to more than twenty percentage points, was based on a combination

[17] The aggregate effect of expectations in each week of the campaign was estimated by subtracting from Hart's actual support in each week the share attributable, on the basis of the total effect of expectations in Figure 6.6, to differences in the two candidates' perceived chances.

[18] Mondale was also directly advantaged by the fact that he was universally recognized, whereas Hart was not. This pure information effect, described in Chapter 4, is not included in the effect of expectations shown in Figure 6.7.

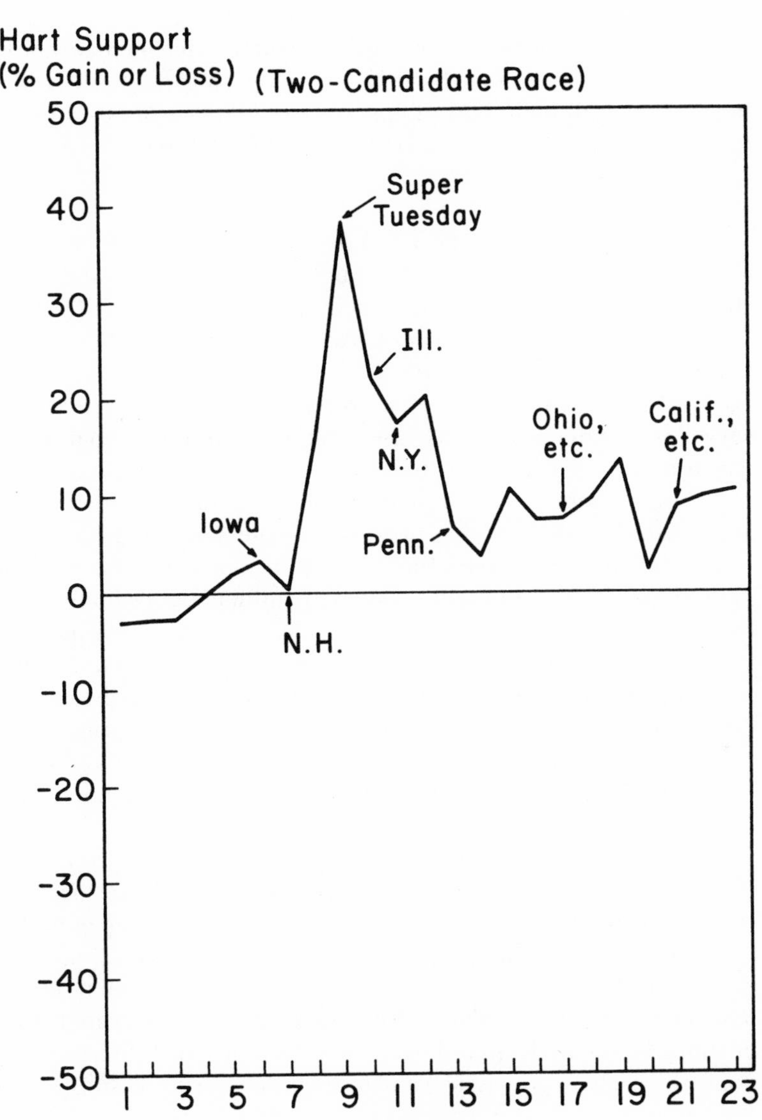

FIGURE 6.7 Aggregate Net Effect of Expectations on Hart Support, 1984.

of internalized, direct, and interactive effects and reflected not only Hart's brief absolute lead in the horse race but also the fact that, as a relatively unknown contender, he benefited more than Mondale could from improving perceptions of his chances. The last eleven weeks of the primary season marked a third phase of the campaign in which Hart's net advantage declined to about eight percentage points; by then he was faring less well in the horse race, and the impact of expectations on decisions to support him continued to decline as prospective voters learned more about him.

This examination of the aggregate role of expectations concludes the analysis scattered through Chapters 4, 5, and 6 of choices between Mondale and Hart in the 1984 NES survey. Before examining some theoretical implications of that role, it may be helpful to summarize the various elements of the analysis in Part II. We saw that information had direct effects on the choices of survey respondents, both because of a recognition threshold below which no candidate is likely to attract appreciable support and because of a more generalized tendency of prospective voters to avoid risk. We also saw that prospective voters' political predispositions and the fit between those predispositions and the political identities of the competing candidates influenced evaluations of the candidates (and therefore choices among them) with increasing force as information accumulated from week to week. Finally, we saw that expectations influenced choices both directly and indirectly through general evaluations in the form of thermometer ratings; they worked in combination with evaluations as well as independently; and their role in determining choices declined with increasing information.

The ability of this set of behavioral regularities to account for the actual choices of survey respondents in the 1984 NES survey is reflected in Figure 6.8. For each week of the 1984 campaign, the figure shows the actual proportion of the NES sample supporting Hart over Mondale, together with the proportion estimated on the basis of my analysis.[19] The fit between actual and estimated proportions is not perfect, and even in weeks for which the proportions themselves are quite similar they can disguise substantial

[19] The estimated shares of support for Hart shown in Figure 6.8 are based on the individual-level statistical results reported in Table A.18 in Appendix C, averaged over the set of respondents interviewed in each week of the NES study.

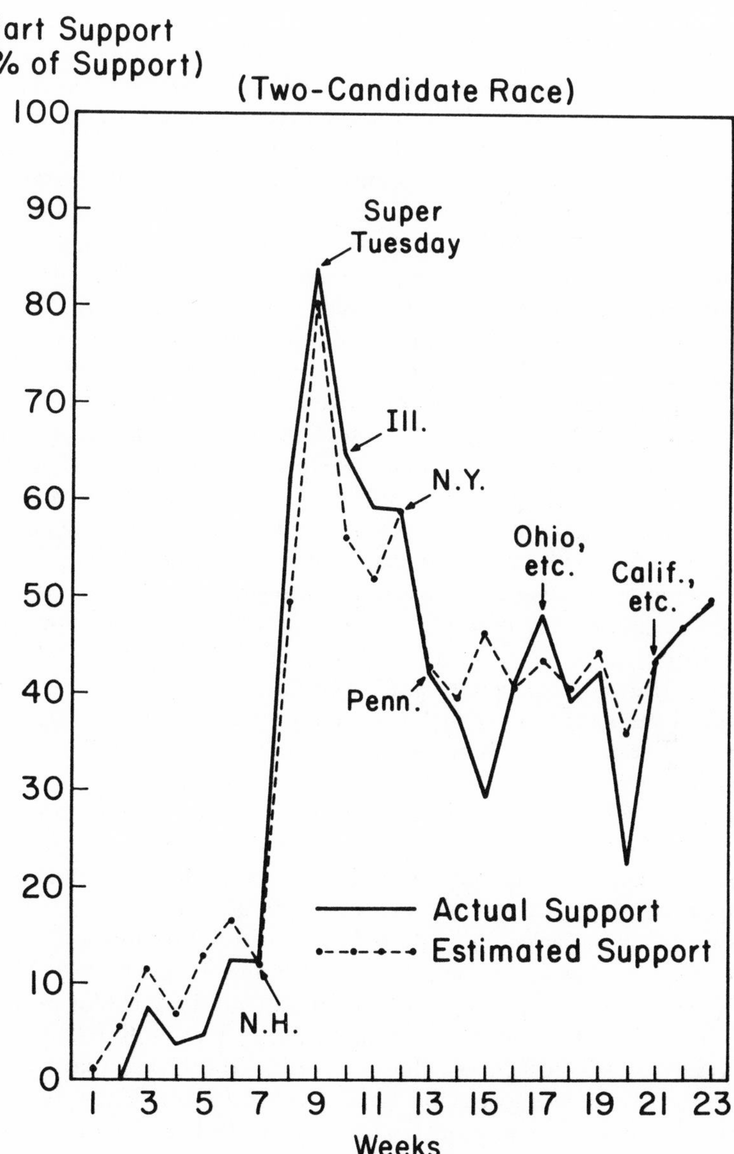

FIGURE 6.8 Actual and Estimated Hart Support, 1984.

counterbalancing errors of fit at the individual level. Nevertheless, it seems clear from Figure 6.8 that this analysis accounts quite successfully for the broad electoral dynamics of the 1984 campaign.

6.3 Why Expectations Matter

As we have seen, one of the great difficulties in any attempt to understand the psychology of momentum is the fact that the same manifest behavior can often be accounted for by a variety of very different psychological mechanisms. For example, the systematic discrepancies between general evaluations of the candidates and choices noted by Shanks et al. (1985: 21) can be plausibly interpreted as evidence of strategic voting (that is, avoiding a "wasted vote" on a candidate with little chance to win, even if he is otherwise quite attractive); but the same discrepancies can also be plausibly interpreted as evidence of the simpler desire to support a winner regardless of his substantive qualities as a candidate. The general fact that prospective voters' expectations about who will win appear to influence their own preferences is insufficient to provide compelling evidence for either one of these specific phenomena. To provide such evidence we must observe behavior that is consistent with one mechanism but not the other.

Some suggestive evidence that strategic calculations do affect prospective voters' choices, independent of their desire to support a winner, is provided in survey data from a March 1976 Field Poll in California described by Brady and Bartels (1982). The Field Poll asked respondents about both their preferences for a variety of paired comparisons between Democratic primary candidates and also their first choice for the Democratic nomination from a complete list of eleven candidates. These two kinds of questions produced somewhat different choices, and the differences appear to have been distinctly nonrandom. For example, seventy-two respondents named Humphrey as their first choice despite preferring Udall or Jackson in a paired comparison, but only ten named Udall or Jackson as their first choice despite preferring Humphrey. Udall and Jackson had already suffered a series of primary losses at this point in the campaign; Humphrey, still inactive, was widely expected to enter the race before the California primary and provide the most viable alternative to Carter. Thus, the preponderant flow of support from Udall and Jackson in (presumably "sincere") paired comparisons to Humphrey in list choices can plausibly be interpreted as an indication of strategic behavior on the part of California Democrats. A simple desire to support a winner provides a less adequate explanation for this pattern of behavior since there is no particular reason to expect such a desire to operate in choices from a complete list of candidates but not in paired comparisons. The crucial fact about paired comparisons that makes them interesting in this context is that survey respondents who treated the paired comparisons realistically as mock elections *would* have reason to behave differently than in choosing a candidate from the complete list; the incentive to avoid a "wasted vote" by supporting a second-best candidate is present in choosing from a complete list of candidates but not in choosing between any pair of candidates.

Another interesting opportunity to distinguish more clearly between strategic voting and a simple desire to support a winner is provided by the experimental election system known as *approval voting*. Under approval voting, participants may cast votes for as many candidates as they wish, rather than for just one. As a result, the dictates of strategic behavior are somewhat different than in the more usual plurality voting system. In particular, voters sometimes have strategic reasons *not* to vote for a candidate who is doing well in an approval voting system, if doing so will dilute the impact of their support for a more preferred alternative.

Richard Niemi and I have explored this aspect of the approval voting system, using a small-scale experiment involving college students during the 1984 primary season (Niemi and Bartels 1984). The respondents—ninety-one undergraduates in an introductory American government course—were asked how they would vote in a Democratic primary both under the usual plurality system and under approval voting.[20] Some of their approval votes clearly reflected strategic thinking. For example, about half of the students whose first choice was Glenn, Jackson, or McGovern also voted for Hart or Mondale as a second choice in order to express a preference between the two front-runners. Conversely, among those who ranked Hart and Mondale, in either order, as their two favorite candidates, several (though not a majority) reported that they would cast a single "bullet vote" for their top choice rather than self-cancelling votes for both front-runners. A few actually pro-

[20] The students all described themselves as Democrats or Independents; Republicans were excluded because their hypothetical choices among Democratic candidates in a pretest often reflected a desire to help Ronald Reagan—for example, by choosing the weakest possible Democratic opponent.

vided this rationale for their behavior in written comments solicited as part of the study.

Although some strategic behavior was evident in the experiment, other students' responses could be accounted for better by a simple desire to "go with a winner." For example, Hart and Mondale supporters who thought the two candidates' chances were about even were *least* likely to "bullet vote" and *most* likely to vote for both of the leading contenders. Thus, the Mondale supporters most likely to cast an additional approval vote for Hart were not those who perceived Mondale as having a comfortable lead in the race, as strategic considerations would suggest, but those who perceived Hart as being even with or ahead of Mondale.

Two hypothetical scenarios in which the candidates' standings in the race were artificially manipulated provided additional examples of approval voting behavior consistent with a desire to support winners but illogical in strategic terms. For example, several students added approval votes for a candidate third or lower in their preference ranking in scenarios where that candidate's chances were described more favorably, despite the fact that doing so diluted a simultaneous vote for a more preferred candidate having a good chance to win. Overall, twenty-two of the twenty-five students who changed their votes from one hypothetical scenario to the other did so in a manner consistent with the notion that they wanted to support winners and avoid losers. Indeed, some of them described their motivations in just that way: "better chance for a winner," "most likely to be a winning vote," "assured that one of my choices would be nominated"—and even simply "I like the front-runner."

The evidence presented in Section 6.2 about how expectations matter provides considerable additional insight regarding the distinct varieties of momentum identified in Section 6.1. To the extent that we can match specific effects of expectations with specific psychological processes, we cannot only demonstrate the existence but also estimate the magnitude of the impact of specific kinds of momentum. As a practical matter the matching will not be airtight: the NES survey was not designed to facilitate the drawing of the relevant behavioral distinctions; and there are intrinsic difficulties in any effort to relate manifest behavior to underlying motivations in a clear and compelling way. But even without attaining a perfect match between evidence and theories, we can use the evidence provided here to draw some interesting tentative conclusions about the nature of momentum.

The internalized effect of expectations illustrated in Figure 6.3 is in certain respects the most problematic of the three effects considered here. It could reflect the impact of cue-taking, with uncertain prospective voters making rational calculations about the substantive information contained in the previous decisions of their fellow voters. Alternatively, it could reflect a sort of contagion, in which casual campaign observers swept up by the atmosphere of success surrounding a winning candidate irrationally confuse success with quality. The empirical effects of these two very different processes are too similar to be clearly distinguishable using currently available data. Thus, from an analytic standpoint it is fortunate that the internalized effect of expectations is the least significant of the three effects in empirical terms. A comparison of Figures 6.3 and 6.4, for example, suggests that the direct effect of expectations on the choices of prospective voters is significantly greater than the internalized effect, at least in the 1984 campaign.

The direct and interactive effects of expectations can be associated more confidently with specific theories of momentum, the interactive effect with what I have called the strategic theory and the direct effect with the simple desire of prospective voters to support a winner. The behavioral distinction between the two effects of expectations closely parallels the psychological distinction between the two theories of momentum. The distinction in each case is between a mechanism enmeshed in the substance of politics and a mechanism independent of the substance of politics.

The fact that prospective voters react in both ways reinforces an important lesson: human beings are both calculating and playful, at once rational political actors and bemused spectators of the political drama unfolding all around them. This variety of perspectives on the political world should not be surprising. What may be surprising, and is certainly politically significant, is the fact that each perspective seems to have a considerable impact on the actual choices of prospective voters. Political calculation and bemused spectating do not go on in separate, watertight compartments. They are inextricably intertwined in the jumble of motivations that shape mass political behavior.

PART III

The Impact of Momentum

CHAPTER SEVEN

Public Opinion and Primary Voting

ALL THE ANALYSIS PRESENTED thus far has been couched in terms of the responses to campaign events of what Shanks et al. (1985: 24) have referred to as "the national audience"—the representative cross-sections of the party rank and file interviewed in Thomas Patterson's surveys in Los Angeles and Erie in 1976 and in the National Election Studies across the country in 1980 and 1984. But poll results do not determine who will be the party's nominee. In the contemporary nominating system, primaries do. Thus, there is some reason to fear that any study focusing entirely on the responses of the national audience to campaign events may be fundamentally misdirected.

There are two major sources of disparity between survey respondents and primary voters. First, they are simply different sets of people. Any survey designed to be representative of party identifiers as a group may be unrepresentative of the particular kinds of party identifiers who participate in primaries. Second, behavior in the voting booth may differ significantly from survey responses. Not only are the circumstances surrounding the choice itself different, but also the political stimuli leading up to the choice are different: primary voting in any state occurs at the end of a more or less intensive state-level campaign, whereas the average survey respondent interviewed elsewhere at the same time may not have been exposed to anything like the same volume of political information and persuasion.

For these reasons, some analysts have discounted the possibility of learning much of interest about primary voting from national surveys. Although national samples impose some important limitations on analyses, I consider them far from useless, even if our only goal is to explain actual primary outcomes. I suspect there are strong, comprehensible connections between the attitudes and perceptions of national survey respondents and the actual behavior of primary voters.

Part III of this book presents direct analyses of primary voting in the five most recent presidential nominating campaigns. In order to connect those analyses to the study of public opinion in Part

II, I examine in this chapter the nature and extent of *compositional* and *contextual* differences between primary voters and survey respondents. Because some kinds of people are more likely than others to vote in primaries, compositional differences are addressed in Section 7.1. And because the same people may behave differently in a primary voting booth after being exposed directly to an active local campaign than they would in an opinion survey conducted at a more typical point in the national primary season, contextual differences are examined in Section 7.2. In Section 7.3 I provide a different kind of connection between public opinion and primary voting by exploring some implications of the analysis of public opinion in Part II for the nature of primary voting in a variety of campaign settings. I propose a typology of primary campaigns and outline the distinctive ways in which the basic elements common to all nominating campaigns—politics, expectations, and uncertainty—play themselves out in each type of campaign, given the general patterns of attitude formation described in Part II.

7.1 Primary Voters

The conventional wisdom among political scientists is that primary voters are unrepresentative of their parties' rank-and-file identifiers, both with respect to their demographic characteristics and with respect to their political views.[1] V. O. Key, Jr. (1956: chap. 5) warned in his study of state-level politics that, for this reason, primaries could provide "the illusion of popular rule." Ranney (1972; 1977) found that primary voters were, indeed, unrepresentative with respect to demographic characteristics (better educated, wealthier, more interested in politics, and with stronger partisan loyalties). Somewhat later, Lengle (1981) used survey data from the 1968 and 1972 primaries in California, with supporting data from some other primary states, to show that Democratic primary voters were unrepresentative of the party constituency not only in demographic terms but also with respect to ideology (more liberal), political style (more "amateur" and participatory), and candidate preference (disproportionately favorable to McCarthy in 1968 and McGovern in 1972). "In today's nomination system," Lengle concluded (1981: 78), ". . . the New Politics faction, its candidates, and

[1] By party *identifiers* I mean those members of the general public who express a psychological attachment to one party or the other, as distinct from those who register as party members or vote for the party's candidates. For the original explication and analysis of the concept, see Campbell et al. (1960: chaps. 6 and 7).

its issue-concerns are advantaged, since the constituency to which these kinds of candidates and issues appeal is over-represented in presidential primary electorates."

The most careful recent study, by Geer (1986), challenged this conventional wisdom by suggesting that voters in recent presidential primaries have not been unrepresentative of the "party following" to any significant degree. Geer used a new definition of the "party following" (the set of general election voters who either identified with the party or voted for its presidential candidate), a new data source (election day "exit polls" rather than door-to-door or telephone surveys), and a new set of primaries (a total of five Republican and seven Democratic primaries—most in 1980 but a few in 1976—in California, Illinois, New York, Ohio, and Pennsylvania). It is difficult to judge which of these differences might be crucial in accounting for the differences between his findings and those of previous analysts. Nevertheless, his work suggests that the question of representation in presidential primaries is less clear-cut than it has sometimes been made to seem.

My interest here is less in the substantive political question of whether primary voters are representative of the party rank and file, however defined, than in the methodological question of whether the party identifiers interviewed in the NES surveys are representative, for the purposes of my own analysis, of actual primary voters. Thus, the relevant comparison is between a sample of party identifiers of the sort relied on in Part II, on one hand, and the subset of identifiers who actually voted in their states' primaries, on the other. Such a comparison is possible in the 1980 NES survey, which includes validated information on primary turnout for each respondent.[2]

For example, Figure 7.1 compares the distribution of opinions about domestic policy for Republican primary voters with that for

[2] Simply asking survey respondents whether or not they voted produces significant overreporting of turnout, particularly when the question refers to a primary election which may have occurred long before the interview. The NES staff went to the precinct of each respondent in the 1980 election survey to determine whether or not the respondent was recorded as having voted in a presidential primary election that year. The subsamples of primary voters analyzed here include only those respondents who cast a verified primary vote; they exclude all respondents living in states not holding presidential primaries in 1980 and may also exclude some respondents who actually voted in a primary but for whom no records could be located. To maximize the number of cases, the comparisons between identifiers and primary voters include all respondents in the year-long 1980 NES study, not just those respondents interviewed during the primary season.

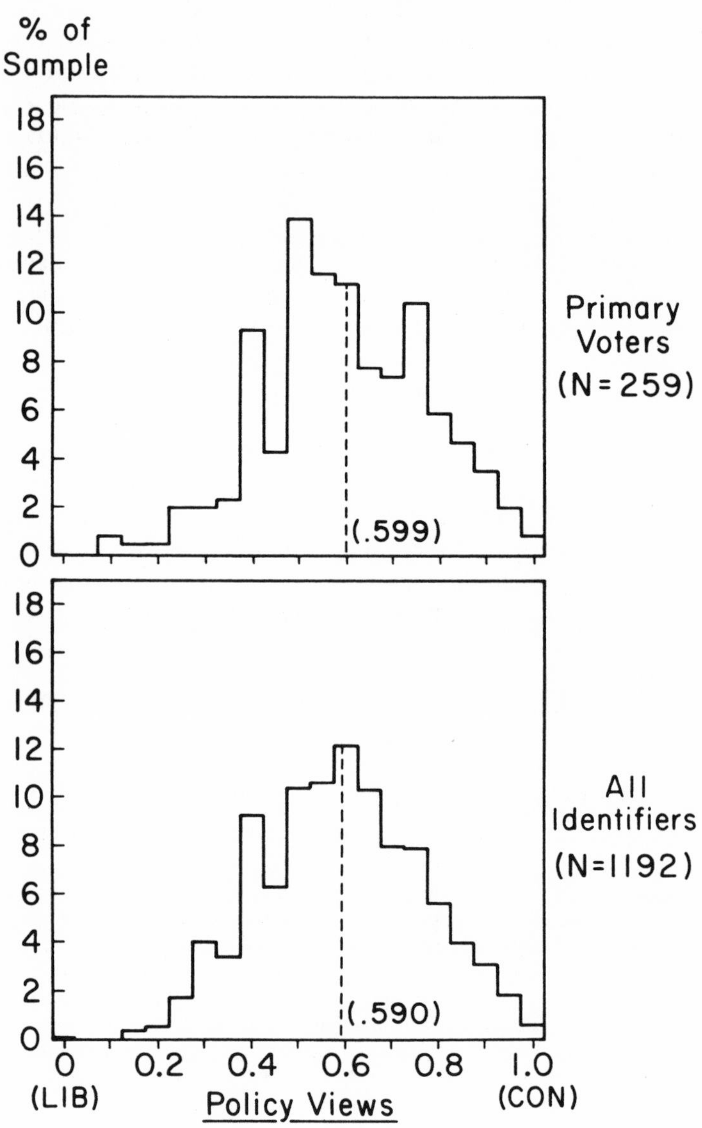

FIGURE 7.1 Domestic Policy Views of Republican Primary Voters and Identifiers, 1980.

all Republican identifiers in the 1980 NES sample.[3] It is evident from the figure that conservative opinions (those to the right of the midpoint) predominated among both groups. On average, the primary voters were slightly more conservative than the party as a whole, but the difference is less than 1 percent of the total length of the scale.

Similar distributions are shown for Republicans' foreign policy positions in Figure 7.2.[4] Republicans tended to be somewhat more conservative about foreign policy than domestic policy, in both the full sample of party identifiers and the subset of primary voters; but, as with domestic policy, the differences between the two groups in their opinions about foreign policy were trivial in magnitude.

Similar comparisons between primary voters and party identifiers are shown for the Democrats in Figures 7.3 and 7.4. In each case the Democrats were noticeably more liberal than the Republicans, but the differences between Democratic identifiers and primary voters were, again, trivial in magnitude. In each case the small difference that did exist suggests that Democratic primary voters were slightly more conservative than rank-and-file Democrats—a difference counter to the conventional wisdom that primary voters are more extreme in their opinions than the rank and file.

Conventional wisdom fares somewhat better on the question of demographic representation. The demographic characteristics of party identifiers and of primary voters are compared in Table 7.1. For both parties, the results are consistent with the notion that primary voters are an unrepresentative subset of the party rank and file. Even here, however, the differences noted most frequently in

[3] "Domestic policy" opinions represent a combination of responses to four separate questions in the 1980 NES survey: abstract liberalism and conservatism, government spending and services, environmental protection versus economic growth, and nuclear power. The answers are scaled so that a respondent with the most extreme conservative position on each question gets an overall score of one and a respondent with the most extreme liberal position on each question gets an overall score of zero.

[4] Foreign policy opinions also represent a combination of responses to four separate questions in the 1980 NES survey: abstract liberalism and conservatism, defense spending, relations with Russia, and Carter's handling of the Soviet invasion of Afghanistan. As with domestic policy opinions, the answers are scaled so that a respondent with the most extreme conservative position on each question gets an overall score of one and a respondent with the most extreme liberal position on each question gets an overall score of zero.

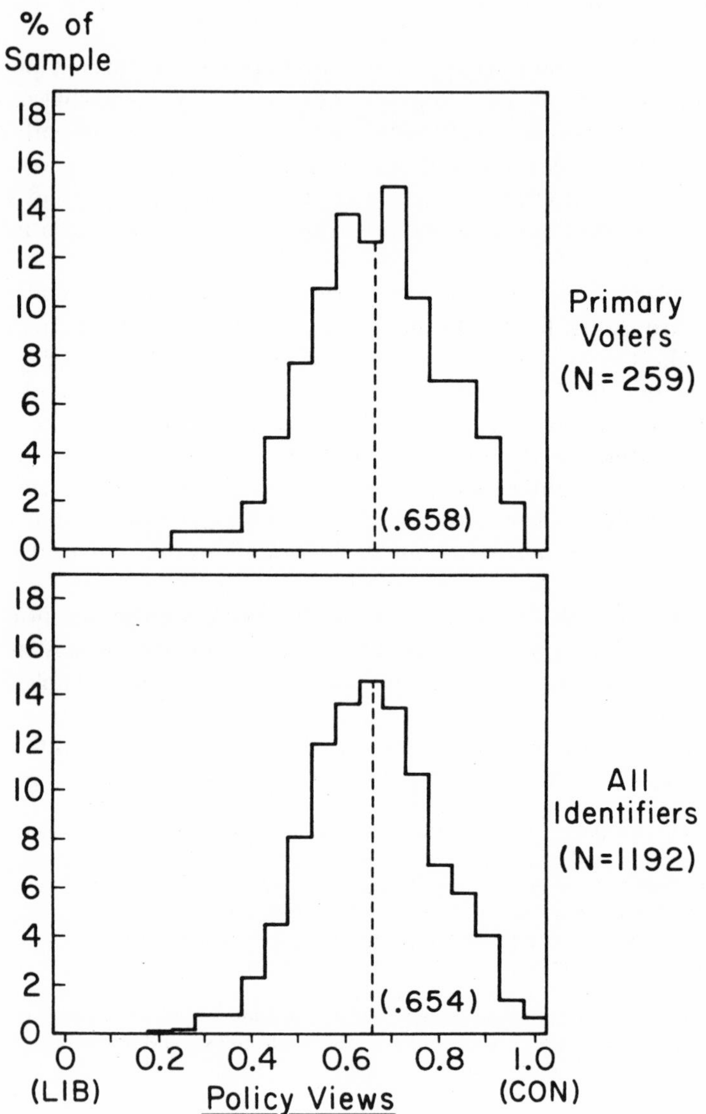

FIGURE 7.2 Foreign Policy Views of Republican Primary Voters and Identifiers, 1980.

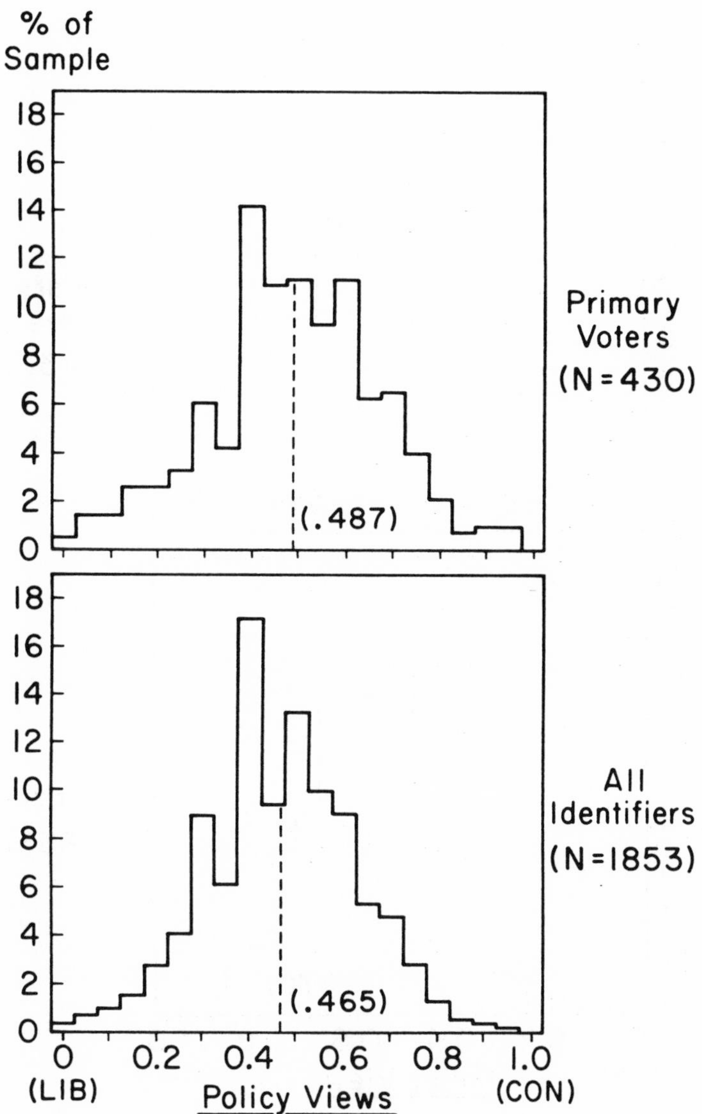

FIGURE 7.3 Domestic Policy Views of Democratic Primary Voters and Identifiers, 1980.

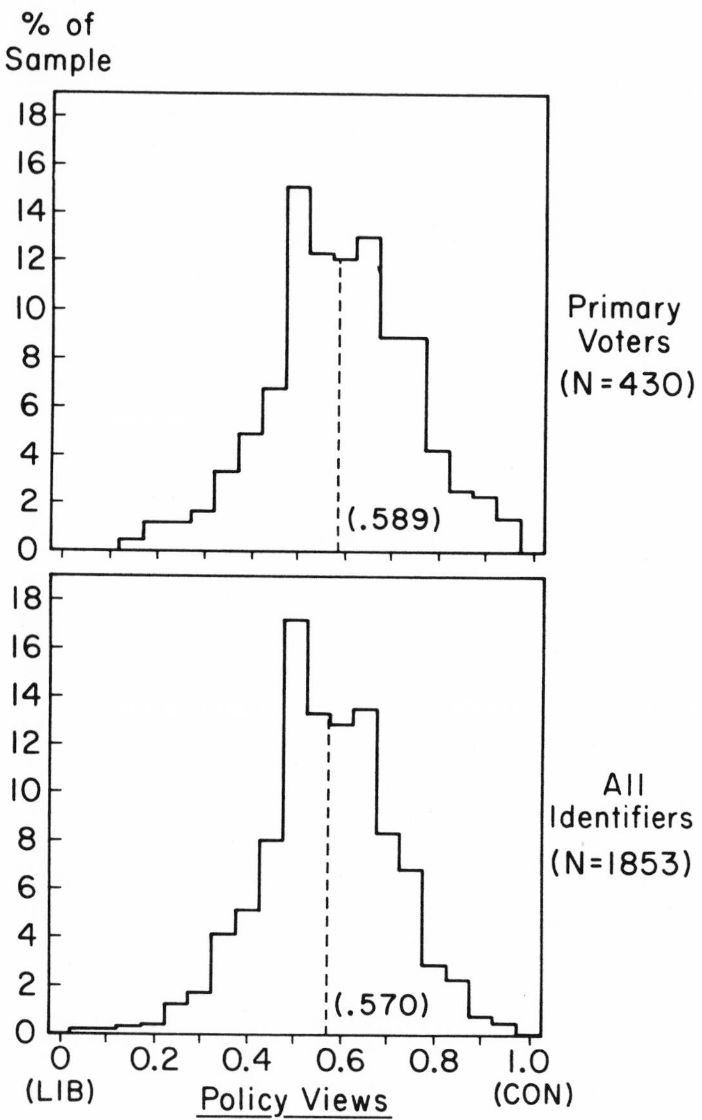

FIGURE 7.4 Foreign Policy Views of Democratic Primary Voters and Identifiers, 1980.

TABLE 7.1 Average Characteristics of Primary Voters and Party Identifiers, 1980

	Republicans		Democrats	
	Party Identifiers (N = 1,192)	Primary Voters (N = 259)	Party Identifiers (N = 1,853)	Primary Voters (N = 430)
Age (in years)	45.2	50.7	45.2	51.3
Education (in years)	12.7	13.1	11.9	12.1
Income (in $1,000s)	15.6	16.2	13.3	13.9
Race (% Black or Hispanic)	4.9	3.1	22.2	16.5
Sex (% Female)	53.8	59.1	59.1	57.0
Home ownership (%)	74.7	82.2	66.3	76.7
Residence in community (in years)	20.2	26.0	23.5	28.8
Church attendance (0–100)	50.4	56.4	45.2	53.9
Interest in the campaign (0–100)	60.3	71.8	54.5	63.8
Political information (0–100; rated by interviewer)	60.6	65.8	52.1	58.9
Media use (0–100)	52.4	57.7	45.8	53.7

Source: Calculated from 1980 NES data.

the literature, those involving education and income, turn out not to be the largest ones. On average, primary voters in 1980 had only a few months more schooling and about $600 more in annual income than party identifiers. More significant differences appear for characteristics related to what might loosely be termed "social stability." On average, primary voters were more than five years older than party identifiers, had lived in their current communities more than five years longer, were 9 percent more likely to own their own homes, and were more frequent churchgoers.[5]

Another difference, and a more important one for my purposes, is that primary voters were more attuned to politics than their parties' rank-and-file identifiers—more frequent users of the media, more informed about public affairs, and more interested in the campaign. These differences are about 10 percent for Republicans and about 15 percent for Democrats. Their significance lies in the fact that, with more exposure and attention to the media and higher levels of information, primary voters would also be expected to differ systematically with respect to the sort of underly-

[5] These differences with respect to "social stability" are consistent with the findings of Wolfinger and Rosenstone (1980) concerning the importance of life cycles and residential mobility in explaining turnout in general elections.

ing uncertainty about the candidates described in Chapter 4. Since we have already seen in Chapters 5 and 6 that uncertainty affects the degree to which prospective voters weigh political predispositions and expectations in making their electoral choices, it follows that primary voters as a group should be expected to differ in this respect as well. The analysis of primary voting in Chapters 8, 9, and 10 will explicitly recognize these differences.

7.2 National and Local Forces

The compositional differences between national samples of party identifiers and primary voters seem sufficiently small to warrant some confidence in the basic relevance of the analysis in Part II for explaining primary voting. But the question of dealing with contextual differences arising from the distinctive political environment of a primary campaign remains. What are the effects of a more or less intensive local campaign on the behavior of primary voters? Do these voters respond in the same way as the "national audience" to the sorts of campaign events and political forces outlined in Part II? Or is each primary a unique event, governed by local forces working in idiosyncratic ways? Any attempt to account for primary outcomes using a simple statistical model confronts these questions, since the usefulness of such an enterprise depends on the presence of underlying regularities in political behavior across a range of primary states. If each primary is a fundamentally unique event, we cannot expect to learn much about primary voting except through state-specific analyses and anecdotes.

The view that individual state primaries are fundamentally unique events was expressed most forcefully by Flanigan and Zingale:

> It is not differing compositions of state electorates in a "nationalized" electorate that have produced different results in different state primaries. Rather, individual state electorates, seeing the candidates in differing campaign contexts, appear to respond differentially, perhaps idiosyncratically, to them. The behavior of various demographic groups in a particular primary tells us little about how the same groupings in other states will react; neither will the preferences expressed in national polls provide much of a basis for projections of the outcomes of particular primaries. (1985: 22)

In one sense Flanigan and Zingale are obviously right. It is clearly not the case that primary outcomes "vary from state to state largely because the marginal distributions of socio-economic and political determinants . . . vary," as Flanigan and Zingale would expect in a "nationalized" primary electorate (1985: 19). The dynamics of expectations and uncertainty play a sufficiently important role in primary voting that they would produce very different outcomes in different states even if primary electorates were demographically identical in every state. But as I have tried to demonstrate in Part II of this book, expectations and uncertainty are no more "idiosyncratic" than other electoral forces and no less amenable to systematic analysis.

The more fundamental question is whether the structure of electoral choice itself varies in idiosyncratic ways from primary to primary. Flanigan and Zingale claimed that it does; for example, the "behavior of various demographic groups in a particular primary tells us little about how the same groupings in other states will react" because "the importance of various determinants of vote choice (issues, personal images, socio-economic and political factors)" is "locally conditioned" (1985: 22, 18). Flanigan and Zingale's evidence for "localized" primary electorates came from a series of primary day exit polls in various states during the 1984 campaign. They found that primary results in specific states bore no clear relationship to the states' aggregate demographic characteristics. Thus, for example, they noted that "Mondale lost some of the primaries with large numbers of union voters, Ohio and Oregon for example, and he won states like North Carolina and Georgia where there were few union voters" (1985: 20). Moreover, they found wide variations across a range of states in the behavior of specific demographic groups. For example, "Members of union households, a group that generally supported Mondale, voted strongly for Hart in certain primaries like Vermont and Massachusetts" (1985: 20).

At this point Flanigan and Zingale's analysis blurs an important distinction: the distinction between similar *effects* and similar *outcomes.* The fact that some states, or even union members in some states, went for Hart is by no means inconsistent with the possibility that their union membership had the same pro-Mondale effect in those states as elsewhere; it simply suggests that the effect of union membership was sometimes more than offset by other factors. This fact is illustrated in Figure 7.5, which shows voting patterns (based on ABC News exit surveys) for a variety of demo-

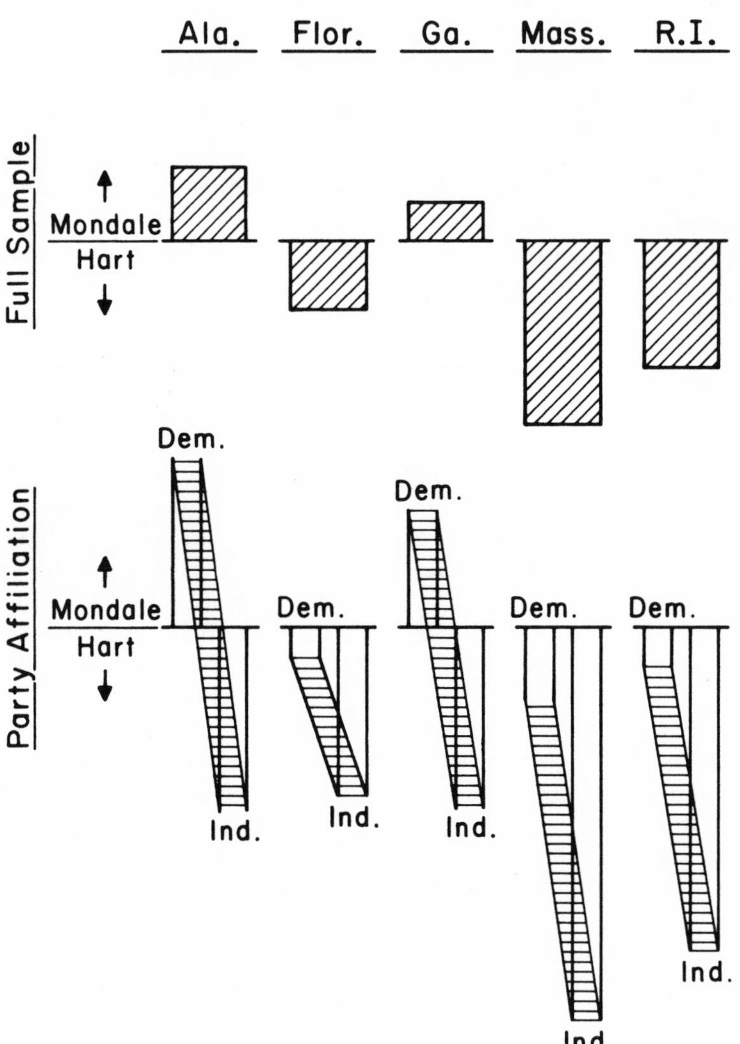

FIGURE 7.5 Selected Demographic Characteristics and Voting in Super Tuesday Primaries, 1984.

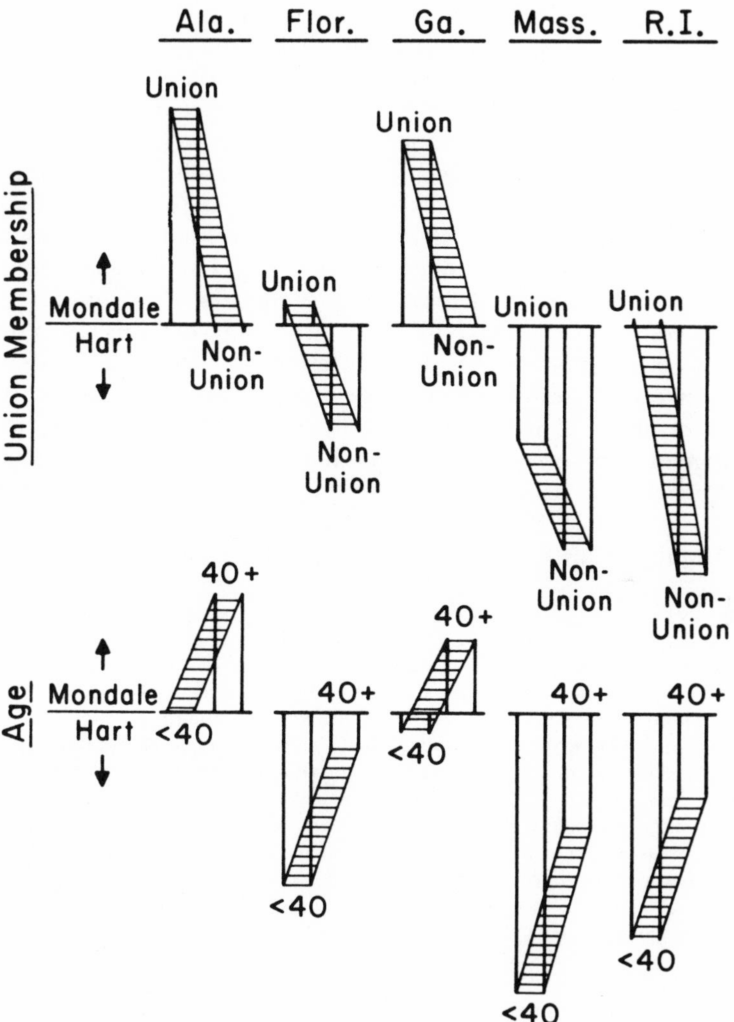

Ala.
Flor.
Ga.
Mass.
R.I.
Union Membership
Mondale
Hart
Union
Non-Union
Age
40+
<40

graphic groups in five states holding their 1984 Democratic primaries on the same day, Super Tuesday.[6] Relative levels of support for Mondale and Hart fluctuated considerably from state to state, both overall and within demographic groups (Democrats and Independents, members of union households and others, voters younger and older than forty years of age). But if we compare the differences between, for example, union households and non-union households within each state, those differences look fairly stable across states. Union households went for Mondale in Florida and for Hart in Massachusettts, but the difference in voting behavior between union households and others was almost exactly the same in each instance. What differed was the mix of other political forces in each state at the time of the primary.

The same point can be made more exhaustively by examining a larger variety of primary states and voting groups. ABC News did exit surveys in thirteen primary states in 1984, and included eight demographic and issue questions that might reasonably be expected to distinguish Mondale supporters from Hart supporters. As a result, we can make ninety-five separate comparisons to determine the apparent effects of different characteristics in different primary states.[7] In ninety-three of the ninety-five cases, the apparent effect is in the expected direction. Notwithstanding the range of local forces at work in each primary state and disregarding whether a particular group gave a plurality of its votes to Mondale or to Hart, the differences between complementary groups were almost always in the same direction in every state.[8] Union

[6] "Exit surveys" are conducted with primary voters as they leave their polling places. The ABC News exit survey data for 1984 appeared (in the form of marginals and simple cross-tabulations) in a volume edited by Smith (n. d.).

[7] The states for which data are available include Alabama, California, Connecticut, Florida, Georgia, Illinois, Massachusetts, New Hampshire, New Jersey, New York, Ohio, Pennsylvania, and Rhode Island. The demographic and issue comparisons include age (over forty versus under forty), race (black versus white), religion (Jews versus non-Jews), income (under $30,000 versus over $30,000), education (noncollege graduate versus college graduate), union membership (union household versus nonunion household), party affiliation (Democrat versus Independent), and concern about unemployment (most important issue versus less important); in each pair I expect the first-named group to support Mondale more than the second-named group. (In nine cases, comparisons based on race or religion were omitted for states in which blacks or Jews comprised less than 5 percent of the exit poll sample.)

[8] The *magnitudes* of the differences are more variable from state to state. These variations are presumably due in part to the phenomenon of political activation described in Chapter 5, in part to the confounding effects of different patterns of

households supported Mondale more than did nonunion households, and so on.

If the effects of various social and political characteristics are reasonably constant across primary states, as these data suggest, then there is no fundamental obstacle to constructing a successful statistical analysis of primary voting across a set of primary states. But, as in any statistical analysis, we must specify and measure the various factors presumed to determine primary outcomes across the range of primary states included in the analysis.

The examination of individual electoral behavior in Part II of this book provides three ways to account for differences in primary outcomes from state to state. First, voters in different states bring to the campaign different sets of political predispositions rooted in different distributions of demographic and social characteristics. Second, the candidates' standings in the primary season horse race change from week to week, and with these changes come changes in the expectations shaping prospective voters' evaluations and choices. Third, and finally, prevailing levels of information change over the course of the primary season, altering the relative weight of predispositions and expectations in evaluations and choices from week to week.

The extent to which these three factors can account for actual primary outcomes is explored in detail in Chapters 8, 9, and 10. But in the remainder of this section I consider an important potential difficulty in applying insights from the individual-level behavioral analysis in Part II to an analysis of primary outcomes at the state level. The difficulty is that, although political characteristics of the various primary states can be observed quite readily, and the expectations of primary voters can reasonably be assumed to approximate those of national survey respondents at the same point in the campaign, prevailing levels of information among primary voters are more difficult to measure in any direct way and less likely to be adequately approximated by corresponding levels of information among survey respondents.

We have already seen in Section 7.1 that primary voters, as a group, are somewhat more interested in politics and somewhat better informed than rank-and-file party identifiers. But this compositional difference may be swamped by a contextual difference reflecting the impact of local campaigning in specific primary

related demographic and political characteristics from state to state, and in part to genuine local differences.

states. One obvious effect of a primary campaign is providing prospective voters with information about the candidates—information which the same prospective voters would not receive under other circumstances. The magnitude of this contextual effect is, of course, an empirical issue. But it seems unlikely that simply adjusting for the relatively minor compositional differences between the party rank and file and the primary electorate will provide a satisfactory measure of the level of information of actual primary voters at any given point in the campaign season.

If any state exhibits the distinctive effects of intensive local campaigning, it ought to be New Hampshire. The state is relatively small, both geographically and in population. The primary comes at the beginning of the campaign season, when public interest is probably at its highest level. The candidates spend an enormous amount of time there—and all the money federal campaign finance law allows.[9] Finally, campaigning occurs at a personal level unmatched in most elections.[10] As one candidate's campaign manager put it, "New Hampshire is the paradigm of retail politicking—one to one, down the street, door to door, over the phone, day after day" (James Friedman, quoted by Moore and Fraser 1977: 91). Here, if anywhere, we should get an excellent, if extreme, illustration of the role of local forces and local context in primary voting.

An illuminating look at the dynamics of primary voting in New Hampshire was provided by David Moore (1985: 5) as part of his effort to challenge the "tenet of faith among most reporters and political analysts these days that New Hampshire is a state where 'retail politics,' not 'wholesale politics,' is required for victory." Moore reported the results of an ABC News/*Washington Post* track-

[9] Under the current law, maximum spending levels in each state are tied to population. According to Federal Election Commission records, major candidates in recent campaigns have spent, on average, about 95 percent of the relatively low maximum spending level for New Hampshire. The vagaries of cost control and accounting in a temporary and often chaotic campaign organization make it virtually impossible to spend much more without incurring considerable risk of exceeding the legal limit, as Reagan actually did in New Hampshire in 1976. Since most of New Hampshire is encompassed in the Boston media market, candidates have also managed to include some additional spending aimed at New Hampshire in their Massachusetts allotments.

[10] Popkin (forthcoming) has estimated that well over half the voters in the 1984 New Hampshire Democratic primary were contacted by at least one of the candidates' campaign organizations and that about a third of the voters actually met one or more of the candidates themselves.

ing survey conducted in the final two weeks before the 1984 New Hampshire primary.[11] Those results are reproduced in Figure 7.6.

The most obvious and important change in preferences over this two-week period was the rapid gain by Hart in the last week of the New Hampshire campaign, a gain apparently made at the expense of all the other candidates. "Such large shifts had not occurred for anyone but Jackson [after his trip to Syria] between March 1983 and early 1984," Moore wrote (1985: 5),

> despite extensive one-on-one campaigning. It is hardly plausible that local organizations or one-on-one campaigning caused these shifts within a one-week period. Clearly, the relentless media coverage of Hart's "better than expected" second place Iowa showing [on February 20th] and Glenn's "very poor" showing there were key to the shifts in voter preference. Ironically, Mondale's organization was rated by many observers as the most extensive and the best financed in the state, yet Mondale's standing among voters dropped the most dramatically.

Moore's example speaks to two important issues raised by my discussion of local context. First, it again illustrates the importance of systematic national forces—in this case, media coverage of Hart's emergence in Iowa—even in a state in which local, idiosyncratic factors are supposedly decisive. And second, it highlights an important respect in which the sound and fury of an active local campaign does produce distinctive behavior among primary voters.

To see this second point, it is useful to compare the responses to Hart's emergence among prospective voters in Moore's New Hampshire polls and among the national campaign audience surveyed by the NES survey. Moore's data suggest that Hart's support in New Hampshire shot up by about twenty-five percentage points in the week between the Iowa caucuses and the New Hampshire primary vote. The corresponding increase in the national audience was similar in quality but very different in quantity: as best we can tell from the NES data, support for Hart in the national Democratic rank and file increased by less than five percentage points in the week after Iowa.[12] Once again, it is prudent to bear in mind that

[11] The survey included a dozen separate cross-sections of registered Democrats and Independents who said they were "certain to vote" in the primary. Each cross-section included between 148 and 446 interviews conducted over a three-day period, with successive waves overlapping to produce one new reading per day.

[12] The 1984 NES data are poorly suited to provide precise estimates of public preferences at a given point. The estimate of Hart's support in the week between the

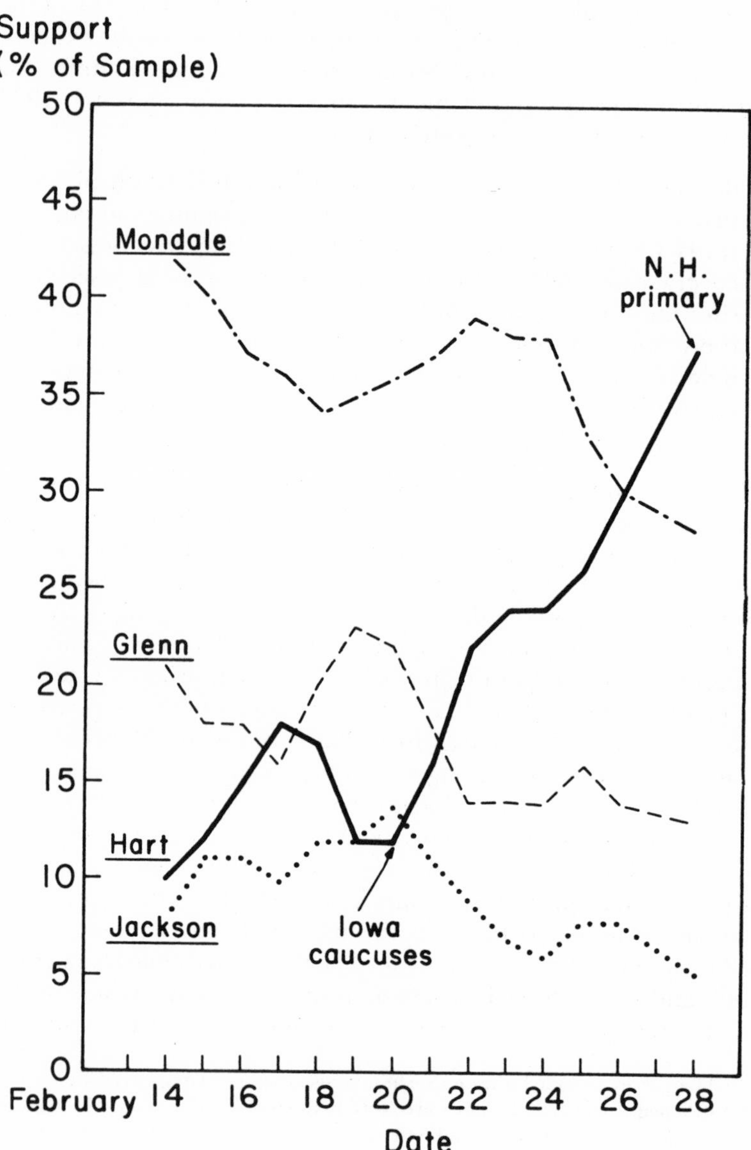

FIGURE 7.6 Trends in Candidate Support Among New Hampshire Democrats, 1984.

New Hampshire is probably the most extreme example of the phenomenon. But even under more typical circumstances, it seems likely that actual primary voters will have substantially more information about the candidates and the race, and will react more forcefully to campaign events, than even a demographically comparable national audience at the same point in the primary season.

Considering this fact, I have structured my statistical analysis of primary voting in a way that makes it possible to estimate from actual primary outcomes the extent to which primary voters exceed survey respondents in their apparent levels of information.[13] These estimates are presented in Figures 7.7 through 7.11, which show average information levels for primary voters and survey respondents (the "National Audience") for every week of every primary campaign since 1976. The information scale shown in the figures, with values ranging from zero to sixteen, is essentially arbitrary, but it is calibrated to correspond exactly to the information scale introduced for the 1984 campaign in Chapter 4. (Indeed, the estimated information levels for survey respondents in Figure 7.11 are merely simplified versions of those shown in Figure 4.9.)[14] As a result, we can compare information levels, both across

---

Iowa caucuses and the New Hampshire primary is based on only fifty-one Democratic survey respondents. But, even if the actual change in Hart's public support was considerably greater than it appeared to be from these fifty-one respondents, we would be left with a significant difference between reactions in the national audience and reactions in New Hampshire.

[13] In order to keep the analysis tractable I assume here that the difference in information levels between survey respondents and primary voters is constant across candidates and over time for each campaign. This assumption probably underestimates the amount of information primary voters have in Iowa and New Hampshire, in part because campaigning begins so much earlier in those states than in the rest of the nation and in part because the candidates focus so much of their personal and organizational effort in those states. In 1988 these two special cases may be even more distinctive. The *National Journal* (18 April 1987, page 954) reported that the Roosevelt Center for American Policy Studies intends to spend $600,000 on educational seminars to bring prospective voters in Iowa and New Hampshire "up to speed" on important issues of public policy.

[14] Both Figure 4.9 and the "National Audience" portion of Figure 7.11 show information levels for the 1984 campaign estimated on the basis of the statistical results in Table A.14 in Appendix C. The difference is that Figure 4.9 shows actual average information levels for the specific respondents interviewed in each week of the 1984 NES survey, while Figure 7.11 shows the corresponding information levels for a single idealized respondent with average personal characteristics (education and media use). The former approach seems more appropriate for descriptive purposes, the latter for comparative purposes (since we lack week-by-week data on personal characteristics for the other campaigns analyzed in this book).

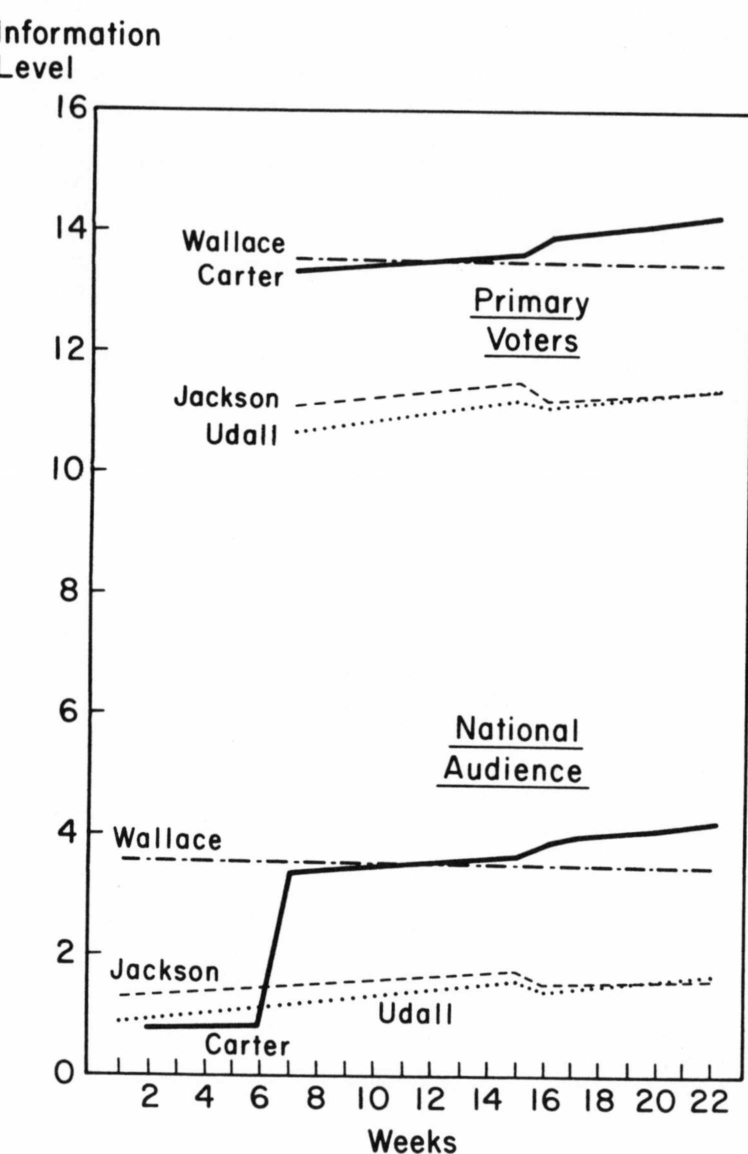

FIGURE 7.7 Average Information Levels for Democratic Primary Voters and National Audience, 1976.

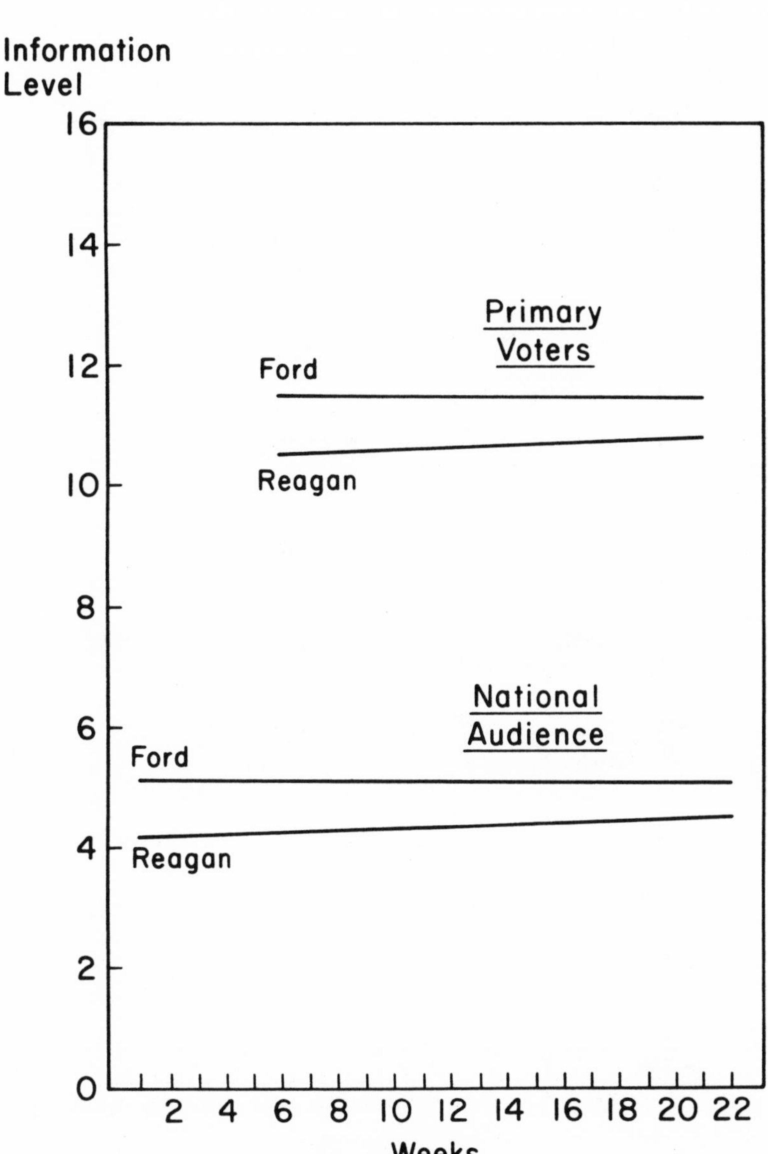

FIGURE 7.8 Average Information Levels for Republican Primary Voters and National Audience, 1976.

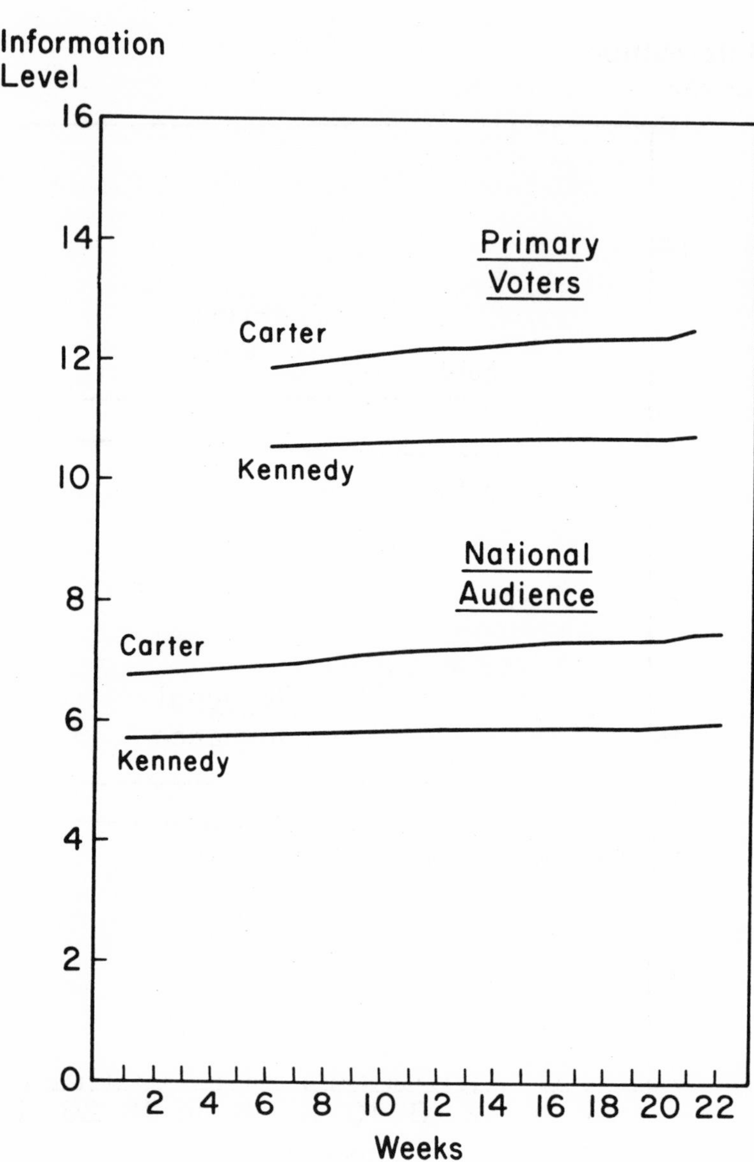

FIGURE 7.9 Average Information Levels for Democratic Primary Voters and National Audience, 1980.

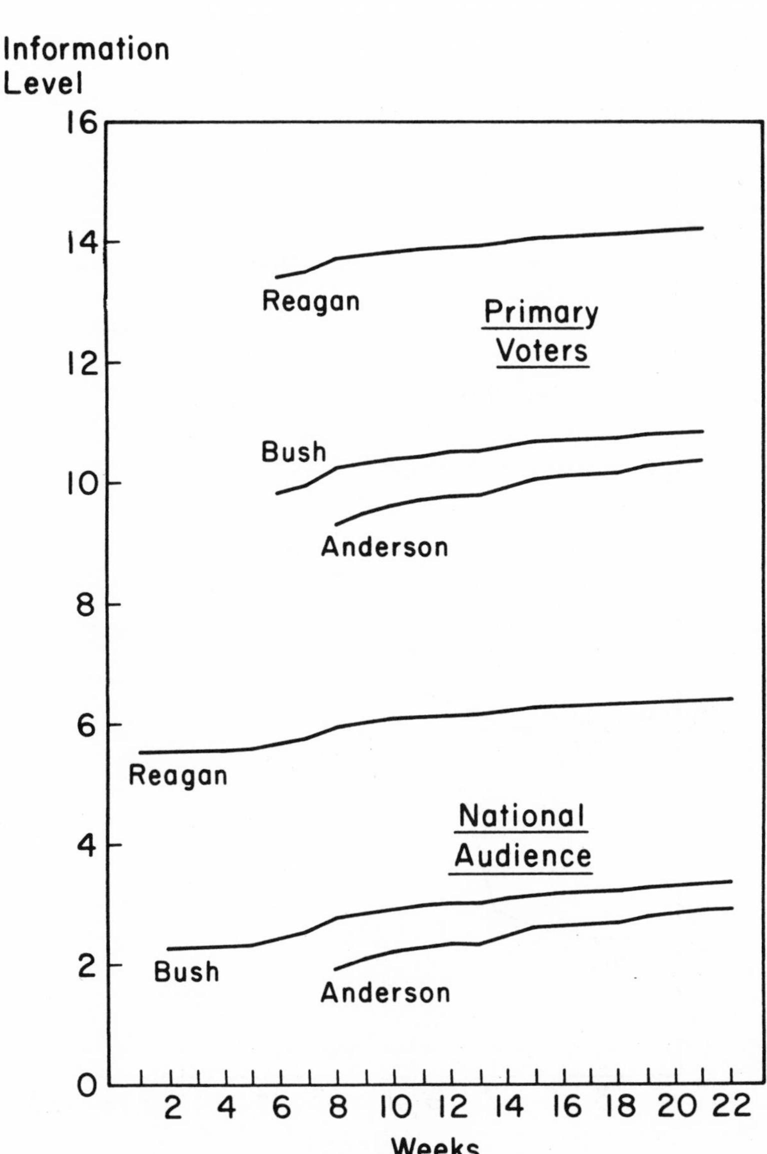

FIGURE 7.10 Average Information Levels for Republican Primary Voters and National Audience, 1980.

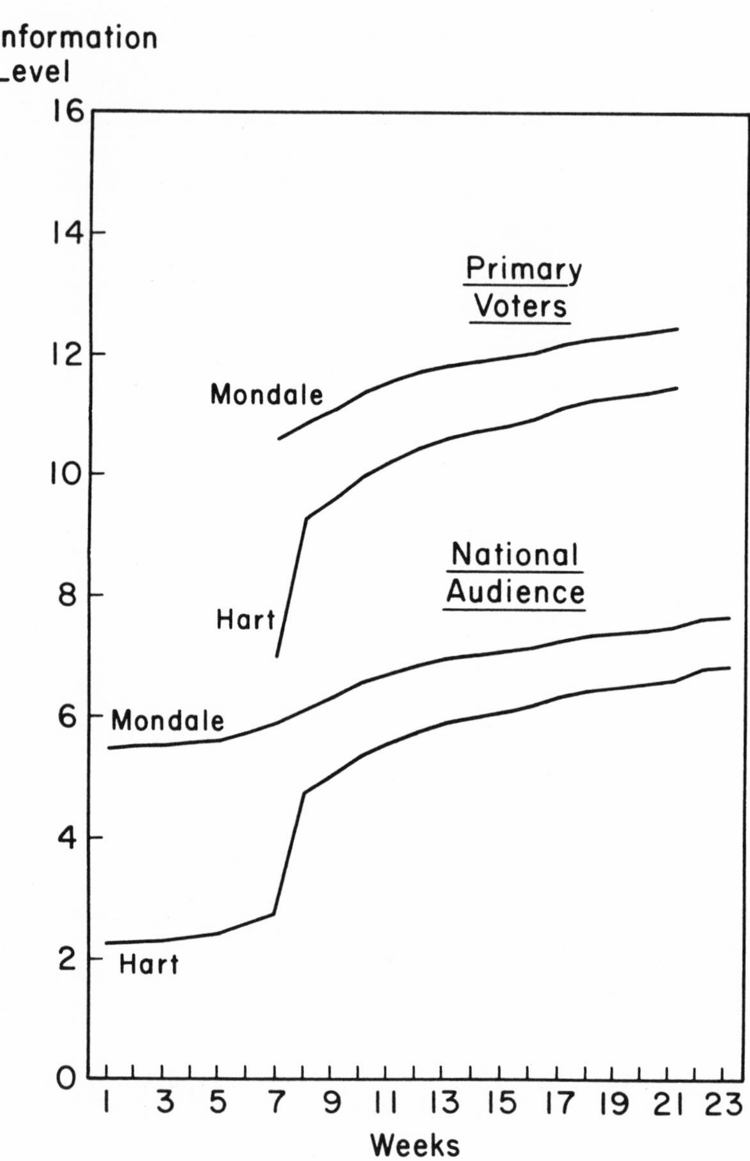

FIGURE 7.11 Average Information Levels for Democratic Primary Voters and National Audience, 1984.

campaigns[15] and between primary voters and the national audience within each campaign.[16] There are some variations among campaigns, but in every case it is clear that primary voters had significantly more information about the candidates than did the national audience at the same time.

This difference between primary voters and the national audience may have significant political consequences if different levels of information lead to different patterns of electoral choice. We saw in Chapter 6 that the weight survey respondents in the 1984 Democratic campaign assigned to expectations and political predispositions seemed to vary with the amount of information they had about the candidates. If the same pattern held for primary voters, their greater overall level of information would make them weigh predispositions more heavily, and expectations less heavily, than survey respondents at the same point in the primary season. As a result, we would reach very different conclusions about the relative impact of political substance and "momentum" among primary voters than we would have reached simply by extrapolating directly from the survey data.

Unfortunately, none of our available data allows for very extensive direct comparisons between primary voters and nonvoters, especially for a variety of different campaigns. However, we *do* have some leverage for assessing the significance of differences in information levels *among primary voters.* In particular, the simulated information levels for each campaign shown in Figures 7.7 through 7.11 can be used to determine whether changes in information levels over time within each campaign did produce variations in the impact of expectations on actual primary voting behavior consis-

[15] The estimated information levels for each campaign are based on both the threshold model of familiarity described in Appendix B.1 and the observed familiarity of survey respondents with each candidate at various stages of the campaign—every week in the case of 1984, and the beginning, middle, and end of the primary season in the cases of 1980 and 1976. The calculations are described in more detail in Appendix C.2, and the statistical results on which they are based are presented in Tables A.10 through A.14.

[16] The estimated information levels for primary voters are based on the levels for survey respondents, multiplied by 1.15 for Democrats and 1.1 for Republicans to reflect compositional differences between the survey samples and the pool of primary voters, and augmented by the constant level of "Local information" estimated separately for each campaign as part of the state-level analyses of primary outcomes described in Chapters 8 through 10. The parameter estimates for "Local information" appear in Tables A.17 through A.22 and A.29 through A.32. All five estimates are quite precise; the lowest of the t-statistics is 6.5.

tent with the pattern identified among survey respondents in the 1984 NES data.

The individual-level analysis in Chapter 6 suggests that, as levels of information increase from week to week, the role of expectations should decrease. This is exactly what appears to have happened in each of the four recent primary campaigns for which we can determine the effect of information on the role of expectations.[17] The pattern is illustrated in Figure 7.12, which shows the declining effect of expectations across the relevant range of information levels for each of these campaigns since 1976.[18] The rate with which the effect of expectations decreased varies considerably across campaigns, but the general pattern is discernible in every campaign.

These results suggest that the apparent role of information in altering the nature of primary choices is peculiar to neither survey data nor the 1984 Democratic campaign. A similar pattern emerges from direct analyses of primary voting in a variety of campaign settings. The generality of this pattern lends some credence to the notion that differences in information levels between primary voters and the national audience of the sort illustrated in Figures 7.7 through 7.11 may have similar significance: the additional information generated by active local campaigns in the primary states may alter the nature of electoral choice for primary voters

[17] The 1976 Democratic campaign is complicated by the fact that several active contenders competed throughout the primary season, with significant variations in their levels of campaign effort from state to state. These complications are discussed in greater detail in Section 8.2.

[18] The estimated effects of expectations in Figure 7.12 are based on the coefficients for "Relative momentum" and "Local information" in Tables A.29 through A.32 in Appendix C. For each campaign, the figure illustrates the estimated effect of a ten-percentage-point increase in a candidate's perceived chances of winning the nomination on his vote share in an otherwise even race. In the 1984 Democratic campaign, for example, an increase of ten percentage points in Hart's perceived chances at the beginning of the campaign, when information was at its lowest level, would have increased his share of the primary vote in an evenly contested state from 50 percent to 61.2 percent—an effect of 11.2 percentage points; at the opposite extreme, an increase of ten percentage points in Mondale's perceived chances at the end of the campaign, when information was at its highest level of the 1984 campaign season, would have *decreased* Mondale's share of the primary vote from 50 percent to 46.9 percent, for an effect of −3.1 percentage points. Neither estimate reflects the additional potential effect of a corresponding (opposite) change in the other candidate's perceived chances; for example, the 11.2 percentage point effect for Hart at the beginning of the campaign is predicated only on a ten-percentage-point increase in his perceived chances and not on a simultaneous decrease in Mondale's chances.

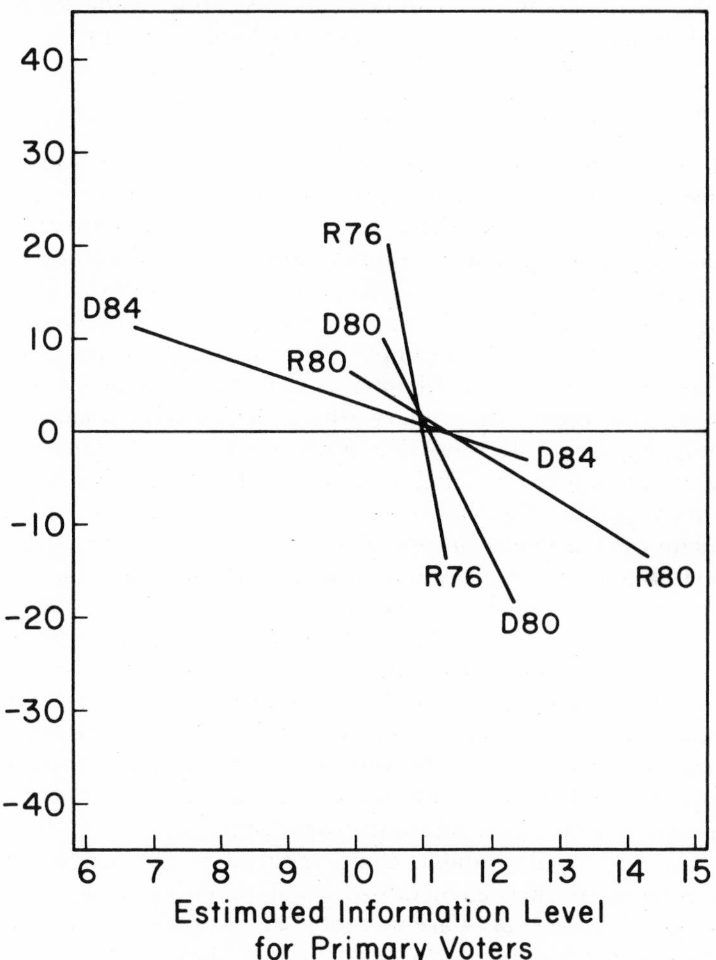

FIGURE 7.12 Information and the Effect of Expectations in Primary Campaigns, 1976–1984.

in important ways. In particular, direct extrapolation from the survey data in Part II would tend, in view of these differences in information levels, to *overestimate* the actual importance of expectations in primary elections, and to *underestimate* the importance of substantive political factors. Direct extrapolation would fail not because the model of choice introduced in Part II is incorrect, but precisely because it appears to apply to primary voters as well as to the national audience. It will be necessary to bear these differences in mind as we transfer our focus of attention from the behavior of party identifiers in the "national audience" to the behavior of actual primary voters exposed to an active local campaign.

7.3 A Typology of Primary Campaigns

Having addressed potential differences in the nature and structure of choice from one primary state to another in Section 7.2, I turn in this section to differences in the nature and structure of choice from one primary season to another. Political scientists have expressed considerable pessimism about the possibility of explaining patterns across nominating campaigns in anything more than a superficial sense. An example of this pessimism is provided by Ceaser's claim (cited in Chapter 1) that the development of any "systematic theory of primary voting" is unlikely "because each campaign is so different." He added (1982: 65): "Primary campaigns are a sea of contingencies, and perhaps the only law of primary voting behavior having any general significance is that a candidate's performance in any given primary is influenced by his performance in the preceding primaries. Doing well tends to help one do better, while doing poorly tends to make one do worse." As it turns out, even this "law" of primary voting behavior fares poorly as a general explanation of primary outcomes. In fact, a candidate's past primary performance matters enormously under some circumstances and almost not at all under others. I aim to explain that fact, using the very differences in political contexts regretted by Ceaser to make some sense out of the "sea of contingencies" washing over recent primary campaigns.

The analysis of candidate choice outlined in Part II of this book is general. Its key elements—political predispositions, expectations, and uncertainty—are present in every primary campaign for all sorts of candidates and voters. But if the basic elements are the same for different primary campaigns, the implications of the analysis are not. Rather, the results in Part II lead us to expect that voters in different kinds of campaigns will behave in significantly different ways.

In this section I focus on one important difference among recent primary campaigns: the environment of information and uncertainty arising from different patterns of political competition in each campaign. Since prevailing levels of information and uncertainty help determine the relative importance of political predispositions and momentum in primary voting, we should find that campaigns involving well-known candidates look significantly different from those involving relatively unknown candidates, and in systematic predictable ways. For this reason, I distinguish three important types of campaigns, each involving a different number of serious, well-known contenders. Primary campaigns since 1972 provide examples of all three types.

Two Major Candidates

Perhaps the simplest possible pattern of political competition is one in which two candidates, both familiar political figures, compete for their party's nomination. In two recent nominating campaigns where this pattern prevailed, one contender was an incumbent president—Gerald Ford in 1976 and Jimmy Carter in 1980. In each case the incumbent faced a serious challenge from an opponent of considerable political standing. In Ford's case the challenger was Ronald Reagan, the leading figure in the conservative wing of the Republican party for more than a decade. In Carter's case it was Edward Kennedy, his party's leading liberal and heir to one of America's most famous political names. As is clear from Figures 7.8 and 7.9, respectively, both challengers were almost as well known as the incumbent presidents they attempted to unseat. And both campaigns were essentially head-to-head contests; no other candidate was a significant factor in either case.[19]

One Major Candidate

There have been two recent campaigns in which a single well-known front-runner was challenged by a large field of less well-known candidates. In the Republican campaign of 1980 the front-runner was Ronald Reagan, and the challengers included John Anderson, Howard Baker, George Bush, John Connally, Phil

[19] In 1980 Jerry Brown also challenged Carter from a base of considerable public familiarity, but Brown's campaign was never taken seriously by politicians or by the press, and only once did he attract as much as 10 percent of any state's primary vote.

Crane, and Robert Dole. In the Democratic campaign of 1984 the front-runner was Walter Mondale, and the challengers included Reubin Askew, Alan Cranston, John Glenn, Gary Hart, Ernest Hollings, Jesse Jackson, and George McGovern.[20] In each campaign, most challengers quickly fell by the wayside while one emerged as the single serious challenger to the front-runner. For the Republicans in 1980 the survivor was George Bush; for the Democrats in 1984 it was Gary Hart. Thus, both campaigns eventually became, essentially, two-candidate races, and each surviving challenger became quite well known by the end of the primary season.[21] But the fact that each began the primary season relatively unknown to the public had significant implications for the nature and success of their respective campaigns.

No Major Candidates

One recent campaign fits neither of these two patterns; there was neither a clear front-runner nor indeed a really well-known contender. In 1976 the Democratic party's most well-known figures—Hubert Humphrey, Edward Kennedy, Edmund Muskie, and George McGovern—were all staying on the sidelines. The active candidates included George Wallace (familiar to 73.8 percent of the Democratic public) and Sargent Shriver (44.3 percent), fairly well known but crippled by political liabilities; neither was given any real chance to win.[22] Beyond these two, the field consisted of a

[20] In each of these campaigns there are some exceptions to the typology which turn out to be more apparent than real. McGovern's previous presidential bid had made him well known, but as an "extremist" and a "loser"; as a result, the press and most politicians never took his 1984 campaign seriously. Jackson's campaign was treated as an important political milestone, but he, too, was given no real chance of winning the nomination. Connally in 1979 and Glenn in 1983 looked like potentially formidable challengers, but both had organizational and strategic problems with their campaigns and (to borrow an overworked description of the Glenn effort) never really got off the launching pad; both dropped out of the race during the first month of the primary season.

[21] Hart's increasing familiarity in 1984 is evident in Figure 7.11; Bush's in 1980 is somewhat less evident in Figure 7.10 because the 1980 NES surveys provide no reading of Bush's level of public recognition before his upset victory in the Iowa caucuses thrust him into the media spotlight.

[22] According to Udall pollster Peter Hart (quoted in Moore and Fraser 1977: 87), "When we looked at the unacceptable quotient [the ratio of favorable to unfavorable impressions for various candidates at the beginning of the 1976 campaign], we found both Shriver and Wallace to be through because both of them had a high percentage of unacceptability." Wallace, though known to more Democrats in February 1976 than Henry Jackson, Morris Udall, and Jimmy Carter put together, was

whole flock of candidates—Birch Bayh, Lloyd Bentson, Jimmy Carter, Frank Church, Fred Harris, Henry Jackson, Milton Shapp, Morris Udall, and others—of whom the best known at the beginning of the campaign was Jackson (familiar to 29.1 percent of the Democratic public).

The analysis in Part II suggests that each of these different types of nominating campaign should produce a distinctive pattern of political behavior on the part of primary voters. For campaigns involving two major candidates, we should expect political predispositions to have an especially powerful impact on primary voting, with momentum based on changing expectations having a decidedly less important role. For campaigns involving no major candidates, we should expect exactly the opposite pattern: political predispositions should be relatively unimportant, and expectations should tend to dominate prospective voters' choices. Finally, in campaigns involving one major candidate, we should expect that major candidate to be considered primarily in terms of substantive political qualities, whereas his relatively unknown challengers should be evaluated primarily on the basis of expectations about their chances; the result would be an intermediate pattern of political behavior, with momentum mattering more than when both candidates are well known but less than when no candidate is well known.

The actual effect of momentum in each recent nominating campaign is estimated and analyzed in detail in subsequent chapters. But it may be useful here to summarize one aspect of those results since it bears directly on the utility of the typology suggested in this section for making some sense of the notable variations in the role of momentum from one campaign to another. Figure 7.13 shows the average effect of momentum on primary voting in each

---

a one-time segregationist of no little notoriety whose identity as a "fringe" candidate was well established in the public consciousness. As if that were not enough, he was also confined to a wheelchair after having been wounded in an assassination attempt during the 1972 campaign. Shriver was known primarily as Edward Kennedy's brother-in-law and as George McGovern's running mate in the drubbing of 1972 (filling in after Thomas Eagleton had been dumped from the ticket). His presidential campaign was "openly ridiculed by most politicians and members of the press" (Witcover 1977: 161). The fact that neither Wallace nor Shriver was a "serious" candidate was not lost on the public; Patterson (1980: 120) found that their perceived chances of being nominated fell well below those of every other candidate in his survey.

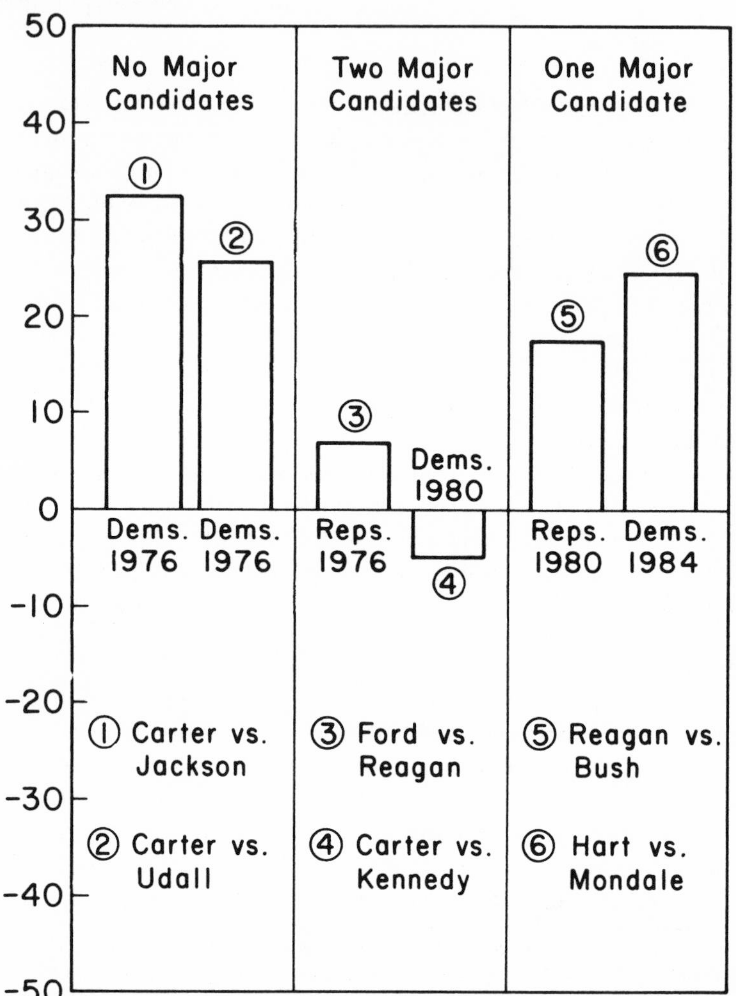

FIGURE 7.13 Political Competition and the Role of Momentum in Primary Campaigns, 1976–1984.

recent campaign, expressed as a percentage of the total two-candidate primary vote.[23]

It is obvious from the figure that momentum mattered much more in some campaigns than in others. For example, Carter gained an average of more than thirty percentage points in each primary state against Henry Jackson in 1976, but actually *lost* an average of five percentage points in each primary state against Edward Kennedy in 1980. The other cases in the figure fall between these two extremes. But important here are the variations in the effect of momentum from one campaign to another, corresponding exactly to the pattern suggested by the typology outlined in this section. Momentum mattered most in the two instances where there was no major candidate (Carter's contests with Jackson and Udall in 1976), somewhat less in the two instances where there was one major candidate (Ronald Reagan for the Republicans in 1980 and Walter Mondale for the Democrats in 1984), and still less in the two instances where there were two major candidates (the contests between Ford and Reagan on the Republican side in 1976 and between Carter and Kennedy on the Democratic side in 1980). This pattern of results suggests that the simple typology outlined in this section may help to account for the very different complexions of recent nominating campaigns.

[23] In each campaign, the effect of momentum is calculated by comparing the actual primary results in each state with projected results from a hypothetical one-day national primary held under the conditions prevailing at the beginning of the primary season. In a one-day national primary, there would be no opportunity for previous weeks' results to affect the behavior of primary voters; thus, momentum of the sort generated in the current sequential primary process would be absent. This is the sense in which the differences between actual results and projected results from the hypothetical one-day primary provide a meaningful estimate of the effect of momentum in each campaign. To preserve comparability across campaigns, each of the estimated effects in Figure 7.13 is based on the first-named candidate's vote share *among voters who chose one or the other of the two candidates indicated in the comparison.* For example, Carter received an average of 90 percent of the votes actually cast for Carter or Jackson in 1976; the statistical analysis in Chapter 8 suggests that he would only have received about 58 percent of the votes cast for either of the two candidates in a one-day national primary; the difference between these two vote shares is thirty-two percentage points, the effect of momentum shown for Carter versus Jackson in Figure 7.13.

CHAPTER EIGHT

Momentum Triumphant: The Case of Jimmy Carter

The sequence or chronological order of primaries are important for obvious reasons. Good or poor showings can have a profound and irrevocable impact on succeeding primaries and a candidate's abilities to raise funds and recruit workers. The press shows an exaggerated interest in the early primaries. . . . [and] we would do well to understand the very special and powerful role the press plays in interpreting the primary results for the rest of the nation. What is actually accomplished in the New Hampshire primary is less important than how the press interprets it for the nation.

The initial delegate-selections [in nonprimary states] will generate some news stories and will be important, but in the long run they will take a back seat to the coverage of the primaries. . . . The prospect of a crowded field, coupled with the new proportional representation rule, does not permit much flexibility in the early primaries. The crowded field enhances the possibility of several inconclusive primaries, with four or five candidates separated by only a few percentage points. Such a muddled picture will not continue long, as the press will begin to make "winners" of some and "losers" of others. The intense press coverage which naturally focuses on the early primaries plus the decent time intervals which separate the March and mid-April primaries dictates a serious effort in all the first five primaries.

Our public strategy would probably be that Florida was the first and real test of the Carter campaign and that New Hampshire would just be a warmup. In fact, a strong surprise in New Hampshire should be our goal, which would have a tremendous impact on successive primaries. Our minimal goals in these early primaries would be to gain acceptance as a serious and viable candidate, demonstrate that Wallace is vulnerable and that Carter can appeal to the Wallace constituency, and show through our candidate and campaign a contrasting style and ap-

> peal. Our maximum goals, which I think are highly attainable, would be [to] win New Hampshire and/or Florida outright, make strong showings in the other early primary states, and beat Wallace.
>
> Late April and early May primaries will dictate difficult and strategic decisions on the allocation of resources. Lack of funds and time will restrict us from running a personal campaign in every state. Hopefully, good press in the early primaries will have solved some of our name-recognition problem and given Jimmy Carter some depth to his new national image. . . . There will be ten primaries in two weeks. If by this point we have knocked Wallace off and led the field in a primary or two, we will be in a strong position to raise funds and enter them all.

These comments, culled from a memorandum written by Hamilton Jordan in 1974 (and quoted by Witcover 1977: 143–46), outline the strategic foundation for the next two years of Jimmy Carter's long quest for the presidency. To a remarkable degree, they also summarize the actual course of the 1976 campaign. Carter won the 1976 Democratic nomination by exploiting exactly those features of the nominating process Jordan emphasized: the impact of early primary successes on the availability of resources and on subsequent primary outcomes; the importance of the press in focusing attention on winners in a crowded field of candidates; and the consequent need to establish viability early, in Carter's case by beating George Wallace and, if possible, by winning outright in one or two of the early primaries. Jordan's only major failing as a political fortune-teller was his inability to foresee the magnitude of the impact these factors would have on his candidate's actual success. Carter easily outperformed the "maximum goals" established in the campaign plan, and he won the nomination more easily than even Jordan was willing to believe possible two years earlier.

8.1 How Carter Won

Carter's domination of the 1976 Democratic primary season was surprising by any standard. But it was particularly surprising given the general expectation in 1975 that no Democratic candidate would be able to achieve a majority before the convention. The pervasiveness of the so-called "brokered convention" scenario was based on several solid political considerations: the large number of active candidates, the absence of a clear front-runner, the new campaign spending regulations, the high level of latent support for noncandidates Hubert Humphrey and Edward Kennedy, and the belief that Wallace would lock up a substantial number of delegates without being able to win the nomination himself. The widespread expectation of a brokered convention is illustrated by the results of Matthews's (1978: 61) content analysis of the *Washington Post* and *New York Times* during the last four months of 1975. Almost half of the direct references to candidate nomination during this period involved Humphrey being drafted. Another third involved other draft or brokered convention scenarios. Only about one in five involved any of the active candidates winning the nomination.

Carter and his advisers appear to have put some stock in the possibility of a brokered convention. Nevertheless, they recognized more clearly than any of their competitors the possibility of at least mounting a serious national campaign on the basis of momentum generated early in the primary season. Carter had originally planned to concentrate his early efforts in New Hampshire and Florida, but as it became clear that the caucuses in Iowa a month earlier might attract substantial attention from the press, the strategy was amended to take advantage of what the candidate himself (quoted by Schram 1977: 8) called "a good chance to build that up with a major media event." His personality, positions, and campaign style were well suited to the politics of the state and to the task of meeting, winning over, and organizing voters by the half-dozens in small face-to-face gatherings. Schram reported after the voting (1977: 22): "Just 50,000 Iowans had gone to the caucuses. Fewer than 14,000 of them voted for Jimmy Carter. In Oyster Bay, Long Island, that would not be enough votes to elect him to the Town Council. But in Iowa, it was more than any other candidate got. In the morning, he appeared on NBC's 'Today' show, the CBS 'Morning News,' and ABC's 'AM America.' Jimmy Carter had popped out of the pack."

Carter's victory in Iowa presented a hidden danger for his campaign because it thrust him more quickly than planned into the forefront of media scrutiny and expectations. But it also gave him a chance to cement his lead by following up on Iowa with another big victory in New Hampshire, where he had been stumping and organizing diligently for months. As Witcover (1977: 238) put it, Carter

> came into New Hampshire as the man to beat, and in spite of his early successes he remained enough of a novelty to catch the

> imagination of voters and the press alike. Again as in Iowa, he had the luxury of running against a highly competitive liberal field—Udall, Bayh, Harris, and Shriver—and the same advantages of an early start and a solid grass-roots organization. This time, it was true, expectations were high, but Carter had the wherewithal to contend with the pressure brought to bear on him.

Carter demonstrated his wherewithal by leading the field again in New Hampshire, garnering 28.4 percent of the primary vote to Udall's 22.7 percent. Given the circumstances—his early focus on New Hampshire, his momentum coming out of Iowa, the absence of Wallace and Henry Jackson—it was hardly a crushing victory. But to the press and the public it was a victory nonetheless, and Carter had become the clear front-runner.

Carter's early victories had important consequences for the scale of his subsequent campaign. National media attention undreamed of a few months earlier suddenly became routine.[1] The flow of campaign contributions increased, and Carter's success began to register in the national opinion polls. Success also began to register in subsequent primary results, shown in Table 8.1. After finishing fourth in Massachusetts, Carter won in Florida to prove that he could beat Wallace in the South. "After Florida," pollster and campaign strategist Patrick Caddell said later, "there was one serious candidacy—Carter's—and everybody else" (quoted by Moore and Fraser 1977: 97). Carter proceeded to demonstrate his vote-getting ability in a major midwestern state by winning in Illinois, held off Morris Udall in Wisconsin, and defeated Henry Jackson in their showdown in Pennsylvania. As a result, he began May campaigning with a big lead in the delegate count.

In the last month of the primary season a pair of new candidates entered the race in earnest—California governor Jerry Brown and Idaho senator Frank Church. Both Brown and Church won most of the primaries they contested, but it was a case of two little too late. Carter's strategy of entering every primary paid off in a steady accumulation of delegates from week to week, while the rest of the party, still waiting in vain for Humphrey to enter the race, divided its votes among Udall, Brown, and Church.

The effect of Carter's accumulation of delegates on his objective

[1] The dynamics of the relationship between the Carter campaign and the media in the spring of 1976 were described by Arterton (1978b: 36–48).

TABLE 8.1 Democratic Primary Results, 1976

		Popular Vote (%)			
		Carter	Udall	Wallace	Other[a]
24 Feb	New Hampshire	28.4	22.7	1.3	
2 Mar	Massachusetts	13.9	17.7	16.7	Jack 22.3
9 Mar	Florida	34.5	2.1	30.5	Jack 23.9
16 Mar	Illinois	48.1	0	27.6	
23 Mar	North Carolina	53.6	2.3	34.7	
6 Apr	Wisconsin	36.6	35.6	12.5	
27 Apr	Pennsylvania	37.0	18.7	11.3	Jack 24.6
1 May	Texas	47.6	0	17.5	Bent 22.6
4 May	Alabama	25.5	1.8	48.9	
	D.C.	39.7	26.0	0	
	Georgia	83.4	1.9	11.5	
	Indiana	68.0	0	15.2	Jack 11.7
11 May	Nebraska	37.6	2.7	3.2	Chur 38.5
18 May	Maryland	37.1	5.5	4.1	Brwn 48.4
	Michigan	43.4	43.1	6.9	
25 May	Arkansas	62.6	7.5	16.5	
	Idaho	11.9	1.3	1.5	Chur 78.7
	Kentucky	59.4	10.9	16.8	
	Nevada	23.3	3.0	3.3	Brwn 52.7
	Oregon	26.7	2.7	1.3	Chur 33.6
	Tennessee	77.6	3.7	10.9	
1 Jun	Montana	24.6	6.3	3.4	Chur 59.4
	Rhode Island	30.2	4.2	0.8	Brwn 31.5[b]
	South Dakota	41.2	33.0	2.4	
8 Jun	California	20.5	5.0	3.0	Brwn 59.0
	Ohio	52.2	21.0	5.7	

Sources: Congressional Quarterly Weekly Reports; Aldrich (1980a).

[a] Other candidates: Jack—Henry Jackson; Bent—Lloyd Bentsen; Chur—Frank Church; Brwn—Jerry Brown. (Only vote shares greater than 10 percent are shown.)

[b] Votes for delegates formally uncommitted but favorable to Brown.

probability of being nominated is shown in Figure 8.1.[2] After the first delegates were selected in Iowa in January, Carter's objective probability of being nominated—based on the delegate count—stood at about 27 percent. He increased his chances to almost 40 percent by winning in New Hampshire, but his fourth-place finish

[2] The objective probabilities shown in the figure are based on weekly delegate counts published by *Congressional Quarterly Weekly Report* and other media sources. They appeared as determinants of subjective public perceptions of the candidates' chances in Chapter 3. Details regarding the translation of delegate counts into probabilities are provided in Appendix A.3. The same procedure is used to estimate objective probabilities of nomination for major candidates in other recent campaigns in Chapters 9 and 10.

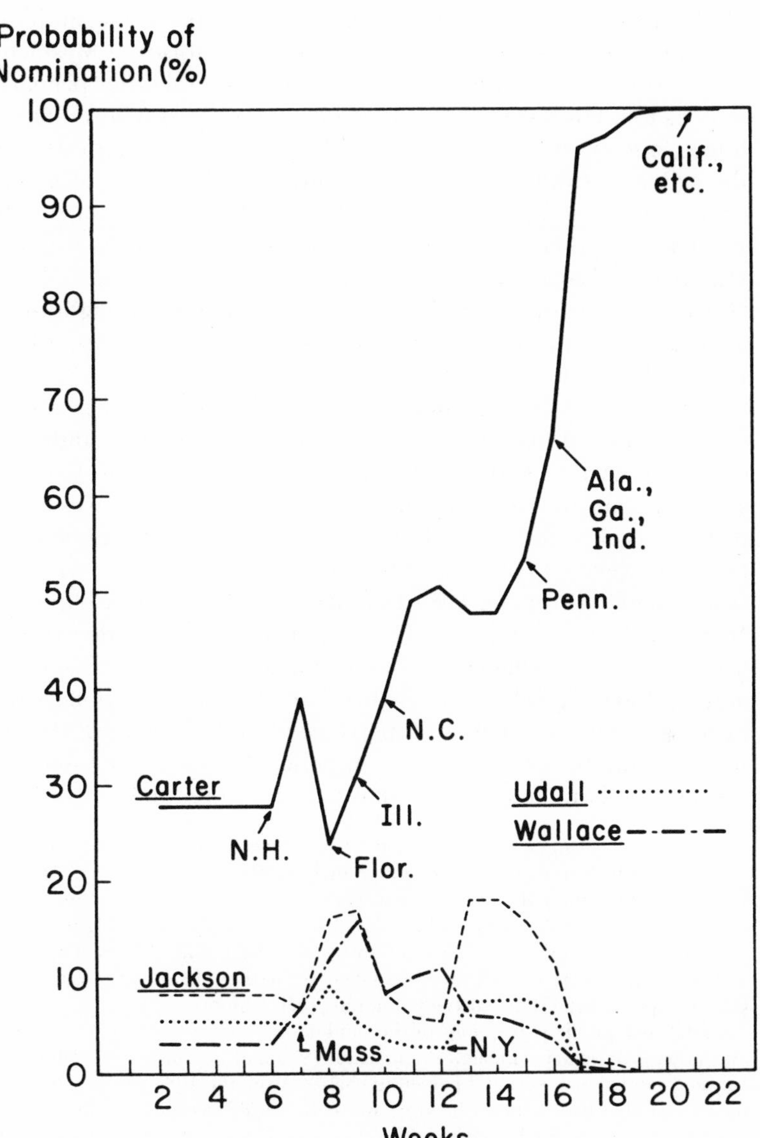

FIGURE 8.1 "Objective" Probabilities of Nomination, Democrats, 1976.

in Massachusetts put a considerable dent in his lead. Fortunately for Carter, the slump was short-lived, as his remarkable string of primary victories in Florida, Illinois, Pennsylvania, and elsewhere generated a steady increase in his chances, mostly at the expense of his three most formidable opponents—Jackson, Udall, and Wallace. Jackson's chances were boosted by his victories in Massachusetts and New York, but his failure to enter several other primaries took its toll. His loss to Carter in Pennsylvania essentially ended his hopes, and by the second week in May (the seventeenth week of the primary season) Carter was the only candidate with any serious chance of winning the nomination. At that point, Udall pollster Peter Hart said later, "it appeared to all the pros that the ballgame was over"; Carter press secretary Jody Powell reported that "Carter was the one candidate running that people thought might actually end up in the White House" (both quoted by Moore and Fraser 1977: 100, 104).[3]

The same set of campaign events is reflected somewhat differently in the estimated subjective perceptions of the candidates' chances shown in Figure 8.2. These subjective chances—based on an empirically derived combination of the objective chances in Figure 8.1, the candidates' cumulative primary vote shares, and the previous week's primary results—parallel the horse race perceptions examined for the 1984 Democratic campaign in Chapter 3.[4] In general, these subjective perceptions tended to underestimate Carter's objective chances and overestimate his opponents'. For example, Carter's subjective chances of winning the nomination never reached as much as 60 percent, even at the end of the primary season, because his various opponents continued to deny him a substantial fraction of the total primary vote. Nevertheless, by

[3] The late challenges by Church and Brown never had any serious chance of derailing Carter's nomination. The one remaining chance for the ABC ("Anybody But Carter") coalition after the Pennsylvania primary was to unite behind a single candidate. The calculations on which the objective probabilities in Figure 8.1 are based do not reflect this possibility, mostly because there is no clear evidence from which to estimate how seriously it was taken at the time. In the event, of course, Carter's opponents did not succeed in uniting their support.

[4] Subjective public perceptions of the candidates' chances in 1976 are estimated on the basis of actual campaign events from 1976 and the observed relationships between campaign events and perceived chances from the 1984 survey data. As in the case of objective chances, the same approach is used to estimate subjective perceptions of the candidates' chances in other recent campaigns in Chapters 9 and 10. A more detailed description of the procedure is provided in Appendix C.1, and the relevant statistical results appear in Table A.9.

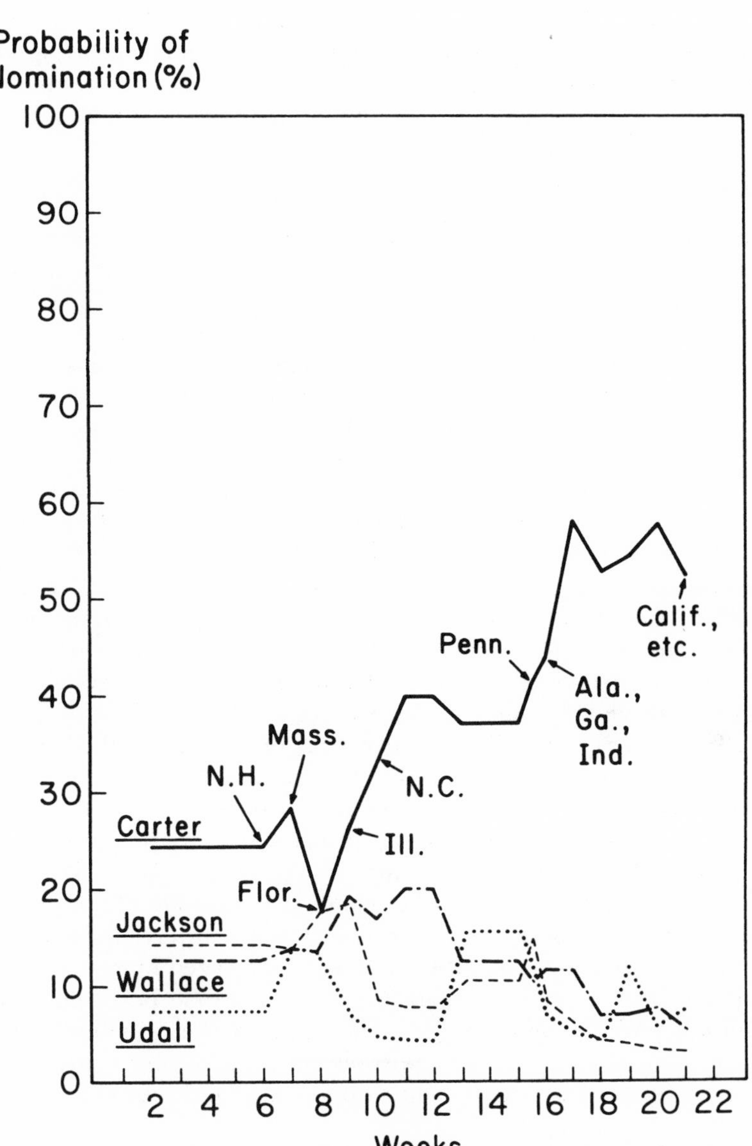

FIGURE 8.2 Estimated Subjective Probabilities of Nomination, Democrats, 1976.

the last month of the primary season Carter had amassed a huge lead even in subjective horse race perceptions. Subjective estimates of his relative odds of winning were in the neighborhood of five-to-one or better against each major opponent even before the final week's primaries. When Carter won in Ohio on the last day of the primary season and began to accept the concessions of his opponents, his nomination had been virtually assured for more than a month—and the convention was still more than a month away.

8.2 Political Substance and Strategy

Why did Carter win? My answer to that question is based on the same set of explanatory factors employed throughout this book: politics, information, and expectations. In this section I show how Carter's performance relative to each of his major opponents varied from primary to primary with variations in the political characteristics of each state's primary electorate. In the final section of this chapter I show how the dynamics of learning, uncertainty, and momentum generated by the sequential structure of the primary process impinged on the static political aspects of each state's primary contest—and how things might have turned out differently had these dynamic factors played no role.[5]

One important complication for any statistical analysis of the 1976 Democratic primary campaign is the fact it involved more candidates over more of the primary season than did the other campaigns examined in this book. In 1980 and 1984, even campaigns with a large number of early contenders saw most of them winnowed out of the race in fairly short order, leaving the field in the middle and later primaries to two major contestants. In 1976, by contrast, at least four Democratic candidates remained active, and significant, for most of the primary season: Jimmy Carter, Henry Jackson, Morris Udall, and George Wallace. In addition, as we have already seen, two other candidates who stayed out of the early primaries mounted serious late challenges: Jerry Brown and Frank Church. Brown and Church each competed in too few primaries to allow a separate statistical analysis of their performances, but it is possible for some purposes to analyze their combined primary vote shares. It is also possible to examine how Carter did against each of his other major opponents—Jackson, Udall, and

[5] The analysis on which these sections are based is described in Appendix B.4 and in Appendix C.6. The relevant statistical results are presented in Tables A.19 through A.28.

Wallace—in each primary state. Thus, my analysis of the 1976 Democratic primary campaign really consists of four separate but interrelated analyses of Carter's fortunes in head-to-head competition with Jackson, Udall, Wallace, and his two late challengers.

As we saw in both Chapters 5 and 7, a variety of social and political characteristics may predispose a given state's primary voters to support one candidate rather than another. To tap these predispositions, I have used a variety of state-level data to represent the significant social and political characteristics of each state's primary electorate.[6] It should not be surprising that the social and political determinants of Carter's success were somewhat different in each of his four head-to-head competitions with different opponents. For example, Carter did up to nineteen percentage points better against Udall in the South than in the rest of the country, other things being equal, but up to eleven percentage points worse against Wallace.[7] And he did relatively poorly against both Jackson and Udall in states with heavily unionized labor forces, but the same pattern did not hold in his contests with Wallace or with Brown and Church.

Interesting differences also appear in the impact of ideology on Carter's performance against each of his major opponents. Indeed, the success of Carter's strategy of competing in virtually every primary depended to a significant extent on just that fact—his ability to attract moderate and conservative votes in his contests with Udall, liberal votes in his contests with Wallace, and so on. To explore more systematically the role of ideology in Carter's primary successes, we need some systematic data on the ideological complexion of the various primary states. Because no such data are readily available, I have constructed my own index of the liberalism of each state's Democratic party.[8] This "liberalism index"

[6] Sources for these data are described in Appendix A.4.

[7] The effects of political factors described in this section represent a combination of the direct effects reported in Tables A.19 through A.22 plus indirect effects mediated by the various candidates' strategic decisions about where to concentrate their campaign effort. The impact of political factors on levels of campaign effort and the impact of campaign effort on primary outcomes are both addressed at the end of this section. The magnitudes of the estimated effects of political factors vary with the closeness of the race between two candidates. For example, Carter's advantage over Udall in southern states was as much as nineteen percentage points in an otherwise even race, but only half as large in a state where Carter was already leading by a four-to-one margin on other grounds.

[8] Other analysts (for example, Wright, Erikson, and McIver 1985) have constructed measures of ideology for states, but not for each party separately within a

is based on a weighted average of past convention voting patterns, general election results, and congressional delegation ideological ratings; thus, it captures something of the ideological positions of both party elites and rank-and-file party voters in each state.[9] The resulting liberalism scores for each state's Democratic party are shown in Table 8.2. They appear to reflect fairly accurately the ideological reputations of the various states, from the District of Columbia and Massachusetts at the most liberal end of the spec-

TABLE 8.2 Democratic Party Liberalism Scores

State	Score	State	Score
D.C.	90.0	Montana	55.1
Massachusetts	85.1	Pennsylvania	54.3
California	75.7	West Virginia	51.9
South Dakota	74.3	Delaware	50.3
Wisconsin	73.3	Virginia	49.7
Oregon	72.5	Arizona	49.1
Vermont	71.6	Indiana	48.6
New York	71.2	Washington	48.3
Rhode Island	71.1	Kansas	48.2
Iowa	70.9	Missouri	46.8
Colorado	67.3	Wyoming	45.9
New Hampshire	64.8	Kentucky	45.6
New Jersey	63.6	Utah	45.1
Alaska	62.4	Nevada	43.2
Connecticut	60.6	Georgia	42.7
Hawaii	59.0	Texas	42.5
Michigan	58.8	North Carolina	42.3
Maine	57.8	Tennessee	41.1
Minnesota	57.8	New Mexico	40.9
Ohio	57.3	Arkansas	38.7
North Dakota	57.1	Louisiana	38.5
Idaho	56.2	South Carolina	36.9
Illinois	55.6	Oklahoma	36.2
Nebraska	55.4	Florida	35.0
Maryland	55.2	Mississippi	34.9
		Alabama	26.0

Source: Original calculations based on past convention voting patterns, general election results, and congressional delegation ideological ratings. See Appendix A.4 for details.

Note: Figures reflect rating on 0–100 thermometer scale.

given state. Party differences can be crucial in states like California, which has a relatively liberal Democratic party but a relatively conservative Republican party.

[9] Details regarding data sources and the construction of the index are provided in Appendix A.4.

trum to Alabama and the other southern states at the most conservative end.

The effects of these ideological differences on Carter's fortunes in the 1976 Democratic primaries are shown in Figure 8.3. The figure shows how Carter's share of the primary vote against each of his three major challengers varied across the range of liberalism scores, holding constant the other political and dynamic factors included in my analysis.[10] As might be expected, the three patterns differ significantly. Carter did relatively well against the liberal Udall in the most conservative states, but his support declined precipitously across the liberal half of the Democratic ideological spectrum. By contrast, against the conservative Wallace, Carter did best in the most liberal states, although the magnitude of this effect was limited by the fact that Carter did so well against Wallace across the ideological spectrum. Finally, the head-to-head competition between Carter and Jackson was only weakly affected by ideology, with Carter doing a little better in ideologically moderate states than in either the most liberal or the most conservative states.[11] This weak and notably curvilinear pattern is consistent with the fact that Carter and Jackson were both perceived as being ideological moderates; thus, primary voters found little to choose between them on ideological grounds.

The political identities of Carter and Jackson are also reflected in the factors that *were* significantly related to their primary fortunes. For example, it should not be surprising that Jackson, a traditional Democrat with strong union ties, did better against Carter in states with heavily unionized workforces than in states where labor unions were relatively weak. My analysis indicates that, in an even head-to-head race, Jackson would have garnered an extra eighteen percentage points against Carter in the strongest union states (Michigan, Pennsylvania, and Illinois) as compared to the least-unionized state (North Carolina). Conversely, Carter did as

[10] The patterns in Figure 8.3 presumably reflect some combination of direct effects (liberal states having more liberal primary voters) and contextual effects (liberal states having more liberal political leaders, newspapers, and so on). It would be interesting from the behavioral standpoint to distinguish between these direct and contextual effects of ideology on primary voting, but it is impossible to do so using aggregate data of the sort available here.

[11] Here, too, the magnitude of the effect was limited by the fact that Carter averaged almost 80 percent of the two-candidate vote against Jackson even in the most ideologically unfavorable primary states. The potential effects of ideology in an otherwise even race between the two candidates would be somewhat more pronounced.

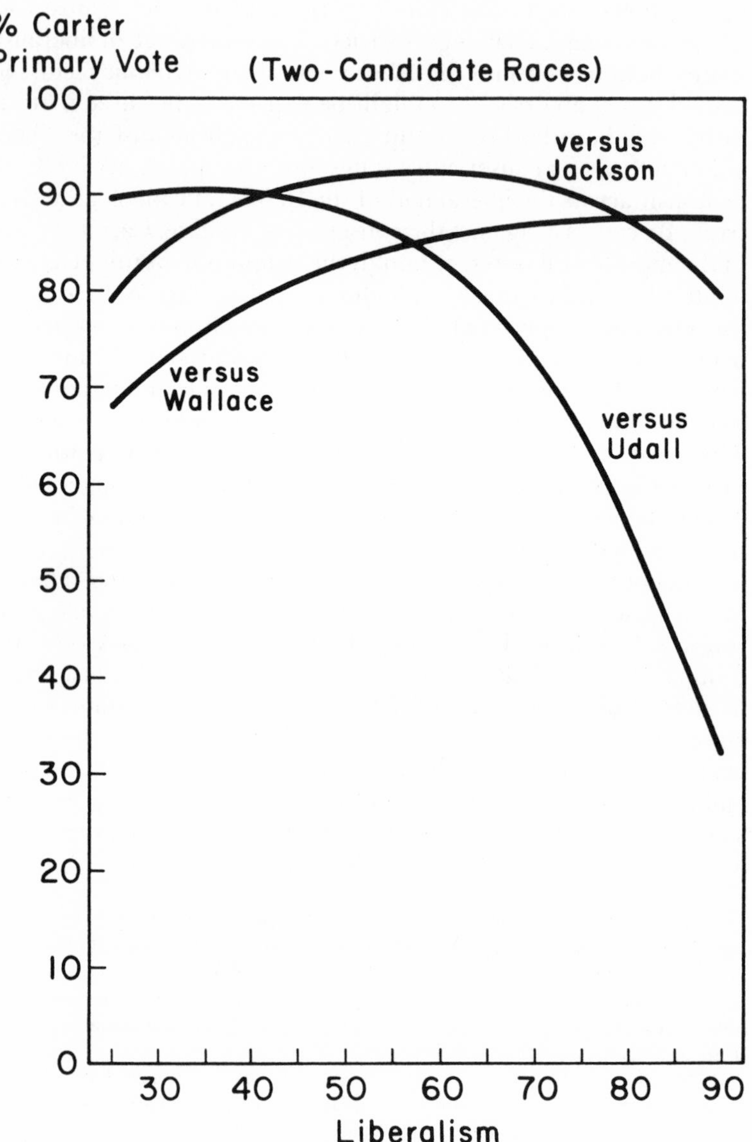

FIGURE 8.3 Ideology and Support for Carter, 1976 Democratic Primaries.

much as ten percentage points better in states like North Carolina, Indiana, and Rhode Island, whose economies are heavily oriented toward manufacturing, than in states like Nevada, Montana, South Dakota, Florida, and the District of Columbia, which have much less extensive industrial establishments.[12] And he did up to ten percentage points better in the most urban primary states than in the most rural primary states.

Somewhat similar patterns appear when we turn to Carter's performance against Udall. The magnitude of Carter's disadvantage against Udall in states with strong union movements was almost exactly the same as it was against Jackson: in an even race, Carter would have done almost eighteen percentage points better in the least unionized primary states than in the most unionized states. Carter's advantages in manufacturing states and in heavily urbanized states were even greater against Udall than against Jackson, amounting to as much as twenty-one percentage points for manufacturing and as much as thirty points for urbanization. In addition, two regional patterns are evident in the contest between Carter and Udall that do not appear in the contest between Carter and Jackson: Carter did up to nineteen percentage points better against Udall in the South than elsewhere, other things being equal, and up to thirty-three percentage points better in the West than elsewhere.[13]

One other characteristic of the various primary states had a significant effect on Carter's showing, not only against Udall and Jackson but also, and less surprisingly, against Wallace. That characteristic was the percentage of blacks in each primary state. Bicker (1978: 108) noted that, in spite of the "continuing show of Carter's strength with different voting blocks in different states," blacks were one of only two major demographic groups to provide Carter with strong and consistent support regardless of who he was running against. This pattern is evident in the fact that Carter did

[12] It may be surprising to note that unionization and industrialization worked in opposite directions in the Carter-Jackson race. Part of the explanation is evident if we consider North Carolina, with more manufacturing employees than any other state but also the weakest union movement of any state. Jackson's traditional New Deal appeal was not particularly compelling in North Carolina, or in other states where unions were weak in spite of significant industrial development.

[13] The western effect was in spite of the fact that the West was Udall's home region. And it does not merely reflect the fact that Udall's campaign was faltering by the time the western states held their primaries; the candidates' relative chances of being nominated are among the other factors held constant in assessing the magnitude of the western regional effect.

significantly better against each of his three major challengers in states with large black populations. Against Jackson and Udall this advantage sometimes amounted to as much as thirty-five percent of the two-candidate vote; against Wallace, somewhat surprisingly, the advantage appears smaller, amounting to about twenty-four percentage points in an otherwise even race.

Neither race nor most other factors mentioned thus far played a significant role in Carter's contests with Brown and Church. Instead, the most crucial factor in those contests was the late challengers' regional advantage in the mostly late western primary states. Other things being equal, Carter did as much as fifty percentage points worse in the West than elsewhere against Brown and Church, plus an additional six or seven percentage points worse in each challenger's home state. The only other important demographic factor in his success against these late challengers was urbanization: Carter did as much as thirty percentage points better in the most rural primary states than in the most urbanized states.

Given the range of political characteristics that influenced primary voting in the 1976 Democratic campaign, it would be useful to have some summary measure of the various candidates' underlying political support in each primary state. Such a measure would be based on the whole range of political predispositions brought to bear on primary voting, but it would factor out the effects of campaign events, campaign strategies, and other short-term influences. I have created just such a measure on the basis of the statistical analysis described in this chapter.[14]

The resulting estimates of Jimmy Carter's underlying political support in each primary state in 1976 are shown in Table 8.3. As expected, the ordering of states by predispositions toward Carter reflects a variety of political factors. Most, though not all, of Carter's best states were in his home region, the South. His worst states were western states in which Brown and Church had strong natural appeals and liberal eastern and midwestern states like Massa-

[14] My measure of underlying political support was constructed by subtracting from Carter's actual support against each of his major opponents the share attributable, on the basis of the statistical results reported in Tables A.19 through A.22 and A.24 through A.28, either to dynamic factors (differences among candidates in information levels or perceived chances of being nominated) or to strategic factors unrelated to the political characteristics of the various primary states. In effect, the resulting levels of underlying support for each state simulate the results of a primary in which all the candidates were equally well known, all had equal chances of being nominated, and the only differences in campaign effort among them were those attributable to differences in the various states' political characteristics.

TABLE 8.3 Underlying Carter Support in Democratic Primary States, 1976

	Carter Support (%)
Georgia	69.0
North Carolina	63.2
Illinois	56.5
Florida	55.6
Tennessee	54.4
Indiana	54.3
Texas	42.4
Oregon	40.4
D.C.	39.9
Arkansas	39.7
Rhode Island	36.2
Maryland	35.1
Nebraska	33.7
Kentucky	28.7
New Hampshire	28.0
Pennsylvania	27.8
Alabama	25.4
Ohio	24.6
Wisconsin	23.2
South Dakota	15.4
Michigan	14.2
Massachusetts	6.2
Nevada	6.2
California	6.1
Montana	5.8
Idaho	5.0

chusetts, Michigan, and Wisconsin in which Udall and Jackson were both relatively strong. However, there are some potential surprises as well. For example, contrary to the impressions of some campaign observers, Carter's critical victory in New Hampshire was won in spite of, not because of, the state's underlying political tendencies; New Hampshire was actually slightly less favorably disposed toward Carter than the average primary state.

Although my method for calculating underlying support does factor out the impact of differences in information and momentum on primary outcomes, it still reflects some accidents of campaign events. In particular, the estimated levels of underlying political support for Carter shown in Table 8.3 reflect not only his own political appeal but also that of his major opponents. Had the field of candidates been different, Carter's underlying political support in each primary state, as measured in Table 8.3, would have been different as well.

Given the number and variety of candidates against whom Carter was competing, it should not be surprising that his primary fortunes did not always reflect his own political identity in any straightforward way. As Bicker put it (1978: 108),

> Several important factors contributed to the appearance of Jimmy Carter as the choice of an ever-broadening base of support within the Democratic Party. The different demographic and ideological bases of the Democratic Party in the primary states and the selective focus of Udall (and other liberal candidates) and Jackson (and other conservative candidates) led to relative ambiguity in Carter's vote-getting ability. Having committed to enter each primary, Carter was heir to the votes not being courted by the candidates entered in the particular state (e.g., the conservative vote in New Hampshire and the liberal vote in Florida). Thus, the networks presented a continuing show of Carter's strength with different voting blocks in different states on successive Tuesday nights. The picture that emerged was of a man who could bring back the Democratic party coalition of FDR days.

In view of the complicated structure of political competition in the 1976 Democratic campaign and the changing field of contenders from state to state, it is necessary to devote some explicit attention to a subject I have mostly chosen to ignore elsewhere in this book—the strategic behavior of the competing candidates.[15] Unlike the candidates in other nominating campaigns since 1976, Carter's 1976 challengers each skipped some primary states entirely in order to concentrate resources and attention in selected contests. Not surprisingly, Carter's performance relative to each of his major opponents depended in part on these strategic decisions. At the same time, the various candidates' decisions to focus campaign effort in one primary state rather than another were influenced by some of the same political and dynamic factors that also influenced primary outcomes directly. Thus, any analysis of the effect of campaign effort on primary outcomes must also consider *why* the various candidates concentrated their effort where they did.

My analysis of campaign strategy is based on Aldrich's (1980a: 232) data on the number of "visitation days" spent in each primary

[15] Candidate strategies are examined in more detail by Brams (1978: chap. 1), Aldrich (1980a: chaps. 6 and 7), and Gurian (1986).

state by each major candidate in 1976. Visitation days ranged from zero (for Carter in four states—Georgia, Arkansas, Kentucky, and Montana—and for each of his opponents in from ten to twenty states) to a maximum of twenty-nine for Udall in Massachusetts. (Carter spent seventeen days in Florida, fifteen in New Hampshire, and fourteen in Pennsylvania, according to Aldrich's data.) Each candidate's allocation of campaign time varied across primary states in ways that make considerable sense, given the political characteristics of those states.[16] For example, Carter devoted disproportional effort to ideologically moderate states and more to his opponents' home states than to his own. Wallace concentrated his efforts disproportionately in the South (devoting about six extra campaign days to the average southern primary state) and in states with relatively small black populations. Brown and Church spent most of their time in the West and in urban states. And Udall's efforts to capture the liberal end of the Democratic ideological spectrum led him to concentrate his campaign in relatively liberal states; controlling for other factors, he spent almost fifteen more campaign days in the most liberal primary states than in the most conservative primary states.

While many of the candidates' strategic choices seem to have been based on the political characteristics of the various primary states, there is also some evidence that campaign effort varied systematically with the candidates' relative standings in the horse race. But these effects were asymmetric, working in different ways for different candidates. For example, Carter's campaign effort *decreased* substantially as his chances of winning the nomination *increased*. This result seems a bit perplexing at first glance, but it probably reflects the fact that Carter was forced by the primary calendar to spread his limited campaign time among more states as the pace of primary voting increased. By contrast, Brown and Church, both of whom entered the race late, were most active when Carter's chances of winning the nomination were greatest. And Carter's early opponents, particularly Jackson and Wallace, showed some tendency to devote less effort to states whose primaries occurred when their own chances of being nominated were relatively poor, presumably because their campaign organizations were becoming more or less moribund as their chances faded.

The impact of the candidates' campaign effort on primary out-

[16] The statistical evidence for the effects described in this paragraph and the following one are presented in Tables A.24 through A.28.

comes is illustrated in Figure 8.4, which shows how primary vote shares varied with campaign effort for two different levels of prevailing support and for two different levels of information—the estimated average levels for Carter at the beginning and end of the 1976 primary season.[17] The marginal impact of an extra day of campaigning varied somewhat with the balance of political forces in a state, as is evident from a comparison of the two sets of curves in the figure, one originating at 50 percent and the other at 10 percent. In general, campaign effort, like everything else in my analysis, tended to matter most in a close race.

Figure 8.4 also reflects my assumption that the marginal value of additional campaign effort declines as the amount of effort already expended increases.[18] The implications of this assumption for campaign strategy vary with a candidate's political circumstances. A candidate already in a strong competitive position in a state appears from the top pair of curves in the figure to receive a substantial payoff from his first few days in the state, but this payoff declines fairly rapidly with increasing effort. By contrast, a candidate who starts out far behind earns almost as much support from his second, third, or even fourth week of campaigning as from his first. This pattern of results suggests that candidates should always spend at least a few days in states they expect to be close, but that they may decide to ignore entirely states where they start off far behind.

A comparison between the "Early" and "Late" curves in Figure 8.4 also shows that, in 1976, the payoff from campaign effort varied with levels of information about the candidates. The magnitude of the differences between the two sets of effects suggests that candidates get significantly greater payoffs from campaigning (especially in close races) when they are relatively unknown, as Carter was at the beginning of the 1976 primary season, than when they are already well known to the public, as Carter was at the end of the 1976 primary season.[19] This result implies that we should ex-

[17] The estimated effects of campaign effort described in the remainder of this section are based on the coefficients for "Campaign effort" and "Effort-Information Interaction" in Tables A.19 through A.22 in Appendix C.

[18] I built the assumption that additional campaigning in a state would have decreasing marginal effects into my analysis by using the square root of campaign days as my measure of campaign effort. My choice of the square root specification accounts for much of the nonlinearity in the estimated effects shown in Figure 8.4.

[19] The difference in campaign effects due to information is surprisingly clear in the data. For example, the probability that the true difference is only half as large as the estimated difference from Appendix C (or smaller) is less than 4 percent.

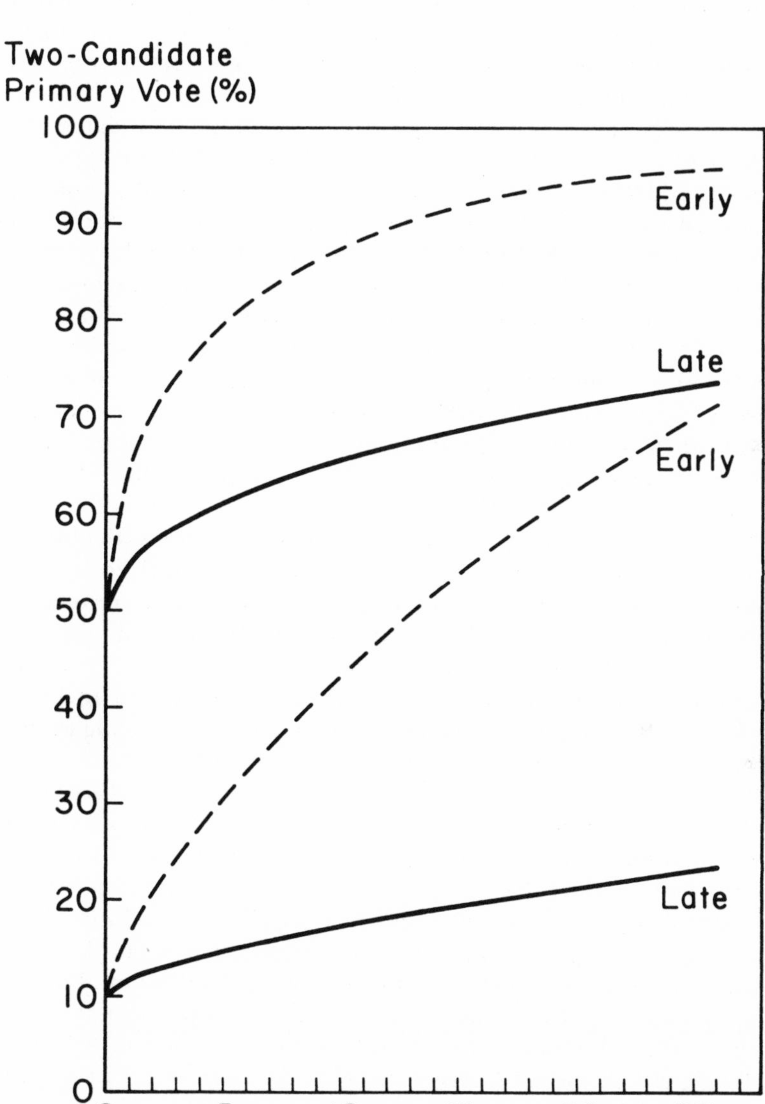

FIGURE 8.4 Campaign Effort and Primary Voting, Democrats, 1976.

pect candidates to concentrate their effort in early primary states, where they are likely to be less well known than in later states. We should also expect relatively unknown candidates to spend more time campaigning than well-known candidates since the payoffs from campaigning are greater for relatively unknown candidates. Both implications seem consistent with impressionistic observations of actual candidate behavior.

In addition to capturing some of the role of the candidates' own strategic decisions about resource allocation on their electoral fortunes, Aldrich's data on campaign effort also make it possible to account for interconnections among the various candidates' fortunes in the crowded field of contenders in the 1976 Democratic primaries. It would not be surprising, for example, to discover that Carter's fortunes in head-to-head competition with Udall depended in part on whether Jackson also mounted an active campaign in a given state. Jackson's presence might draw votes away from Udall, given their similar appeals to liberals, union members, and other elements of the traditional New Deal coalition. Therefore, Carter would do better against Udall in states where Jackson mounted an active campaign.

The data suggest some important interconnections of this sort among the candidates. For one thing, an active campaign by Jackson did appear to drain some votes away from Udall in head-to-head competition with Carter. A state-by-state analysis suggests that Jackson's campaign cost Udall about 15 percentage points against Carter in Massachusetts, 11.8 percentage points in Pennsylvania, and about 4.5 percentage points each in Michigan and Wisconsin; both of the last two states were sufficiently close for Udall to have won had Jackson not been in the race. Curiously, however, the relationship was not symmetric: active campaigning by Udall hurt rather than helped Carter in head-to-head competition with Jackson.

A similar asymmetry was present in the effect of Jackson's campaign effort on Wallace and Wallace's campaign effort on Jackson: Carter did somewhat worse against Wallace in states where Jackson campaigned most actively, but he did slightly better against Jackson in the primaries in which Wallace was most active. All these effects, except the last, were of roughly the same order of magnitude: in each instance, five days of campaigning by a third candidate could have altered the result of an otherwise even head-to-head race by a little more than seven percentage points. However, the effect of Wallace's campaign effort on the division of the primary vote between Carter and Jackson was only about a third as large as each of the other three effects.

8.3 What Might Have Been

Having described the role of political substance and strategy in the 1976 Democratic primaries, I study the impact of dynamic forces arising from the sequential nature of the primary process. I begin by examining the effect of expectations about the candidates' chances of winning the nomination on primary outcomes. After showing that expectations did affect primary voting, I estimate how the 1976 Democratic primaries might have turned out under very different circumstances: in a primary system from which the dynamic aspects of the current nominating process were entirely eliminated. The projected results of such a system—a one-day national primary—provide a dramatic illustration of the impact of momentum on the actual results of the 1976 Democratic primaries under the existing sequential primary system.

Figure 8.5 shows the estimated effect of expectations about the candidates' chances on primary voting in the 1976 Democratic campaign.[20] The three separate curves in the figure illustrate how Carter's fortunes in head-to-head competition with each of his major challengers—Jackson, Udall, and Wallace—varied with perceptions of his standing in the horse race.[21] Carter's estimated share of the primary vote was relatively high in each of these head-to-head competitions, even for perceived chances of being nominated as low as one in twenty.[22] But Carter's estimated vote share increased steadily with increasingly favorable perceptions of his

[20] The estimated effects in Figure 8.5 are based on the coefficients for "Relative momentum" and "Local information" in Tables A.19 through A.22 in Appendix C.

[21] The statistical analysis in Appendix C.6 on which these curves are based assumes that the direct effect of differences in perceived chances on primary voting is the same for each pair of candidates. Differences in the shapes of the curves arise, first, from the different indirect effects of chances on primary votes generated by differences in the candidates' resource allocation strategies noted in Section 8.2, and second, from the fact that a given increase in Carter's subjective chances of being nominated generated corresponding decreases of different magnitudes in his various opponents' subjective chances, also reflected in the figure.

[22] Each of the three curves in Figure 8.5 is constructed to reflect Carter's actual average performance against each of his major opponents for the primary season as a whole. Each curve also reflects the candidates' average information levels for the entire primary season; similar changes in expectations would have somewhat different effects earlier or later in the campaign, especially for candidates (like Carter) about whom voters learned a great deal during the primary season.

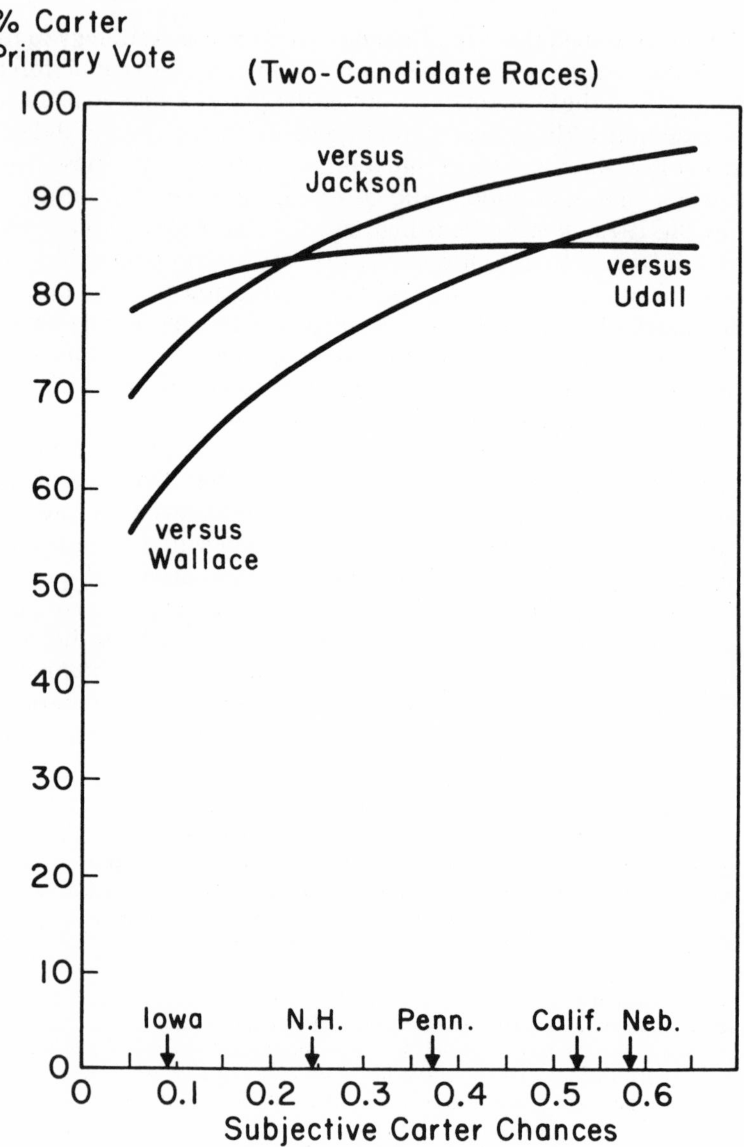

FIGURE 8.5 Expectations and Primary Voting, Democrats, 1976.

chances, particularly against Jackson and Wallace. For the actual range of expectations about Carter's chances in the 1976 campaign, his estimated share of the two-candidate vote against Jackson ranged from about 74 percent (for perceived Carter chances of about 9 percent before the Iowa caucuses) to almost 95 percent (for perceived Carter chances of about 58 percent at the time of the Nebraska primary). Against Wallace, the corresponding range is from about 60 percent at the low point of Carter's perceived chances to about 88 percent at the high point. Only Udall did about as well against Carter regardless of their perceived chances: across the range of expectations shown in the figure, Carter's share of the two-candidate vote against Udall only varied between about 80 and 85 percent.

Another way to look at the effects of expectations on primary voting—and perhaps a better way to judge the import of those effects—is to explore their implications for the actual results of the 1976 Democratic primaries. To do that, we need a baseline for comparison: a set of projected primary results, purged of the apparent effects of changing expectations from week to week, with which to compare the actual primary outcomes. A baseline of just this sort is provided by the projected results of a one-day national primary, in which every state would vote at the same time and under the same dynamic circumstances.

Jimmy Carter's projected performance in a one-day national primary for the 1976 Democratic nomination is shown in Table 8.4. The projections are based on the assumption that, in a one-day national primary, information about Carter and perceptions of his chances would both have remained constant at the levels prevailing at the time of the first primary in New Hampshire. Similarly, I assume that each of Carter's opponents would have been as well known in each primary state as they were in New Hampshire and that expectations about their chances of being nominated would also have remained constant at the New Hampshire levels.[23] Given these assumptions, it is possible to simulate the results of a one-day national primary simply by subtracting from the actual primary

[23] It is important to note that this procedure does not remove the effect of Carter's early victory in the Iowa caucuses from his projected performance in subsequent primaries. It is impossible to do so given the available data because we lack a measure of public familiarity with Carter before he emerged in Iowa; Patterson's panel survey, on which the estimated information levels in Figure 7.7 are based, did not begin until after the Iowa caucuses and the beginning of the associated Carter media blitz.

TABLE 8.4 Projected Performance in One-Day National Democratic Primary, 1976

		Carter Vote (Multi-Candidate Race %)		
		Actual Results	National Primary	Difference
24 Feb	New Hampshire	28.4	28.4	—
2 Mar	Massachusetts	13.9 (J)	5.1 (J)	8.8
9 Mar	Florida	34.5	15.5 (W)	19.0
16 Mar	Illinois	48.1	28.1 (W)	20.0
23 Mar	North Carolina	53.6	24.4 (W)	29.2
6 Apr	Wisconsin	36.6	12.3 (U)	24.3
27 Apr	Pennsylvania	37.0	12.3 (J)	24.7
1 May	Texas	47:6	17.7 (W)	29.9
4 May	Alabama	25.5 (W)	5.5 (W)	20.0
	D.C.	39.7	13.0 (U)	26.7
	Georgia	83.4	38.6	44.8
	Indiana	68.0	22.9 (W)	45.1
11 May	Nebraska	37.6 (Ch)	16.6 (Ch)	21.0
18 May	Maryland	37.1 (B)	12.8 (B)	24.3
	Michigan	43.4	9.5 (U)	33.9
25 May	Arkansas	62.6	16.4 (W)	46.2
	Idaho	11.9 (Ch)	4.3 (Ch)	7.6
	Kentucky	59.4	15.0 (W)	44.4
	Nevada	23.3 (B)	7.8 (B)	15.5
	Oregon	26.7 (Ch)	10.3 (Ch)	16.4
	Tennessee	77.6	26.8 (W)	50.8
1 Jun	Montana	24.6 (Ch)	7.6 (Ch)	17.0
	Rhode Island	30.2 (B)	11.2 (B)	19.0
	South Dakota	41.2	9.5 (U)	31.7
8 Jun	California	20.5 (B)	6.2 (B)	14.3
	Ohio	52.2	13.8 (U)	38.4
	AVERAGES	40.9	15.1	25.8

Note: Actual or projected winner, if other than Carter: (B) Jerry Brown; (Ch) Frank Church; (J) Henry Jackson; (U) Morris Udall; (W) George Wallace.

results in each state the share of Carter's support attributable to differences between the levels of information about the candidates and subjective chances actually prevailing at the time of the state's primary and the levels prevailing at the time of the New Hampshire primary.[24]

[24] In the 1976 Democratic campaign an additional complication is caused by the fact that candidates shaped their campaign strategies, sometimes voluntarily and sometimes involuntarily, in response to the primary calendar. As David and Ceaser noted in a related context (1980: 36), "had the rules been different, the strategies of the candidates would also have been different in certain respects. Behavior cannot be expected to be constant under different institutional arrangements." To ac-

The same projected differences between Carter's actual performance and his performance in a one-day national primary are presented graphically in Figure 8.6. For each week of the primary season, the figure shows Carter's apparent gain in primary vote shares as a result of the sequential, dynamic aspect of the existing nominating process. This momentum effect begins at zero for the first primary in New Hampshire because the projected results of the one-day national primary, shown in Table 8.4, are based on the assumption that political circumstances in the national primary would have been exactly like those prevailing at the time of the first primary in New Hampshire. But the estimated weekly effect of momentum increased to almost thirty percentage points in each primary state by the time of the North Carolina primary four weeks later, before leveling off to a relatively steady twenty-five percentage points or so in the remaining primaries.

The behavioral implications of these projections are obvious and striking: they suggest that millions of Democratic primary voters who supported Carter would not have done so in a one-day national primary. But in order to assess the political impact of this behavioral effect, it is necessary to determine whether Carter's projected performance in a one-day national primary would have been sufficiently strong for him to win his party's nomination even without the aid of momentum. In part, this means determining how the other candidates would have done in a national primary. It is clear from both Table 8.4 and Figure 8.6 that momentum played a critical role in Carter's 1976 campaign. But neither the table nor the figure clearly indicates how the votes Carter would have lost in a one-day primary would have been distributed among the other candidates or how they would have altered the overall political picture going into the 1976 Democratic convention.

More detailed projections, showing not only Carter's share of the one-day primary vote in each state but those of his major opponents as well, are presented in Table 8.5.[25] These projections

count for the likely impact of a one-day national primary on the candidates' strategies, I also subtracted from the actual primary results those portions apparently due to fluctuations in the various candidates' levels of campaign effort, except fluctuations arising systematically from the political characteristics of each primary state, which would presumably have persisted in a one-day national primary. Nevertheless, the projected results in Tables 8.4 and 8.5 are unrealistically contingent on the field of candidates actually competing in each primary state in the sequential primary system.

[25] For simplicity, the projections ignore the potential impact of momentum on the vote shares of minor candidates by assuming that the total vote for Carter, Jack-

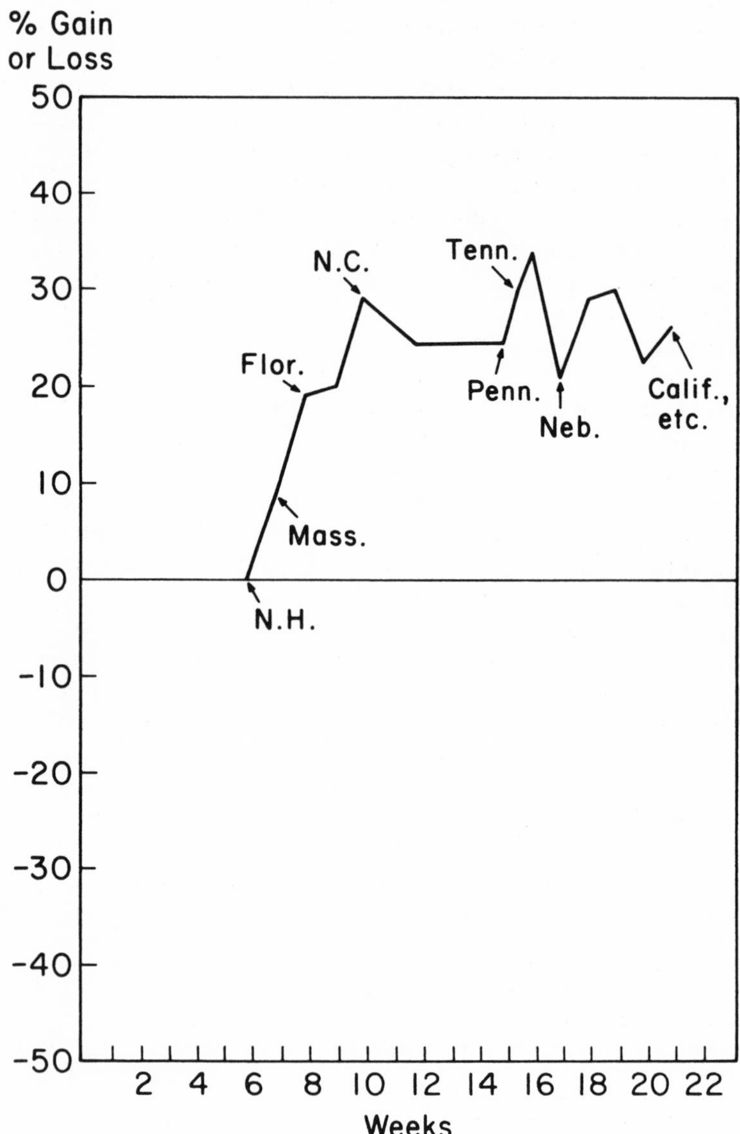

FIGURE 8.6 Effect of Momentum on Carter's Weekly Performance, 1976 Democratic Primaries.

TABLE 8.5 State-by-State Projections for One-Day National Primary, 1976

			Actual Results (%)	National Primary (%)
24 Feb	New Hampshire	Carter	28.4	28.4
		Udall	22.7	22.7
2 Mar	Massachusetts	Jackson	22.3	27.4
		Wallace	16.7	20.2
		Udall	17.7	17.5
		Carter	13.9	5.1
9 Mar	Florida	Wallace	30.5	42.9
		Jackson	23.9	27.8
		Carter	34.5	15.5
16 Mar	Illinois	Wallace	27.6	38.4
		Carter	48.1	28.1
23 Mar	North Carolina	Wallace	34.7	52.2
		Carter	53.6	24.4
		Jackson	4.3	11.7
6 Apr	Wisconsin	Udall	35.6	50.4
		Jackson	6.4	14.8
		Wallace	12.5	12.7
		Carter	36.6	12.3
27 Apr	Pennsylvania	Jackson	24.6	42.8
		Udall	18.7	18.1
		Wallace	11.3	17.4
		Carter	37.0	12.3
1 May	Texas	Wallace	17.5	39.7
		Bentsen	22.2	22.2
		Carter	47.6	17.7
4 May	Alabama	Wallace	48.9	67.7
		Carter	25.5	5.5
	D.C.	Udall	26.0	44.3
		Carter	39.7	13.0
	Georgia	Carter	83.4	38.6
		Wallace	11.5	34.1
		Jackson	0.7	13.1
		Udall	1.9	8.5
	Indiana	Wallace	15.2	32.9
		Jackson	11.7	32.8
		Carter	68.0	22.9

Table 8.5 State-by-State Projections for One-Day National Primary, 1976 (*cont.*)

			Actual Results (%)	National Primary (%)
11 May	Nebraska	Church	38.5	38.5
		Carter	37.6	16.6
		Wallace	3.2	11.2
		Jackson	1.5	9.5
		Udall	2.7	7.6
18 May	Maryland	Brown	48.4	45.4
		Wallace	4.1	15.8
		Carter	37.1	12.8
		Udall	5.5	12.4
		Jackson	2.4	11.1
	Michigan	Udall	43.1	61.8
		Wallace	6.9	16.9
		Carter	43.4	9.4
		Jackson	1.5	6.0
25 May	Arkansas	Wallace	16.5	50.7
		Carter	62.6	16.4
		Jackson	1.9	10.3
		Udall	7.5	9.8
	Idaho	Church	78.7	77.7
		Wallace	1.5	6.3
	Kentucky	Wallace	16.8	49.8
		Carter	59.4	15.0
		Udall	10.9	13.8
		Jackson	2.7	10.0
	Nevada	Brown	52.7	48.4
		Wallace	3.3	13.0
		Jackson	2.5	11.4
		Church	9.0	8.3
		Carter	23.3	7.8
		Udall	3.0	5.0
	Oregon	Church	33.6	35.6
		Brown	24.7	26.2
		Carter	26.7	10.3
		Jackson	1.2	6.8
		Wallace	1.3	6.0
		Udall	2.7	5.2
	Tennessee	Wallace	10.9	44.1
		Carter	77.6	26.8
		Jackson	1.7	16.2
		Udall	3.7	6.6

Table 8.5 State-by-State Projections for One-Day National Primary, 1976 (*cont.*)

			Actual Results (%)	National Primary (%)
1 Jun	Montana	Church	59.4	48.8
		Udall	6.3	13.7
		Jackson	2.7	13.5
		Wallace	3.4	12.7
		Carter	24.6	7.6
	Rhode Island	Brown[a]	31.5	31.1
		Church	27.2	26.9
		Carter	30.2	11.2
		Udall	4.2	11.0
		Jackson	1.3	8.8
		Wallace	0.8	6.2
	South Dakota	Udall	33.4	54.2
		Carter	41.2	9.5
		Jackson	1.0	6.9
		Wallace	2.4	6.7
8 Jun	California	Brown	59.0	55.1
		Wallace	3.0	12.8
		Udall	5.0	9.7
		Church	7.4	6.9
		Carter	20.5	6.2
		Jackson	1.1	5.3
	Ohio	Udall	21.0	35.8
		Wallace	5.7	21.4
		Carter	52.2	13.8
		Jackson	3.2	13.5
		Church	13.9	11.4

Note: Only candidates with projected vote shares greater than 5 percent are shown.

[a] Vote for delegates formally uncommitted but favorable to Brown.

suggest that, in addition to losing a substantial fraction of his actual share of the primary vote, Carter in a one-day national primary would have lost almost every one of his most crucial primary victories. He would still have carried New Hampshire and his home state, Georgia, but he would have lost Pennsylvania to Henry Jack-

son, Udall, Wallace, Brown, and Church combined would have been the same in a one-day national primary as in the actual sequential primary process. This simplification probably produces slight overestimates of the actual percentages for all six major candidates in the one-day national primary, but it has no impact on their vote shares relative to each other.

son, Wisconsin, Michigan, and Ohio to Morris Udall, and Florida, Illinois, North Carolina, and Texas to George Wallace.

One of the worst features of the one-day national primary, from Carter's point of view, is that he would have lost his critical southern base to Wallace. The importance of the South to Carter's success is evident from the actual primary results in Table 8.1—Carter won outright majorities in North Carolina, Georgia, Arkansas, Kentucky, and Tennessee, a near-majority in Texas, and a crucial plurality in Florida. The nature and importance of Carter's southern base is equally evident in Table 8.3, which shows that four of the five states in which Carter's underlying support was greatest were Georgia, North Carolina, Florida, and Tennessee. But in a one-day national primary, Carter would have lost every one of these states except Georgia, mostly because he would have lacked what became one of his most important resources: the argument that he, unlike Wallace, had demonstrated he could win the nomination. As his press secretary, Jody Powell, put it later (quoted by Moore and Fraser 1977: 88), "One of the major things we had going for us against Governor Wallace in Florida was that Jimmy Carter . . . was a Southerner with a real chance to win the nomination. Obviously, there's no better way to do that than to go 'way the hell off yonder to New Hampshire and win a primary."

In a national primary system, with every state voting on the same day, there simply would not have been any opportunity for Carter to produce either that early demonstration victory or any of the additional reinforcing demonstrations that followed. And conversely, Wallace would not have suffered from the self-reinforcing perception generated by his repeated primary defeats that he was washed up as a major political figure. Instead, he would have averaged about 47 percent of the southern primary vote and about 16 percent outside the South—figures only six to eight percentage points lower than in the 1972 primary season.

While Wallace would have been the biggest winner in a national primary system, Udall and Jackson would also have benefited significantly at Carter's expense. Jackson would have more than doubled his share of the total primary vote, from 6.3 to 13.5 percent. Udall would have increased his share of the primary vote from 9.3 to 14.2 percent, leaving him just behind Carter in that respect, but more important, instead of going through the entire primary season without a single victory, he would have won five primaries—Michigan, Ohio, Wisconsin, South Dakota, and the District of Columbia—to Carter's two.

Table 8.6 summarizes the implications of momentum for the primary season as a whole. In a one-day national primary, Carter would have lost almost two-thirds of his actual primary vote. George Wallace would have been, far and away, the most successful primary vote-getter, with Carter, Udall, Brown, and Jackson each getting about half of Wallace's total vote. Udall and Jackson would have gained total votes; Church would have gained slightly, and Brown would actually have lost votes, mostly because Jackson, Udall, and Wallace would have been somewhat stronger contenders in California if that primary had been held under the circumstances actually prevailing some fifteen weeks earlier.

The results are, if anything, even more striking when we turn from primary votes to primary victories. Wallace would have led the field with nine victories, but only two would have been outside the South, in Illinois and Indiana. Udall would have followed winning five states, then Brown and Church with four each, and Carter and Jackson with two each.

Of course, it is impossible to determine with any exactitude what would have happened at the convention under these circumstances. Carter's chances of winning the Democratic nomination without clearly dominating the primaries were considered slim even by his own advisers. In a March strategy memorandum (quoted by Schram 1977: 113), pollster Patrick Caddell wrote: "I don't think there is any question that we must win Wisconsin, avoid embarrassment in New York, and beat Jackson in Pennsylvania, and then in Indiana, to effect a quick kill in the primaries. My position is, unless we can put together a first-ballot victory or damn close to it, this party will deny us the nomination. Popular with the elites, we are not." Had it not been for momentum, my analysis suggests, Carter would have won neither Wisconsin, Pennsylvania, Indiana, nor Florida, Illinois, and North Carolina, which had already been won when Caddell wrote his memo. He would not have put together a first-ballot victory or come "damn close to it." It is hard to believe, under these circumstances, that Jimmy Carter would have been the Democratic nominee.

What *would* have happened is less certain. With Wallace the clear plurality choice, but—presumably—anathema to a majority at the Democratic convention, and with the party's remaining support scattered so evenly among several candidates, we might well have ended up with what everyone had been expecting before the primary season began: a brokered convention.

TABLE 8.6 Projected Aggregate Results of One-Day National Democratic Primary, 1976

	Total Primary Votes	
	Actual results	National primary
George Wallace	2,491,000	4,785,000
Jimmy Carter	6,890,000	2,512,000
Morris Udall	1,620,000	2,478,000
Jerry Brown	2,476,000	2,391,000
Henry Jackson	1,106,000	2,358,000
Frank Church	789,000	848,000
Others	2,061,000	2,061,000
TOTAL	17,433,000	17,433,000
	Primary Vote Shares	
	Actual results %	National primary %
George Wallace	14.3	27.4
Jimmy Carter	39.5	14.4
Morris Udall	9.3	14.2
Jerry Brown	14.2	13.7
Henry Jackson	6.3	13.5
Frank Church	4.5	4.9
Others	11.8	11.8
TOTAL	100.0	100.0
	States Carried	
	Actual results	National primary
George Wallace	1	9
Morris Udall	0	5
Jerry Brown	4	4
Frank Church	4	4
Jimmy Carter	16	2
Henry Jackson	1	2
Others	1[a]	1[a]
TOTAL	27	27

[a] Favorite son Robert Byrd won the West Virginia primary with 89 percent of the vote. George Wallace was the only major candidate to contest the state.

CHAPTER NINE

Trench Warfare: The Reagan and Kennedy Challenges

IF JIMMY CARTER'S 1976 CAMPAIGN was an example of nominating politics as blitzkrieg, the two campaigns examined in this chapter hark back another generation to World War I and the more elemental warfare of the western trenches. In each case an incumbent president with serious liabilities faced a major challenge within his own party. And in each case the challenge was mounted not by an unknown candidate of little consequence but by a major political figure with a strong and longstanding claim to the party's loyalty. Neither incumbent would get the newcomer's benefit of the doubt that Carter got in 1976, and neither challenger would be rolled over by a few quick primary victories. Both campaigns would be long, slow wars of attrition.

In some sense, these two campaigns represent the opposite end of the spectrum from Carter's campaign in 1976. Thus, a study of how they were waged and why they finished as they did provides a useful illustration of familiar political and dynamic forces at work in a very different setting. And the resulting differences in outcomes provide an object lesson regarding the importance of political context in shaping the dynamics of every nominating campaign.

9.1 REAGAN VERSUS FORD

By any estimate, Gerald Ford entered the 1976 campaign as an orthodox conservative Republican president. Under most circumstances, the combination of orthodox conservatism and incumbency would have been sufficient to assure his nomination without serious opposition. But in 1976 circumstances were abnormal in two important respects. First, Ford himself was a very atypical incumbent. Having been appointed to the vice presidency by Richard Nixon, he was thrust into the presidency when Nixon resigned in disgrace. He spent most of his first year in office attempting to distance himself from Nixon, after having granted him a controversial blanket pardon, and to convince the country that he could be more than a caretaker, do-nothing president. To make matters worse, he had never been involved in a national political campaign; indeed, he had never run for any public office outside his home congressional district in Michigan.

Ford's second, and bigger, problem was that the candidate ready and willing to challenge him was the hero of conservative Republicans for more than a decade, Ronald Reagan. Witcover (1977: 70) summarized the situation from the conservatives' perspective:

> What was so farfetched about the party that so loved Ronald Reagan giving him its presidential nomination? Sure, Jerry Ford was in the White House, and he had always been regarded as a conservative. But he was Nixon's choice, not the choice of the party out around the country. And for all his conservative rhetoric and use of the veto against the Democratic Congress, he was presiding over a federal budget out of balance by a colossal $66.5 billion. Moreover, he was not the kind of leader to stir passions, to excite the voters, to give life to the old GOP ideology.

Reagan's performance in the 1976 primaries demonstrated that *he* was the kind of candidate who *could* excite the voters—at least, Republican primary voters comfortable with "the old GOP ideology." After a narrow loss in New Hampshire and a string of subsequent defeats in Massachusetts, Florida, and Illinois, Reagan won in North Carolina to keep himself in the race. With only one primary in the month of April, he used the subsequent breathing space to raise new money for major challenges in more congenial states in May. His victory by a margin of more than two-to-one in Texas on May 1, followed by equally crushing victories in Alabama and Georgia and a close win in Indiana three days later, changed the complexion of the race. As his campaign manager, John Sears, put it later (in Moore and Fraser 1977: 42),

> the Texas primary . . . [was] the point at which most people began to feel that we might have a chance of getting nominated. The North Carolina event had been an interesting phenomenon to a lot of people and created interest in what might happen in May, but until we won in Texas, and indeed until we followed up that win with some victories on the following Tuesday, most people did not feel that the Reagan race was going to be significant.

Reagan's successes in early May ensured that his challenge would remain significant. He matched Ford vote for vote in the remaining primary season and battled down to the wire for uncommitted delegates before losing the nomination at the convention.

State-by-state primary results are shown in Table 9.1, along with a record of delegates won by each candidate. The candidates' objective probabilities of being nominated at each stage in the campaign, estimated on the basis of weekly delegate counts from caucus as well as primary states, are shown in Figure 9.1. The figure clearly reflects the outlines of the campaign as just described: Ford's march through the early primaries, Reagan's reprieve in North Carolina, the significance of his dramatic comeback beginning in Texas. It also reflects Ford's regaining of the delegate lead late in the campaign, when even a small margin in the delegate race could have significant implications for the candidates' relative chances of being nominated. Finally, the figure reflects, albeit less

TABLE 9.1 Republican Primary Results, 1976

		Popular Vote (%)		Delegates	
		Ford	Reagan	Ford	Reagan
24 Feb	New Hampshire	49.4	48.0	18	3
2 Mar	Massachusetts	59.6	32.9	28	15
9 Mar	Florida	52.8	47.2	43	23
16 Mar	Illinois	58.9	40.1	75	11
23 Mar	North Carolina	45.9	52.4	25	28
6 Apr	Wisconsin	55.3	44.4	45	0
1 May	Texas	32.7	66.8	0	100
4 May	Alabama	33.9	66.1	0	37
	Georgia	31.7	68.3	0	48
	Indiana	48.7	51.3	9	45
11 May	Nebraska	45.4	54.4	7	18
	West Virginia	56.8	43.2	28[a]	0
18 May	Maryland	57.9	42.1	43	0
	Michigan	64.9	34.3	55	29
25 May	Arkansas	35.6	62.9	10	17
	Idaho	24.9	74.3	5	16
	Kentucky	50.9	46.9	19	18
	Nevada	28.8	66.2	5	13
	Oregon	50.3	45.8	16	14
	Tennessee	49.8	49.0	21	22
1 Jun	Rhode Island	65.3	31.2	19	0
	South Dakota	44.0	51.2	9	11
8 Jun	California	34.5	65.5	0	167
	New Jersey	72.1	27.9	67[a]	0
	Ohio	56.6	43.4	91	6

Sources: Congressional Quarterly Weekly Reports; Aldrich (1980a).
[a] Delegates formally uncommitted but favorable to Ford.

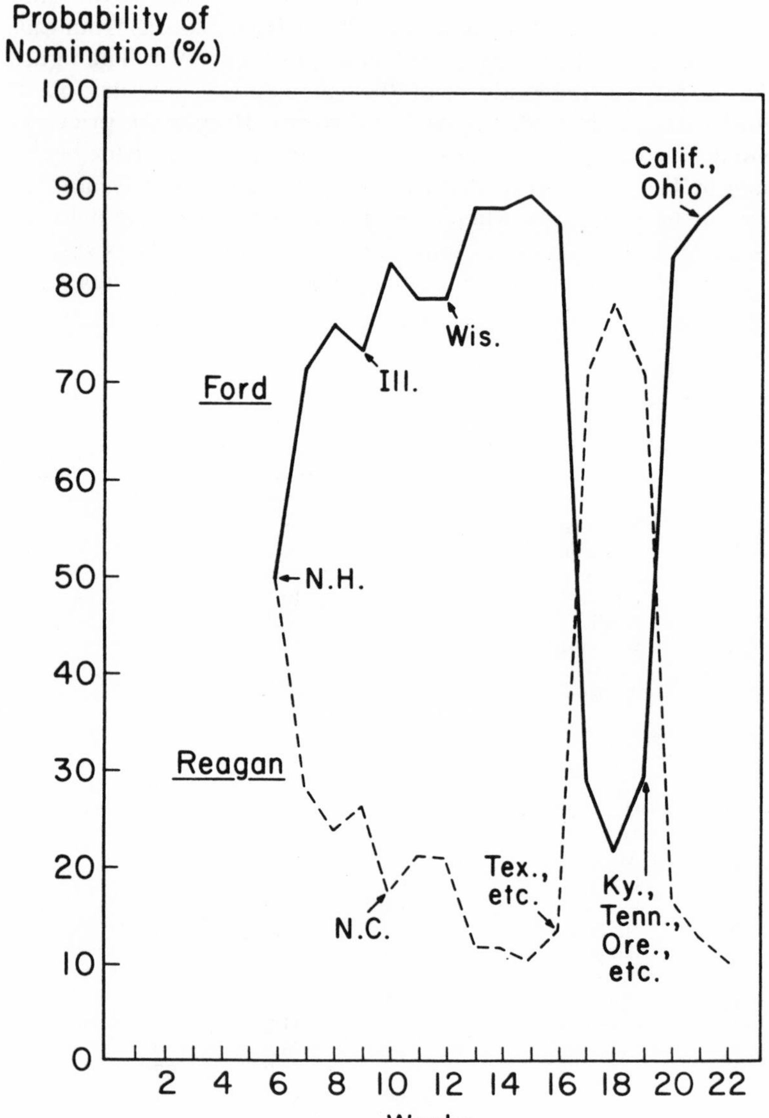

FIGURE 9.1 "Objective" Probabilities of Nomination, Republicans, 1976.

directly, the closeness of the Ford–Reagan race. Reagan's estimated probability of being nominated stood at 10 percent at the end of the primary season—a significant deficit, but the only instance among the five campaigns examined in this book in which a losing candidate's objective probability of winning was still greater than zero at the end of the primary season.

The implications of these objective probabilities for the subjective perceptions of primary voters are shown in Figure 9.2. As in the Democratic race, the estimated subjective probabilities reflect the same trends as the objective probabilities, but with smaller variations from week to week. In effect, campaign observers appear to have been "conservative" in their use of weekly delegate counts to project the candidates' chances.[1] The changes in subjective probabilities from week to week also reflect the assumption, built into the model on which they are based, that the effect of a single surprising result will be less marked late in the campaign, when existing expectations based on accumulated experience are more strongly held. For example, it is evident in Figure 9.2 that Ford's very narrow victory in New Hampshire had a greater impact on expectations than Reagan's much more dramatic sweep of all 100 delegates in the Texas primary, precisely because expectations were more labile at the beginning of the campaign than after two months of mostly one-sided primary results. Because the Reagan sweep in Texas was insufficient to counteract Ford's previous string of victories, it was interpreted as a possible fluke, until additional Reagan victories by similar margins later in the week demonstrated the real strength of Reagan's challenge. As Sears put it, "until we followed up that win [in Texas] with some victories on the following Tuesday, most people did not feel that the Reagan race was going to be significant." By contrast, Ford's victory in New Hampshire came at a time when there was little contrary information to be overcome; thus, it had an immediate and powerful impact on public perceptions of the race.

Before examining the effect of these perceptions on primary voting, it will be useful to survey the political terrain on which the dynamic aspects of the Ford–Reagan contest were overlayed. Reagan's challenge to his own party's incumbent president in 1976 was a dramatic manifestation of a longstanding political struggle be-

[1] This finding of "conservatism" in the use of new information parallels the results of a long and elaborate experimental research tradition in the psychology of decision making. A useful summary and abundant references are available from Slovic and Lichtenstein (1971: 693–98).

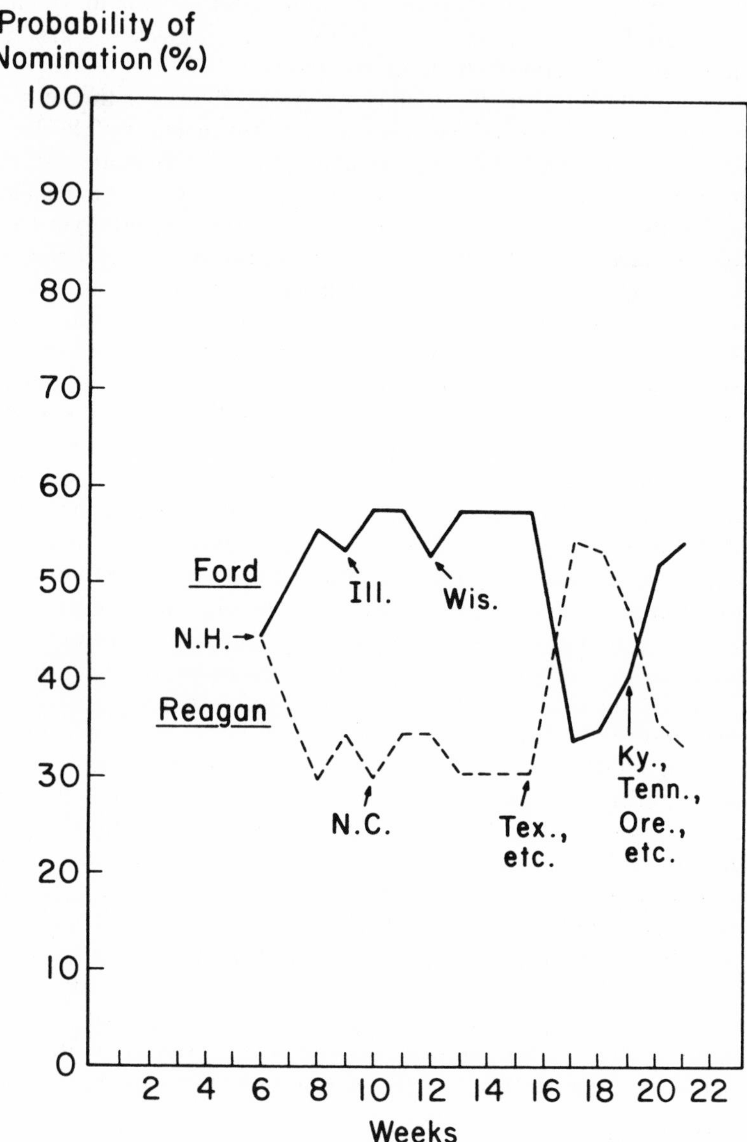

FIGURE 9.2 Estimated Subjective Probabilities of Nomination, Republicans, 1976.

tween two powerful competing factions within the Republican party. One of those factions was the strongly conservative western and southern wing of the party symbolized for a generation by Reagan and Barry Goldwater. This conservative faction often dominated the party at the grass-roots level, but its political agenda—based on the values of entrepreneurship, Christianity, and patriotism—had never been wholeheartedly adopted by Republican administrations. The Republican party-in-government had always been dominated by an opposing faction, more moderate in its political tendencies and concentrated primarily in the Northeast and Midwest. Although clearly a conservative on most important issues of public policy, Gerald Ford was in and of this moderate Republican establishment. By challenging the incumbent president, Reagan challenged the tendency of his party's moderate governing faction to contest presidential elections on its own terms and shape public policy to its own tastes.

Even a casual examination of the primary results in Table 9.1 makes it clear that the candidates' primary support was closely tied to this longstanding ideological division between extreme conservatives on one side and moderates on the other. Reagan's biggest primary victories came in Idaho, Nevada, Georgia, Texas, Alabama, and California—all strongly conservative Republican states in the West and South. By contrast, Ford's biggest victories came in New Jersey, Rhode Island, Michigan, and Massachusetts—all traditional strongholds of the moderate Republican establishment.

To examine more systematically the relationship between ideology and primary voting, I have constructed an index of party ideology for each state's Republican party. Like the Democratic "liberalism index" introduced in Chapter 8, this Republican "conservatism index" is based on a weighted average of past convention voting patterns, general election results, and congressional delegation ideological ratings.[2] The conservatism scores assigned to each state's Republican party are shown in Table 9.2. The general ordering of states corresponds well with preconceptions about the relative ideological positions of the various state parties, from Idaho and Mississippi at the conservative end of the spectrum to Massachusetts and Rhode Island at the liberal end.

The conservatism scores in Table 9.2 make it possible to exam-

[2] Details regarding data sources and the construction of the index are provided in Appendix A.4.

Table 9.2 Republican Party Conservatism Scores

Idaho	79.9	Colorado	67.1
Mississippi	79.5	Missouri	66.4
North Carolina	79.0	Illinois	63.6
Alabama	78.5	North Dakota	63.6
Georgia	77.6	Wisconsin	62.9
Louisiana	77.6	West Virginia	62.6
Oklahoma	76.5	Hawaii	61.3
California	75.5	Delaware	61.2
Florida	75.4	Washington	60.8
Texas	74.9	New Hampshire	60.4
South Carolina	74.7	South Dakota	60.3
Nebraska	72.9	Iowa	60.2
Tennessee	72.9	Alaska	58.7
Arizona	72.8	Maryland	56.7
Virginia	72.5	Minnesota	52.4
Wyoming	72.3	New Jersey	50.9
Kansas	71.2	Maine	50.6
Indiana	71.0	Pennsylvania	50.2
New Mexico	71.0	Vermont	49.9
Arkansas	70.9	Michigan	47.8
Utah	70.6	Oregon	47.2
Montana	69.6	New York	43.8
Nevada	68.1	Connecticut	42.3
Ohio	68.1	Rhode Island	37.0
Kentucky	67.6	Massachusetts	32.6

Source: Original calculations based on past convention voting patterns, general election results, and congressional delegation ideological ratings. See Appendix A.4 for details.

ine more systematically the relationship between ideology and primary voting implied by Reagan and Ford's most dramatic successes. That relationship is illustrated in Figure 9.3. The figure is certainly consistent with an ideological interpretation of the Ford–Reagan contest: moving from left to right across the figure, Ford's share of the primary vote declined precipitously in increasingly conservative states. The magnitude of this relationship, implying a difference of about thirty percentage points in Ford's vote share between the most liberal Republican states like Massachusetts and Rhode Island and the most conservative states like Idaho and Alabama, suggests that even relatively modest ideological differences were of crucial importance in the see-saw 1976 campaign. Had Reagan been able to broaden his ideological appeal, even marginally, he might well have been his party's nominee.

FIGURE 9.3 Ideology and Support for Ford, 1976 Republican Primaries.

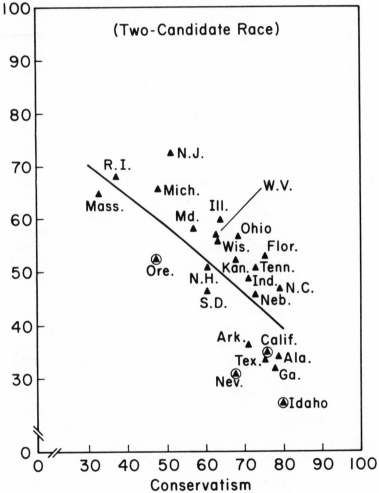

Of course, to claim that ideology was important is not to claim it as the *only* important factor in the 1976 Republican race. A variety of other factors helped shape the responses of primary voters to the Reagan challenge. One of these factors can be discerned directly from Figure 9.3, where western primary states (the four states circled in the figure) stand out as being among Ford's worst states at each level of conservatism. This regional pattern in the primary results should not be surprising, given the western regional basis of the conservative faction within the Republican party, Reagan's governorship of California, and his image as an essentially western figure. Ford also did worse in the West than elsewhere because most western primaries occurred in late May, the height of Reagan's late-season surge. But even after controlling for this coincidence of the primary calendar and the other political characteristics (especially the conservatism) of each primary state, it appears that Ford did as much as fourteen percentage points worse in the western states than would otherwise have been expected.[3]

In addition to this purely regional effect, Ford did better in states with heavily unionized labor forces. Presumably he did so partly because he was friendlier, or at least less hostile, toward the union movement than Reagan was; congressmen from Michigan, even conservative congressmen from Grand Rapids, seldom flourish as active enemies of labor. In addition, the proportion of each state's nonagricultural labor force belonging to unions probably serves as a proxy for other, unmeasured, political and social characteristics of the state, including which industries it relies on for jobs and the balance it strikes between the competing demands of businesses and workers. In any case, after controlling for other relevant factors, Ford's support was more than thirteen percentage points greater in the most heavily unionized states like Michigan and West Virginia than in the least unionized states like North Carolina.

Taken together, these essentially static political factors can account for much of the variation from state to state in Ford's actual primary performance. This fact is illustrated in Table 9.3, which shows for each primary state underlying levels of support for Ford, calculated on the basis of the political factors considered

[3] This estimate, like all of the empirical assertions in this chapter about the factors influencing 1976 Republican primary results, is based on the statistical results presented in Table A.29 in Appendix C.

TABLE 9.3 Underlying Ford Support in Republican Primary States, 1976

	Ford Support (Two-Candidate Vote %)
New Jersey	82.3
Rhode Island	79.2
Michigan	77.5
Massachusetts	76.5
Maryland	71.5
New Hampshire	71.5
Illinois	71.4
West Virginia	71.3
Ohio	70.1
Wisconsin	68.2
Oregon	66.9
Kentucky	66.6
Tennessee	65.2
Indiana	63.8
Nebraska	61.2
South Dakota	61.0
Florida	58.9
North Carolina	56.4
Arkansas	51.0
Alabama	48.8
California	48.7
Georgia	46.3
Texas	44.8
Nevada	44.5
Idaho	38.1

here.[4] Ford's underlying levels of support range from less than 40 percent in Idaho to more than 80 percent in New Jersey. It is not surprising, given the factors associated with support for Ford, that his best states were ideologically moderate northeastern states like New Jersey, Rhode Island, Michigan, and Massachusetts. Nor is it surprising that Ford's worst primary states were the most conservative, southern, and western states like Idaho, Nevada, Texas, Georgia, California, and Alabama. But the magnitude of the difference in Ford's underlying political support in these different states, amounting in some cases to more than 40 percent of the potential primary vote, emphasizes the importance of old-fashioned politics in determining the outcome of the 1976 Republican nominating campaign.

[4] Underlying support for Ford was calculated by subtracting from the actual primary figures the portion of each state's primary result attributable, on the basis of my statistical analysis, to differences between the candidates in levels of public recognition and perceived chances of winning the nomination.

In spite of the pronounced, longstanding factional cleavages activated by the Ford–Reagan contest, the actual results in specific primary states also depended significantly on the more fluid, dynamic element of momentum generated by changes from week to week in expectations about the candidates' chances of being nominated. The impact of expectations on primary voting is illustrated in Figure 9.4 for two distinct patterns of information about the candidates, those prevailing at the beginning and the end of the 1976 primary season.[5]

The difference between these two effects highlights the importance of information in conditioning the responses of primary voters to the campaign horse race. At the beginning of the primary season there was a moderately strong positive relationship between expectations and primary voting, particularly for increases in Ford's perceived chances of the sort following his victory in the New Hampshire primary.[6] In contrast, by the end of the primary season the effect of expectations was essentially zero in the range of Ford's actual perceived chances and actually slightly negative for changes in a pro-Reagan direction. These results are consistent with the general pattern, noted in Chapters 6 and 7, that expectations matter most in the early stages of a primary season, when information about the candidates is relatively scarce.

The implications of these results for the course of the 1976 Republican primary season are examined in Section 9.3. However, it may be useful here to compare the magnitude of the momentum effect implied by my analysis with an independent estimate from another source. A fairly direct comparison is possible in one important instance. Witcover (1977: 425) reported the results of polls conducted in Florida by Reagan's pollster, Richard Wirthlin, before and after Ford's narrow victory in New Hampshire. Ten days before the New Hampshire vote, Wirthlin had Ford ahead by 49 to 46 percent, only three percentage points, but in a poll conducted a few days after the New Hampshire vote, the margin had soared to 51 to 34 percent, seventeen percentage points. "Reagan and Ford both figured there would be some linkage between New

[5] The estimated effect of expectations in the 1976 Republican campaign is based on the coefficients for "Relative momentum" and "Local information" in Table A.29 in Appendix C.

[6] It appears from the figure that primary voters would have been slightly less sensitive to a Reagan victory in New Hampshire, since the effect of *decreases* in Ford's perceived chances from the starting point in late February was somewhat less steep.

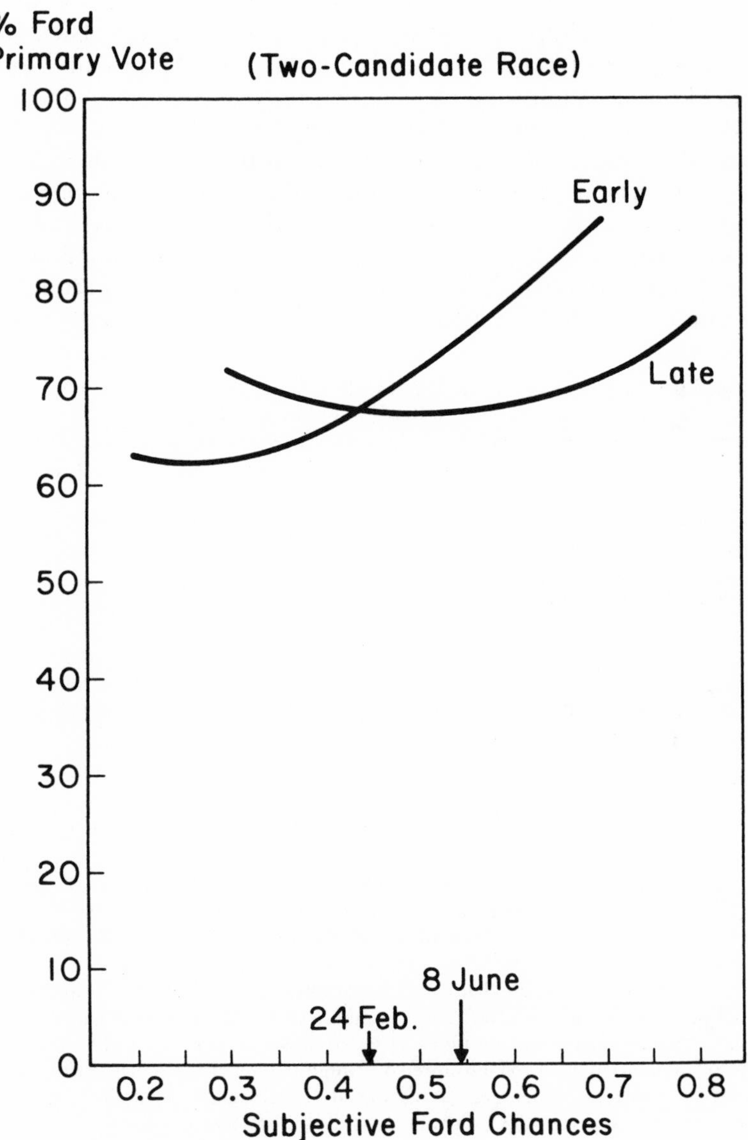

FIGURE 9.4 Expectations and Primary Voting, Republicans, 1976.

Hampshire and Florida," Witcover commented, "but neither expected that the momentum for Ford would be so great."

Table 9.4 compares the momentum effect indicated by Wirthlin's Florida polls and the estimated effect from my statistical analysis of actual primary outcomes. The effect of Ford's New Hampshire victory implied by my analysis can be calculated by comparing two projected results of the Florida primary—one based on the candidates' chances before New Hampshire and the other based on those after New Hampshire.[7] The resulting estimated effect is a fifteen percentage point increase in Ford's margin, which nearly matches Wirthlin's estimate of fourteen percentage points.[8] It is also consistent with Wirthlin's own analysis of the impact of the New Hampshire primary in previous nominating campaigns, from which he concluded that "we could expect either a gain or loss of about fifteen to eighteen percentage points in the

TABLE 9.4 Two Estimates of the Effect of New Hampshire Momentum on Candidate Support in Florida Republican Primary, 1976

	Ford (%)	Reagan (%)	Ford's Margin (%)
Wirthlin Polls			
Mid-February	49	46	+3
After New Hampshire	51	34	+17
Difference	+2	−12	+14
Projections[a]			
Before New Hampshire	37.0	63.0	−26
After New Hampshire	44.5	55.5	−11
Difference	+7.5	−7.5	+15

[a] These projections are based on statistical analysis of primary outcomes.

[7] Both projections are less favorable to Ford than Wirthlin's corresponding polls, presumably because the polls were taken too early to reflect an unrelated surge toward Reagan near the end of the Florida primary campaign (Witcover 1977: 429–30).

[8] In Table 9.10 I estimate that Ford's actual vote share in the Florida primary was 15.8 percentage points greater than it would have been in a one-day national primary. That estimate translates into a 31.6 percentage point increase in Ford's margin from before the New Hampshire vote until the time of the actual Florida vote. There is a difference between the estimated 15 percentage points here and the estimate of 31.6 percentage points in Table 9.10; the former reflects only the impact of New Hampshire, whereas the latter reflects the combined impact of Ford's victories in both New Hampshire and Massachusetts.

primaries following."[9] In this instance, the reasonableness of my estimated momentum effect is strongly supported by outside evidence.

The degree to which the complete set of political and dynamic factors considered here can account for the actual results of the 1976 Republican primaries is shown in Table 9.5. The table compares Ford's actual share of the two-candidate vote in each primary state with his estimated share based on the factors considered in this section. The difference between actual and estimated results is less than ten percentage points for all but one of the twenty-five primary states. Perhaps more remarkably, the error of estimation is less than four percentage points for most states and less than four and a half on average. From these results (that is, the comparison between actual and estimated vote shares) the factors considered here provide a reasonably complete account of actual primary outcomes in the Ford–Reagan campaign.

9.2 Kennedy versus Carter

For more than a decade, from the summer of 1968 through the fall of 1979, Democratic presidential politics revolved in large part around the offstage presence of Edward Kennedy. Kennedy was not only the heir to America's most famous political name, but he was also a talented and powerful politician in his own right and the acknowledged leader of his party's liberal wing. In popularity polls among Democratic voters, he consistently outshone the party's active presidential contenders in 1972 and again in 1976. According to conventional wisdom, whenever Kennedy finally decided he wanted the party's nomination, he would get it.

By the fall of 1979 Kennedy had made his decision to run. The political situation at the time must certainly have seemed propitious. Jimmy Carter, the incumbent Democratic president, was reaching lows in public approval unmatched by Richard Nixon in the midst of Watergate. Democratic officeholders nervous about

[9] The Wirthlin quotation appeared in Moore and Fraser (1977: 36). Wirthlin continued, "I turned from being a skeptic to being a strong supporter of the momentum hypothesis." A somewhat lower estimate of the effect of previous New Hampshire victories was provided by Beniger's (1976) study of primary results and national poll standings from 1952 to 1972. Beniger estimated a win in New Hampshire was worth an average gain of 8.4 percentage points in the next national poll and a loss in New Hampshire cost a candidate about 1 percentage point. The result is an average net change of a little less than 10 percentage points in the winning candidate's margin of support among the national campaign audience.

TABLE 9.5 Actual and Estimated Results of Republican Primaries, 1976

	Ford Support (Two-Candidate Vote %)		
	Actual	Estimated	Difference
New Jersey	72.1	60.7	+11.4
New Hampshire	50.7	42.8	+7.9
Tennessee	50.4	43.7	+6.7
North Carolina	46.7	40.4	+6.3
Florida	52.8	48.4	+4.4
Ohio	56.6	52.5	+4.1
Oregon	52.3	48.6	+3.7
Nebraska	45.5	42.0	+3.5
Kentucky	52.0	49.2	+2.9
California	34.5	31.8	+2.7
Maryland	57.9	55.9	+2.0
Illinois	59.5	57.6	+1.9
Wisconsin	55.5	56.2	−0.7
Indiana	48.7	49.7	−1.0
West Virginia	56.8	58.0	−1.2
Michigan	65.4	66.9	−1.5
Idaho	25.1	25.7	−1.6
Rhode Island	67.7	70.2	−2.6
South Dakota	46.2	48.9	−2.7
Nevada	30.3	35.4	−5.0
Alabama	33.9	40.5	−6.6
Georgia	31.7	38.8	−7.1
Massachusetts	64.4	71.9	−7.5
Arkansas	36.1	43.8	−7.7
Texas	32.9	42.1	−9.2

Notes: Average error = 4.4%. Serial correlation of average weekly residuals = −0.166.

running on a Carter ticket were, literally, lining up to urge Kennedy into the race (Reid 1980: 65–66). And in spite of his own glaring liability—Chappaquiddick and the issue of "character"—Kennedy was beating Carter handily in every national poll.

Kennedy officially entered the campaign in November. It would have been hard to imagine, even a few weeks before, that by then his campaign would already be heading rapidly downhill. The dramatic reversal of fortunes began in a disastrous nationally televised interview with Roger Mudd, in which Kennedy could neither explain coherently why he wanted to be president nor dispel the perception he was still holding back on Chappaquiddick. But as bad as the Mudd interview was for Kennedy, it was only the day's second most important blow to his presidential hopes. In one of those remarkable ironies of political history, an even more important event occurred that same day in Tehran, where the U.S. embassy was overrun and its personnel taken hostage by Islamic militants.

Kennedy's campaign problems and the burst of patriotic support for Carter in the early weeks of the hostage crisis were largely responsible for a remarkable turnabout in the complexion of the race: after trailing Kennedy two-to-one in the polls at the beginning of November, Carter was actually leading by the end of the year. Moreover, the continuing hostage crisis, and the Soviet invasion of Afghanistan in December, gave Carter good reasons to stay in the White House, keeping the full burden of campaign scrutiny on Kennedy. In Iowa, where Carter and Kennedy had been scheduled to debate, the president withdrew from the debate, stayed out of the state, and swept the caucuses with almost 60 percent of the vote. For Kennedy it was the first in what would become a long series of defeats.

Table 9.6 shows the state-by-state results of the 1980 Democratic primaries. In the end, Kennedy lost twenty-three primaries and won ten. But five of his ten victories came in the last week of the primary season, when the outcome of the Carter–Kennedy race was no longer in any real doubt. Of the twenty-five primaries held through the end of May, Kennedy won five and lost twenty, losing sixteen of those by twenty-five percentage points or more.

The effect of these primary results on the candidates' objective probabilities of being nominated are shown in Figure 9.5, and the corresponding subjective perceptions of the candidates' chances are shown in Figure 9.6. Except for brief swings reflecting Kennedy's victories in Massachusetts, New York, and Connecticut, both figures reflect an almost steady march by Carter through the primary season. Kennedy's perceived chances of being nominated fell below 20 percent by the end of the primary season, and his objective chances fell to zero.

As in every primary campaign, public expectations of the sort shown in Figure 9.6 were overlayed on a static political landscape, profoundly shaping observed patterns of primary voting. Indeed, it is interesting to note how closely the Democratic landscape of 1980 resembled that of 1976 in certain key respects. Despite the major differences between the two campaigns, for example, the impact of ideology on support for Carter was apparently quite similar in both instances. In each case, after controlling for other fac-

TABLE 9.6 Democratic Primary Results, 1980

		Popular Vote (%)		Delegates	
		Carter	Kennedy	Carter	Kennedy
24 Feb	New Hampshire	47.1	37.3	10	9
4 Mar	Massachusetts	28.7	65.1	77	0
	Vermont	73.1	25.5	5	7
11 Mar	Alabama	81.6	13.2	43	2
	Florida	60.7	23.2	75	25
	Georgia	88.0	8.4	62	0
18 Mar	Illinois	65.0	30.0	163	16
25 Mar	Connecticut	41.5	46.9	26	28
	New York	41.1	58.9	129	151
1 Apr	Kansas	56.6	31.6	23	14
	Wisconsin	56.2	30.1	48	26
5 Apr	Louisiana	55.7	22.5	50	1
22 Apr	Pennsylvania	45.4	45.7	95	90
3 May	Texas	55.9	22.8	108	38
4 May	D.C.	36.9	61.7	12	5
	Indiana	67.7	32.3	53	27
	North Carolina	70.1	17.7	66	3
	Tennessee	75.2	18.1	51	4
13 May	Maryland	47.5	38.0	34	24
	Nebraska	46.9	37.6	14	10
20 May	Oregon	58.2	32.1	26	13
27 May	Arkansas	60.1	17.5	25	6
	Idaho	62.2	22.0	9	7
	Kentucky	66.9	23.0	45	5
	Nevada	37.6	28.8	8	4
3 Jun	California	37.7	44.8	140	166
	Montana	51.6	37.2	13	6
	New Jersey	37.9	56.2	45	68
	New Mexico	41.9	46.1	10	10
	Ohio	51.0	44.1	89	72
	Rhode Island	25.8	68.3	6	17
	South Dakota	45.9	48.2	9	10
	West Virginia	61.9	38.1	21	10

Sources: Congressional Quarterly Weekly Report; Moore (1981).

tors, Carter's support peaked in moderately liberal primary states like Illinois and Pennsylvania and declined in both more conservative and more liberal states.[10] This similarity is evident in Figure 9.7, which shows the estimated relationship between liberalism and support for Carter, net of other factors, for both campaigns. The

[10] The estimated effect of ideology in the 1980 campaign is based on the statistical results presented in Table A.30 in Appendix C. Table A.30 is also the source for the estimated effects of other political and dynamic factors in the 1980 Democratic campaign presented in this chapter.

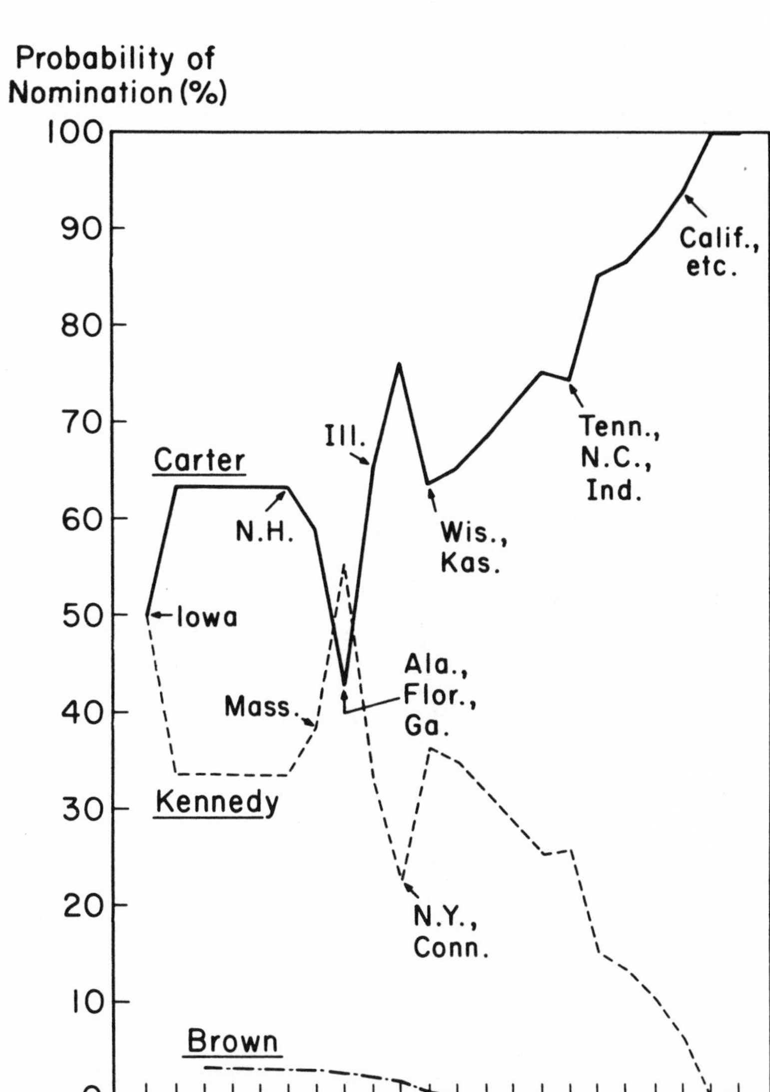

FIGURE 9.5 "Objective" Probabilities of Nomination, Democrats, 1980.

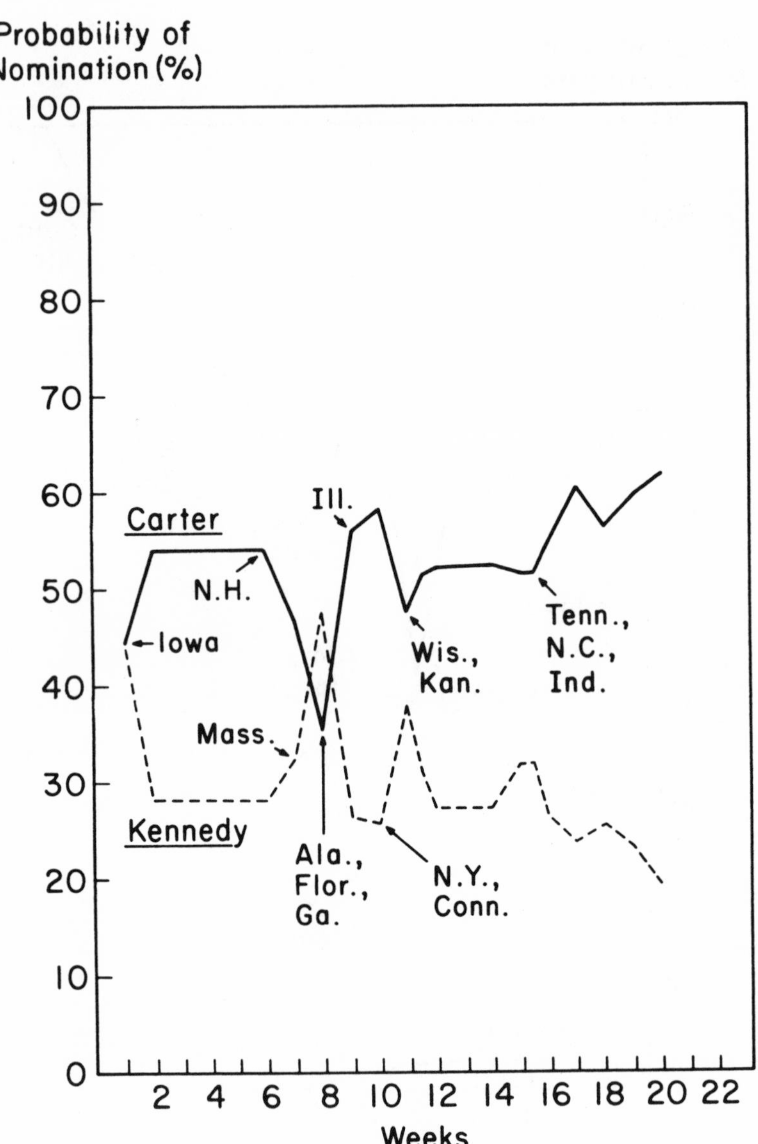

FIGURE 9.6 Estimated Subjective Probabilities of Nomination, Democrats, 1980.

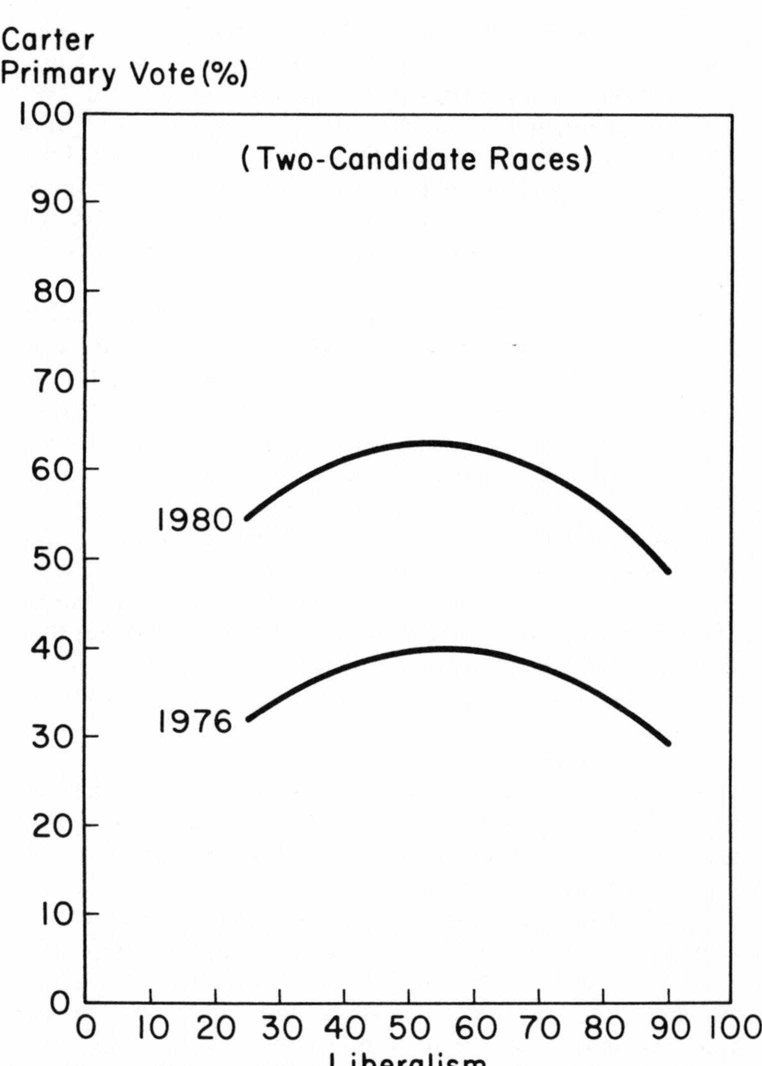

FIGURE 9.7 Ideology and Support for Carter, 1976 and 1980 Democratic Primaries.

two curves are virtually identical, except that Carter's share of the vote at every level of ideology was substantially greater in 1980 than it had been in 1976.

How, then, can we account for the common impression that ideology was a more important factor in 1980 than in 1976? The apparent difference between the two campaigns is largely the result of changes in the regional effects held constant in Figure 9.7. With different fields of challengers in each campaign, different combinations of regional advantages and disadvantages worked to mask the apparent effect of ideology in 1976 and to reinforce it in 1980. In 1976, as we saw in Chapter 8, Carter did unusually well in his own home region, the South, but did worse in the West—the home region of his two late challengers, Jerry Brown and Frank Church. Since both the South and the West are relatively conservative, these regional effects had little impact on the apparent effect of ideology.

Not surprisingly, 1980 saw a different pattern of regional effects. Carter's regional bonus in the eight southern primary states averaged more than seven percentage points, and Kennedy's corresponding bonus in the seven northeastern states averaged almost twice that—nearly fifteen percentage points. In addition, both candidates enjoyed home state advantages over and above their regional advantages: Carter's in Georgia amounted to more than five percentage points, and Kennedy's in Massachusetts was more than twelve. Because the northeastern states, particularly Massachusetts, are among the most liberal Democratic states, whereas the southern states are among the most conservative, imposing these regional and home state bonuses on the underlying ideological effects for 1980 shown in Figure 9.7 creates a very different impression than in 1976—an impression of strong ideological cleavage between liberal and conservative primary states.

In addition to ideological, regional, and home state effects, two demographic characteristics of primary states had significant effects on the 1980 Democratic results: 1980 unemployment levels were positively related to support for Carter; and levels of urbanization were negatively related to support for Carter. It may seem bizarre for unemployment to be positively related to support for an incumbent Democratic president, but a look at the specific states where unemployment was lowest and highest in 1980 suggests an explanation for the pattern. Three of the four states with unemployment levels below 5 percent were Kansas, Nebraska, and South Dakota—Midwestern farm states with their own reasons to be dissatisfied with Carter's performance.[11] Conversely, many of the states with the highest unemployment levels in 1980 were in other respects natural strongholds of Carter support. Six of the eight states with the highest unemployment levels were Illinois, Indiana, Ohio, Pennsylvania, West Virginia, and Kentucky—the heart of a region in which Carter's unusual blend of traditional morality, sympathy with blacks, and simultaneous appeal to small town and labor interests had always been favorably received. Apparently these common unmeasured characteristics of the high- and low-unemployment states were sufficiently powerful to swamp the effect of unemployment itself. Thus, Carter did about eight percentage points worse in the states with the lowest unemployment levels than he did in the states with the highest unemployment levels in 1980.[12]

The other significant demographic characteristic of primary states was urbanization: Carter did substantially better in more rural states than in those with greater urban concentrations. Comparing the two extremes of the distribution of primary states, urbanization alone accounted for two-thirds of the thirty-six percentage point difference in Carter's performance between Vermont (34 percent urban, 73 percent for Carter) and the District of Columbia (100 percent urban, 37 percent for Carter). Part of this effect presumably reflects Carter's own rural background and down-home style; Kennedy's contrasting image must also have played a role.

The combined effect of these factors and static factors not explicitly included in the model is summarized in Table 9.7. The table shows underlying levels of support for Carter in each of the Democratic primary states, reflecting Carter's performance in each state net of the effect attributable to momentum. The ordering of states makes considerable sense, with Georgia and the other southern primary states grouped at the top of the list and Massachusetts and the other northeastern primary states grouped at the bottom. But two points deserve particular notice. First, the average level of support across the range of primary states is quite favorable to Carter; only eight of the thirty-four states had "natural" majorities for Kennedy. Second, Iowa and New Hampshire both look like

[11] Farm states had been hard hit by high interest rates and by the 1979 oil price shock. In addition, Carter had just imposed an embargo on grain sales to the Soviet Union in reaction to the Soviet invasion of Afghanistan.

[12] The lowest state unemployment level in 1980 was 4.1 percent in Nebraska; the highest level was 9.6 percent in Indiana.

TABLE 9.7 Underlying Carter Support in Democratic Primary States, 1980

	Carter Vote (Two-Candidate Race %)
Georgia	81.6
Arkansas	79.3
Tennessee	76.6
Kentucky	76.4
Idaho	75.9
North Carolina	75.7
Alabama	72.3
West Virginia	66.3
Texas	65.0
Louisiana	63.5
Oregon	62.8
Montana	62.7
Indiana	62.3
Illinois	60.5
Maryland	59.4
Nebraska	59.4
Nevada	59.2
Vermont	58.9
Kansas	58.4
Ohio	58.3
Iowa	56.2
Wisconsin	54.5
South Dakota	53.5
Florida	52.5
New Mexico	52.4
California	50.5
New Jersey	44.9
New Hampshire	42.6
Connecticut	41.7
Pennsylvania	40.0
New York	36.1
D.C.	32.0
Rhode Island	31.4
Massachusetts	18.1

relatively favorable locales for a Kennedy challenge; his decisive losses in both states should have suggested early in the campaign that Kennedy's challenge could be successful only in expressive or symbolic terms, not as a vehicle for actually unseating an unpopular incumbent and certainly not for replacing him with Kennedy.

9.3 Momentum as a Double-Edged Sword

A major feature of the 1980 Democratic primary campaign was that voters seemed to care little for either major candidate. As Schram put it (1980: 87), "Jimmy Carter was viewed by the public as seriously flawed when he began his campaign to win renomination and he was viewed much the same when he finally had the nomination numerically won. His victory came not because he was especially beloved or even greatly respected; it came mostly because he was considered less objectionable than his chief opponent." Lemann's characterization of the situation (1980: 31) was even balder: "Carter's strongest point was that he wasn't Kennedy and Kennedy's strongest point was that he wasn't Carter."

The day after the primary results in Illinois increased Carter's probability of being nominated from 66 to 78 percent, by my calculation, his pollsters began to report a "dramatic shift" in voting patterns. Patrick Caddell (quoted by Schram 1980: 109) told the president and his advisers that "apparently people are now suddenly willing to vote for Kennedy even though they do not care for him. . . . Now that people believe that Carter will be the party's nominee, they are focusing upon Carter almost exclusively, and they are deciding they do not like what they see." In effect, Carter's increasing likelihood of being renominated forced primary voters to ignore his strongest point and focus their attention increasingly on reasons not to vote for him. A few days later Caddell's partner, John Gorman, commented (quoted by Schram 1980: 112), "Ted Kennedy has disappeared as a factor in this election. It's Carter versus Carter. And Carter is going to get murdered."

It may be unrealistic to expect that a systematic statistical analysis of the sort provided here could faithfully reflect the reality of a campaign in which "It's Carter versus Carter" implies that "Carter is going to get murdered." Nevertheless, my analysis appears to do just that. The same principles used to analyze voting behavior in other recent nominating campaigns produce for the 1980 Democratic campaign exactly the sort of negative result suggested by the quotations from Caddell and Gorman. This negative result is illustrated in Figure 9.8, which shows the effect of Carter's chances on his primary support at the beginning and end of the 1980 Democratic primary season.[13] At the beginning of the campaign the estimated effect of expectations on primary voting was essentially zero. But by the end of the primary season the esti-

[13] The estimated effects of horse race expectations in the 1980 Democratic campaign are based on the coefficients for "Relative momentum" and "Local information" in Table A.30 in Appendix C.

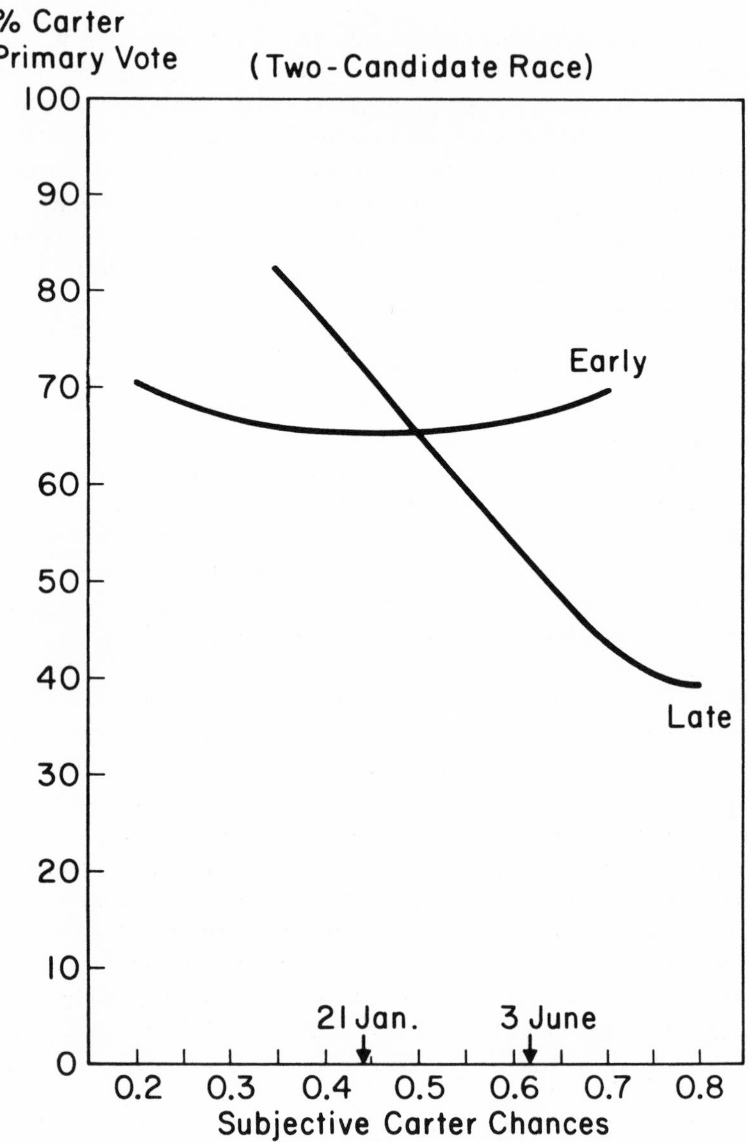

FIGURE 9.8 Expectations and Primary Voting, Democrats, 1980.

mated effect was decidedly negative, just as we would expect on the basis of Schram's and others' observations.

The implications of this increasingly negative relationship between chances and primary support in the 1980 Democratic campaign are traced in Table 9.8 and in Figure 9.9. Table 9.8 presents simulated results for each state from a one-day national primary,

TABLE 9.8 Projected Results of One-Day National Democratic Primary, 1980

		Carter Vote (Two-Candidate Race %)		
		Actual Results	National Primary	Difference
20 Jan	Iowa caucuses	65.4	65.4	—
26 Feb	New Hampshire	55.8	52.3	3.5
4 Mar	Massachusetts	30.6 (K)	24.6 (K)	6.0
	Vermont	74.1	67.9	6.2
11 Mar	Alabama	86.1	79.4	6.7
	Florida	72.3	62.0	10.4
	Georgia	91.3	86.7	4.6
18 Mar	Illinois	68.4	69.4	−1.0
25 Mar	Connecticut	46.9 (K)	51.4	−4.5
	New York	41.1 (K)	45.5 (K)	−4.4
1 Apr	Kansas	64.2	67.5	−3.3
	Wisconsin	65.1	63.9	1.2
5 Apr	Louisiana	71.2	72.0	−0.7
22 Apr	Pennsylvania	49.8 (K)	49.6 (K)	0.3
3 May	Texas	71.0	73.3	−2.3
6 May	D.C.	37.4 (K)	41.0 (K)	−3.6
	Indiana	67.7	70.9	−3.2
	North Carolina	79.8	82.2	−2.3
	Tennessee	80.6	82.9	−2.3
13 May	Maryland	55.6	68.4	−12.8
	Nebraska	55.5	68.3	−12.8
20 May	Oregon	64.5	71.4	−6.9
27 May	Arkansas	77.4	85.0	−7.5
	Idaho	73.9	82.3	−8.4
	Kentucky	74.4	82.7	−8.3
	Nevada	56.6	68.2	−11.6
3 Jun	California	45.7 (K)	60.1	−14.4
	Montana	58.1	71.2	−13.1
	New Jersey	40.3 (K)	54.6	−14.4
	New Mexico	47.6 (K)	61.9	−14.3
	Ohio	53.6	67.4	−13.8
	Rhode Island	27.4 (K)	40.3 (K)	−12.9
	South Dakota	48.8 (K)	63.0	−14.2
	West Virginia	61.9	74.4	−12.5
AVERAGES		60.6	65.5	−4.9

Note: (K) indicates actual or projected Kennedy victory.

in which the effect of momentum in each state would be based not on the circumstances actually prevailing when the state's primary was held but on the circumstances prevailing at the beginning of the primary season. Figure 9.9 shows the differences between these simulated results and the actual primary results for each week of the 1980 campaign. Each week's effect is the average difference between Carter's actual share of the two-candidate vote and the simulated share from a one-day national primary shown in Table 9.8. In each case, the ups and downs in the effect of momentum from week to week follow almost exactly the pattern implied by the comments of Carter's pollsters about negative voting. Indeed, the impact of momentum appears from the figure to have turned against Carter precisely at the time of the Illinois primary, as suggested by Caddell and Gorman. After Kennedy's victories in New York and Connecticut put some life back into the race, Carter's negative momentum was neutralized until his near-victory in Pennsylvania and clear victories in Texas, Indiana, North Carolina, and Tennessee in the subsequent week erased his last real chance of losing the nomination. At that point Carter's negative momentum returned with a vengeance, costing him an average of almost 12 percent of the vote in primaries held during the last four weeks of the campaign.

There is no evidence that this rather striking finding of negative momentum in the 1980 Democratic campaign is a statistical fluke. The overall match between estimates based on the finding and actual primary results, shown in Table 9.9, is reasonably close—the average error in estimating Carter's share of the two-candidate vote is less than four percentage points—and the nature of the errors in specific states suggests no obvious relationship to the dynamics of the campaign. The parameters on which the finding of negative momentum is based are estimated fairly precisely.[14] And the results hold up under a variety of alternative formulations of the underlying statistical model, including the simple formulation described in Section 7.3 where the effect of expectations on primary results is assumed to be unaffected by variations in information either across candidates or over time.

The 1980 Democratic results were generated by the same basic set of political and dynamic forces analyzed in this book for other

[14] The parameter estimates and their standard errors are reported in Table A.30 in Appendix C. The t-statistics for the relevant parameter estimates are 2.2, 1.9, and 24.4.

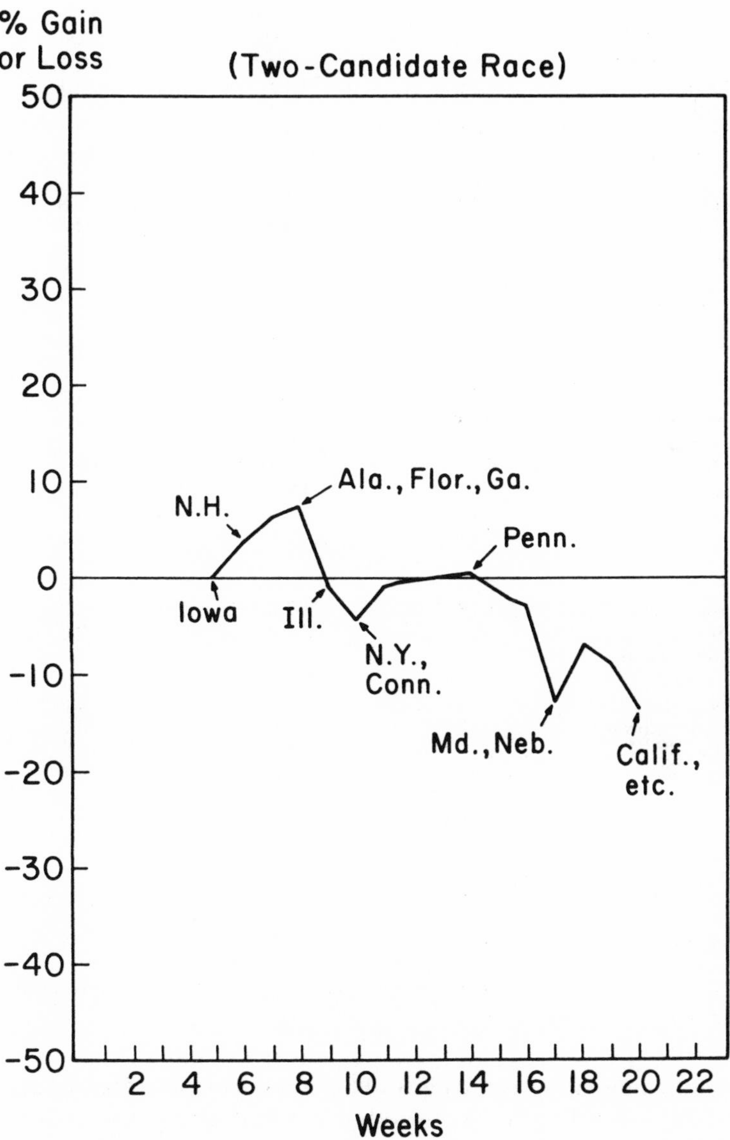

FIGURE 9.9 Effect of Momentum on Carter's Weekly Performance, 1980 Democratic Primaries.

TABLE 9.9 Actual and Estimated Results of Democratic Primaries, 1980

	Carter Vote (Two-Candidate Race %)		
	Actual	Estimated	Difference
Idaho	73.9	64.8	+9.1
Kentucky	74.4	66.1	+8.3
Nevada	56.6	50.2	+6.4
California	45.7	40.5	+5.2
Vermont	74.1	69.3	+4.8
Oregon	64.5	59.9	+4.6
Maryland	55.6	51.7	+3.9
Tennessee	80.6	76.9	+3.7
Connecticut	46.9	43.6	+3.3
Illinois	68.4	65.3	+3.2
Texas	71.0	69.5	+1.6
Alabama	86.1	84.6	+1.5
Massachusetts	30.6	29.4	+1.2
New York	41.1	40.4	+0.7
Arkansas	77.4	76.7	+0.7
Nebraska	55.5	54.8	+0.7
Georgia	91.3	90.8	+0.5
Kansas	64.2	63.8	+0.4
North Carolina	79.8	79.6	+0.2
D.C.	37.4	38.8	−1.3
Iowa	65.4	67.8	−2.3
Ohio	53.6	56.2	−2.6
Rhode Island	27.4	30.0	−2.6
Montana	58.1	60.8	−2.7
Wisconsin	65.1	67.9	−2.8
New Hampshire	55.8	59.0	−3.2
Indiana	67.7	71.3	−3.6
Louisiana	71.2	75.6	−4.3
Pennsylvania	49.8	55.9	−6.0
Florida	72.3	78.6	−6.3
New Jersey	40.3	46.9	−6.6
South Dakota	48.8	55.9	−7.1
New Mexico	47.6	54.8	−7.2
West Virginia	61.9	71.3	−9.4

Notes: Average error = 3.8%. Serial correlation of average weekly residuals = 0.156.

recent nominating campaigns. That they look so different from the corresponding results for other recent campaigns is testimony to the fact that a few basic forces can combine and interact in many different ways. The contrast is particularly striking if we compare the Carter–Kennedy contest in 1980 with the Ford–Reagan race in

1976. In the latter case, broadly similar circumstances produced significantly different results.

Table 9.10 shows the projected results of a one-day national primary for the 1976 Republican campaign. Unlike Carter in 1980, Ford in 1976 benefited significantly from the sequential nature of the actual primary process. The projected results suggest that his average share of the vote in a national primary would have been more than seven percentage points less than his actual average share. More importantly, instead of carrying fourteen primary states to Reagan's eleven, Ford would have carried only eight states in a national primary to Reagan's seventeen. He would have lost Florida in March, Wisconsin in April, Kentucky, Oregon, and Ten-

TABLE 9.10 Projected Results of One-Day National Republican Primary, 1976

		Ford Vote (Two-Candidate Race %)		
		Actual Results	National Primary	Difference
24 Feb	New Hampshire	50.7	50.7	—
2 Mar	Massachusetts	64.4	57.1	7.3
9 Mar	Florida	52.8	37.0 (R)	15.8
16 Mar	Illinois	59.5	50.6	8.9
23 Mar	North Carolina	46.7 (R)	34.6 (R)	12.1
6 Apr	Wisconsin	55.5	46.8 (R)	8.7
1 May	Texas	32.9 (R)	24.9 (R)	7.9
4 May	Alabama	33.9 (R)	28.0 (R)	5.9
	Georgia	31.7 (R)	26.1 (R)	5.6
	Indiana	48.7 (R)	41.9 (R)	6.8
11 May	Nebraska	45.5 (R)	39.2 (R)	6.3
	West Virginia	56.8	50.4	6.4
18 May	Maryland	57.9	50.7	7.2
	Michigan	65.4	58.5	6.9
25 May	Arkansas	36.1 (R)	29.9 (R)	6.2
	Idaho	25.1 (R)	20.2 (R)	4.9
	Kentucky	52.0	45.0 (R)	7.1
	Nevada	30.3 (R)	24.7 (R)	5.6
	Oregon	52.3	45.3 (R)	7.1
	Tennessee	50.4	43.4 (R)	7.0
1 Jun	Rhode Island	67.7	60.9	6.7
	South Dakota	44.0 (R)	39.0 (R)	7.2
8 Jun	California	34.5 (R)	28.0 (R)	6.5
	New Jersey	72.1	65.6	6.5
	Ohio	56.6	49.0 (R)	7.6
AVERAGES		48.9	41.9	7.0

Note: (R) indicates actual or projected Reagan victory.

nessee in May, and Ohio on the last day of the primary season in June.

There is no precise way to translate these hypothetical primary results into conclusions about what would have happened at the convention had momentum played no role in the 1976 Republican campaign. Nevertheless, given the extraordinary closeness of the actual race,[15] it seems likely that the six victories attributed to momentum in my state-by-state projections were crucial to Ford's nomination. The victories in Wisconsin and Ohio were particularly important because those states conducted "loophole" primaries, in which large numbers of delegates could be won on the basis of very narrow popular vote margins.[16] Overall, it appears, Ford would probably have trailed Reagan by two to three hundred delegates in a one-day national primary, rather than leading by fifty delegates as he actually did at the end of the sequential primary process. Under these circumstances, it seems unlikely he would have been the Republican nominee. Thus, it appears that momentum was decisive in the 1976 Republican campaign, although its behavioral effect on primary voters was modest by the standards of the campaigns examined in Chapters 8 and 10.

[15] Straffin (1977: 702) estimated that Ford did not achieve the critical "bandwagon" level of delegate strength until more than a month after the end of the primary season.

[16] In "loophole" primaries the winning candidate in each congressional district receives all the delegates from that congressional district, no matter how narrow his margin of victory.

CHAPTER TEN

Coming Up Short: George Bush and Gary Hart

THE TWO CAMPAIGNS ANALYZED in this chapter reflect a mixture of elements from the contrasting political worlds analyzed in Chapters 8 and 9. Neither involved an incumbent president, but each had a clear front-runner. In each case the front-runner faced a crowded field of would-be challengers, most of whom were "winnowed out" in the early stages of the campaign. In each case one relatively unknown candidate did emerge from the early primaries as a serious challenger. But in each case the challenge fell short, leaving the original front-runner as the party's eventual nominee.

The historical experience of these two similar campaigns raises some interesting broader questions about the dynamics of the modern presidential nominating process. Under what circumstances do relatively unknown candidates emerge as major challengers? What kinds of political resources do front-runners have to withstand such challenges? And how does the presence of other candidates impinge on the dynamics of the campaign? This chapter addresses those questions in the context of the Bush and Hart challenges.

10.1 Bush versus Reagan

By late 1979, Ronald Reagan was once again an active candidate for the Republican presidential nomination. But his situation in 1979 was more favorable in several respects than it had been four years earlier. His strongest potential opponent, Gerald Ford, had decided (at least provisionally) not to run. In the absence of another Ford–Reagan showdown, a crowded field of lesser candidates scrambled for early visibility and support. Moreover, since 1976 explicit ideological conservatism had become even more a matter of consensus within the Republican party. The entire field of challengers, with the single exception of longshot liberal John Anderson, had adopted most of the conservative themes Reagan had espoused for years; instead of competing on ideological grounds, each billed himself as a younger Reagan, a sexier Reagan, Reagan with a better resumé, Reagan with better jokes. And the Democratic opposition was in apparent disarray, with the incumbent president and his main challenger both looking quite incapable of winning a general election. What better time for Reagan?

Among the Republican challengers, only George Bush appeared to be making any real progress as the 1980 campaign began in earnest. But even for Bush, Ronald Reagan was the quite-possibly-immovable object. Bush's pollster, Robert Teeter, recalled a year later (in Moore 1981: 2) that "there was never any certainty whether Bush or anyone else could beat Ronald Reagan. I think the key was that you had to get yourself in a position so that if something happened and the opportunity that Ronald Reagan could be defeated presented itself, you were the alternative to Reagan."

Bush solidified his position as the alternative to Reagan by winning an upset victory in the Iowa caucuses in January. The victory itself was a slim one; Bush's margin amounted to less than ten thousand votes. But the impact of the victory on perceptions of the race was revolutionary. In a matter of days Bush became "the hottest property in American politics" (Cannon and Peterson 1980: 137). The cover story in *Newsweek* magazine announced, "Bush Breaks Out of the Pack." Public opinion polls suddenly showed him even with Reagan in support among rank-and-file Republicans. And a poll conducted among luncheon guests at the National Press Club one week after Bush's Iowa breakthrough turned up 185 Washington insiders who expected Bush to be the Republican nominee; only 29 were still betting on Reagan (Greenfield 1982: 12). There was no longer any doubt that, if Reagan continued to falter, Bush would be the beneficiary.

The only problem, from Bush's perspective, was that there was no more faltering. Reagan intensified his campaign activities, performing particularly well in two New Hampshire debates. Later he also reorganized his campaign staff, replacing the professionals responsible for his insulation from the voters in Iowa with a more comfortable team dominated by old California associates. Meanwhile, Bush himself was failing to build a substantive, issue-oriented basis for his newfound support. According to his own campaign manager, James Baker (quoted by Germond and Witcover 1981: 118), "We had solved the George Who problem in Iowa. We did not answer the question of George Why." With a less firmly entrenched organization than in Iowa and an often unimpressive campaign style, Bush gave New Hampshire Republicans no good reason not to vote for Reagan; they did vote for Reagan over Bush by more than two to one. Bush's old friend, "Big Mo," was precipitously reversed before the primary season was even a week old. Reagan finished the remaining primaries without a serious stumble and won the nomination easily.

The week-by-week primary results are shown in Table 10.1. The

TABLE 10.1 Republican Primary Results, 1980

		Popular Vote (%)		
		Reagan	Bush	Anderson
26 Feb	New Hampshire	49.6	22.7	4.3
4 Mar	Massachusetts	28.8	31.0	30.7
	Vermont	30.1	21.7	29.0
8 Mar	South Carolina	54.7	14.8	0
11 Mar	Alabama	69.7	25.9	0
	Florida	56.2	30.2	9.2
	Georgia	73.2	12.6	8.4
18 Mar	Illinois	48.4	11.0	36.7
25 Mar	Connecticut	33.9	38.6	22.1
1 Apr[a]	Kansas	63.0	12.6	18.2
	Wisconsin	40.2	30.4	27.4
5 Apr	Louisiana	74.9	18.8	0
22 Apr[b]	Pennsylvania	42.5	50.5	2.1
3 May	Texas	51.0	47.4	0
6 May	Indiana	73.7	16.4	9.9
	North Carolina	67.6	21.8	5.1
	Tennessee	74.1	18.1	4.5
13 May	Maryland	48.2	40.9	9.7
	Nebraska	76.0	15.3	5.8
20 May	Michigan	31.8	57.5	8.2
	Oregon	54.5	34.7	10.1
27 May[c]	Idaho	82.9	4.0	9.7
	Kentucky	82.4	7.2	5.1
	Nevada	83.0	6.5	0
3 Jun	California	80.2	4.9	0
	Montana	87.3	9.7	0
	New Jersey	81.3	17.1	0
	New Mexico	63.7	9.9	12.1
	Ohio	80.8	19.2	0
	Rhode Island	72.0	18.6	0
	South Dakota	82.1	4.2	6.3
	West Virginia	85.6	14.4	0

Sources: Congressional Quarterly Weekly Report; Moore (1981).

[a] Anderson suspended his campaign for the Republican nomination on April 2.

[b] Anderson announced his independent campaign for the presidency on April 27.

[c] Bush formally withdrew from the race on May 26.

major candidates' objective probabilities of being nominated, based on the weekly delegate count, are shown in Figure 10.1. These objective probabilities emphasize the speed with which Reagan regained control of the race in New Hampshire and immediately thereafter. He regained the lead with his victory in New Hampshire, and convincing victories in South Carolina, Alabama, Florida, and Georgia in the next two weeks gave him a practically insurmountable delegate cushion. From then on there was no real contest, and Bush's real chances of being nominated fell to zero even before he actually dropped out of the race in late May.

The subjective public perceptions of the candidates' chances corresponding to these objective probabilities are shown in Figure 10.2. They, too, suggest that Reagan's early lead disintegrated in Iowa, but that it was quickly regained in the three weeks separating the New Hampshire primary in late February and the Illinois primary in mid-March. Bush's perceived chances hovered around the 20 percent mark for the remainder of the primary season, mostly on the strength of his sizable share of the cumulative primary vote.

Although Reagan's campaign was broader-based in 1980 than it had been in 1976, his popularity did not completely overshadow the continuing cleavage in the Republican ranks between moderates and more extreme conservatives. Bush, like Ford in 1976, was certainly a conservative, but one who was in and of the moderate Republican establishment. As a result, the contest between Bush and Reagan in 1980 was to some extent a replaying of the factional conflict of 1976. As in 1976, Reagan did significantly better in the most conservative Republican primary states than in those with more moderate political tendencies. Across the range of conservatism from Idaho at one extreme to Massachusetts at the other, the difference in Reagan's share of the two-candidate vote attributable to this ideological cleavage was about twenty percentage points.[1]

In addition to reflecting the Republican party's longstanding ideological divisions, the results of the 1980 primaries were affected by several campaign-specific factors. Each candidate enjoyed a significant home state advantage, about twenty-four percentage points for Bush and nine percentage points for Reagan.[2]

[1] The estimated effects of ideology and other factors on primary voting in the 1980 Republican campaign are shown in Table A.31 in Appendix C.

[2] These two different percentage point shifts are based on an underlying effect constant by assumption for both candidates. The difference in their magnitudes reflects the assumption built into my statistical analysis that any given political or

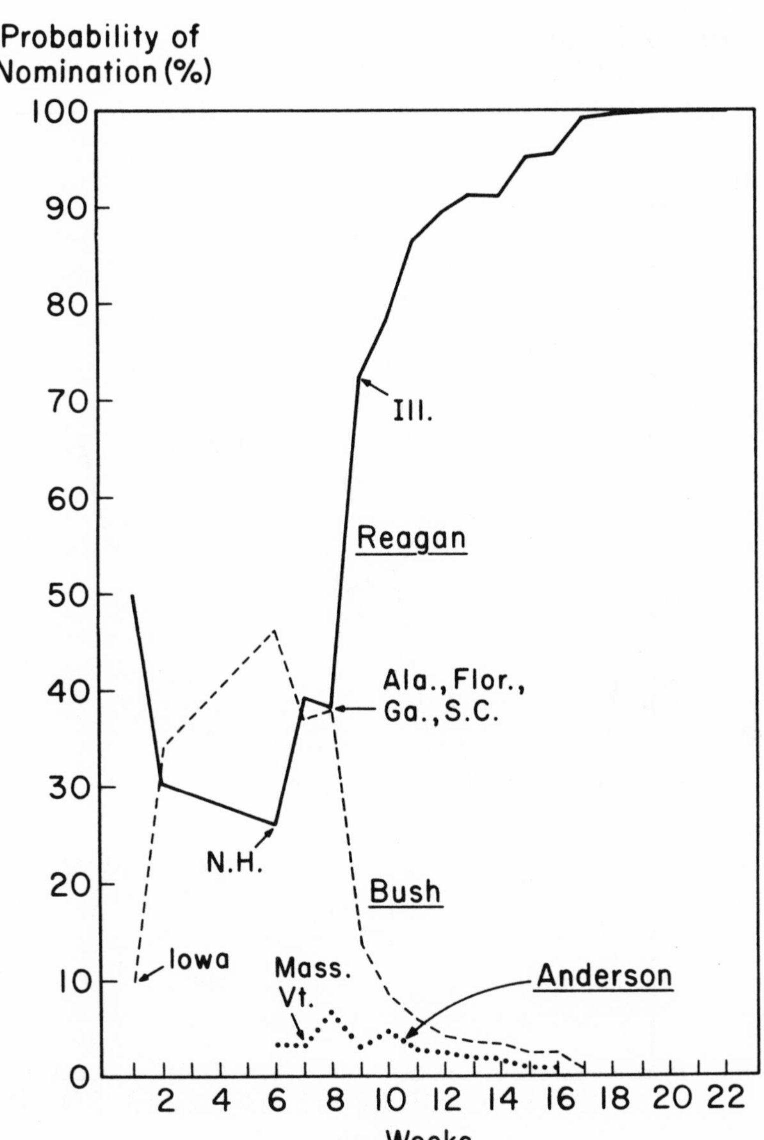

FIGURE 10.1 "Objective" Probabilities of Nomination, Republicans, 1980.

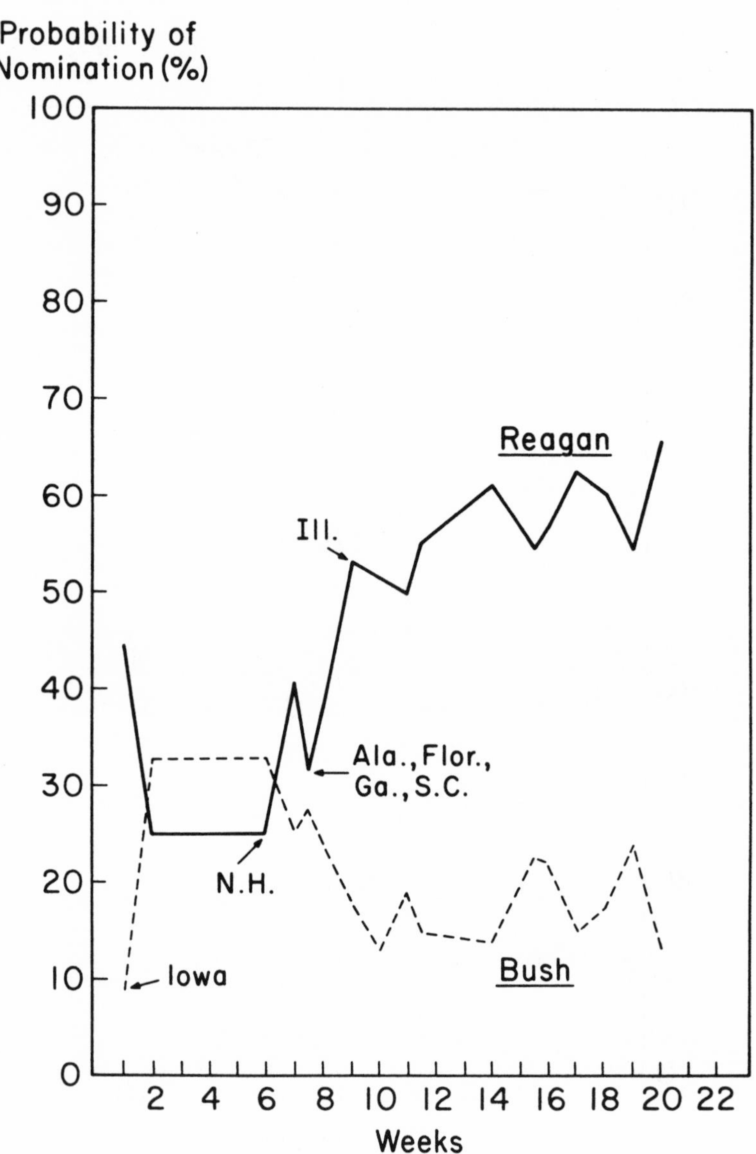

FIGURE 10.2 Estimated Subjective Probabilities of Nomination, Republicans, 1980.

In addition, Reagan did better in relatively rural states and in states with low unemployment rates. The difference between his performance in the most urban states and his performance in the most rural states, net of other factors, amounted to almost thirteen percentage points. The effect of unemployment created a similar range of results—except in Michigan, where an unemployment level exceeding 12 percent cost Reagan sixteen percentage points more than in the next most hard-hit primary state.

As in every recent nominating campaign, these static political factors provide only a partial explanation of each state's primary outcome. A fuller explanation requires that we also consider the dynamic forces generated by the sequential nature of the primary process—particularly, in this instance, the significant changes during the primary season in prospective voters' information about George Bush and their perceptions of his chances of winning the nomination. Furthermore, we must supplement the set of dynamic factors considered in other primary seasons to account for an additional complication in the 1980 Republican race: Bush, unlike most other major challengers, formally withdrew from the race before the end of the primary season.

Table 10.2 shows the combined impact of these dynamic forces on the results of the 1980 Republican primaries—the effects of changes in information and expectations of the sort examined for other recent campaigns and of Bush's early withdrawal from the race.[3] The table compares the actual primary results with projected results from a one-day national primary, in which these dynamic forces would have played no role.

At first glance the results seem puzzling; they suggest that Bush did worse in the actual sequential system than he would have done in a one-day national primary, where momentum would not have been a factor. However, the one-day primary simulated in Table 10.2 reflects the circumstances prevailing at the time of the New Hampshire primary, *after* Bush's Iowa victory and subsequent

dynamic factor will make a greater difference in close primaries than in primaries where either candidate is dominant on other grounds. Reagan's two home states (Illinois, his boyhood home, and California) were carried with 81.5 and 94.2 percent of the two-candidate vote; Bush's two home states (Connecticut and Texas) were lost with 46.8 percent and won with 51.8 percent, respectively.

[3] The estimated effects of these factors are based on the coefficients for "Relative momentum," "Local information," and "Bush withdrawal" in Table A.31 in Appendix C.

TABLE 10.2 Projected Results of One-Day National Republican Primary Following Iowa Caucuses, 1980

		Bush Vote (Two-Candidate Race %)		
		Actual Results	National Primary	Difference
26 Feb	New Hampshire	31.4	31.4	—
4 Mar	Massachusetts	51.8 (B)	48.5	3.3
	Vermont	41.9	38.7	3.2
8 Mar	South Carolina	21.3	38.6	−17.3
11 Mar	Alabama	27.1	39.4	−12.3
	Florida	35.0	48.4	−13.5
	Georgia	14.7	23.1	−8.4
18 Mar	Illinois	18.5	21.7	−3.1
25 Mar	Connecticut	53.2 (B)	68.1 (B)	−14.8
1 Apr	Kansas	16.7	25.8	−9.1
	Wisconsin	43.1	56.7 (B)	−13.7
5 Apr	Louisiana	20.1	29.4	−9.3
22 Apr	Pennsylvania	54.3 (B)	65.5 (B)	−11.2
3 May	Texas	48.2	66.3 (B)	−18.1
6 May	Indiana	18.2	29.9	−11.7
	North Carolina	24.4	38.2	−13.8
	Tennessee	19.6	31.9	−12.3
13 May	Maryland	45.9	56.3 (B)	−10.4
	Nebraska	16.8	23.4	−6.6
20 May	Michigan	64.4 (B)	77.7 (B)	−13.3
	Oregon	38.9	55.0 (B)	−16.1
27 May	Idaho	4.6	31.5	−26.9
	Kentucky	8.0	45.4	−37.4
	Nevada	7.3	42.7	−35.4
3 Jun	California	5.8	26.2	−20.4
	Montana	10.0	39.2	−29.2
	New Jersey	17.4	54.9 (B)	−37.6
	New Mexico	13.5	47.4	−33.9
	Ohio	19.2	57.9 (B)	−38.7
	Rhode Island	20.5	60.0 (B)	−39.4
	South Dakota	4.9	22.9	−18.0
	West Virginia	14.4	49.4	−35.0
AVERAGES		26.0	43.5	−17.5

Note: (B) indicates actual or projected Bush victory.

emergence into public prominence.[4] Thus, the comparison is between a simulated situation in which Bush's momentum coming out of Iowa would have had a direct and relatively immediate impact on every primary state and the actual situation in which that momentum was quickly diluted by Reagan's victories in New Hampshire and elsewhere.

[4] My analysis of the 1980 Republican campaign, and thus the projections shown

Therefore, it is not surprising that Bush would have fared better in the simulated one-day primary. Bush was not the victim of the sort of negative momentum that seemed to operate in the 1980 Democratic campaign. Rather, his own short-lived momentum based on the early win in Iowa was overwhelmed by Reagan's more durable momentum.

The state-by-state projections in Table 10.2 suggest that Bush was still benefiting slightly from momentum in the week after New Hampshire, and indeed that momentum was decisive in his close victory in the Massachusetts primary. But Reagan's growing dominance in subsequent weeks swung the dynamics of the campaign in his direction, eventually costing Bush potential primary victories in seven states, including Texas, New Jersey, and Ohio. Not surprisingly, Bush's concession reduced even further his already low vote shares in the later primaries. My calculations suggest that in the eleven primaries held after his formal withdrawal Bush's share of the two-candidate vote averaged about fifteen percentage points less than it would have had he remained an active candidate. Potential Bush supporters either accepted the inevitable and voted for Reagan, or, perhaps more likely, they simply did not bother to vote at all. Although even their support would not have put Bush within striking distance of Reagan in any of the eleven affected states, it would have transformed the last two weeks of the primary season from a triumphal march into a somewhat more competitive race.

The role of momentum in Reagan's string of primary victories is also apparent in Figure 10.3, which shows the difference between Reagan's actual average support in each week of the primary season and his projected support in a one-day national primary. Although there are ups and downs, the overall trend is one of increasing Reagan gains from week to week. Between late March and late May these gains amounted, on average, to between

---

in Table 10.2, begin with the New Hampshire primary. I have omitted the Iowa caucuses from the analysis because I lack a reliable estimate of the level of public uncertainty about Bush before Iowa; the first wave of the 1980 NES survey began the week after Bush's Iowa victory. The analysis of primary voting appears relatively insensitive to this omission. For example, if Iowa was included in the analysis by simply extrapolating back from observed uncertainty about Bush in later weeks of the campaign, the parameter estimates indicating the effects of various factors on support for Reagan would differ by an average of about 7 percent for static political factors and about 18 percent for dynamic factors. However, the projected results of a one-day primary held at the time of the Iowa caucuses would differ significantly with different assumptions about how much prospective voters knew about Bush before his big upset in Iowa.

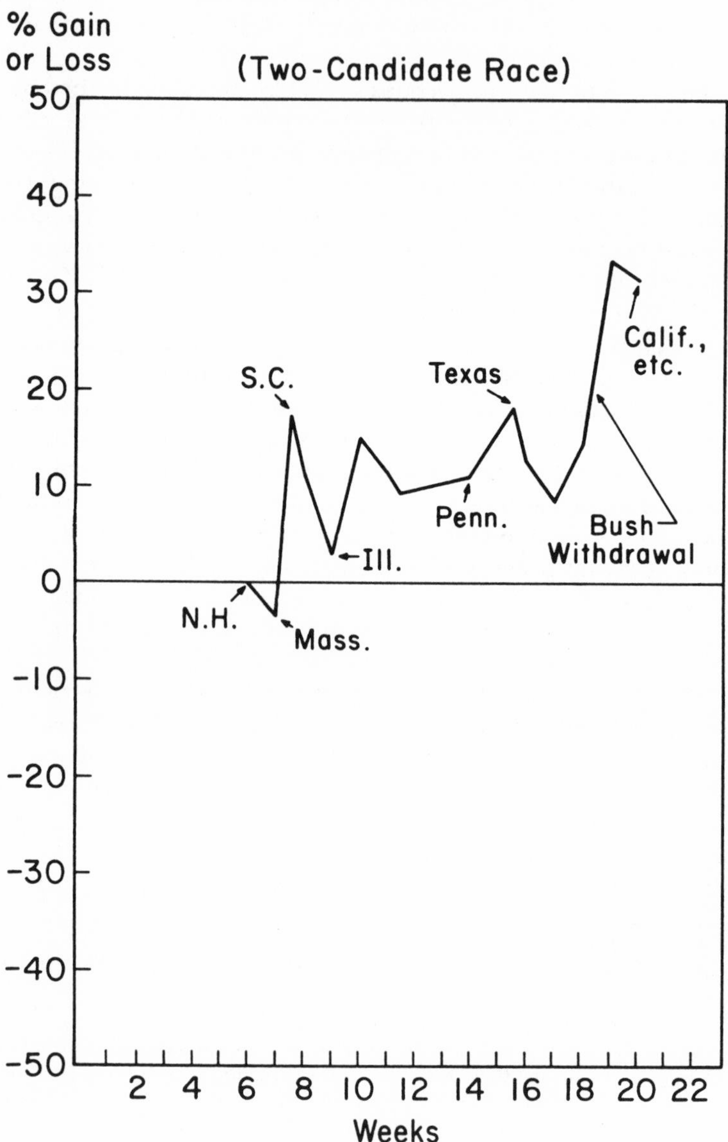

FIGURE 10.3 Effect of Momentum on Reagan's Weekly Performance, 1980 Republican Primaries.

10 and 15 percent of the two-candidate vote. This bonus due to momentum, combined with Reagan's underlying political support among Republican primary voters, was more than sufficient to assure his nomination. Bush's withdrawal from the race, which more than doubled the difference between Reagan's actual support in the last two weeks of the primary season and the support he might have expected in a one-day national primary, was merely icing on the cake.

The estimated results of the 1980 Republican primaries, based on my statistical analysis of all the political and dynamic factors considered in this section, are compared with the actual primary results in Table 10.3. The correspondence between actual and estimated results is a little less close for this campaign than for most of the other campaigns analyzed in this book; the average error in each state is almost five percentage points. Much of this average error results from especially serious misses in two states—Wisconsin (in which Reagan's vote share is overestimated by almost eighteen percentage points) and Indiana (where it is underestimated by almost fifteen percentage points). The average error for the other thirty primaries is slightly less than four percentage points, a degree of statistical fit consistent with that achieved for other recent campaigns. Why the Wisconsin and Indiana results are so poorly accounted for by the statistical analysis is an open question.[5]

10.2 Hart versus Mondale

Some of the aura of "inevitability" surrounding Walter Mondale's campaign for the 1984 Democratic nomination has no doubt faded from memory in the light of subsequent events. A useful bit of perspective may be provided by recalling the lead paragraph of Hedrick Smith's *New York Times* campaign story on the morning of the 1984 New Hampshire primary: "With Senator John Glenn continuing to fade and no new challenger emerging strongly, Walter F. Mondale now holds the most commanding lead ever re-

[5] One obvious source of error is the index of conservatism introduced in Chapter 9 as a measure of each state's Republican party ideology. To account for the residuals in Table 10.3, conservatism would have to be badly overestimated in Wisconsin and badly underestimated in Indiana by the index scores in Table 9.2. While such errors are possible, they seem unlikely, especially since no corresponding evidence for them appears in the residuals from the 1976 Republican analysis. Reagan's vote share in 1976 was underestimated by 1.6 percentage points in Wisconsin and overestimated by 0.6 percentage points in Indiana.

TABLE 10.3 Actual and Estimated Results of Republican Primaries, 1980

	Reagan Vote (Two-Candidate Race %)		
	Actual	Estimated	Difference
Indiana	81.8	67.1	+14.6
Illinois	81.5	73.4	+8.1
Georgia	85.3	78.7	+6.6
Louisiana	79.9	73.6	+6.3
Connecticut	46.8	41.2	+5.6
Tennessee	80.4	75.2	+5.2
Rhode Island	79.5	75.0	+4.4
Alabama	72.9	69.9	+3.3
Nebraska	83.2	80.3	+2.9
South Dakota	95.1	92.4	+2.7
New Jersey	82.6	80.1	+2.6
Massachusetts	48.2	45.9	+2.2
Oregon	61.1	59.2	+1.9
Kansas	83.3	82.7	+0.6
Idaho	95.4	94.8	+0.6
Nevada	92.7	92.2	+0.5
New Hampshire	68.6	68.4	+0.2
West Virginia	85.6	86.0	−0.4
Kentucky	92.0	93.0	−1.0
California	94.2	95.4	−1.2
Montana	90.0	91.4	−1.4
South Carolina	78.7	80.4	−1.7
New Mexico	86.5	89.3	−2.8
Ohio	80.8	85.0	−4.1
Michigan	35.6	41.1	−5.5
Texas	51.8	57.4	−5.6
Vermont	58.1	63.9	−5.8
North Carolina	75.6	81.7	−6.1
Maryland	54.1	62.7	−8.6
Pennsylvania	45.7	55.3	−9.6
Florida	65.0	75.6	−10.5
Wisconsin	56.9	74.6	−17.7

Notes: Average error = 4.7 percent. Serial correlation of average weekly residuals = −0.271.

corded this early in a Presidential nomination campaign by a non-incumbent, according to the latest New York Times/CBS News Poll." By the time the primary season began, Mondale was not only leading by a commanding margin in the polls, but he had also secured the support of the AFL-CIO—the first time the union had ever made a formal endorsement in a nominating campaign. He had organized support from the women's movement, from the teachers' union, and from other powerful interest groups. And he had the backing of most important Democratic party officials, including the vast majority of the "super delegates" with reserved seats at the Democratic convention.[6] Mondale's strategy, as Orren put it (1985: 57), would be to "act as a staunchly partisan Democrat, build a traditional coalition, and seize the nomination by force of organization."

Mondale's strategy happened to be an accurate reflection of his own preexisting political identity as a New Deal loyalist, a committed liberal, and a party insider; four years as Jimmy Carter's vice president did little to alter that identity, except to saddle Mondale with some of Carter's unpopularity. Mondale's strategy was also well suited to the circumstances of the 1984 campaign. With Ted Kennedy out of the running, Mondale was the natural representative of the party's traditional liberal elements. His major active challenger, John Glenn, oriented his campaign not toward traditional Democratic interests but toward a "constituency of the whole." Glenn emphasized popular appeal over party organization, the future over the past, and centrism over liberalism. Jesse Jackson competed with Mondale for the black vote, but he was not widely viewed as a serious contender outside his own "Rainbow Coalition." Gary Hart and Alan Cranston offered liberal voters additional alternatives to Mondale, but both aimed their appeals at somewhat different segments of the liberal Democratic audience. Hart offered a campaign of "new ideas" and "new leadership" aimed at the liberals of the 1960s and 1970s rather than at liberals raised in the party's New Deal tradition, and Cranston cast himself almost entirely as a candidate of the nuclear freeze movement.

Mondale's "inside" strategy worked to perfection in Iowa, where he won with 48.9 percent of the caucus vote. But Hart, far behind

[6] Beginning with the 1984 campaign, party rules called for about 15 percent of the party's convention seats to be reserved for Democratic congressmen chosen by their colleagues and not formally committed to any candidate. In 1984 these "super delegates" were selected before the beginning of the public primary and caucus season, and most supported Mondale.

with 16.5 percent, was close enough to garner a burst of media coverage as the interesting newcomer who had performed "better than expected." In the subsequent week, in New Hampshire, Hart succeeded in parlaying his momentum into a convincing upset victory. Hedrick Smith's story in the next morning's *New York Times* was headlined "The Campaign Reshaped." *Newsweek* proclaimed "Hart's Charge," with the blue-eyed candidate smiling from the cover. Suddenly it had become a two-man race, and Mondale was the second man.

Hart won again the following week in Vermont with an astounding 70 percent of the primary vote to Mondale's 20 percent. As the candidates approached the next week's crucial Super Tuesday primaries, Hart was riding high, and, as we saw in Chapter 3, he was beginning to attract the front-runner's share of scrutiny from the media and from his opponents. Meanwhile, a stunned Mondale considered pulling out of the race, but he decided instead to redouble his efforts in Alabama and Georgia in hopes of staving off Hart's knockout blow. Mondale did succeed in holding off Hart, but only barely. He lost in Florida, Massachusetts, and Rhode Island but managed to win in Alabama and Georgia (in the latter instance by only three percentage points). Although it was not pretty, by media standards it was good enough to count as a draw. Mondale had survived to fight in more congenial states in the subsequent month—especially Illinois, New York, and Pennsylvania—and eventually won ten primaries and garnered a bare plurality of the total primary vote. The state-by-state results for the entire primary season are shown in Table 10.4.

The major candidates' objective probabilities of winning the nomination at each stage in the 1984 campaign are shown in Figure 10.4. What is most striking about these probabilities is the magnitude of Mondale's lead in the delegate race, even in his dark period after Hart's New Hampshire upset. Given his early cushion of "super delegates," Mondale's objective probability of winning the nomination never dropped below 60 percent, and after his rebound began in earnest in Illinois a few weeks later he dominated the remainder of the delegate-hunting season.[7]

[7] Mondale's delegate lead, and hence his objective probability of nomination, was bolstered by Hart's failure to file full delegate slates in several states. Intent on surviving the early contests in Iowa and New Hampshire, the Hart organization in January 1984 failed to file full slates for March and April primaries in Florida, Illinois, and Pennsylvania. As a result, Hart's success in attracting primary votes in

Table 10.4 Democratic Primary Results, 1984

		Popular vote (%)		
		Mondale	Hart	Jackson
28 Feb	New Hampshire	27.9	37.3	5.3
6 Mar	Vermont	20.0	70.0	7.8
13 Mar	Alabama	34.6	20.7	19.6
	Florida	32.1	40.0	12.4
	Georgia	30.5	27.3	21.0
	Massachusetts	25.5	39.0	5.0
	Rhode Island	34.4	45.0	8.7
20 Mar	Illinois	40.5	35.2	21.0
27 Mar	Connecticut	29.1	52.6	12.0
3 Apr	New York	44.8	27.4	25.6
	Wisconsin	41.1	44.4	9.9
10 Apr	Pennsylvania	45.1	33.3	16.0
1 May	D.C.	25.6	7.1	67.3
	Tennessee	41.0	29.1	25.3
5 May	Louisiana	22.3	25.0	42.9
8 May	Indiana	40.9	41.8	13.7
	Maryland	42.5	24.3	25.5
	North Carolina	35.6	30.2	25.4
	Ohio	40.3	42.1	16.4
15 May	Nebraska	26.6	58.2	9.1
	Oregon	27.3	58.9	9.5
22 May	Idaho	30.1	58.0	5.7
5 Jun	California	37.4	41.2	19.6
	New Jersey	45.1	29.5	23.6
	New Mexico	36.2	46.5	11.9
	South Dakota	38.5	51.2	5.2
	West Virginia	53.7	37.1	6.7

Sources: Congressional Quarterly Weekly Report; Orren (1985).

Conversely, Hart's objective probability of being nominated, based on the weekly delegate count, never reached 30 percent. This was in marked contrast to his subjective probability as estimated by the public, shown in Figure 10.5, which peaked at almost 50 percent after New Hampshire and remained at about 25 percent through the second half of the primary season. The contrast reflects Hart's continued strong competition in the primaries; indeed, he received about as many votes as Mondale in the primary season as a whole. His only problem was that Mondale had already accumulated a sufficient delegate margin to make Hart's showing in the later primaries essentially irrelevant.

those states, especially in Florida on Super Tuesday, was not fully reflected in the delegate tallies (Kamarck 1986: 189–90).

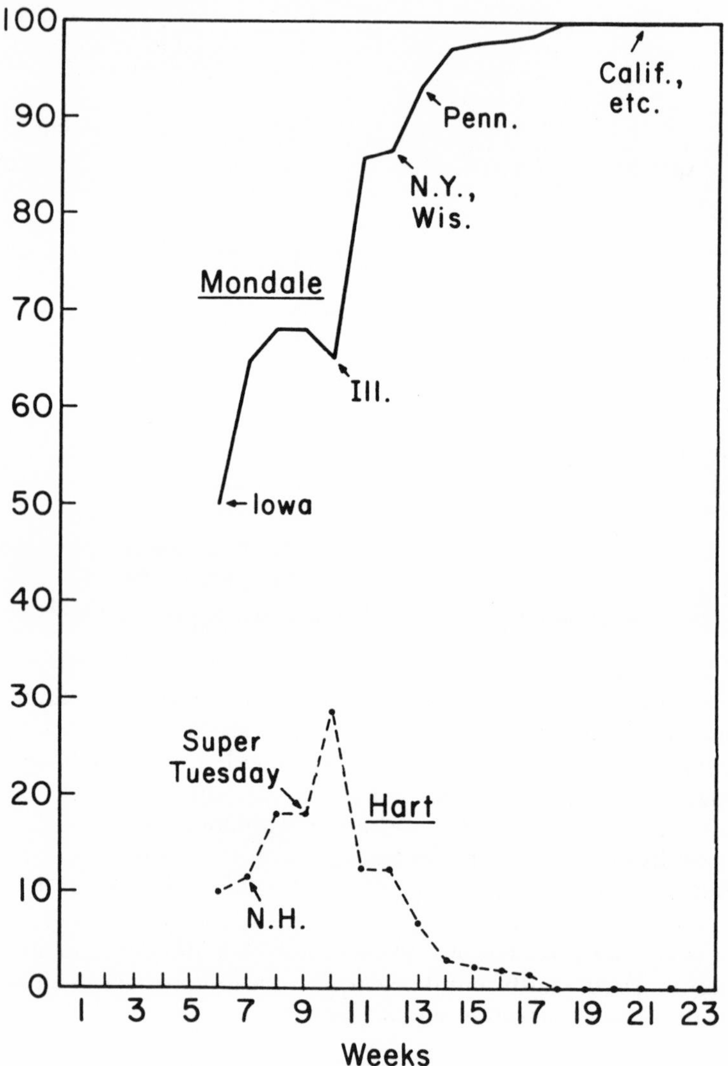

FIGURE 10.4 "Objective" Probabilities of Nomination, Democrats, 1984.

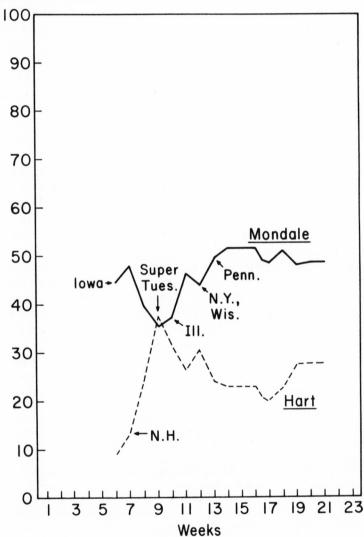

FIGURE 10.5 Estimated Subjective Probabilities of Nomination, Democrats, 1984.

The political bases of Mondale's primary support were, for the most part, consistent with his identity as a traditional New Deal Democrat.[8] First, support for Mondale was positively related to the proportion of blacks in each primary state.[9] Controling for other factors, Mondale's performance in states with very few blacks (New Hampshire, Vermont, and several western states) was almost fifteen percentage points worse than his performance in states with large numbers of blacks (the states of the deep South) and more than thirty percentage points worse than in the District of Columbia (with a black population of more than 70 percent).[10] Support for Mondale also varied with urbanization; other things being equal, he did about sixteen percentage points better against Hart in the most heavily urbanized states (including the District of Columbia and New Jersey) than in the most rural states (Idaho, Vermont, and some of the Plains states).

However, Mondale did significantly worse than would otherwise be expected in states which were strongholds of John Anderson's independent candidacy in the 1980 general election. Anderson's support in 1980 was drawn from many of the same sources as Hart's in 1984—young people, professionals, those dissatisfied with both sides of the traditional liberal-conservative debate and eager for "new ideas." This emerging group has gone by various names. For Anderson it was the Volvo, Brie, and Doonesbury set; during Hart's campaign a new summary label gained wide currency—Yuppies. But the supporters and their political characteristics were similar in the two instances. Thus, it should be no surprise to find that Hart did particularly well in many of the same places where Anderson did. Still, the magnitude of the effect may be surprising. Holding constant other relevant factors, Hart's share of the two-candidate vote in the 1984 Democratic primaries varied by as much as forty-seven percentage points between the states most hospitable to Anderson in 1980 (all of New England)

[8] For another view of the role of political factors in determining the outcomes of the 1984 Democratic primaries, see Parent, Jillson, and Weber (1987). Their conclusions are essentially congruent with those reported here, although their analysis took no explicit account of dynamic forces in the primary campaign.

[9] The results of my statistical analysis relating Mondale's primary support in each state to various political and dynamic factors appear in Table A.32 in Appendix C.

[10] One other factor held constant in these comparisons is the share of each state's primary vote won by Jesse Jackson. Part of Mondale's apparent advantage in states with large concentrations of blacks was diluted by Jackson's success in appealing to black voters. Jackson's impact on Mondale's performance is discussed in more detail in Section 10.3.

and those where Anderson made little progress (most of the South).

Finally, the division of the primary vote between Mondale and Hart was systematically related to the ideological complexions of the various primary states. In view of the fact, noted in Chapter 5, that Mondale and Hart were perceived by the public to be almost identical in their overall ideological positions, it would be surprising to find a strong, consistent pattern of disproportional support for either candidate in the most liberal or the most conservative primary states. But a pattern quite similar to the one observed in both the 1976 and 1980 Democratic campaigns does appear. Hart in 1984, like Carter in the earlier campaigns, won his largest shares of the primary vote, other things being equal, in ideologically moderate states. His support trailed off both in the most conservative states and, to a somewhat greater degree, in the most liberal states. This pattern of support and the very similar pattern of support for Jimmy Carter in the 1980 campaign are illustrated in Figure 10.6.

In Section 10.3 I examine the combined effect of these underlying political factors on the Hart–Mondale race in each primary state. But first it may be helpful to provide a preliminary assessment of the role of dynamic forces in shaping voters' reactions to the candidates and the campaign. The analysis of survey data in Part II of this book suggested that expectations about the candidates' chances had a powerful impact on prospective voters' preferences in the contest between Hart and Mondale and that changing expectations from week to week of the primary season accounted for much of the corresponding change observable in the distribution of preferences. If the connections I have tried to draw between the behavior of survey respondents and primary voters are reasonable ones, we should also find a strong relationship between changing expectations and observable changes in primary outcomes from week to week.

In assessing the consistency of the individual- and aggregate-level data, however, it is important to remember the systematic differences between the two settings embodied in my analysis. In particular, the differences in information levels between survey respondents and actual primary voters at the same point in the primary season—differences illustrated in Figure 7.11—would lead us to predict that expectations would be less strongly related to preferences among primary voters than among rank-and-file party identifiers in the "national audience."

FIGURE 10.6 Ideology and Support for Hart in 1984 and Carter in 1980.

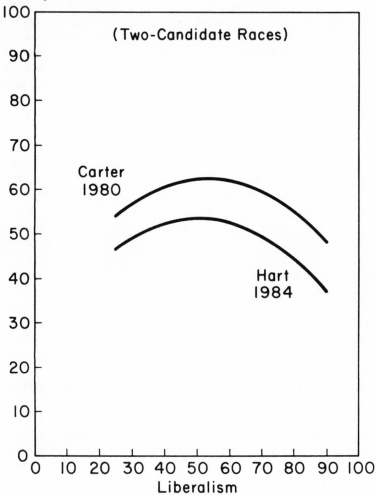

As it turns out, a comparison of the two relationships produces exactly the predicted pattern of differences. Once we account for those differences, the magnitude of the impact of expectations on preferences is remarkably similar among survey respondents and primary voters. In fact, the estimated magnitude of the impact of expectations on actual primary outcomes differs by only about 8 percent from the magnitude predicted on the basis of the analysis of survey data in Part II, given the differences in information levels between the two settings. This degree of consistency between the two very different analyses is encouraging indeed.[11]

The implications of this analysis for the impact of expectations on primary voting in the 1984 campaign are illustrated in Figure 10.7. It is clear from the figure that expectations had a very significant effect on the candidates' primary showings and that the nature of that effect itself varied significantly with changes in the electoral setting between the beginning and end of the 1984 primary season. At the beginning of the campaign, when Hart was a relatively unknown quantity and even Mondale was noticeably less familiar to the public than he would be later in the primary season, the impact of expectations on primary support was very strongly positive. Over much of the relevant range of expectations, an increase of five percentage points in Mondale's perceived chances, and a corresponding decrease of five percentage points in Hart's perceived chances, would have altered the candidates' shares of the two-candidate vote by ten percentage points or more. Alternatively, to take an example more in line with the actual experience of the 1984 campaign, a decrease in Mondale's perceived chances of the magnitude generated by Hart's New Hampshire upset, about eight and a half percentage points, appears from Fig-

[11] The comparison is embodied in the parameter estimate for "Relative momentum" in Table A.32. The meaning of the parameter estimate and its connection to the analysis of survey data in Part II are discussed more fully in Appendix C.6. A further comparison between the analysis of primary outcomes described in this chapter and the analysis of survey data described in Part II is available from the estimated effect in Table A.32 of "Relative risk aversion." Because the effect of risk aversion, like that of momentum, is keyed to the expected effect based on the analysis in Part II, the parameter estimate for risk aversion in Table A.32 reflects the consistency between the individual- and aggregate-level results. For risk aversion, the estimated effect on primary outcomes in Table A.32 matches the effect expected on the basis of the analysis of survey data in Part II to within 12 percent. As with the effect of momentum, this degree of consistency provides some reassurance that my analysis has successfully accounted for the important differences between the survey setting and the voting booth.

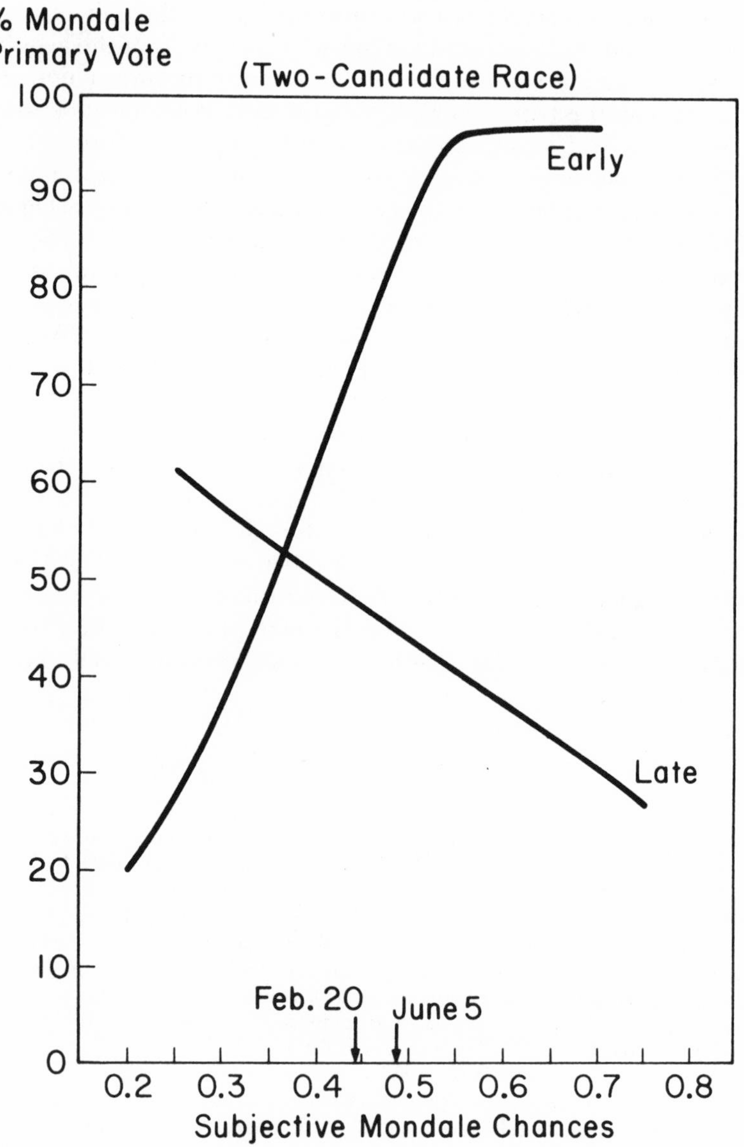

FIGURE 10.7 Expectations and Primary Voting, Democrats, 1984.

ure 10.7 to imply a decline of about twenty percentage points in Mondale's share of the two-candidate primary vote.

The apparent effect of expectations on primary voting at the end of the campaign is also significant, but significantly negative, as Figure 10.7 also makes clear. The pattern is one we have already seen in other recent campaigns. For sufficiently high levels of information—and both Mondale and Hart were quite familiar to the public by the end of the 1984 primary season—the effect of clinching the nomination was to reduce the prospective winner's primary support and increase the prospective loser's. This pattern in the primary voting data corresponds to a similar pattern in the survey data on respondents' preferences in the 1984 NES survey, shown in Figure 6.1. There, we saw that the proportion of the Democratic rank and file preferring Mondale as the party's nominee dipped noticeably at the end of the primary season and that the proportion preferring Hart increased noticeably—in spite (or rather, because) of the fact that perceptions of the candidates' relative chances were moving in the opposite direction.

In combination, the political and dynamic factors considered here account for most of the variation from state to state in actual primary outcomes during the 1984 campaign. A comparison of Mondale's actual share of the two-candidate vote in each state and the share estimated on the basis of my statistical analysis is presented in Table 10.5. The average error for the twenty-eight states included in the analysis is 4.3 percentage points. In only one state, Rhode Island, did Mondale's estimated share of the two-candidate vote differ from his actual share by more than 8.5 percentage points. These results suggest that the set of political and dynamic factors included in the analysis provide a reasonably good accounting for the actual results of the 1984 Democratic primaries.

10.3 How to Start a Brush Fire (And How to Stop One)

The parallel histories of the Bush and Hart campaigns—an early win against an established front-runner, a meteoric emergence as the only serious challenger to that front-runner, and a failure to sustain the resulting momentum long enough to win the nomination—suggest two important general questions about the workings of the modern nominating process. First, how does a candidate like Bush or Hart get started? And second, how does he get stopped? In this section I attempt to sketch some answers to those general questions.

TABLE 10.5 Actual and Estimated Results of Democratic Primaries, 1984

	Mondale Vote (Two-Candidate Race %)		
	Actual	Estimated	Difference
Rhode Island	43.3	33.3	+10.1
Tennessee	58.5	50.2	+8.3
West Virginia	59.1	51.2	+8.0
Maryland	63.6	56.6	+7.0
New Mexico	43.8	37.5	+6.3
New Jersey	60.5	54.3	+6.1
North Carolina	54.1	48.2	+5.9
South Dakota	42.9	39.9	+3.0
Iowa	74.8	71.8	+3.0
New York	62.0	59.9	+2.2
Massachusetts	39.5	39.0	+0.5
California	47.6	47.4	+0.2
D.C.	78.3	78.2	+0.1
Pennsylvania	57.5	57.6	−0.0
Idaho	34.2	34.3	−0.2
Alabama	62.6	63.2	−0.6
New Hampshire	42.8	44.4	−1.6
Georgia	52.8	55.3	−2.5
Illinois	53.5	56.9	−3.4
Vermont	22.2	25.7	−3.5
Florida	44.5	48.2	−3.7
Oregon	31.7	35.9	−4.2
Nebraska	31.4	35.9	−4.6
Connecticut	35.6	42.2	−6.6
Indiana	49.5	56.1	−6.7
Louisiana	47.1	54.7	−7.6
Ohio	48.9	56.5	−7.6
Wisconsin	48.1	56.5	−8.5

Notes: Average error = 4.3 percent. Serial correlation of average weekly residuals = −0.171.

One crucial ingredient in the making of a brush fire like Bush's or Hart's is pure, unadulterated luck. Of course, luck plays a role in every political campaign. But the institutional structure of the modern nominating process serves, in certain respects, to emphasize the role of chance factors in determining the outcome of the process. Most obviously, different arbitrary sequences of state primaries can produce very different results.[12]

[12] This is not to suggest that the candidates themselves have no impact on the

Hart's great good fortune in this respect is evident in Table 10.6, which shows levels of underlying political support for Mondale in each of the Democratic primary states in 1984. The most striking thing in the table is that Mondale's two worst states (or, from the opposite perspective, Hart's two best) were the very first two primary states—New Hampshire and Vermont. These states provided fertile ground for a Hart bandwagon; neither is heavily urbanized, each is less than 1 percent black, and both were notable strongholds of Anderson's independent candidacy in 1980.[13] To

TABLE 10.6 Underlying Mondale Support in Democratic Primary States, 1984

	Mondale Support (Two-Candidate Race %)
D.C.	89.3
Maryland	80.2
Alabama	79.7
New Jersey	78.4
West Virginia	77.4
New York	77.1
Tennessee	76.5
Pennsylvania	74.0
North Carolina	73.2
Georgia	72.4
Illinois	69.8
Indiana	69.4
Ohio	68.9
California	68.3
Louisiana	67.5
Iowa	66.8
Wisconsin	65.6
Florida	65.4
New Mexico	64.9
Rhode Island	64.3
South Dakota	64.1
Massachusetts	60.6
Idaho	54.5
Oregon	53.3
Nebraska	52.9
Connecticut	52.3
New Hampshire	47.1
Vermont	32.6

primary calendar. Efforts to rearrange the ordering of primary states for the political benefit of one or another contender have become standard gambits in the preseason maneuvering of the competing candidates' camps. My point is that many important features of the calendar, such as the primacy of Iowa and New Hampshire, are historical accidents with significant and arbitrary political consequences.

[13] The underlying levels of support shown in Table 10.6 also include support

have precisely these two primaries scheduled in successive weeks, with no other contests to distract the attention of the press and the public, was a stroke of good luck. To have them scheduled in the first two weeks following Hart's emergence in Iowa, in the most intensive period of media coverage and public interest, with Hart himself a virtually blank slate on which a national audience could project its own picture of an ideal candidate, was a stroke of luck almost too good to be true.

Ironically, much of Hart's good luck flowed from the successful efforts of Walter Mondale to manipulate the 1984 primary calendar. Mondale's partisans in the Democratic party hierarchy supported exemptions from the party's "window rule" to allow Iowa and New Hampshire to maintain their first-in-the-nation status. Moreover, Mondale's strategists made a successful attempt to minimize the time between these early contests and the key Super Tuesday primaries in the mistaken belief that a week or two would be insufficient time for any successful challenger to exploit the momentum generated by better-than-expected showings in the earliest public tests of support; but, of course, Hart's momentum peaked within a week or ten days after his New Hampshire upset. Finally, Mondale's supporters, worried about the possibility of losing badly in the early southern primaries, succeeded in adding Massachusetts and Rhode Island to the Super Tuesday calendar; in fact, Hart won easily in Massachusetts and Rhode Island, and Mondale's victories in the South saved his campaign from extinction.[14]

---

unaccounted for by factors explicitly included in my analysis. In New Hampshire and Vermont this residual support may include some actually due to momentum coming out of Iowa but not captured by the momentum variables in my analysis. However, Hart's residual support amounted to only 1.6 percent of the two-candidate vote in New Hampshire and 3.5 percent in Vermont. Even without this residual support, the political characteristics of these two states would easily have made them the two most favorable states for Hart's campaign.

[14] A firsthand account of the Mondale camp's efforts to shape the primary calendar for their candidate's benefit was provided by Kamarck (1986). "Once Ted Kennedy had dropped out of the nomination race in late 1982," Kamarck wrote (1986: 63–64), "it was clear that Mondale would have a substantial financial and organizational lead over his rivals and that 'frontloading' the calendar would work to his advantage. The frontloading theory rested on the twin assumptions that Mondale would win Iowa and New Hampshire and that no other candidate would have the time to muster enough resources to run in many contests simultaneously. Both assumptions turned out to be wrong. Mondale lost the New Hampshire primary and found out that momentum was enough of a resource in and of itself to obviate the need for other more standard resources such as money and organiza-

The results of Mondale's cleverness and Hart's good luck are dramatically clear in Figure 10.8, which shows how Hart's actual performance in the 1984 Democratic primaries differed from his projected performance in a one-day national primary conducted at the time of the Iowa caucuses, before his real emergence. It appears from the comparison that Hart gained almost thirty percentage points in three weeks due to the dynamic effects of his second-place finish in Iowa and his primary victories in New Hampshire and Vermont. This advantage declined somewhat in the next seven weeks—the middle portion of the primary season corresponding to Mondale's gradual comeback—before rebounding again in the last month of the primary season.

A state-by-state comparison of actual and projected results, shown in Table 10.7, highlights the importance of momentum in Hart's campaign. In the static one-day primary Hart would, it appears, have averaged about 25 percent of the two-candidate vote, almost exactly half of his actual average support. And he would have won not fifteen primaries, but one. The brush fire would never have begun.

Hart was lucky in having an early primary calendar well suited to his own political identity—and in the fact that the sequential, dynamic nature of the primary process allowed him to capitalize on his early successes in later primaries. But if a congenial primary calendar is the first ingredient for a successful brush fire, a congenial field of candidates is the second. Hart was lucky in sharing the field not only with Mondale, but also with a third force who proved to be a persistent thorn in what would otherwise have been one of Mondale's least vulnerable sides. That third force was Jesse Jackson.

Jackson competed throughout the 1984 primary season, drawing 18 percent of the vote on average and performing especially well in states with significant black populations.[15] Given his apparent appeal to minority voters it is not surprising that Jackson drew votes disproportionately from Mondale, who (as we saw in Sections 5.1 and 10.2) was viewed significantly more favorably than Hart by blacks. In states where Jackson did especially well, he did so pri-

---

tion." On the basis of her own and others' experiences, Kamarck concluded that "[c]alculations on the part of presidential candidates as to the most desirable sequence of contests are as often wrong as they are right" (1986: 69).

[15] The correlation between support for Jackson and the percentage of blacks in each primary state was 0.94.

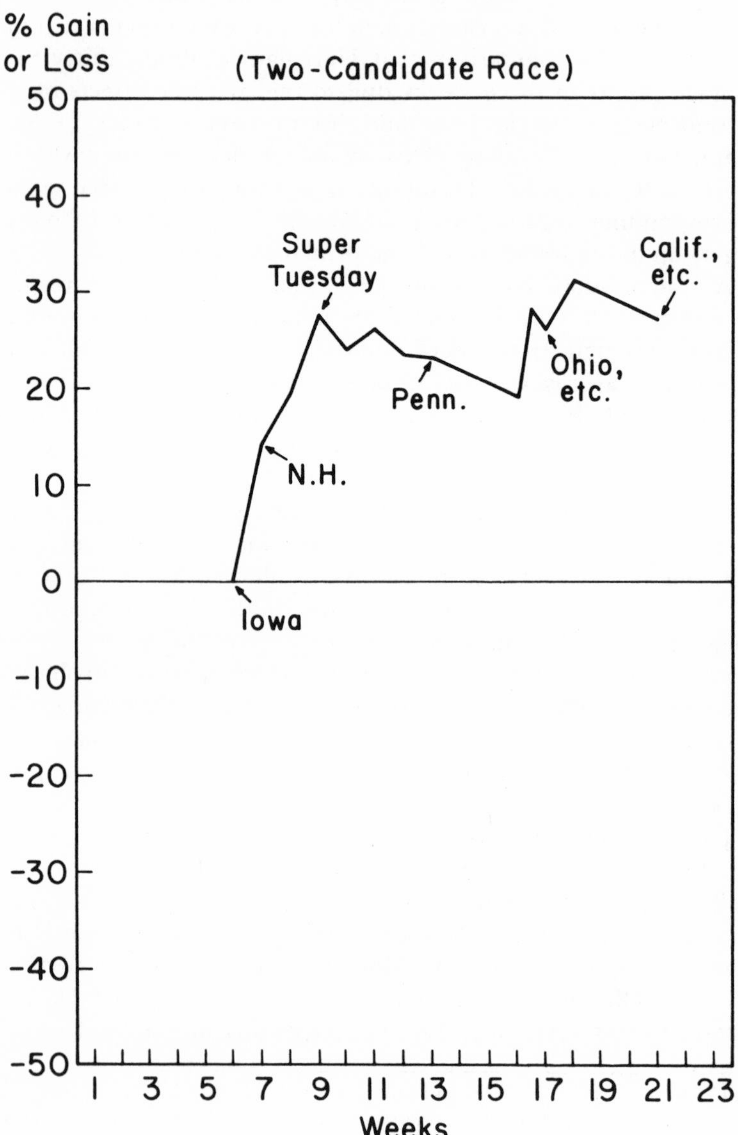

FIGURE 10.8 Effect of Momentum on Hart's Weekly Performance, 1984 Democratic Primaries.

TABLE 10.7 Projected Results of One-Day National Democratic Primary, 1984

		Hart Vote (Two-Candidate Race %)		
		Actual Results	National Primary	Difference
20 Feb	Iowa caucuses	25.2	25.2	—
28 Feb	New Hampshire	57.2 (H)	43.3	14.0
6 Mar	Vermont	77.8 (H)	58.4 (H)	19.4
13 Mar	Alabama	37.4	14.7	22.7
	Florida	55.5 (H)	26.4	29.0
	Georgia	47.2	20.5	26.7
	Massachusetts	60.5 (H)	30.6	29.9
	Rhode Island	56.7 (H)	27.4	29.3
20 Mar	Illinois	46.5	22.7	23.8
27 Mar	Connecticut	64.4 (H)	38.3	26.1
3 Apr	New York	38.0	16.8	21.2
	Wisconsin	51.9 (H)	26.2	25.7
10 Apr	Pennsylvania	42.5	19.3	23.2
1 May	D.C.	21.7	7.6	14.2
	Tennessee	41.5	17.3	24.2
5 May	Louisiana	52.9 (H)	24.6	28.2
8 May	Indiana	50.5 (H)	23.0	27.5
	Maryland	36.4	14.3	22.0
	North Carolina	45.9	19.9	26.0
	Ohio	51.1 (H)	23.4	27.7
15 May	Nebraska	68.6 (H)	37.6	31.0
	Oregon	68.3 (H)	37.3	31.0
22 May	Idaho	65.8 (H)	36.2	29.7
3 Jun	California	52.4 (H)	24.0	28.5
	New Jersey	39.5	15.8	23.8
	New Mexico	56.2 (H)	26.9	29.4
	South Dakota	57.1 (H)	27.6	29.5
	West Virginia	40.9	16.5	24.4
AVERAGES		50.3	25.8	24.6

Note: (H) indicates actual or projected Hart victory.

marily at Mondale's expense, as evidenced by the negative effect of Jackson's vote on Mondale's share against Hart.

An estimate of Jackson's effect on the Hart–Mondale race is shown in Table 10.8, which compares Mondale's actual share of the two-way vote in each primary state with an estimate of what his share would have been with Jackson out of the race.[16] On average,

[16] The simulated Mondale vote was obtained by subtracting the effect of Jackson's campaign—in effect, setting Jackson's share of the primary vote in each state to zero. This procedure probably produces an underestimate of Jackson's true effect on the campaign since it takes no account of the dynamic implications of Mondale's resulting gain in each primary on the outcomes of subsequent primaries.

TABLE 10.8 Effect of Jackson's Campaign on Mondale–Hart Race, Democratic Primaries, 1984

	Mondale Vote (Two-Candidate Race %)		
(Jackson %)	Actual	Without Jackson	Difference
D.C. (67.3)	78.3	88.0	−9.7
Louisiana (42.9)	47.1 (H)	58.3	−11.2
New York (25.6)	62.0	68.1	−6.1
Maryland (25.5)	63.6	69.6	−5.9
North Carolina (25.4)	54.1	60.6	−6.5
Tennessee (25.3)	58.5	64.8	−6.3
New Jersey (23.6)	60.5	66.2	−5.7
Georgia (21.0)	52.8	58.2	−5.4
Illinois (21.0)	53.5	58.9	−5.4
California (19.6)	47.6 (H)	52.7	−5.1
Alabama (19.6)	62.6	67.3	−4.7
Ohio (16.4)	48.9 (H)	53.2	−4.3
Pennsylvania (16.0)	57.5	61.6	−4.0
Indiana (13.7)	49.5 (H)	53.0	−3.6
Florida (12.4)	44.5 (H)	47.8 (H)	−3.2
Connecticut (12.0)	35.6 (H)	38.6 (H)	−2.9
New Mexico (11.9)	43.8 (H)	46.9 (H)	−3.1
Wisconsin (9.9)	48.1 (H)	50.7	−2.6
Oregon (9.5)	31.7 (H)	33.9 (H)	−2.2
Nebraska (9.1)	31.4 (H)	33.5 (H)	−2.1
Rhode Island (8.7)	43.3 (H)	45.6 (H)	−2.3
Vermont (7.8)	22.2 (H)	23.7 (H)	−1.4
West Virginia (6.7)	59.1	60.8	−1.7
Idaho (5.7)	34.2 (H)	35.5 (H)	−1.4
New Hampshire (5.3)	42.8 (H)	44.2 (H)	−1.4
South Dakota (5.2)	42.9 (H)	44.3 (H)	−1.3
Massachusetts (5.0)	39.5 (H)	40.8 (H)	−1.3
Iowa caucuses (1.5)	74.8	75.1	−0.3
AVERAGES	49.7	53.7	−4.0

Note: (H) indicates actual or projected Hart victory.

it appears that Jackson cost Mondale about 4 percent of the primary vote, but in states where Jackson did particularly well the effect was correspondingly greater. In five states—Wisconsin, Louisiana, Indiana, Ohio, and California—Jackson apparently drew enough votes from Mondale to cost him primary victories. Had Jackson not been in the race, Hart would have won eleven primaries instead of the sixteen he actually did win, trailing Mondale by more than a million votes (more than twice the actual margin of 430,000). Thus, Mondale would have been left as the clear winner for the primary season as a whole—even without his super delegates and in spite of Hart's momentum.

The 1980 Republican primary season also had a third force in the person of John Anderson. Anderson's emergence in March was one of the biggest stories of the primary season, and his campaign was received with sufficient public enthusiasm to propel him into the general election as an independent alternative to the major parties' candidates. But Anderson's importance in the 1980 Republican primary season was no match for Jackson's in 1984, in spite of the fact that his presence did affect the division of support between the two major candidates. For one thing, Anderson dropped out of the primary campaign at the beginning of April to contemplate his independent candidacy in the general election. Then too, Anderson's support came not at the expense of the front-runner, as did Jackson's, but at the expense of challenger George Bush. And finally, given these facts, the 1980 Republican race simply never became sufficiently close fought for the "Anderson difference" to have any real impact.

These points are illustrated in Table 10.9, which shows the apparent effect of Anderson's campaign on the 1980 Republican primary outcomes. It appears from the table that Anderson drained a little more than 5 percent of the two-candidate vote from Bush during the period of Anderson's own active candidacy and about half that much over the primary season as a whole. Had he remained an active candidate, his effect, measured in percentage terms, might have rivaled Jackson's in 1984. But even then he would have made no real difference in the outcome of the 1980 campaign, except to make Reagan's dominance a little more clear-cut than it already was. Had Anderson not run at all, Bush might have won two more early primaries, in Vermont and Wisconsin. But he would still have been the loser in twenty-eight of the thirty-four primaries—twenty-three by margins of two-to-one or more. To this extent Reagan truly was what his opponents feared—an immovable object of his party's respect and affection.

What lessons should we draw from Reagan's success? In a perceptive analysis of the 1980 election, Jeff Greenfield attributed that success to the importance of what he called "the real campaign"—roughly, what I have been referring to as political predispositions or underlying political support.

> George Bush did not win the Republican Presidential nomination. And at least part of the explanation for this outcome lies in

TABLE 10.9 Effect of Anderson's Campaign on Reagan–Bush Race, Republican Primaries, 1980

	Reagan Vote (Two-Candidate Race %)		
(Anderson %)	Actual	Without Anderson	Difference
Illinois (36.7)	81.5	72.7	+8.8
Massachusetts (30.7)	48.2 (B)	37.9 (B)	+10.3
Vermont (29.0)	58.1	48.2 (B)	+9.9
Wisconsin (27.4)	56.9	47.6 (B)	+9.4
Connecticut (22.1)	46.8 (B)	39.3 (B)	+7.4
Kansas (18.2)	83.3	79.6	+3.8
New Mexico (12.1)	86.5	84.5	+2.1
Oregon (10.1)	61.1	57.8	+3.3
Indiana (9.9)	81.8	79.7	+2.1
New Hampshire (9.8)	68.6	65.6	+3.0
Maryland (9.7)	54.1	50.8	+3.3
Idaho (9.7)	95.4	94.8	+0.6
Florida (9.2)	65.0	62.1	+2.9
Georgia (8.4)	85.3	83.8	+1.5
Michigan (8.2)	35.6 (B)	33.1 (B)	+2.5
South Dakota (6.3)	95.1	94.7	+0.4
Nebraska (5.8)	83.2	82.1	+1.1
Kentucky (5.1)	92.0	91.4	+0.5
North Carolina (5.1)	75.6	74.3	+1.3
Tennessee (4.5)	80.4	79.4	+1.0
Pennsylvania (2.1)	45.7 (B)	45.0 (B)	+0.7
Alabama	72.9	72.9	0
California	94.2	94.2	0
Louisiana	79.9	79.9	0
Montana	90.0	90.0	0
Nevada	92.7	92.7	0
New Jersey	82.6	82.6	0
Ohio	80.8	80.8	0
Rhode Island	79.5	79.5	0
South Carolina	78.7	78.7	0
Texas	51.8	51.8	0
West Virginia	85.6	85.6	0
AVERAGES	74.0	71.7	+2.3

Notes: (B) indicates actual or projected Bush victory. During Anderson's active campaign, his average effect on Reagan's percentage of the two-candidate vote was 5.2 percent.

a simple fact of modern campaign life: the politics of momentum is a highly incomplete account of how Presidential politics works. It is an accurate account of a pattern that emerges with some frequency in an age of mass-media politics; but that pattern is by no means dominant, and is fully capable of being over-

> whelmed by other, more enduring political patterns. To put it most simply: there was never any reason to vote for George Bush for President. In premising his campaign on the factor of momentum, George Bush stripped his effort of any substantive or ideological rationale; and a campaign lacking such a rationale is almost impossible to sustain against a candidate who has labored long and hard to build a *political*, as opposed to a *strategic* case for his candidacy; which is what Ronald Reagan had been doing within the Republican Party for sixteen years. (Greenfield 1982. 42)

My analysis is entirely consistent with Greenfield's in suggesting that the impact of momentum in presidential nominating politics is a contingent impact; it greatly depends upon a particular set of political circumstances—a relatively unknown challenger, a newsworthy early surprise, a favorable primary calendar. It is clear from the cases examined in this chapter that a front-runner's substantive political appeal may overwhelm the impact of momentum, as it did for Reagan against Bush and for Mondale against Hart. But it should also be clear that political substance need not always triumph over dynamics. Inevitability is often a product of selective retrospection.

In spite of their early images of invulnerability, and their very genuine and formidable political resources, both Reagan and Mondale were sorely tested by the dynamics of the primary season—and very nearly found wanting. It is hard to believe that either, at the nadir of his fortunes, would have shared Greenfield's faith that it is "almost impossible to sustain" a campaign of momentum against a campaign of ideology, organization, and political experience. Had Reagan been a bit less sharp in a heated New Hampshire debate, had Hart had a few more days to campaign in the South before Super Tuesday, had Mondale been a bit less surefooted in negotiating the thicket of intraparty politics in Illinois, things might easily have turned out very differently. Perhaps next time they will.

PART IV

The Import of Momentum

CHAPTER ELEVEN

The Primary Season as "Caucus-Race"

> "What *is* a Caucus-race?" said Alice; not that she much wanted to know, but the Dodo had paused as if it thought that *somebody* ought to speak, and no one else seemed inclined to say anything.
>
> "Why," said the Dodo, "the best way to explain it is to do it." (And, as you might like to try the thing yourself, some winter day, I will tell you how the Dodo managed it.)
>
> First it marked out a race-course, in a sort of circle, ("the exact shape doesn't matter," it said,) and then all the party were placed along the course, here and there. There was no "One, two, three, and away!" but they began running when they liked, and left off when they liked, so that it was not easy to know when the race was over. However, when they had been running half-an-hour or so, and were quite dry again, the Dodo suddenly called out, "The race is over!" and they all crowded round it, panting, and asking, "But who has won?"
>
> Lewis Carroll, *Alice's Adventures in Wonderland*

Lewis Carroll's imaginative procedure for drying out in Wonderland (1865: 53) provides a charming and prescient description of a political process that was not invented in the "real" world for another hundred years. Like Carroll's caucus-race, the modern presidential nominating process is run on a rather arbitrary course ("the exact shape doesn't matter"), with contenders placed along the course, here and there, some ahead and some behind. They begin running when they like, and leave off when they can no longer attract money or volunteers or media attention. And because it is not always easy to keep track of who is ahead and who is behind, we often find ourselves turning to the Dodos of the press corps, panting, to ask, "But who has won?"

In this chapter I attempt to make some sense of this Alice-like process by applying the lessons contained in the first ten chapters of this book to some significant questions of political accountability and institutional design. In Section 11.1 I focus on the political parties and on the role of the presidential nominating process as an arena for intraparty political competition. In Section 11.2 I describe some proposed reforms of the nominating process and evaluate them in the light of my empirical analysis of recent primary campaigns. In Section 11.3 I attempt to provide an overall reckoning of the advantages and disadvantages inherent in the contemporary dynamic process of presidential nomination.

11.1 "All the Party Were Placed Along the Course"

Any political party, at any given point in its history, faces a few pressing questions of ideology and strategy. These questions arise from the tensions and contradictions inherent in the effort to build and maintain a minimally cohesive governing coalition in a fractious and rapidly changing political world. One function of the presidential nominating process is providing an arena in which each party's pressing historical questions can be aired, contested, and eventually resolved.[1]

Given the importance of historical evolution to the health of the party system, any successful nominating process must be capable of facilitating more or less orderly transformations in party ideology and strategy without succumbing to mere rampant factionalism. The greatest defender of the elite-centered party system, E. E. Schattschneider, argued that that system alone could successfully coordinate and manage such transformations:

> The immobility and inertia of large masses are to politics what the law of gravity is to physics. This characteristic compels people to submit to a great channelization of the expression of their will, and is due to *numbers*, not to want of intelligence. An electorate of sixty million Aristotles would be equally restricted. The people are a sovereign whose vocabulary is limited to two words, "Yes" and "No." This sovereign, moreover, can speak only when spoken to. As interlocutors of the people the parties frame the question and elicit the answers. (1942: 52)

If Schattschneider was right—if a mass-based nominating process is incapable of posing and resolving pressing political issues without the help of some coterie of grand interlocutors—then the current procedures for choosing presidential nominees can only lead to mischief. But perhaps Schattschneider was mistaken about the potential for orderly, democratic change within the parties. The record of the modern nominating process in wrestling with the era's most pressing historical questions of party ideology and strategy provides some evidence that he was.

For the Democratic party of the 1970s and 1980s, the overriding historical issue has been the search for a new coalition and a new ideology to replace those handed down, inevitably eroded over time, from the glory days of Franklin Roosevelt's New Deal. The

[1] Sundquist (1983) and others have described major examples of intraparty struggles to adapt to new issues.

collapse of the Solid South in the 1950s and 1960s left the New Deal coalition short of a natural majority in presidential politics. The Democratic position has been further eroded by two decades of growing public disenchantment with the basic philosophy of federal activism underpinning the policy innovations of the New Deal and the Great Society. Thus, there has been only one Democratic president in the last twenty years—and one whose exceptional background and priorities seemed to prove the rule that the Democratic party can now win the presidency only by recasting or repudiating traditional Democratic politics.

The record of the presidential nominating process in reflecting and resolving the Democratic party's internal struggle over its future must be described as mixed. In 1972, the second half of the Democratic primary season did provide a fairly clear choice between representatives of the party's two most important competing factions at the time: Hubert Humphrey and George McGovern. With McGovern's nomination and subsequent landslide defeat in the general election and with a gradual cooling of passions following the winding down of the Vietnam War, the New Left faction which McGovern represented began to fade from view; the party was left with no clear alternative to its traditional New Deal identity. Jimmy Carter in 1976 filled this political vacuum very successfully, but without articulating any new ideology or building any new coalition of more than personal scope. Although Carter was able to be elected—something no other Democrat since Lyndon Johnson has managed to do—he lacked the political resources to weather an oil shortage, foreign setbacks, economic dislocations, and a self-diagnosed "national malaise."

In 1984, with Carter gone from the scene, the Democratic party resumed its long search for a new coalition. The most obvious ideological possibility was a package combining the liberal social stance of the 1970s with a less ambitious, more pragmatic economic policy. The natural base for this new ideology was the growing class of young voters, especially the smaller subset of relatively well-educated young middle-class white-collar workers, raised to take for granted women's rights, sexual freedom, and marijuana on the one hand and unemployment, stagflation, and persistent poverty on the other. Independent candidate John Anderson began to speak to part of this incipient class in 1980, but its first prominent champion within the Democratic party was Gary Hart in 1984.

In retrospect it is easy to forget that Hart was far from being the most obvious alternative to Walter Mondale in the 1984 Democratic campaign; John Glenn was, in prospect, a very attractive representative of the party's substantial moderate and conservative constituency, and he was also much better known than Hart. Mondale and Glenn were, in some sense, natural primary season opponents.[2] The early collapse of Glenn's campaign provides some important lessons about the nature of the contemporary presidential nominating system.[3] But the fact that Hart emerged to replace Glenn as the main alternative to Walter Mondale in the 1984 Democratic primaries must, from my historical perspective, be counted as a considerable success for the nominating process. That Hart's challenge was unsuccessful may indicate that he was the wrong person for the job, or that he was ahead of his time, or simply that the path he followed will ultimately prove another dead end in the search for a new Democratic majority. Perhaps 1988 will tell.

On the Republican side the record is, if anything, more favorable. The historical shift in the party's center of gravity, away from the small towns of the Northeast and Midwest and toward the cities and suburbs of the Sun Belt, has been reflected in and facilitated by the party's nominating process. A new breed of conservative Republicans, already capable in 1964 of capturing the party's organizational apparatus, has been forced by the demands of the modern primary-centered nominating process to become a powerful electoral force as well. The unsuccessful effort to unseat Gerald Ford as the Republican nominee in 1976 was a political watershed not only for Ronald Reagan, but also for his faction and his party. The electoral consequences of this political mobilization have marked the history of the subsequent decade.

In some sense, though, the Republicans' most pressing problems are just beginning. With Reagan retiring from the scene, the 1988 campaign will mark the beginning of the party's search for a genuine electoral majority in the post-Reagan era. The Reagan coalition of economic and social conservatives—a coalition diffuse enough to include Wall Street bankers, blue-collar patriots, and devout creationists—will have to be recast and reinforced if it is to withstand the test of time. Given the fragility of past Republican

[2] This point is illustrated by the fact that thermometer ratings for Mondale and Glenn in the 1984 NES primary season survey were negatively correlated. By contrast, Mondale and Hart tended to appeal to the same broad segments of the party rank and file (Shanks et al. 1985: 28).

[3] These lessons are drawn in a forthcoming study of Glenn's presidential candidacy by Richard Fenno.

gains, and the variety of would-be inheritors of Reagan's mantle of leadership, the future of the party is very much open. For better or worse, the nature of the contemporary nominating process will help shape that future.

11.2 "The Exact Shape Doesn't Matter"

Do the rules of the political game determine its outcome? Reformers of all stripes have been tinkering with the rules of the nominating process for almost twenty years now in the belief that those rules are important, that the exact shape of the process really does matter. And they are not finished yet. In this section I survey some possible further reforms of the nominating process and attempt to assess their potential political consequences.

Regional Primaries

Probably the most frequently suggested reform of the current nominating process would produce one or another form of regional primary system. States would continue to hold their primaries on different days, but each day's primaries would be concentrated in a single region of the country. The candidates might compete in New England in late February, in the South in March, in the industrial Midwest in April, and so on. Any regional primary system would have both a practical and an abstract advantage. The abstract advantage is simply that a thoroughgoing regional system would eliminate some of the confusion and clutter which some observers seem to find so offensive in the current system. The political significance of such neatness would, of course, be negligible. The practical advantage of a regional primary system is its possible reduction in the wear and tear on candidates and their bank accounts resulting from constant cross-country campaigning. Given the complaint that successful presidential candidates must be wealthy athletes (Polsby and Wildavsky 1984: 225), a system that lowered the financial and athletic hurdles by concentrating each week's or month's primaries in a single region might be a genuine improvement.

The major disadvantage of a regional primary system is that it would reduce and perhaps eliminate the opportunity for relatively unknown candidates to compete effectively, while preserving and perhaps increasing the temptation inherent in the current system to draw conclusions about campaign progress on the basis of biased information. Some commentators have argued that "regions would be heterogeneous and large" (Crotty and Jackson 1985: 228). But the larger the regions, the more a regional primary system would handicap candidates lacking name recognition, organization, and cash. In any event, we have seen in Chapters 8, 9, and 10 that even large regions are notably unheterogeneous by national standards and that their distinctive political characteristics frequently tend to advantage some candidates and disadvantage others.[4] To concentrate all the primaries occurring in a given week in one region would magnify the impact of these regional advantages and disadvantages, perhaps even providing the illusion of a broad, sweeping victory for a candidate whose real support is largely confined to a single part of the country.

Proponents of the regional primary plan have recognized the disproportionate influence of whichever region happens to vote first. To mitigate this unfairness, most versions of the plan provide either for a random ordering of regions or for a regular rotation in which each quadrenniel campaign would have a different section of the country voting first. Either method would ensure a measure of fairness in the long run, although it is hard to imagine that a candidate deprived of the nomination by an unlucky ordering of regions would take much comfort in the fact that a more propitious ordering might come along four, eight, or twelve years hence.

Further "Front-Loading"

Twenty years ago the primary calendar looked very different than it does today. Of course, there were fewer primaries, but those primaries were also distributed differently over the three months of the primary season. When Lyndon Johnson withdrew from the 1968 presidential campaign at the end of March, only one primary had already occurred, and the most important primaries were more than two months away. By contrast, when John Glenn withdrew from the 1984 campaign in mid-March, the most crowded week of the primary calendar had already passed, and a large fraction of the delegates to the national convention were already committed.

[4] Geer (1986: 142–43) described a plan designed by Stephen Dunne to create a grouped primary system with "ideologically balanced" regions. But even if we set aside the difficulty of balancing regional ideological characteristics over long periods of time, and for both parties simultaneously, my analysis in Chapters 8, 9, and 10 suggests that primary outcomes will continue to differ significantly and systematically by region, even after controlling for the effects of ideology.

Several factors have combined to produce the trend toward earlier primaries. Perhaps the most important has been the obvious importance of early states in the dynamics of momentum under the contemporary nominating process. The trend toward front-loading will take another major step forward in 1988. According to current plans, summarized in Table 11.1, the Super Tuesday primary in early March will become significantly more super than it was in 1984, with simultaneous primaries in no fewer than fifteen states and caucuses in at least four more.

The expanded set of Super Tuesday primaries for 1988 has the look of a de facto regional primary. Ten new southern and border states are added to the list of three southern and two northeastern states carried over from 1984. The rationale for this change, organized and promoted by conservative southern politicians in both

TABLE 11.1 Tentative 1988 Primary and Caucus Schedule

11 Jan	Michigan caucuses—Republicans only
8 Feb	Iowa caucuses
16 Feb	New Hampshire
23 Feb	South Dakota[a]
28 Feb	Maine caucuses
1 Mar	Vermont
5 Mar	South Carolina—Republicans only Wyoming caucuses
8 Mar	Alabama, Arkansas, Florida, Georgia, Kentucky, Louisiana, Maryland, Massachusetts, Mississippi, Missouri, North Carolina, Oklahoma, Rhode Island, Tennessee, Texas
15 Mar	Illinois, Ohio
29 Mar	Connecticut
5 Apr	New York, Wisconsin
26 Apr	Pennsylvania
3 May	Indiana
10 May	Nebraska, West Virginia
17 May	Oregon
24 May	New Jersey
7 Jun	California, Montana, New Mexico

Source: Congressional Quarterly Weekly Report (23 August 1986, page 2000); updated by the author on the basis of press reports and information provided by the Democratic Party Compliance Review Commission.

Note: This tentative schedule shows projected dates for all primaries, and for caucuses through 8 March.

[a] South Dakota's plan to hold a primary in February is in violation of Democratic party rules.

parties, is to increase the influence of the southern states' primaries in the nominating process as a whole.[5] With Iowa and New Hampshire clinging to their first-in-the-nation status, the theory goes, the only way for the South to wield its due influence is to put together a delegate bonanza too big for either the candidates or the press to downplay.

Ironically, this effort to bolster the clout of the southern states in the nominating process may actually make Iowa and New Hampshire even more important in shaping either or both parties' choices. For example, a relatively liberal candidate who emerged from those early contests with significant momentum might be able to sustain that momentum long enough to make a strong showing in the South, winning votes far out of proportion to his underlying political support in the region. That is what happened in 1984. The candidates most eager to make their stands in Dixie, and most attractive to conservative Democratic leaders in the region—John Glenn, Ernest Hollings, and Reubin Askew—were practically eliminated from the race after New Hampshire. Southern voters who wanted a viable alternative to Walter Mondale were left, even by Super Tuesday, with the rather unpalatable prospect of supporting a Kennedyesque liberal intellectual who had managed George McGovern's presidential campaign and who, for good measure, had barely set foot in the region as recently as three weeks earlier.

Gary Hart's success in the South on Super Tuesday, 1984—carrying Florida and strongly challenging Mondale in Alabama and Georgia—had less to do with his substantive political identity than with the momentum generated by his victory in New Hampshire.[6] Southern voters whose primaries occurred later in the season confronted the same unpalatable choices faced by voters in the South on Super Tuesday, but they did so in large part because the results from the South on Super Tuesday were so powerfully shaped by what had happened earlier in Iowa and New Hampshire.

These considerations suggest that early primaries may fail to provide the political advantage expected by politicians in the states crowding the primary calendar in early March. But even if those

[5] The political origins of the southern primary and a survey of claims and counterclaims about its likely effects were presented by Stanley and Hadley (1987).

[6] The statistical results summarized in Table 10.6 suggest that Hart's levels of underlying support against Mondale in these three states ranged between 20 and 35 percent. His actual shares of the two-candidate primary vote were nearly twenty percentage points higher.

state-specific advantages do materialize, they may produce significant costs for the nominating process as a whole. The competition for clout among the various states may produce the worst of both possible worlds: a process in which the idiosyncratic effects of early outcomes in Iowa and New Hampshire have the greatest possible impact on subsequent primary results but with minimal scope for campaigning by the candidates and learning by prospective primary voters.

A National Primary

Opinion polls have found with impressive consistency that the American public would prefer a national primary to the existing system by which they nominate potential presidents. A national primary would be simple, comprehensible, and consistent with other aspects of American political practice. It could be quick, at least by comparison with the current system. And it would eliminate in a single stroke the entire dynamic edifice of momentum characteristic of the existing nominating process.

It may seem paradoxical that, although extensive front-loading of the primary calendar would probably maximize the importance of dynamic forces in the presidential nominating process, a more thoroughgoing move in the same direction would have precisely the opposite effect. A national primary system would outdo even a super Super Tuesday of the sort scheduled for 1988 by concentrating the entire primary season on a single day. But in so doing it would recast the dynamics of the nominating process, producing a result very different from anything we are likely to see in 1988.

The crucial difference between a front-loaded primary system and a national primary system is not quantitative but qualitative. In a front-loaded system of the sort gradually evolving, more and more states fall under the direct and immediate influence of momentum generated in Iowa and New Hampshire. As journalist David Broder put it, "The bigger the bloc of votes available the next Tuesday, the larger the premium for winning New Hampshire."[7] By contrast, in a national primary of the sort contemplated here, Iowa and New Hampshire would vote on the same day as every other state. There would be no opportunity for early demonstration victories of the sort that launched Jimmy Carter in 1976, George Bush in 1980, and Gary Hart in 1984.[8]

[7] "The Southern Primary: Another Mistake," in the *Washington Post*, 12 March 1986, page A23.

[8] Actually, candidates would probably attempt with some success to generate

In describing the effect of momentum in recent nominating campaigns, I have repeatedly drawn on comparisons between the actual results of sequential state primaries and the projected results of a national primary, in which party voters in every state would go to the polls on the same day. These comparisons suggest that, at least under some political circumstances, a national primary would produce starkly different results. Whether the differences would be good or bad is a question raised, though not resolved, in Section 11.3.

Approval Voting

The reforms described so far would alter the timing of primary voting. Political scientist Steven Brams and others have suggested a different sort of reform proposal—one that would alter the *method* of primary voting in a fundamental way. Rather than being forced to vote for a single candidate, primary voters would be allowed to cast "approval votes" for as many candidates as they wanted to support. The winning candidate would be the one receiving the greatest number of approval votes, whether or not this plurality amounted to a majority of the primary electorate.[9]

Approval voting would be feasible in almost any sort of election. But it seems particularly appropriate for primary elections, in which the problem facing the party is precisely to settle upon a widely acceptable candidate for the general election. Critics of the existing nominating process (for example, Polsby 1983) have complained that current procedures have the opposite tendency, encouraging candidates to appeal to narrow factions within the party in the hope of attracting the relatively small number of committed supporters required to finish first in a multicandidate race. Under approval voting some voters would cast two, three, or more votes. To win, candidates would need more votes and thus a wider range of support. As a result, Brams has argued, approval voting would benefit ideologically moderate candidates and others with broad popular appeal (Brams 1978: 228).

Another effect of approval voting, of particular relevance for

early tests of strength in pseudo-events like straw polls. However, these events would lack the visibility and legitimacy of official delegate-selection activities.

[9] For a detailed description of approval voting and its theoretical properties, see Brams and Fishburn (1983). The earliest empirical study—a simulation of approval voting outcomes based on thermometer ratings of candidates for the Democratic presidential nomination in 1972—was by Joslyn (1976). Additional references are available in Niemi and Bartels (1984).

the analysis presented in this book, is its recasting of some, though by no means all, the dynamic and strategic considerations involved in primary voting. I have already alluded in Chapter 6 to some evidence suggesting that approval voters in a sequence of presidential primaries would be no more immune than plurality voters to being swayed by expectations about the primary season horse race (Niemi and Bartels 1984). But the *ways* in which they would be swayed are somewhat different. In plurality elections the desire to "go with a winner" and the incentive to vote strategically generally work in the same direction: both advantage the front-runner. Under approval voting these two factors would sometimes conflict: the desire to support a winner would continue to push prospective voters toward the front-runner; but strategic considerations would sometimes produce extra votes for other candidates, mitigating somewhat the aggregate effect of momentum.[10]

The Role of the Media

The major news media play such a prominent role in the contemporary presidential nominating process that criticisms of the process often turn out to be criticisms of the role of the media in the process. The press may be charged with focusing on the horse race to the exclusion of political substance, with lavishing unwarranted attention on straw polls and other pseudo-events, or with trivializing the nominating process by treating it as a series of familiar prepackaged images: face-to-face campaigning in a living room in Iowa; the candidate shaking hands with factory workers on a snowy New Hampshire morning; the campaign headquarters staffed by enthusiastic volunteers; angry charges and countercharges between the candidates in dramatic public debates.

The news media may be guilty as charged, on these counts and others. It may even be true, although this is less clear, that a steady diet of high-minded political substance from a reformed media establishment would make primary voters wiser and more responsi-

[10] Consider, for example, the situation facing a prospective strategic voter who liked both Walter Mondale and Gary Hart in 1984. Under approval voting, the closer the race between the two candidates became, the greater the voter's incentive would have been to distinguish between them by approving of one but not the other. But the farther either candidate fell behind in the race, the less costly it would have become on strategic grounds to cast approval votes for *both* candidates. Unfortunately, the strategic implications of approval voting are too complicated to permit any confident general prediction about the balance likely to emerge between different strategic and dynamic incentives in an actual campaign setting.

ble. But the media are to would-be reformers what Tweetie is to Sylvester: tempting but ultimately untouchable. Electoral procedures can be and are routinely altered. Even a change as sweeping as the establishment of a single national primary is entirely feasible. But in the American political system, the behavior of the media is dictated not even by the most powerful legislators or reform commissions, but by the media themselves. If they are to be reformed, it must be a voluntary, self-initiated process.

The autonomy of the media makes it imperative that any proposal for reform be consistent with the media establishment's own view of its commercial interests and journalistic responsibilities. A call for high-minded substance and education about the issues is likely to have the same bracing effect on real life as a call for universal brotherhood, cheap gas, or perpetual sunshine. But it is quite another matter to propose changes in style and emphasis that would let the media do better what they already want to do: tell a coherent story, provide some dramatic interest to the race, and compete successfully with other media for the attention of their audience.

One failure of the media not endemic to the nature of the news business is the failure to recognize what Greenfield (1982: 15) called "the enduring political terrain of American politics." Reporters focus on speeches, organizational shake-ups, and other events of the moment, ignoring more important underlying political forces. Patterson (1980: 49–53) documented this pattern in the explanations provided by the press of primary outcomes in the 1976 Republican campaign. The party's enduring factional cleavage, a major element in the explanation of primary outcomes provided in Chapter 8, received only occasional attention from reporters. Instead of focusing on the substance of ideological and factional conflict, Patterson found (1980: 50–51), "the press usually cited campaign promises, events, strategies, styles, and organizational activities as the reasons behind the developments in the Ford–Reagan race." As a result, reporters were often surprised along with their readers and listeners when primary outcomes reflected enduring regional and ideological divisions rather than "newsworthy" changes in organizational structures or campaign tactics.

There are difficulties inherent in covering the "enduring political terrain." As Greenfield himself noted,

> [the] facts underlying the real campaign cannot be filmed or taped, and they make for very poor drama. They lack the dazzle

> of colorful balloons ascending from a crowd, the whiff of grapeshot accompanying angry charges from candidate to candidate, the compelling soundtrack provided by a brass band. And since they do not change from day to day, they cannot be touched on day after day on the evening news programs without running the risk of repetition.

Still, it seems likely that a smart reporter, motivated by the ever-present competitive incentive to handicap and interpret campaign events more successfully than the competition, could make good use of the underlying patterns of support identified in my analysis. An important advantage of primary campaigns in this regard is that, in contrast to other kinds of campaigns, the enduring political terrain of the nominating season *does* change from week to week with changes in the primary venue. With some journalistic imagination, underlying political forces could be merged with changing electoral circumstances to produce a coherent story at once dramatic, substantive, and a step ahead of day-to-day campaign events.

11.3 "But Who Has Won?"

Does the best man—or woman—win? In some sense, that is the central question to be asked of any electoral institution. But it is a question we are not well equipped to answer, either in general terms or in the more specific context of presidential nominating politics. The problem is not so much in agreeing on a list of important criteria for a "good" presidential nominee; different analysts tend to produce similar enough lists.[11] The problem is rather in determining how successful the system has been in producing good candidates by these criteria. Have recent nominees been able politicians? Persons of strong moral fiber? Responsive to the political views of the electorate?

At a conference of reporters and politicians in early 1980, Alan Baron argued that the presidential nominating process does tend to produce, if not "good" nominees, at least appropriate ones (Foley et al. 1980: 90):

> It's been said time and time again here that George Bush won Iowa because he spent 28 days in Iowa and got a lot of organizers and did a great job. Well, I don't know the numbers, but Phil

[11] Compare, for example, Hess (1978: 25–37), Ceaser (1979), and Brady and Johnston (1985: 1–10).

> Crane I'm sure did about as much work as George Bush did in Iowa. In 1976 Fred Harris and Mo Udall and Birch Bayh did a lot of work in Iowa. You don't win voters by shaking their hands only. The fact is you've got to start with the product. In 1976 Jimmy Carter, better than any other candidate running, understood where the country was, what people wanted in the president . . . and Jimmy Carter gave it back to them.

If Baron is correct, then the process itself is not at fault. Perhaps, to paraphrase Carter's own successful slogan, America is getting presidential nominees as good as its people. But the point is not self-evident; certainly less sanguine views of Carter's nomination have been put forward by other political observers.

Analysts could also evaluate the products of the contemporary presidential nominating process in comparison to the real or imagined products of some alternative process. Could we expect more from the nominees produced by a national primary or by an old-style convention system? One way to address this question is to engage in what Brady (1985b: 7) has referred to as the "enjoyable parlor game" of selective comparison: McGovern versus Roosevelt, Reagan versus Harding, or whatever historical examples seem appropriate for making the desired point. The difficulties involved in making such comparisons in a balanced and convincing way should be obvious. In view of these difficulties, Brady (1985a; 1985b) has suggested a different, perhaps less problematic, standard of judgment. Following the lead provided by recent democratic theory, his analyses have focused on "the process of decision rather than its substance" (1985a: 3). The goal then is to identify the most important features of the process of decision itself and, if possible, to judge whether those features are healthy or unhealthy for the process as a political institution.

Since my focus in this book has been on the dynamics of the contemporary presidential nominating process, it seems particularly appropriate to consider here whether the sequential nature of the process enhances or detracts from its capacity as a political institution. Critics and supporters alike often forget that the contemporary nominating process, or any potential alternative process, must be thought of not only as a mechanism for selecting nominees, but also as an integral part of the broader process of presidential selection.[12] Thus, a nominating system must be judged not only by the nominees it produces but also by its consequences

[12] A notable exception is Polsby (1983).

for the behavior and fortunes of those nominees in the subsequent general election.

The phenomenon of "negative momentum" in the later stages of some recent nominating campaigns provides one troubling example of the possible linkage between the nominating process and the broader electoral system of which it is a part. My analysis of recent campaigns in Chapters 8, 9, and 10 produced repeated instances of this rather surprising pattern. The most striking example occurred in 1980, when Carter's increasing certainty of nomination actually cost him, on average, about 10 percent of the vote in the last month of the primary season. But in other campaigns the same pattern appeared, especially for well-known candidates. Negative momentum seems to have relatively little impact on the selection of nominees; indeed, it arises most potently after the nomination is actually or practically locked up. But if we consider the nominating process as the beginning of the fall campaign, it should be clear that a systematic tendency for prospective nominees to lose the support of their party's primary voters late in the primary season could have serious consequences. In relatively benign cases, it could produce a perception of lagging popularity going into the national convention. In more drastic cases, like Carter's in 1980, it could fuel an increasingly bitter intraparty struggle, seriously tarnishing a nominee's image and precipitating defections from the party ticket in the general election.

It is impossible to tell for sure whether the pattern of negative momentum reflects the overly enthusiastic efforts of the media to "dewheel" front-runners (Chapter 3), the unavoidable difficulty of maintaining enthusiastic support in a fickle and mostly uninterested public throughout a long and sometimes boring primary season, or simply the inherent political weaknesses of recent front-runners. But whoever is to blame, the fact that familiarity breeds contempt in the contemporary system bodes ill for prospective nominees and for the system as a political institution.

The potential for frequent and troubling second thoughts about prospective nominees seems especially great in a system with the remarkable openness to new candidates exhibited by the contemporary nominating process. In many political systems positions of party leadership are earned through decades of toil in the party organization. In contemporary American politics the same positions are sometimes seized, almost literally overnight, by candidates with negligible party credentials and very short histories as national public figures. "In December 1974," James M. Perry recalled later (in Moore and Fraser 1977: 73), "a Gallup poll asked voters to select their first choice for the [Democratic] nomination from a list of thirty-one names, including George Wallace, Hubert Humphrey, Henry Jackson, George McGovern, John Lindsay, Adlai Stevenson, Ralph Nader, Walter Mondale, on through Terry Sanford and Kevin White—but not including Jimmy Carter." It is hard to imagine any other process of presidential selection that could produce a winner who, eighteen months earlier, was not even considered among the top thirty prospects for the job within his own party.

The dangers inherent in this openness have been pointed out by Robert Scheer, among many others. "There's a special problem with the drawn out system of primaries and caucuses," Scheer argued (Foley et al. 1980: 44).

> What it allows is for an unknown to get in. These people do not have a track record. They don't have 12 years in the Senate and five in the House. They don't have things you can hang them with. You got a guy like Carter and you wrap him up, or get a guy like Caddell or Rafshoon wrapping him up, he doesn't have anything you can pin him on except some myths about what went on in Georgia. By the time you unravel that and find out some of the reality, the election is over anyway.

Obviously, one way to avoid getting nominees without track records would be to replace the current sequential primary process with a national primary system. My analysis in Chapter 8 suggests that Carter, for one, would never have been nominated in a national primary. Without the momentum generated by the dynamics of the current system, only major contenders—candidates with substantial name recognition, financial support, and organizational resources—would have any real chance of being nominated. The problem with that solution is that it would preclude serious consideration of not only shallow, dangerous newcomers but also those who are able, independent, and purposeful. Openness, like many other salient features of the nominating process, has both good and bad consequences. It sometimes forces primary voters to choose among unknown alternatives, but it also provides flexibility and opportunity.

Ken Bode of NBC News emphasized the advantages of openness in the presidential nominating process (Foley et al. 1980: 126):

> One of the things this process has to have is a measure of accountability in both parties. It's got to be possible to challenge

the leadership and stewardship of the incumbent president. Any time you have a single simultaneous test in six or eight or 10 places at one time, you advantage the guy who is the front-runner, the incumbent. Insurgents, challengers have got to have time to raise money slowly, build momentum slowly, have a few tests in Iowa and New Hampshire and move across the country. That's very important if you're going to have any accountability in a nominating system and it's vital in this democracy.

Obviously, reasonable observers may disagree about the relative importance of the virtues and vices of openness in the contemporary nominating process.[13] The best of both worlds would be a process that both preserved the advantages of openness described by Bode and minimized the disadvantages pointed out by Scheer. But can we have it both ways? My analysis suggests that a sequential nominating process much like the one that now exists is capable, in principle, of providing an attractive compromise of just this sort between openness and chaos. We have already seen a variety of indications that a sequential nominating process is capable of producing reasoned collective judgments even about relatively unknown candidates. The analyses in Chapter 5 and elsewhere suggest that substantive political factors do appear to be important considerations in every nominating campaign. The public does learn a fair amount over the course of the primary season about the political identities of the competing candidates and weighs that information when evaluating the candidates. Moreover, my analyses of primary voting in Part III suggest that information is especially plentiful in the local political context generated by a primary election; thus, actual prospective voters tend to be substantially better informed than the national audience at the same time. As a result, it is hard to point to an instance in which the existing sequential process has produced the "wrong" nominee, at least as measured by what we can tell after the fact about the competing candidates' underlying levels of political support.

The greatest failing of the existing sequential process is that it works least well in these respects precisely when producing the virtues of openness—when an unknown candidate emerges in the early stages of a nominating campaign. Substantive political infor-

[13] Disagreements seem to reflect, in part, the formative political experiences of the observers themselves: Democrats shaped by the events of 1968 seem most likely to emphasize the virtues of openness; those for whom the Carter era is most salient seem most likely to emphasize the vices of openness.

mation is then in short supply; perceptions about the horse race, largely disconnected from substantive political considerations, play a crucial role in shaping choices among the candidates. And that is when reckless enthusiasm could most easily produce an irrevocable mistake.

It seems clear that an ideal nominating process would somehow facilitate more informed decisionmaking. Such a process would be sequential, but with sufficient time between events for the press and the public to absorb and reflect upon each new turn before coming to the next. Particularly in the early stages of the campaign, when the heat of momentum can be hottest, the process would minimize the likelihood of unstoppable brush fires for candidates wrapped up in myths.

This line of argument suggests that one crucial parameter of institutional design in the contemporary nominating process is the frequency of primaries relative to the speed at which the public learns about the candidates. What do prospective voters know, and when do they know it? Once a bandwagon begins to roll, how long does it take people to recover their bearings and begin to evaluate a new candidate critically, as a political leader rather than as a media phenomenon?

No clear, precise answers to these questions emerge from the historical record, but some relevant evidence does exist. First, a comparison of the experiences of George Bush and Gary Hart is suggestive. Bush upset Ronald Reagan in Iowa to become the (first) hot new candidate of the 1980 campaign, but in the month separating the Iowa caucuses and the first primary in New Hampshire his momentum fizzled, and he lost in New Hampshire by a substantial margin. Hart emerged by finishing a distant second to Walter Mondale in Iowa in 1984, and yet he parlayed his momentum into a big win in New Hampshire one week later, followed in rapid succession by additional victories in primaries and caucuses in Vermont, Maine, and Wyoming within the next ten days. Hart's bandwagon only began to slow on Super Tuesday—three weeks after his original emergence in Iowa. There are, of course, a variety of explanations for these contrasting patterns of events. But one worth considering is that the "shelf life" of momentum in its most intense and uncritical form may be no more than two or three weeks.

The evidence presented in this book, although by no means conclusive, is consistent with the notion that a period of three weeks may provide a critical "cooling off" period after an early-season surprise. Most notably, the changing relationship between predispositions toward Gary Hart and evaluations of him, shown in Figure 5.2, suggests that about three weeks are required for prospective voters to begin to sort out what a new candidate is about and how his political views and values measure up to their own. The contrast in timing between changes in overall familiarity with Hart and changes in more specific familiarity with his character traits and issue stands (Figure 4.3) likewise suggests that specific perceptions may take three weeks or so to catch up with respondents' willingness to make overall judgments about a candidate.[14] Finally, the estimated magnitude of issue projection for Hart in the weeks after his New Hampshire upset (Figure 5.7) reinforces the impression that a few weeks are required for prospective voters to form realistic political judgments about a surprising newcomer.

If that impression is correct, it suggests there may be a world of difference between a sequential process of the sort outlined in Table 11.1, in which New Hampshire follows Iowa by one week and the first month of the public campaign is dotted with half a dozen separate events, and a sequential process in which key events are separated by longer opportunities for learning and reflection. A saner primary calendar of the latter sort could probably be established only through legislation; political parties are not sufficiently centralized to impose any orderly system on unwilling state affiliates. But once established, such a calendar might partially mitigate the dangers inherent in the dynamics of the current system and yet preserve the flexibility and openness that make the current system more attractive than the most obvious alternative, a one-day national primary.

At stake is the capacity of the nominating process to facilitate

[14] Popkin (forthcoming) has noted the potential significance of a "pseudo-certainty" effect, in which prospective voters believe they know more about a new candidate than they really do know. The lag between overall judgments and specific perceptions in Figure 4.3 may reflect exactly that phenomenon. Brady's analysis of the development of "stable" and "distinct" images of the character traits of the various candidates for the 1984 Democratic nomination (1985a: 23–25) seems to suggest that learning occurs more slowly than I have indicated here. For example, Brady calculated on the basis of linear trend lines that respondents in the 1984 NES survey took twenty to thirty weeks to develop images of Gary Hart that were as stable and distinct as the images they had of Walter Mondale at the beginning of the primary season (1985a: 25). However, a week-by-week inspection of Brady's data (1985a: Figure 6) suggests that, even by his criteria, most of the gap between Hart and Mondale had disappeared within six weeks or so after the New Hampshire primary.

sober political evaluation. Richard Leone, a Mondale campaign adviser (quoted by Moore 1986: 71–72), recalled after the 1984 election that his candidate's hopes in the dark days after Hart's New Hampshire upset rested on just this sort of sober evaluation—on the possibility that

> the degree of positive television coverage, the intensity of media hype about Hart, and the necessarily shallow nature of his support, since people were moving to him in droves and knew very little about him at a very early stage, would inevitably lead to a reconsideration—who is this person who has suddenly been thrust into the forefront? . . .
>
> People would wake up the next morning and wonder whom they had spent the night with and start to think about what it all meant.

In 1984, the reconsideration did come in time for Mondale to survive and eventually win the nomination, but the timing was almost too close. A less precarious nominating process would retain the opportunity for a candidate like Hart to emerge into prominence, but it would also give prospective voters a little more time to "wake up the next morning" and consider their choices in the cool light of day.

As these lines are being written—one week after the 1986 midterm elections—the whole process is gearing up to begin again in earnest. Vice president Bush has already raised $24 million for 308 potentially grateful Republican candidates at the state and local levels, his office reports. Democratic congressman Richard Gephardt of Missouri has made a dozen visits to Iowa. And Representative Jack Kemp of New York has cornered the endorsements of half of New Hampshire's Republican county chairmen.[15] Whether any of these candidates will be successful in 1988 is beyond my ability to predict. Indeed, having said what I can about who *has* won in recent presidential nominating campaigns, it is dis-

[15] These signs of early activity were reported in a front page article by E. J. Dionne in the *New York Times* (10 November 1986). Early Republican precaucuses in Michigan, the first formal announcement of candidacy by former governor Pierre duPont of Delaware, and the highly public testing of the waters by television evangelist Pat Robertson drew national media coverage even before the 1986 elections. But there are limits. In the popular comic strip "Bloom County" (5 October 1986), a penguin named Opus was tarred and feathered for attempting to draw the attention of a harried housewife to the incipient 1988 campaign.

heartening to have so little to add on the very interesting subject of who *will* win in future campaigns.

According to some versions of the philosophy of science, genuine prediction is the fundamental bench mark against which any scientific theory must be tested. It is as well to admit straightaway that, by that criterion, nothing in this book—nothing in the sum total of academic and journalistic writing on presidential nominating politics—can be billed as a serious scientific theory. In spite of everything we know about the role of political predispositions in primary voting, we do not know which candidate will succeed in appealing to the independent and unpredictable voters of Iowa and New Hampshire. In spite of everything we know about the patterns of media coverage in past campaigns, the press may react differently to the next unexpected winner. In spite of everything we know about the dynamics of learning and uncertainty in past campaigns, we cannot guess what voters will learn about the candidates who emerge with momentum in 1988. And in spite of everything we know about the circumstances in which momentum is most likely to be important, we do not know whether it will be decisive in the choice of a nominee, as it has been at times in the past. The string of surprises that has marked the recent history of presidential nominating politics will probably not end any time soon, but the surprises themselves should not be surprising. Politics is still an art as well as a science.

CHAPTER TWELVE

The Dynamics of Public Choice

THE INSTITUTIONAL QUESTIONS SURROUNDING the presidential nominating process will be settled, in the end, on the basis of political experience and political values. But whatever may happen in the institutional realm, the phenomenon of momentum seems to me to have important implications as well for the way political scientists think about electoral behavior and public choice. In this chapter I wish to suggest that the intellectual ramifications of the analysis presented in this book may in fact be quite far-reaching, highlighting a significant limitation of a major branch of our existing political theory and of the more fundamental liberal philosophy from which that branch of theory has evolved.

This branch of political theory will be referred to here as the "classical theory of public choice." Its central problem is: How can individual preferences be combined into a single collective choice? The basic result of a generation of probing into this problem suggests it is not as simple as it first appears; indeed, within the most refined conceptual framework of modern liberal democratic theory it may be impossible for individual preferences to be fairly and coherently aggregated into a collective choice. Chapter 12 provides a brief examination of this startling puzzle in the classical theory of public choice. Having outlined the results and implications of the theory itself, I proceed to argue that the force of the dilemma it creates may depend crucially upon a basic assumption of liberal philosophy, an assumption which turns out to be unduly limiting in many actual political settings. By relaxing this assumption it is possible to envision a dynamic version of the theory of public choice in which some of the formidable difficulties highlighted by the classical static theory may actually disappear.

12.1 The Classical Theory of Public Choice

> In any election, when there are only *two* issues to vote on . . . and when the Chairman is able to give a casting vote, it is clear that there *must* be a majority for one or other issue, and in this case open voting is the obvious course.

> But wherever there are three or more issues to vote on, any one of the following three cases may exist in the minds of the electors:
>
> (α) *There may be one issue desired by an absolute majority of the electors.*
>
> (β) *There may be one issue which, when paired against every other issue separately, is preferred by a majority of electors.*
>
> (γ) *The majorities may be 'cyclical'*, e.g. *there may be a majority for* A *over* B, *for* B *over* C, *and for* C *over* A.
>
> The words of the Ordinance are 'THAT CANDIDATE FOR WHOM THE GREATEST NUMBER OF VOTES SHALL HAVE BEEN GIVEN SHALL BE DEEMED ELECTED.'
>
> It seems to me that this may be complied with by either of two modes of election:
>
> In case (α) *If a candidate be declared elected who, when all are voted on at once, has an absolute majority of votes.*
>
> In case (β) *If a candidate be declared elected who, when paired with every other separately, is preferred by the majority of those voting.*
>
> But that it is *not* complied with by the following mode:
>
> In case (γ) *If a candidate be declared elected, though it is known that there is another who, when paired with him, is preferred by the majority of those voting.*

This brief passage was taken from a little pamphlet printed at Oxford in 1876. Its author, an eccentric and somewhat timid Christ Church mathematics don named C. L. Dodgson, had a considerable theoretical understanding of the possible pitfalls of majority voting. He recognized that, if there are more than two alternatives to be voted upon, no one will necessarily command a majority; he argued that in this case one alternative may still be a reasonable choice if it can command a majority against each of the other alternatives in pairwise competition; but he realized that even this second criterion might fail to produce a definite winner if the pattern of individual preferences created "cyclical" majorities, with no one alternative commanding a majority against each of the others. Each of these aspects of the "paradox of voting" had been discovered by Condorcet a century earlier, and each would be periodically rediscovered by future generations. But this particular exposition of the paradox is an especially interesting one, aside from its directness and clarity, because Dodgson was the same Dodo whose peculiarly prescient caucus-race we met in Chapter 11, a man whose quirky imaginative genius won him literary immortality as Lewis Carroll.[1]

The practical difficulties inherent in applying mass electoral procedures to complex choices are reflected in the pathologies identified by Dodgson for Oxford's system of plurality voting, but plurality voting is only one of many possible voting schemes. Might not some other scheme produce more satisfactory results? Since World War II a substantial and in some ways quite sophisticated theoretical literature has grown up around exactly this question. The results are not encouraging. Under the standard assumptions of modern economic theory, public choice theorists have demonstrated the logical impossibility of constructing *any* attractive, consistent procedure for making collective choices from unrestricted sets of three or more alternatives. In this section I review the pessimistic conclusions of public choice theory. I will primarily focus on the outstanding single work in the tradition, Kenneth Arrow's *Social Choice and Individual Values* (1951), but most of my discussion will apply as well to the extensive body of more or less consistent related literature leading to and following from Arrow's book.

Arrow and his successors address the central problem: How can individual preferences be combined into a single collective choice? As it stands, this question asks much less than we might want it to, since many conceivable methods of preference aggregation are quickly ruled out of consideration by our shared ideas about the nature of democratic choice. For example, one possible method would be to make the collective preference always correspond with the individual preference of whoever happened to be the strongest (or richest or smartest) single individual. Obviously, we would want to say that such a procedure does not satisfy some minimum requirements for a fair and reasonable method of democratic choice.

The real problem, then, is to identify methods which aggregate individual preferences into collective preferences while simultaneously satisfying some minimum conditions of fairness and rea-

[1] Dodgson's work on the theory of elections was reprinted, with extensive commentary, by Black (1958: 189–238); the quoted passage appears at page 226. A fascinating and tragic connection between this work and the famous Alice books is provided by Black's suggestion (1958: 199–200) that Dodgson's interest in electoral procedures stemmed primarily from his repressed desire to thwart, in the world of college politics, the father of the real-life Alice and his superior at Christ Church, Dean H. G. Liddell. On Dodgson's identification of himself with the Dodo, see Gardner (1960: 44). For a survey of earlier work on the theory of elections by Condorcet and others, see Black (1958: 156–88).

sonableness. In a brilliant effort to illuminate this problem, Arrow (1951) analyzed a set of four such conditions which he considered necessary for any reasonable process of public choice to satisfy.[2]

1. *Unrestricted domain*: All logically possible orderings of the alternatives must be admissible as individual preference orderings. No possible pattern of preferences can be ruled out *a priori* because, for example, it is odd or untraditional.

2. *Unanimity principle*: If any alternative is preferred to another by every individual, then it must also be preferred by the collectivity. A process lacking this property could produce distressing collective choices with which the individual members of the collectivity were in unanimous disagreement.

3. *Non-dictatorship*: No individual's personal preferences must necessarily determine the collective preference. This condition rules out the cases mentioned above in which, for example, the strongest single individual always gets his way, regardless of everyone else's preferences.

4. *Independence of irrelevant alternatives*: The collective choice between two alternatives must depend only on the individual preferences between those two alternatives, not on comparisons involving any other alternatives. This condition rules out certain procedures, such as the "Borda count," which assign scores to alternatives on the basis of overall individual rankings and then attempt to sum these scores across individuals. Such procedures are eliminated because their results can be changed by adding new alternatives to the list, even if those new alternatives would never themselves be selected.

The gist of Arrow's result is that these four conditions, taken together, are incompatible with coherent collective choice. In particular, Arrow's *general possibility theorem* demonstrates that, if all four conditions hold, it is possible for *any* method of collective choice to produce *intransitive* social orderings of the alternatives.[3] The existence of such an ordering makes the rationality of any collective choice fundamentally problematic; any choice must result in an outcome to which some other would have been collec-

[2] The conditions listed here represent a reworking of Arrow's original set. See Arrow (1963: 96–100).

[3] An intransitive social ordering is one in which there is no clear, stable ranking of alternative from best to worst. For example, with three alternatives, A, B, and C, we might have A preferred to B, B preferred to C, and C preferred to A.

tively preferred.[4] In the felicitous image suggested by Rae (1980), public choice becomes an Escher stairway, promising to lead ever upward to more preferred alternatives but occasionally leaving us unexpectedly back where we started.

For the special case of majority voting, Arrow's theorem proves that in a given set of alternatives there may be no one alternative preferred by a majority to each of the other alternatives. In this respect, it merely formalizes the "paradox of voting" pointed out by Dodgson and others. However, the force of Arrow's result comes not just from the force of the original paradox of majority voting but from the proof that *any conceivable* aggregation procedure satisfying Arrow's four conditions involves analogous logical difficulties. Thus, the theorem is often interpreted as an *impossibility* theorem because it demonstrates the impossibility of ensuring rational collective choice using any procedure that satisfies Arrow's four conditions.

Critical reaction to Arrow's theorem has been decidedly mixed. After scattered early attempts to downplay the paradox, specialists in the field have come to believe that it is both mathematically irrefutable and of major theoretical significance. Summarizing the trend of research, Plott (1976: 511–12) wrote:

> intrigued and curious about this little hole, researchers, not deterred by the possibly irrelevant, began digging in the ground nearby. . . . What they now appear to have been uncovering is a gigantic cavern into which fall almost all of our ideas about social actions. Almost anything we say and/or anyone has ever said about what society wants or should get is threatened with internal inconsistency. It is as though people have been talking for years about a thing that cannot, in *principle*, exist, and a major effort now is needed to see what objectively remains from the conversations.

The reaction to Arrow's theorem among nonspecialist political scientists has been markedly less apocalyptic. Although not seeming to doubt the technical correctness of the result, many do seem to harbor the belief that it is not of central relevance. For one thing, although public choice theorists have gone to great lengths to study the theoretical probability of paradoxical outcomes, they

[4] Technically, this is only true if the intransitivity occurs at the "top" of the preference ordering—that is, if no single alternative is preferred to all the rest. But it appears likely on theoretical grounds that this will be the usual situation. See Plott (1976: 532), Riker (1980: 441–42), and references therein.

have had quite limited success in pointing to actual occurrences in real voting situations.[5] Perhaps more importantly, the axiomatic structure on which the theorem is built strikes many political scientists with different theoretical orientations as inappropriately simple-minded for practical application to problems of interest. Under these circumstances, it may be quite rational for critics to see the pessimistic conclusions of public choice theory as a reflection not on the nature of the real political world but on the unreality of the theory itself and its underlying logic. As Bluhm (1987: 290) put it, our most interesting and most pressing political questions

> will not be answered by a political science that is centrally concerned with the summation of preferences. An adequate science must rather be concerned with the formation of preferences. It must seek to answer the quest[ion] of how we can develop, in democratic fashion, a rational understanding of the problems before us and a rational and agreed upon approach to the solution of those problems. It will be a political science concerned with the definition and implementation of the common good.

In the next section I examine the major theoretical limitation of the classical theory of public choice and of the broader philosophical tradition of which it is a part. I aim to determine to what extent the criticisms offered by competing traditions of political theory are valid and in the longer run to determine whether the classical theory can be adjusted to take due account of these criticisms while retaining the rigor and clarity which make it attractive in the first place.

12.2 A Crucial Limitation of the Classical Theory

The formal mathematical theory developed by Arrow and his successors is a fundamentally liberal creation. Its intellectual pedigree can be traced through the neoclassical economists to the great utilitarians and from there to the origins of liberal theory in the sev-

[5] Most estimates of the frequency of paradoxical outcomes are based on avowedly unrealistic assumptions about the distribution of actual preference patterns. For examples, see the articles by Weisberg and Niemi and by Bjurulf in Niemi and Weisberg (1972). For a rare empirical study, see Bowen's analysis in the same volume of U.S. Senate roll call votes. Among 111 bills studied, Bowen found only 13 for which the probability of a voting cycle was greater than zero and only 3 for which the probability was greater than 0.5.

enteenth century. This entire line of intellectual development shares important concerns and assumptions, of which I wish to focus on one as the distinctive element which justifies the common designation, "liberal": namely, the assumption that individual preferences over a set of relevant alternatives are to be taken as the unchanging, unanalyzed, predetermined basis for public choice. Arrow himself, in noting the theoretical limitations of his work, recognized the tradition behind this assumption. His study assumed, he wrote (1951: 7–8), "that individual values are taken as data and are not capable of being altered by the nature of the decision process itself. This, of course, is the standard view in economic theory (though the unreality of this assumption has been asserted by such writers as Veblen, Professor J. M. Clark, and Knight) and also in the classical liberal creed."

This "standard view" has indeed been criticized on a variety of philosophical, technical, theoretical, and empirical grounds. For example, Frank Knight argued vigorously against the treatment of preferences as givens in traditional economic analyses.

> Of the various sorts of data dealt with in economics, no group is more fundamental or more universally and unquestioningly recognized as such than human wants. We propose to suggest that these wants which are the common starting-point of economic reasoning are from a more critical point of view the most obstinately unknown of all the unknowns in the whole system of variables with which economic science deals. Economics has always treated desires or motives as facts, of a character susceptible to statement in propositions, and sufficiently stable during the period of the activity which they prompt to be treated as causes of that activity in a scientific sense. Wants, it is suggested [here], not only are unstable, changeable in response to all sorts of influences, but it is their essential nature to change and grow; it is an inherent necessity in them. The chief thing which the commonsense individual actually wants is not satisfactions for the wants which he has, but more, and *better* wants. The things which he strives to get in the most immediate sense are far more what he thinks he ought to want than what his untutored preferences prompt. (Knight 1951: 20–22)

Knight was only one of a long string of important thinkers, otherwise steeped in the liberal theory, who resisted the traditional conception of preferences as given. Among the classical political economists, Adam Smith preceded his more famous theory of market capitalism with an ambitious attempt to understand the psychological development of values, *The Theory of Moral Sentiments*. John Stuart Mill rejected the belief of his father and Jeremy Bentham that no distinction is necessary between utilities derived from different objects or activities; the younger Mill held not only that some preferences are "higher" or more noble than others but also that society ought to be designed so as to facilitate the development of higher preferences among the industrial masses.

About the same time, of course, a much more radical break with the liberal tradition was being made by Karl Marx. Much of Marx's analysis followed from his conviction that individual preferences, far from being exogenous, are in fact wholly determined by economic circumstances. In this sense, primarily, Marx may be thought of as the antiliberal theorist par excellence. Marx's followers have continued to criticize the "standard view in economic theory" for ignoring the fact that some consumer preferences are the result of "genuine" interests, whereas others are based on "false consciousness" resulting from various forms of social and economic coercion. Within the traditional theory this distinction is declared irrelevant; and since consumer preferences appear to have much the same economic consequences regardless of how they come to be formed, it is impossible to deny *within the perspective of the theory* that the traditional approach is sensible. The point of the Marxist criticism is that a theory that treated preferences as endogenous would be superior precisely because it encompassed phenomena outside the range of the traditional approach.

The reformulation of social theory by the great turn-of-the-century sociologists, especially Emile Durkheim and Max Weber, can be thought of as in part a reaction against the stark dichotomy posed by the liberal and Marxist views concerning the theoretical status of preferences.[6] Durkheim and Weber were too sophisticated either to accept the Marxist doctrine of economic determinism or to ignore the processes by which social circumstances and interactions helped shape the values and preferences motivating social action. Their goal, which has dominated much of the subsequent development of sociology, was to construct an empirical theory on the middle ground between the Marxist simplification on one side and the liberal simplification on the other.

Among economists the main line of development was in a quite

[6] This thesis is central to the synthesis of classical sociological theory presented by Parsons (1937).

different direction. The formalization of economic theory in terms of marginal utility in the late nineteenth century was a great theoretical step forward; the resulting "neoclassical" edifice has dominated economic theory ever since. But from the standpoint adopted here, neoclassical economics was also a major step backward. By common consent, enforced by considerable technical success, individual preferences once again became the unanalyzed basis for rational economic behavior. To the extent that some economists continued to concern themselves with how preferences emerged, they tended—like Veblen, Clark, and Knight—to remain outside the mainstream of economic analysis.

In the course of this process, the explicitly political concerns of political economy as practiced by John Stuart Mill were excised first from economics and later from the new synthesis of economics and politics reflected in the classical theory of public choice. This theoretical framework was developed to analyze behavior in the economic realm, where preferences, often formed over long periods of time, are repeatedly tested against experience; the framework has been translated bodily to the political realm, where preferences are often much more complex, less strongly developed, and less persistently applicable to a rapidly changing environment. The translation has produced a vigorous, interesting, and occasionally profound body of new political analysis, but the disquieting feeling persists that the body has no heart. The real differences between economic and political circumstances, and between the nature and significance of economic preferences on one hand and political preferences on the other, may make the theoretical structure designed to deal with economic phenomena inadequate for dealing with some important aspects of political life—not for any reason of principle, but simply as a matter of practical fact.

The possibility of a serious mismatch between theory and reality is evident if we simply compare the characteristic concerns and assumptions of the classical theory of public choice with the most salient features of the particular concrete political process described in this book. The classical theory treats as previously determined the set of alternatives from which choices are to be made, but we have seen that in presidential nominating campaigns the effective set of competing candidates sometimes changes from week to week. The classical theory treats the electorate as fixed, but we have seen that in nominating campaigns decision making is fragmented among different self-selected electorates at different points in the process. Finally, the classical theory assumes that decision makers have sufficient information to judge the relative merits of the alternatives, but we have seen that in nominating campaigns some candidates begin virtually unknown to the public and the struggle for mere recognition is centrally important to the success of those candidates' campaigns.

Most importantly, the classical theory of public choice is essentially static in character. It posits individual decision makers endowed with arbitrary sets of preferences which remain fixed throughout the choice process; these individual preferences must simply be tabulated and aggregated into some corresponding "collective preference." But we have seen that in nominating campaigns preferences are dynamic, subject to significant change as a result of learning and momentum.

Presidential nominating campaigns are of special interest because they present situations in which the dynamic elements of political choice are particularly striking. The sequential nature of primary elections, the emphasis of the news media on outcomes to the seeming exclusion of substance, and the generally low levels of public knowledge and interest during the primary period combine to create highly favorable conditions for the short-run responsiveness of individual preferences to changes in the preference expressed by other political actors. In this respect, the modern presidential nominating process provides an unusually vivid example of the potential mismatch between a theoretical framework with static and exogenous preferences and a political world with dynamic and endogenous preferences. Still, there are many other political choices for which the assumption of a static, individualistic choice process probably does considerable violence to reality. Individual decision makers may be strongly influenced over time by the persuasive efforts of other political actors. Collective choices may result from a sequence of separate decisions, each of which affects subsequent steps in the process. Choices may involve not so much an assessment of preferences at a specific time as a "standing decision"—or "nondecision"—about political institutions and procedures. In each of these cases, the classical theory of public choice must be adapted to a dynamic situation in which the shaping and mutual adjustment of individual preferences is an important aspect of a real political process. A theory taking preferences as given is less appropriate in each case than one recognizing the fact that, as Edelman (1971: 8) put it, "political actions chiefly arouse or satisfy people not by granting or withholding their stable, substantive demands but rather by changing their demands and expectations."

Perhaps ironically, the most important theoretical consequence of this practical fact may be to simplify the basic problem of public choice in its classical form: the problem of aggregating diverse individual preferences into a consensus or majority for a single alternative. Arrow's theorem and related results in the static tradition indicate that this problem is insoluble in a static world of arbitrary preferences. Reflected in the work of Shepsle (1979) and others but noted most explicitly by Riker (1980), the implication of Arrow's result is that the actual outcome of political processes must be determined not by preferences alone but also by the structure of the political insititutions which channel preferences in particular ways. The point of my analysis is that the reciprocal shaping of preferences involved in the dynamics of momentum may provide precisely that sort of institutional structure, assuring a determinate solution to what would otherwise be a literally insoluble problem of preference aggregation.

The idea that preference aggregation can be facilitated through the institutional encouragement of preference change is by no means new. Dodgson proposed a solution of this sort to deal with the possibility of cyclical majorities raised in his Oxford pamphlet (Black 1958: 227). If majorities are found to be cyclical, he wrote, "opportunity shall be given for further debate. . . . The Chairman shall inform the meeting how many alterations of votes each issue requires to give it a majority over every other separately. If . . . any elector wish[es] to alter his paper, he may do so: and if the cyclical majorities be thereby done away with, the voting shall proceed by former Rules."[7] Dodgson's procedure is only one of a wide variety of actual or potential mechanisms for facilitating the mutual shaping and adjustment of individual preferences in a truly social process of collective choice. I aim here not to proliferate such examples but to suggest that the mechanisms they involve may play an important role in mitigating the dilemma inherent in the classical theory of public choice.

Because the contemporary presidential nominating process provides an especially vivid example of a dynamic choice process, it

[7] Dodgson also recognized the possibility of strategic voting. To place some check on the deliberate creation of cycles through strategic voting, he recommended that every voter begin by listing his preferences in writing; thus, strategic deviations from those preferences on subsequent ballots would be evident to and presumably discouraged by the assembly.

also provides an especially vivid example of how such processes may result in coherent majority choices, in spite of the theoretical difficulties predicted by the static classical theory of public choice. Arrow's theorem and related work suggest that the probability of arriving at a majority choice from a set of several competing candidates should be very small. Some important institutional features of the nominating process, such as public funding of minor candidates and proportional representation in many primary and caucus states, reinforce that pessimistic conclusion.[8] But actual experience with the presidential nominating process has been exactly the opposite of what we are led to expect on theoretical grounds. Every recent campaign—no matter how many candidates it involved, what specific rules were used to translate votes into delegates, or how complicated the electorate's preferences may have been—has produced a clear winner. The problem of preference aggregation central to the classical theory has been overcome, time and time again, by the dynamic features of the nominating process described in this book.[9]

This striking example suggests that generalizing the classical theory of public choice to incorporate dynamic elements in the real political world may also soften the pessimistic implications of the theory in its purely formal aspects. On one hand, an explicitly dynamic representation of political choice would reflect more faithfully the reality insisted upon by a long line of political theorists and observers; on the other, it might provide an illuminating way out of Arrow's formal dilemma, a dilemma interpreted by its enthusiasts as a profound undermining of the goal of much traditional political thought.

Lest we be too quick to congratulate ourselves on this escape, it may be worth pointing out that the solution existed long before the problem itself was posed in the precise technical language of

[8] Of course, from the perspective of political columnists the prospect of a deadlocked nominating process is a source not of pessimism but of great cheer. The drama inherent in "brokered convention" scenarios makes them perennial sources of media speculation, despite the rarity of their actual occurrence. For a recent example, see Paul Taylor's tale in "Sometimes Accidents Happen," *Washington Post National Weekly Edition*, 13 April 1987, p. 7.

[9] Hence the response by David Broder to Taylor's "brokered convention" scenario cited in footnote 8: "The System Won't Permit It," *Washington Post National Weekly Edition*, 13 April 1987, p. 7. "The nominating system we have," Broder claimed flatly, "does not permit late-starting candidacies or brokered conventions. . . . Forget it. It doesn't happen."

modern economics.[10] Consider Stavely's (1972: 155) description and analysis of the ancient Romans' choice, by lot, of the first voting unit in their traditional sequential voting process:

> This *centuria praerogativa* not only voted before the rest of the assembly; it also had the result of its vote announced before the remainder of the centuries were called. It was therefore in a position to set a pattern for the voting and to exercise not a little influence on the uncommitted members of later centuries. Cicero indeed speaks of it as the "omen of the elections" and makes the somewhat extravagent claim that the consular candidate who was put in first place by the prerogative century invariably secured election. The reason for the institution of the practice of conferring a prerogative vote upon one unit remains a matter for conjecture; but as it dated from the latter part of the third century, when the number of candidates at elections was probably on the increase and the verdict of an ever-growing electorate was becoming less predictable, there is much to be said for the view that it was designed to ensure a speedy and decisive result to electoral contests by discouraging too great a spread of votes among the several candidates.

Here is a dynamic choice process, complete with momentum, to serve precisely the aggregative function of the modern dynamic process of presidential nomination. If anything, the ancients' institutional engineering was more conscious, and more consciously sophisticated, than that of their modern counterparts. In each election they chose their Iowa or New Hampshire by lot for two reasons which may still seem compelling. "For one thing," Stavely explained (1972: 155), "the election campaign would have been reduced to a mockery if the identity of such an influential voting unit had been predetermined in any way. For another, the influence which it did exert was likely to be more effective if its selection could be represented to the more superstitious among the voters as a manifestation of divine will."

If our modern secular polity is no longer very interested in manifestations of divine will, it does at least still put some stock in the luck of the draw. And the complaint that the contemporary presidential nominating process has been "reduced to a mockery" precisely by the preordained importance of Iowa and New Hampshire

[10] Here I draw with gratitude on the classical education of Stanley Kelley.

is very much alive.[11] Perhaps, in politics as elsewhere, there is really nothing new under the sun.

12.3 Liberal Democracy in a Dynamic World

The analysis of presidential nominating politics provided in this book suggests that the classical theory of public choice, with its emphasis on the problem of aggregating fixed, arbitrary preferences into a single collective choice, does not do justice to the fluid, dynamic aspects of the real social choice process leading to the nomination of a presidential candidate. In a modern nominating campaign, where preferences sometimes appear to change substantially in a matter of days or weeks, it simply does not make sense to insist upon a theoretical framework in which preferences are taken as given. If observable preference changes were random, they might require only a minor modification in the conceptual structure represented by the classical theory of public choice. But the preference changes I have documented in this book are not random: they work in systematic, predictable ways, not as the result of exogenous political events but as an integral part of the process of choice itself.

This fact is important because it may offer an escape from the fundamental problem posed by the classical theory of public choice—the problem of how to aggregate preferences to arrive at a coherent collective decision. My analysis suggests that, at least under some circumstances, quite diverse individual preferences can be shaped and modified by social interaction to produce, if not a consensus, at least a genuine majority for a single alternative. Thus, an explicitly dynamic perspective contributes toward vitiating the formal dilemma constructed by Arrow.

A determined advocate of the classical theory might well argue that nothing I have written directly falsifies that theory. At some fundamental level, the argument would go, preferences *are* static; what changes is how those underlying preferences relate to concrete electoral choices. Given changes over time in the field of competing candidates, the strategies of those candidates, the amount and kind of information possessed by voters, and their expecta-

[11] For a representative condemnation of the "crazy," "wacky," and "demeaning" courtship of political activists and ordinary voters in Iowa and New Hampshire by contemporary presidential candidates, see Paul Taylor's article, "Is This Any Way to Pick a President?" *Washington Post National Weekly Edition*, 13 April 1987, pp. 6–7.

tions about the behavior of other voters, static underlying preferences produce different electoral behavior. Formal theorists working in the classical tradition have recently begun to explicate the ways in which voters in a dynamic, low information environment might bring their underlying preferences to bear on electoral choices. The potential fruitfulness of this approach is illustrated in McKelvey and Ordeshook's (1982) paper on the role of polls and endorsements in elections with limited information. The results of such theorizing are in many respects consistent with my own focus on both underlying political predispositions and the changing interactions between those predispositions and the dynamic factors arising from the sequential nature of the primary process. But the *interpretation* imposed on those results by classical theorists seems to me defective in two important respects.

First, the fundamental focus, almost as a matter of faith, on underlying static preferences tends, in practice, to obscure many of the most interesting questions surrounding any real process of electoral choice. What are the underlying preferences that drive political behavior in a given campaign? How are connections made between alternatives at the level of underlying preferences and alternatives in the form of living, breathing candidates? How do these connections change with new information and changing political circumstances? None of these questions is excluded in principle from the classical theory. But the traditional concerns of the classical theory and the difficulties involved in representing complicated dynamic processes with simple, tractable models of voting behavior have combined to focus attention elsewhere. Eminently important political issues—from why momentum exists in the contemporary nominating process to why we got Jimmy Carter but not Gary Hart—go unexamined.

At a deeper level, the problem with the classical theory is that it leaves fundamentally unsettled the philosophical status of individual preferences and public choices in a dynamic political world. The results of the classical theory strike a significant blow at the very idea of democratic choice by suggesting that no choice process can really reflect the popular will in a coherent way. If we are to have democracy at all, the classical theorists argue, it can be only a very weak form of democracy in which clear majorities can sometimes block the reelection of unpopular incumbents. "The kind of democracy that thus survives," Riker wrote (1982: 244), "is not . . . popular rule, but rather an intermittent, sometimes random, even perverse, popular veto."

Can there be more to democratic choice than this? The thrust of my analysis is that, in a dynamic political world, there can be. Social interaction can produce genuine consensus from diverse individual predispositions. What is still missing is a firm philosophical basis on which to construct a normative judgment about whether any particular process of social interaction or any particular social outcome is good or bad. Within the classical perspective, a consensus produced by dynamic forces is inherently suspect because it is inherently social: it involves more than the mechanical aggregation of fixed individual preferences. But once we move beyond this philosophical prejudice, liberal democratic theory provides little systematic basis for addressing fundamental normative questions about the dynamics of public choice.

This lacuna reflects the fact that, once we admit dynamic factors into our analyses of public choice in an explicit way, we confront a fundamental ambiguity in the liberal notion of an optimal social outcome. Under the classical theory, a choice process need only aggregate an arbitrary set of individual preferences fairly and efficiently into a single collective decision. But once we recognize that preferences are shaped, in part, by the process of public choice itself, we lose this firm bench mark for what a satisfactory choice should be. Should such a choice reflect as accurately as possible the original, "unsocialized" preferences of individual choosers? Or should it reflect the "socialized" preferences that result from interactions among decision makers in real processes of political choice?

Dodgson, for one, was inconsistent on this point. As we have seen, he advocated procedures designed to avoid cyclic majorities in committee settings, including opportunities for debate and provision by the chairman of information about the distribution of members' preferences. But he also advocated, for public elections lasting several days, that early returns should be kept secret so as not to influence later voters (Cohen 1982: 109). His first proposal seems to base public choice on socialized preferences, the second on unsocialized preferences.

Neither distinct set of preferences is obviously more "genuine" than the other. To the extent that important differences exist between them, any choice of one over the other implies a willingness to disregard at least some real preferences of real participants in the process of choice. This is not merely an abstract possibility; the problem arises in the real political world as well. At the 1980 Democratic convention, for example, supporters of Edward Kennedy argued that delegates committed to Jimmy Carter on the basis of public preference expressions several weeks or months old should be "freed" to reflect current public preferences, presumably more favorable to Kennedy.[12] Disregarding the factual premises and political motivations involved in this argument, it seems clear that the unresolved normative issue underlying the policy argument arises from precisely the dynamic forces I have focused on here.

Not surprisingly, traditional liberal political philosophy provides no clear resolution of this underlying normative issue. We could hardly expect that it would, given the persistent unwillingness of traditional liberal theorists to focus systematic attention on the questions of where preferences come from and how they change. My point here is simply that, given the current state of theoretical development, the dependence of individual preferences on dynamic social forces provides a considerable logical stumbling block for any traditional justification of liberal, individualistic institutions based on the autonomy of those preferences.

Although a few theorists have attempted to integrate the traditional liberal emphasis on autonomous individual preferences with an explicit recognition of the powerful dynamic forces at work in many real processes of collective choice, so far no one has succeeded in producing a living, fertile offspring from two such disparate parents. Perhaps, once the autonomy of subjective preferences is denied, modified liberal positions can provide only precarious stops on the way to a strong alternative emphasis on objective interests. Given such an emphasis, the attractiveness of alternative choice procedures would depend on their ability to represent objective interests effectively, without particular regard for expressed public preferences. Thus, it should not be surprising that some analysts who have addressed the issue of preference formation most directly have tended to arrive at an unliberal conclusion: any public choice must be justified not only, perhaps not even primarily, in terms of the degree to which it reflects any specific set of expressed preferences but in terms of its correspondence with objective interests of one kind or another.

If there is a liberal resolution to be found, it will require a rein-

[12] Actually, the call for an "open convention" originated with unaligned Democratic politicians equally unenthusiastic about Carter and Kennedy as potential nominees (Kamarck 1986: 315–24). However, given the fact that Carter could win under the existing rules and Kennedy could not, the movement naturally attracted Kennedy supporters willing to shake things up in the hope that their candidate could find a way to win once existing delegate commitments were suspended.

terpretation—along lines as yet unrecognized—of what preferences are and of how and why they should be satisfied. The socially shaped preferences developed by individuals living in a dynamic political world may ultimately provide a suitable basis from which to reach collective choices. But a philosophical justification of political institutions in such a world will have to extend beyond traditional liberalism and its static, asocial conception of the process of public choice. The result will be a fundamental change in our inherited ideas about politics.

Appendixes

APPENDIX A

Data

A.1 Media Content

Each of the last three primary seasons has produced a major media content analysis. In 1976, Thomas Patterson followed all three network newscasts, *Time* and *Newsweek*, and four local newspapers in conjunction with his multiwave, year-long panel study of political attitudes in Erie, Pennsylvania, and Los Angeles (Patterson 1980). In 1980, Michael Robinson and Margaret Sheehan followed the "CBS Evening News" and the UPI wire (Robinson and Sheehan 1983). And in 1984, Henry Brady also followed the UPI wire (Brady 1985a).

Throughout this book I have treated media content as a single undifferentiated flow. My choice of a specific medium to measure content in any given instance—newspaper stories, the UPI news wire, or network television news—was dictated almost entirely by the availability of data. Fortunately, detailed studies of campaign coverage suggest the various media are similar in most important respects. Some of Patterson's (1980) data from the 1976 primary season are shown in Table A.1 by way of illustration. On every dimension, network television news, newspapers, and news magazines were virtually indistinguishable in their emphases. Thus, it does not seem unreasonable, for my purposes, to treat the media as a monolithic information source in the nominating process.

One disadvantage of the 1980 and 1984 wire service data is that they provide no indication of which stories carried on the wire actually appeared in print or of how prominently they were placed. Another more general difficulty in using the various content analyses is that each has its own focus and procedures; direct comparisons across campaigns are often impossible. To circumvent these problems I organized a modest content analysis of my own, executed by C. Lawrence Evans and Paul Janaskie. For each of the three most recent primary seasons, Evans and Janaskie measured the proportion of each day's front page devoted to campaign stories in the *New York Times, Washington Post, Houston Chronicle*, and *Rochester Democrat and Chronicle*. The resulting data are limited by the fact that stories are not allocated to candidates to produce can-

TABLE A.1 Comparisons Across Media of Primary News Content, 1976

	Network evening newscasts	Newspapers (Erie, Pa., and Los Angeles)	National News Magazines
Stories about "game" (winning and losing, strategy, logistics, appearances, hoopla) rather than "substance"	64	62	62
Strategy and momentum as explanations for Republican primary outcomes	22	16	20
Coverage of first-place finisher, Democratic primaries	59	57	62
Coverage of Carter, Democratic primaries	48	44	54

Source: Patterson (1980: 29, 51, 45, 46).
Note: Percentages reflect portion of total newscast, newspaper, or news magazine devoted to primary campaign coverage.

didate-specific coverage scores. Nevertheless, they provide a workable standardized measure of temporal variations in the general intensity of media coverage during each campaign.[1] They are shown, aggregated by week, in Tables A.2 through A.6.

A.2 SURVEY DATA

My analyses in Part II of individual reactions to the nominating campaign are based, for the most part, on data from the 1984 National Election Study (NES) survey. The survey was conducted by the Center for Political Studies of the Institute for Social Research at the University of Michigan under the direction of Warren E. Miller. The 1984 study included both the traditional pre- and post-election surveys in the fall and an innovative "continuous monitoring" element. Beginning in mid-January and continuing through late November, approximately seventy-five respondents were interviewed each week. Interviews, conducted by telephone, lasted about forty minutes on average. Each week's respondents were se-

[1] The data shown in the tables and used throughout my analysis are simple averages of the front page shares for the four separate newspapers. To avoid home-state distortions, I have dropped the *New York Times* from the average for the weeks before and after New York, Connecticut, and New Jersey primaries, the *Rochester Democrat and Chronicle* for the weeks before and after New York primaries, and the *Houston Chronicle* for the weeks before and after Texas caucuses.

TABLE A.2 Democratic Campaign Coverage, 1976

Week	N.Y. Times	Wash. Post	Hous. Chron.	Roch. Dem. & Chron.	Average
14–20 Jan	2.0	5.5	1.1	1.8	2.6
21–27 Jan	3.8	2.8	1.0	1.4	2.2
28 Jan–3 Feb	0.5	1.1	1.6	0.5	0.9
4–10 Feb	2.4	3.7	3.6	0	2.4
11–17 Feb	1.7	1.5	3.1	2.2	2.1
18–24 Feb	2.2	5.3	0	0	1.9
25 Feb–2 Mar	10.2	12.2	4.4	6.9	8.4
3–9 Mar	14.7	10.6	1.2	6.5	8.2
10–16 Mar	5.2	12.3	4.6	7.5	7.4
17–23 Mar	10.4	7.2	1.7	7.2	6.6
24–30 Mar	9.5	4.6	1.5	10.7	6.6
31 Mar–6 Apr	10.2[a]	5.9	2.8	12.8[a]	5.1
7–13 Apr	17.5[a]	12.3	2.0	7.1[a]	8.4
14–20 Apr	1.7	5.8	1.5	4.4	3.4
21–27 Apr	7.4	8.0	1.5	2.7	4.9
28 Apr–4 May	20.3	19.7	11.4[a]	16.1	15.7
5–11 May	11.1	12.3	9.6	5.8	9.7
12–18 May	6.9	11.3[a]	2.1	10.9	7.2
19–25 May	6.1	7.7[a]	1.6	5.8	4.9
26 May–1 Jun	11.6	4.5	0.3	7.7	6.0
2–8 Jun	10.1	3.9	1.3	4.6	5.0
9–15 Jun	17.6	16.9	1.2	12.3	12.0

Source: Original data gathered by C. Lawrence Evans and Paul Janaskie.

Note: Coverage is estimated by measuring percentage of front page devoted to campaign.

[a] Home-state coverage; adjusted before averaging.

lected through a random digit dialing procedure intended to obtain a statistically representative sample of the noninstitutionalized adult population. Weekly response rates varied between 53 and 69 percent and averaged approximately 60 percent.

My analysis is based only on the responses of people interviewed during the primary season—the twenty-three-week period beginning in mid-January and ending in mid-June. Because my focus is entirely on the Democratic campaign, I have limited the analysis to respondents who either identified with or "leaned" toward the Democratic party. Given this restriction, the number of usable responses for each week of the 1984 primary season ranges from twenty-four to fifty-three and averages almost thirty-eight. The definition of sample weeks and the actual weekly sample sizes are shown in Table A.7.

In addition to the 1984 NES survey, I have made some use of

TABLE A.3 Republican Campaign Coverage, 1976

Week	N.Y. Times	Wash. Post	Hous. Chron.	Roch. Dem. & Chron.	Average
14–20 Jan	4.6	0	0.8	0	1.4
21–27 Jan	2.5	0	0	0	0.6
28 Jan–3 Feb	3.0	0.7	1.5	1.9	1.8
4–10 Feb	4.0	2.5	0.7	4.0	2.8
11–17 Feb	2.3	4.5	5.3	2.0	3.5
18–24 Feb	2.9	5.2	1.4	7.2	4.2
25 Feb–2 Mar	10.5	8.4	2.7	7.8	7.4
3–9 Mar	6.8	6.2	1.6	4.7	4.8
10–16 Mar	4.6	4.9	4.5	5.6	4.9
17–23 Mar	3.0	3.2	0.3	5.9	3.1
24–30 Mar	7.3	2.5	3.3	8.1	5.3
31 Mar–6 Apr	4.6	3.8	1.7	5.7	4.0
7–13 Apr	3.8	3.3	2.8	3.6	3.4
14–20 Apr	4.9	1.6	2.0	3.4	3.0
21–27 Apr	1.9	4.7	1.7	3.5	3.0
28 Apr–4 May	9.9	7.3	9.8[a]	11.3	8.2
5–11 May	7.6	5.4	3.4	14.2	7.6
12–18 May	9.4	16.0[a]	3.4	6.6	6.6
19–25 May	3.8	6.9[a]	1.9	9.7	5.1
26 May–1 Jun	4.6	4.2	1.9	7.3	4.5
2–8 Jun	4.7	3.3	0	6.6	3.6
9–15 Jun	10.0	10.5	2.9	4.8	7.0

Source: Original data gathered by C. Lawrence Evans and Paul Janaskie.
Note: Coverage is estimated by measuring percentage of front page devoted to campaign.
[a] Home-state coverage; adjusted before averaging.

data from other primary season surveys. The 1980 NES survey included two separate national cross-sections, one in late January and February with 1,008 respondents and the other in April with 965 respondents. Almost 85 percent of the January-February respondents were reinterviewed in June. I have relied on these data for estimates of information levels for the various candidates during the 1980 primary season. They also provided the basis for my earlier analysis of momentum in the 1980 campaign (Bartels 1985), in which some of the ideas presented in this book appeared in preliminary form.

For 1976 there is no corresponding preconvention element in the NES survey. Instead, I have relied on Patterson's survey in Los Angeles and Erie, Pennsylvania—a five-wave panel study with the first three waves occuring in February (1,002 respondents), April (897 respondents of whom 772 had been previously interviewed),

TABLE A.4 Democratic Campaign Coverage, 1980

Week	N.Y. Times	Wash. Post	Hous. Chron.	Roch. Dem. & Chron.	Average
16–22 Jan	0.5	4.5	1.3	0.8	1.8
23–29 Jan	3.3	4.2	0	1.7	2.3
30 Jan–5 Feb	0	2.5	0	4.9	1.8
6–12 Feb	5.2	4.2	0.9	2.1	3.1
13–19 Feb	0	2.6	0	0.4	0.8
20–26 Feb	3.6	2.2	0	2.4	2.0
27 Feb–4 Mar	4.6	1.9	1.5	4.6	3.2
5–11 Mar	4.9	1.1	1.5	6.1	3.4
12–18 Mar	4.3	3.2	3.1	5.5	4.0
19–25 Mar	7.7[a]	3.0	0.7	16.5[a]	2.3
26 Mar–1 Apr	8.3[a]	5.8	0.9	6.2[a]	3.9
2–8 Apr	2.4	2.9	1.2	1.8	2.1
9–15 Apr	0	0	0	0	0
16–22 Apr	2.4	2.4	1.6	0	1.6
23–29 Apr	4.2	4.7	0.5	2.3	2.9
30 Apr–6 May	2.8	2.5	4.9[a]	4.1	2.6
7–13 May	3.5	1.9[a]	0	0.9	1.4
14–20 May	0.8	1.5[a]	0	0.4	0.4
21–27 May	0.6	0.9	0	0	0.4
28 May–3 Jun	8.0[a]	3.1	0.5	0	1.4
4–10 Jun	14.3[a]	10.7	2.3	2.5	5.9
11–15 Jun	0	5.5	0	0	1.4

Source: Original data gathered by C. Lawrence Evans and Paul Janaskie.
Note: Coverage is estimated by measuring percentage of front page devoted to campaign.
[a] Home-state coverage; adjusted before averaging.

and June (907 respondents of whom 720 were in the original panel). Details of the sampling procedure and an indication of the range of content are available in Patterson's (1980) published report. The data themselves are available through the Inter-university Consortium for Political and Social Research, as are all the NES data sets.

The analysis of contextual forces in Chapter 7 makes some use of data from exit polls conducted in thirteen primary states in 1984 by ABC News. These data are summarized in the form of various cross-tabulations in an ABC News election handbook edited by Smith (n. d.). The range of questions available in the exit polls is, of course, much narrower than in the major academic surveys, and there is little in the way of documentation regarding the sampling design, sample sizes, or possible selection bias.

Finally, my comparison in Chapter 7 of the characteristics of pri-

TABLE A.5 Republican Campaign Coverage, 1980

Week	N.Y. Times	Wash. Post	Hous. Chron.	Roch. Dem. & Chron.	Average
16–22 Jan	4.5	2.5	1.7	0.8	2.4
23–29 Jan	1.5	2.8	0	1.5	1.4
30 Jan–5 Feb	0.9	0.8	0	0	0.4
6–12 Feb	1.2	0	2.3	0	0.9
13–19 Feb	0.9	2.6	1.0	1.8	1.6
20–26 Feb	5.7	6.4	3.6	4.4	5.0
27 Feb–4 Mar	8.9	5.6	4.6	8.0	6.8
5–11 Mar	15.3	13.4	8.7	12.5	12.5
12–18 Mar	7.9	6.3	2.7	2.3	4.8
19–25 Mar	6.5[a]	6.5	0.7	4.2	4.2
26 Mar–1 Apr	2.2[a]	3.2	0.9	3.0	2.7
2–8 Apr	2.4	2.0	1.2	3.3	2.2
9–15 Apr	0	0	0	0	0
16–22 Apr	7.1	8.2	0	0.8	4.0
23–29 Apr	3.1	10.4	2.3	1.5	4.3
30 Apr–6 May	2.9	0.8	3.4[a]	1.5	1.5
7–13 May	0.8	3.0[a]	0	0.9	0.6
14–20 May	0.8	0.8[a]	0	0.4	0.4
21–27 May	5.0	3.0	2.2	4.0	3.6
28 May–3 Jun	3.0	1.1	0	0.5	1.2
4–10 Jun	3.0	2.7	2.3	0	2.0
11–15 Jun	3.5	0	0	0	0.9

Source: Original data gathered by C. Lawrence Evans and Paul Janaskie.
Note: Coverage is estimated by measuring percentage of front page devoted to campaign.
[a] Home-state coverage; adjusted before averaging.

mary voters and party identifiers in 1980 is based on data from the autumn (pre- and postelection) waves of the NES survey. These data have the advantage of including verified information on primary turnout, and they are based on a sufficiently large sample to permit reasonably precise estimates of the characteristics of primary voters; there are 1,192 Republican identifiers of whom 259 were verified primary voters, and 1,853 Democratic identifiers of whom 430 were verified primary voters.

A.3 Measuring Chances

In Chapter 3 I examine the causes, and in Chapter 6 the effects, of prospective voters' perceptions of the various candidates' chances of winning the nomination. The data on perceptions of

TABLE A.6 Democratic Campaign Coverage, 1984

Week	N.Y. Times	Wash. Post	Hous. Chron.	Roch. Dem. & Chron.	Average
11–17 Jan	3.9	8.2	1.2	4.2	4.4
18–24 Jan	0.8	3.5	0.7	1.7	1.7
25–31 Jan	2.1	4.4	0	0	1.6
1–7 Feb	2.6	3.4	7.6	1.0	3.6
8–14 Feb	1.1	1.4	5.7	0.3	2.1
15–21 Feb	4.0	9.3	10.0	7.0	7.6
22–28 Feb	5.4	16.7	4.7	11.0	9.4
29 Feb–6 Mar	15.6	26.7	8.0	10.3	15.2
7–13 Mar	9.2	20.0	7.4	15.0	12.9
14–20 Mar	17.7	24.6	10.7	13.1	16.5
21–27 Mar	11.4[a]	11.4	4.1	15.0	9.9
28 Mar–3 Apr	16.0[a]	16.0	2.4	19.1[a]	8.7
4–10 Apr	6.6[a]	8.5	5.9	10.3[a]	6.8
11–17 Apr	2.1	12.1	2.0	1.3	4.4
18–24 Apr	2.5	11.4	0	0.7	3.6
25 Apr–1 May	4.4	7.5	6.4	2.6	5.2
2–8 May	6.9	13.0	10.4[a]	5.0	7.6
9–15 May	3.0	11.5	1.7	1.8	4.5
16–22 May	2.8	6.6	1.5	0.8	2.9
23–29 May	3.4	5.2	2.1	0.7	2.8
30 May–5 Jun	4.4	6.8	0.1	3.2	3.6
6–12 Jun	11.0	14.1	3.3	6.1	8.6
13–15 Jun	2.0	2.0	6.7	0	2.7

Source: Original data gathered by C. Lawrence Evans.
Note: Coverage is estimated by measuring percentage of front page devoted to campaign.
[a] Home-state coverage; adjusted before averaging.

chances are taken from the 1984 NES survey.[2] Respondents' perceptions of each candidate's chances of winning the nomination were measured using items of the following form: "Now let's talk about who is likely to win the *Democratic nomination for President.* We will be using a scale which runs from 0 to 100, where 0 represents no chance for the nomination, 50 represents *an even chance,* and 100 represents *certain* victory. Using this 0 to 100 scale, what do you think *Walter Mondale's* chances are of winning the nomina-

[2] Patterson's 1976 study asked respondents to rate the candidates' chances of winning the nomination on a one-to-seven scale. The 1980 NES survey asked which candidate was "most likely" to win each party's nomination, but it did not ask for direct estimates of the various candidates' chances. Neither format is as convenient for my purposes as the relatively direct probability format used in the 1984 NES survey.

TABLE A.7 NES Democratic Primary Season Sample, 1984

Week	Dates	Number of Respondents
1	11–17 January	24
2	18–24 January	28
3	25–31 January	28
4	1–7 February	37
5	8–14 February	39
6	15–21 February	32
7	22–28 February	51
8	29 February–6 March	45
9	7–13 March	33
10	14–20 March	53
11	21–27 March	46
12	28 March–3 April	30
13	4–10 April	49
14	11–17 April	39
15	18–24 April	29
16	25 April–1 May	39
17	2–8 May	36
18	9–15 May	37
19	16–22 May	39
20	23–29 May	40
21	30 May–5 June	39
22	6–12 June	37
23	13–15 June	38
TOTAL		868

Note: Number of respondents shown for each week includes Democratic identifiers and "leaners" only.

tion?" Responses to these questions resist interpretation as probability estimates in any literal sense. For example, some respondents assigned a total probability estimate of *400* percent to the six candidates they were asked about (Mondale, Glenn, Cranston, Jackson, Kennedy, and Hart); the *average* respondent assigned a total probability of more than *200* percent. These peculiarities may simply reflect the well-documented fact that untrained respondents have difficulty assigning coherent probabilities to uncertain events. Alternatively, they may result from the use of the phrase "even chance" in the question, which seems to suggest that a candidate with one chance in six (an "even chance" relative to each of the other candidates) should be assigned a "probability" of 50.

To approximate more closely a genuine probability measure, I rescaled the raw "chances" reported by respondents in two ways. First, I raised the raw scores (divided by 100) to the 2.5 power. The resulting probabilities still run from zero to one, but a raw score of

50 turns into a transformed score of .177 (approximately one-sixth). This transformation reduces the average total "probability" assigned by each respondent to about 1.2. To remove remaining individual differences, I then normalized each respondent's probabilities to sum to one.

There are four kinds of missing data to confront in dealing with these perceptions of chances. If the respondent did not recognize the candidate's name in an earlier question, I attribute a "chances" score of zero. If the respondent recognized the candidate's name but did not know where to place him on the chances scale, I attribute a score of 50, before making any of the adjustments described in the preceding paragraph. If the respondent was interviewed in a week in which the "chances" question was not asked for Gary Hart (i.e., before the New Hampshire primary), I attribute a raw score of 50 or zero for Hart depending upon whether or not the respondent could rate him on the thermometer scale. If the respondent was interviewed after "chances" questions were dropped for a candidate (after Connecticut for Cranston, after Pennsylvania for Glenn), I attribute a score of zero for that candidate.

In Chapter 3 and elsewhere I relate public perceptions of the candidates' chances to three distinct kinds of campaign events. Together, these three kinds of events are intended to measure the objective political environment shaping expectations about the candidates' chances at any given point in the primary season.[3] For related efforts, see Aldrich's (1980a: 94–99) measure of "competitive standing" and Marshall's (1981) measure of "media verdicts."

Cumulative Primary Vote Shares

This measure reflects each candidate's share of the total vote cast in all previous primaries and in the Iowa caucuses, with two adjustments. First, the candidates' percentages in each state are weighted not by the number of votes cast in the state but by the amount of media coverage devoted to the campaign in the subsequent week.[4] When there is more than one primary in a single week, each candidate's vote share is the average of his vote share in each state, with states weighted by the number of delegates at stake in each. Second, to reflect the fact that primary victories and defeats gradually fade from memory, previous results are dis-

[3] The analysis relating subjective perceptions of chances to these specific campaign events is described in Appendix C.1.

[4] The media coverage data are described in Appendix A.1.

counted by 10 percent each week in determining the cumulative average (for example, Mondale's victory in the Iowa caucuses in 1984 loses half its effect by the time of the Pennsylvania primary seven weeks later).

Last Week's Vote Shares

Public perceptions of the candidates' chances do seem to respond to cumulative primary results over the course of the campaign season. But they respond with special force, at any given point in the campaign, to the *most recent* primary results. Presumably this fact reflects the emphasis of the media on current rather than old news and the rather uncritical attitude of both the media and the public toward primary victories—even when those primary victories have minimal significance for the candidates' objective chances of winning the nomination. My measure of last week's result for each candidate is his share of the primary vote in the most recent primary.[5] When there is more than one primary in a single week, each candidate's vote share is the average of his vote share in each state, with states weighted by the number of delegates at stake in each.

"Objective" Probabilities of Nomination

This measure is based on a comparison of each candidate's share of the delegates selected at a given point in the campaign with the share of remaining delegates he would have to win to achieve a convention majority. The accumulation of delegates increases a candidate's "objective" probability of being nominated in two distinct ways: by reducing the number of remaining delegates he needs to win and by increasing his expected share of delegates in the remaining weeks.[6] The difference between each candidate's expected share of remaining delegates and the share he needs to win a convention majority is translated into a probability estimate on the basis of historical experience from the five campaigns ana-

[5] Because primaries are not scheduled on a regular weekly basis, the most recent primary sometimes occurred two or more weeks before the current week's primary. I have not attempted to take special account of such situations.

[6] The first delegates to appear in the weekly delegate counts for 1984 were "super delegates"—party and public officials chosen by their colleagues and formally uncommitted. In fact, most of these super delegates favored Mondale. I counted super delegates in determining how many remaining delegates each candidate needed to win the nomination, but I did not count them in the share each candidate had won so far; success in winning super delegates is not directly indicative of future success in winning primary and caucus delegates.

lyzed in this book.[7] These estimated probabilities were then normalized to sum to one for all the candidates each week.

A.4 State-level Data

The analyses of primary outcomes in Chapters 8, 9, and 10 include a variety of proxy measures for the political predispositions of each state's primary electorate. Data on race (percent black), urbanization (percent living in Standard Metropolitan Statistical Areas), unionization (percent of nonagricultural work force belonging to labor unions), and unemployment (annual percent) were gathered by Paul Janaskie from the *Statistical Abstract of the United States.* Regional effects were estimated using the following conventions:

The south includes the eleven states of the old Confederacy—Alabama, Arkansas, Florida, Georgia, Louisiana, Mississippi, North Carolina, South Carolina, Tennessee, Texas, and Virginia.

new england includes Connecticut, Maine, Massachusetts, New Hampshire, Rhode Island, and Vermont.

The northeast includes all of New England plus New Jersey, New York, and Pennsylvania.

The west includes Arizona, California, Colorado, Idaho, Montana, Nevada, New Mexico, Oregon, Utah, Washington, and Wyoming.

Ideology Scores

The items used to construct the Democratic party liberalism index described in Section 8.2 included 1968 convention voting (support for Eugene McCarthy versus Hubert Humphrey), 1972 convention voting (support for George McGovern plus Shirley Chisholm), 1964 general election voting (support for Lyndon Johnson), and average 1978 ideological ratings for each state's Democratic congressmen (Americans for Democratic Action rating minus Americans for Constitutional Action rating).

[7] A logit analysis was used to estimate the apparent probability of being nominated associated with each week's observed difference between each candidate's current share of delegates and the share of remaining delegates he needed to win. For example, if a candidate's current share was 30 percent less than the share of remaining delegates he needed to win, his estimated probability of winning was 24 percent. If his current share was 10 percent more than the share of remaining delegates he needed to win, his estimated probability of winning was 94 percent.

The items used to construct the Republican party conservatism index described in Section 9.1 included 1964 convention voting (support for Goldwater), 1968 convention voting (support for Reagan versus George Romney, Nelson Rockefeller, and Clifford Case), 1972 general election voting (support for Nixon plus American Independent candidate John Schmitz), and average 1978 ideological ratings for each state's Republican congressmen (Americans for Constitutional Action rating minus Americans for Democratic Action rating).

In each case, the relevant data were taken from Runyon et al. (1971), Barone et al. (1979), Bain and Parris (1973), and various issues of *Congressional Quarterly Weekly Report.* Weights were assigned to the items on the basis of principal components analyses, and the principal component scores were rescaled so that the lowest and highest possible, not actual, scores were zero and one hundred. The Republican and Democratic indices were scaled in opposite directions to emphasize the fact that they are not directly comparable. A liberalism score of fifty indicates something about the ideological position of a given state's Democratic party relative to other states' Democratic parties but nothing about its ideological position relative to a Republican party with a liberalism score of fifty.

APPENDIX B

Models

B.1 A Threshold Model of Familiarity

My analysis of information and uncertainty in Chapter 4 and elsewhere requires the translation of dichotomous observable indicators ("knowing something about" a candidate, willingness to rate the candidate on a feeling thermometer) into continuous measures of the underlying levels of uncertainty on which the manifest responses are presumably based. The model used here to make that translation parallels the model introduced elsewhere (Bartels 1986) to measure uncertainty about candidates' issue positions. The basic assumption in each case is that the manifest indicators are produced by a threshold response rule: if the underlying level of uncertainty is below the threshold, a survey respondent will rate the candidate, claim to "know something about him," or place him on an issue scale; if the underlying level of uncertainty exceeds the threshold, the respondent will refuse to rate the candidate, claim not to know something about him, or refuse to place him on the issue scale.

More precisely, I assume that respondent i will rate candidate j if and only if

(1) $1/V_{ij} > T$,

where V_{ij} is the unobserved variance of an underlying evaluation of candidate j by respondent i (an evaluation of the sort illustrated in Figure 4.4), $1/V_{ij}$ is the "precision" of the evaluation, and T is an unobserved response threshold constant across respondents and candidates.

In addition, I assume that the underlying precision of an evaluation, $1/V_{ij}$, is systematically related to characteristics of the respondent i, the candidate j, and the response setting. For example, we might suppose that precision increases with increases in the education of the respondent, the prominence of the candidate's previous political activities, and the attention being paid to the candidate by the news media at a given point in the primary season. Thus, we might stipulate that

(2) $1/V_{ij} = b_{cj}\,(\text{Characteristic}_{ci}) + e_{ij}$

where c indexes a set of characteristics of the respondent and the response setting, the e_{ij}s are independent, normally distributed random variables with mean zero and identical variance for each respondent, and the b_{cj}s are parameters constant across respondents, though not necessarily across candidates.

Under these assumptions, the probability that respondent i will be willing to rate candidate j is

$$\text{(3)} \qquad \text{prob}\,[1/V_{ij} > T]$$
$$= \text{prob}\,[b_{cj}\,(\text{Characteristic}_{ci}) + e_{ij} > T]$$
$$= \text{prob}\,[-e_{ij} < b_{cj}\,(\text{Characteristic}_{ci}) - T]$$

$$\text{(4)} \qquad = \Phi\,[b_{cj}\,(\text{Characteristic}_{ci}) - T].$$

Given my assumptions about the distributions of the e_{ij}s, equation (4) is a straightforward probit model relating the probability of an observable outcome (respondent i being willing to rate candidate j) to a series of observable respondent characteristics. Although we cannot directly estimate the response threshold T, we can estimate (up to an arbitrary positive scale factor) the impact of the various characteristics on the precision of respondents' underlying uncertain evaluations. In addition, we can use our estimates of the b_{cj} parameters (plus observed characteristics) to construct estimates of underlying uncertainty for each respondent for each candidate, up to an arbitrary linear transformation. These estimates can then be used to explore the impact of uncertainty on other aspects of political behavior.

The specific sets of characteristics I have used to estimate uncertainty for recent primary campaigns are described in Appendix C.2. The tables in that appendix list the resulting estimates of the b_{cj} parameters for each campaign. The resulting estimates of average information levels over time in each recent primary campaign are illustrated in Figures 7.7 through 7.11.

B.2 Issue Perceptions

The analysis of issue perceptions in Section 5.3 is based on a model of response for issue placement questions introduced by Brady and Sniderman (1985). The basic logic of the model is that respondents attempt simultaneously to minimize error in their placements of candidates on issue scales and to minimize incongruity between their placements of the candidates and their own issue positions. I have elaborated Brady and Sniderman's basic model in two ways: first, to reflect the presumed effect of information about the candidates on respondents' desire to minimize errors in placing the candidates; and second, to reflect the presumed effect of interest in the campaign on respondents' desire to minimize incongruities between their placements of the candidates and their own positions on the issues.[1]

In particular, I assume that respondent i chooses a perceived candidate position on issue k that *minimizes*

$$(5) \quad (1 + S_{jk}\text{Info}_{ij})(\text{Actual}_{jk} - \text{Perceived}_{ijk})^2 + (1 + R_{jk}\text{Interest}_i)(Q_{jk} + P_{jk}\text{Therm}_{ij})(\text{Own}_{ik} - \text{Perceived}_{ijk})^2$$

where Actual_{jk} is candidate j's "true" position on issue k (an unknown parameter to be estimated in the model); Perceived_{ijk} is respondent i's perception of where candidate j stands on issue k; Own_{ik} is respondent i's own preferred position on issue k; Therm_{ij} is respondent i's overall evaluation of candidate j; Info_{ij} is respondent i's level of information about candidate j; Interest_i is respondent i's level of interest in the campaign; and P_{jk}, Q_{jk}, R_{jk}, and S_{jk} are parameters assumed to be constant across respondents.

Respondent i's psychologically optimal perceived position for candidate j on issue k, chosen to minimize expression (5), is

$$(6) \quad \text{Perceived}_{ijk} = (\,(1 + S_{jk}\text{Info}_{ij})\text{Actual}_{jk} + (1 + R_{jk}\text{Interest}_i)(Q_{jk} + P_{jk}\text{Therm}_{ij})\text{Own}_{ik}\,) \,/\, (\,(1 + S_{jk}\text{Info}_{ij}) + (1 + R_{jk}\text{Interest}_i)(Q_{jk} + P_{jk}\text{Therm}_{ij})\,)$$

This expression can be used to estimate the unknown parameters of the model, including the "true" candidate positions (which serve, essentially, as intercept terms). The S_{jk} parameters reflect the extent to which increasing information about the candidates increases the weight attached to the candidates' true positions in respondents' perceptions of the candidates' positions. (Since increasing information presumably makes the candidates' true positions more salient, these parameters are expected to be positive.) The R_{jk} parameters reflect the extent to which increasing interest in the campaign increases the weight attached to congruity with the respondents' own positions. (Since increasing interest presum-

[1] I applied a slightly different version of Brady and Sniderman's model to perceptions of George Bush's issue positions in early 1980 in an unpublished paper, "Where Candidates Come From: The Case of George Bush," presented at the 1984 meeting of the Political Methodology Group in Ann Arbor, Michigan. The results of that analysis are broadly consistent with the results for the 1984 campaign presented in Appendix C.4.

ably makes issue congruity more important to respondents, these parameters are also expected to be positive.)

The P_{jk} and Q_{jk} parameters reflect the impact of congruity with the respondents' own positions, relative to the impact of the candidates' true positions, on respondents' perceptions of where the candidates stand. In particular, the Q_{jk} parameters express the extent to which respondents strive for congruity between their own positions and those of candidates to whom they assign neutral overall evaluations. Brady and Sniderman (1985), following the standard terminology in social psychology, refer to this as a "false consensus" effect. The P_{jk} parameters express the extent to which respondents strive to agree with candidates they like and disagree with candidates they dislike. Brady and Sniderman refer to this as a "focussed" or "partisan" projection effect; both effects are also expected to be positive.

In Appendix C.4, a model of this form is applied to data from the 1984 NES survey on perceptions of where Walter Mondale and Gary Hart stood on the issues of defense spending, government spending and services, and abstract ideology. The results from that analysis, presented in Table A.16, are the basis for the substantive discussion of issue perceptions in Section 5.3.[2]

B.3 Candidate Choice

In this section I describe a model relating prospective voters' choices of one candidate or another to observable political factors and dynamic circumstances. The model is used to analyze the choices of survey respondents in Part II, especially in Chapter 6; it also informs the model of choice for actual primary voters described in Appendix B.4.

[2] To avoid confounding the effects of information and interest, the measure of information actually employed in the analysis reported in Table A.16 is an aggregate-level measure rather than an individual-level measure. For each week of the campaign, information about the candidates is approximated by cumulative media coverage. The precise relationships, estimated from logit analyses like those described in Appendix C.2 applied to respondents' willingness to place the candidates on the issues, are:

$$\text{Mondale Information} = 1.321 + .00403 \text{ (Cumulative Coverage)}$$

and

$$\text{Hart Information} = .01334 \text{ (Cumulative Coverage)}.$$

Not surprisingly, these relationships suggest that Mondale started out with a considerable head start in issue information levels but that respondents learned more quickly about Hart's issue positions during the campaign.

The model includes three basic elements: the first relates political predispositions and expectations about the horse race to ratings of the various candidates expressed in the form of thermometer scores; the second relates thermometer scores and dynamic factors (levels of information and perceptions of the candidates chances) to an unobserved overall "utility" attached to the prospect of supporting each candidate; and the third relates these unobserved "utilities" to the observable behavior of prospective voters.

The first of these three elements of the overall model is based on the presumption that prospective voters' ratings of each candidate depend in part on pre-existing political predispositions and in part on the candidate's chances of winning the nomination. More specifically, I suppose that predispositions determine ratings with increasing force as the prospective voter's information about a candidate increases and that expectations determine ratings with *decreasing* force as information increases. The first interaction with information reflects the process of political activation referred to in Section 5.2; the second allows for the possibility that the media and the public may tire of the horse race, or turn to more reliable cues about which candidate to support, as the campaign proceeds and substantive information becomes more plentiful.

The model specification created to capture these various possibilities is

$$\text{(7)}\quad \text{Therm}_{ij} = .5 + H_j\,(\,(\text{Predisp}_{ij} - .5)(\text{Info}_{ij}) + (1 - K_j(\text{Info}_{ij}))(M_j + N_j(\text{Expect}_{ij})^{1/2})\,)$$

where Therm_{ij} is respondent i's thermometer rating of candidate j on a scale running from zero to one; Predisp_{ij} is respondent i's predisposition toward candidate j, similarly measured on a scale running from zero to one; Info_{ij} is respondent i's current level of information about candidate j; Expect_{ij} is respondent i's subjective estimate of candidate j's chances of winning the nomination;[3] e_{ij} is a stochastic disturbance term; and H_j, K_j, M_j, and N_j are constant parameters to be estimated.

The second part of my model of candidate choice deals explicitly with the divergence, noted in Chapter 6, between thermometer

[3] Here and elsewhere I use the square root of respondents' expectations about the candidates' chances rather than the probability estimates themselves to account for evaluations and choices. This choice of functional form reflects my a priori belief that increases in perceived chances probably have diminishing marginal returns. Where it is possible to judge, the square root transformation also seems slightly superior to the untransformed probability estimates in empirical terms.

ratings and actual preferences for one candidate or another in a context of concrete choice. I presume that prospective voters' propensities to support a given candidate are based not only on thermometer ratings but also on the amount of information they have about the candidate, their perceptions of the candidate's chances, and an interaction between thermometer ratings and perceived chances. The latter two possibilities correspond to the direct and interactive effects of expectations referred to in Section 6.2.[4]

The model specification created to capture these aspects of the prospective voter's decision calculus is

$$(8)\qquad U_{ij} = A + B\ \text{Rate}_{ij} + C\ \text{Info}_{ij} + D\ \text{Therm}_{ij} + E\ \text{Therm}_{ij} (\text{Expect}_{ij})^{1/2} + F\ (\text{Expect}_{ij})^{1/2} + G\ (\text{Expect}_{ij})^{1/2}\ \text{Info}_{ij} + d_{ij}$$

where U_{ij} is the "utility" voter i associates with supporting candidate j; Rate_{ij} is a dummy variable taking the value one if respondent i can rate candidate j and zero otherwise; d_{ij} is a stochastic disturbance term arising from idiosyncratic features of respondent i's judgments about the candidates (or from perceptual errors); and A, B, C, D, E, F, and G are constant parameters to be estimated.[5]

Given propensities to support each of two competing candidates generated by equation (8), we may ask how a prospective voter might reasonably arrive at a decision to vote for one of these candidates rather than the other.[6] The third part of my model consists of the simple assumption that the prospective voter will compare the stochastic utilities she associates with the two candidates and choose the candidate for whom the associated utility is greatest.[7] Thus, for candidates A and B, the voter chooses candidate A if

$$(9)\qquad U_{iA} > U_{iB}$$

and candidate B otherwise.[8] Rewriting equation (8) as

[4] The internalized effect of expectations from Section 6.2 is represented by the Expectations term in equation (7).

[5] I assume here that the parameters A, B, C, D, E, F, and G are constant across candidates as well as across prospective voters.

[6] The principle suggested here can easily be extended to situations in which there are three or more candidates; however, practical complications arise which make the more general version difficult to analyze mathematically. I skirt these difficulties by restricting my attention to the two-candidate case.

[7] The principal of utility maximization implied by this assumption plays a major role in formal analyses of decision making. See, for example, Lindley (1985).

[8] This formulation introduces an apparent asymmetry into the comparison of candidates, since B will be chosen if $U_{iA} = U_{iB}$ exactly. But utility distinctions can,

(10) $U_{ij} = S_{ij} + d_{ij}$

where S_{ij} summarizes all of the systematic factors on the right side of the equation, condition (9) implies that

(11) $(S_{iA} + d_{iA}) > (S_{iB} + d_{iB})$

(12) $(S_{iA} - S_{iB}) > (d_{iB} - d_{iA})$

The *probability* that this condition is satisfied can be represented by the cumulative probability distribution of the random variable $(d_{iB} - d_{iA})$ evaluated at the point $(S_{iA} - S_{iB})$. Under the assumptions that d_{iA} and d_{iB} have a multivariate normal distribution with mean zero, variances V_A and V_B, and covariance C_{AB} for each respondent, the relevant probability is

(13) $\text{prob}\,(U_{iA} > U_{iB}) = \Phi\,(\,(S_{iA} - S_{iB}) / (V_A + V_B - 2\,C_{AB})^{1/2}),$

where Φ represents the cumulative normal function.

This expression implies that respondents' observable choices of one candidate over the other will be related to the systematic portions of their associated utilities, S_{iA} and S_{iB}, by a probit function.[9] The parameters relating respondents' unobserved utilities to political characteristics and dynamic circumstances in equation (8) are estimable up to an arbitrary positive constant of proportionality.[10] The relevant parameter estimates for choices between Walter Mondale and Gary Hart in the 1984 NES survey are presented in Table A.18 in Appendix C.

B.4 Individual Behavior and Primary Outcomes

Having developed in Appendix B.3 a model of individual electoral choice, I turn here to the development of a corresponding model of state-level primary outcomes. The most elegant approach, in theoretical terms, would be to derive the aggregate-level model directly from the individual-level model set out in Appendix B.3. Unfortunately, that approach is impracticable here because of the

in principle, be made sufficiently fine that an exact equality will be extremely unlikely.

[9] See, for example, McFadden (1976).

[10] The arbitrary constant of proportionality reflects the fact that the scale of the unobserved evaluations is itself arbitrary. The constant of proportionality also absorbs the expression in the denominator of equation (13) representing the standard deviation of the difference in perceptual errors.

complexity of the individual-level model. And even if it were practicable, the resulting aggregated model would be ill-suited to answer the sorts of questions we presumably want to ask of the state-level data. For example, average state-level characteristics would often appear in two different places in the model because they affect predispositions toward each candidate separately. As a result, precious observations would be squandered in estimating separate predispositions for each candidate imprecisely because of the collinearity inherent in such a model, and we would learn little about the reactions of primary electorates to the dynamic aspects of the nominating campaign.

My alternative approach is to work with a state-level model informed by, but not explicitly derived from, the individual-level model in Appendix B.3. As in the individual-level model, I assume that the unobserved utilities which prospective voters associate with each candidate are based in part on political predispositions and in part on dynamic factors. And as in the individual-level model, I assume that the impact of expectations about the candidates' chances decreases with increasing levels of information. But here I assume that the resulting unobservable utilities determine voters' electoral choices exactly, without the stochastic term d_{ij} which appeared in equation (8) in the individual-level model.

Given this simplifying assumption, we have

$$(14) \qquad U_{ij} = W\,(\text{Predisp}_{ij}) + Y\,(1 - Z\,\text{Info}_{jt})\,(\text{Expect}_{jt}),$$

where Predisp_{ij} is voter i's predisposition toward candidate j; Info_{jt} is the level of information about candidate j; assumed here to be identical for all voters in a given week t of the primary season; and Expect_{jt} is a shared public perception, identical for all voters in a given week t of the primary season, of candidate j's chances of winning the nomination.[11]

The corresponding condition for choosing one candidate, A, over another, B, is

$$(15) \qquad [W\,(\text{Predisp}_{iA}) + Y\,(1 - Z\,\text{Info}_{At})\,(\text{Expect}_{At})] > [W\,(\text{Predisp}_{iB}) + Y\,(1 - Z\,\text{Info}_{Bt})\,(\text{Expect}_{Bt})],$$

which can be rearranged to produce

[11] In this simplified version of the model I ignore individual variation in both levels of information and perceived chances. Such variation is, in any case, impossible to capture using the available aggregate-level data.

$$(16) \quad [W\,(\text{Predisp}_{iA} - \text{Predisp}_{iB}) + Y\,(\text{Expect}_{At} - \text{Expect}_{Bt}) - YZ\,(\text{Info}_{At}\,\text{Expect}_{At} - \text{Info}_{Bt}\,\text{Expect}_{Bt})] > 0$$

(again at the individual level).

If we aggregate this relationship across individuals in a given primary state s and if we assume that individual predispositions for each candidate are normally distributed within each state, we get

$$(17) \quad (\%_{sA}) = \Phi\,[W\,(\text{Predisp}_{sA} - \text{Predisp}_{sB}) + Y\,(\text{Expect}_{At} - \text{Expect}_{Bt}) - YZ\,(\text{Info}_{At}\,\text{Expect}_{At} - \text{Info}_{Bt}\,\text{Expect}_{Bt})]$$

where $\%_{sA}$ is the observed share of the primary vote for candidate A over candidate B in state s, and Predisp_{sA} and Predisp_{sB} are the average predispositions toward the candidates in state s. Taking the inverse of the cumulative normal function on each side gives

$$(18) \quad \Phi^{-1}\,(\%_{sA}) = [W\,(\text{Predisp}_{sA} - \text{Predisp}_{sB}) + Y\,(\text{Expect}_{At} - \text{Expect}_{Bt}) - YZ\,(\text{Info}_{At}\,\text{Expect}_{At} - \text{Info}_{Bt}\,\text{Expect}_{Bt})]$$

Equation (18) represents an observable relationship between the political characteristics of a given state, including the dynamic circumstances prevailing at the time of the state's primary, and the outcome of that primary.

APPENDIX C

Statistical Results

C.1 Expectations

My analyses of public expectations about the candidates' chances of being nominated are based on two distinct sets of statistical results. The individual-level analysis in Chapter 3 is based on a model involving objective campaign events, predispositions toward the candidates, and media use. My presumption is that, given some specific set of campaign circumstances, respondents favorably predisposed toward a candidate on political grounds may view the candidate's chances more optimistically than respondents disposed to dislike the candidate. I also presume that any given set of campaign circumstances may have a greater effect on the expectations of respondents who are relatively heavy users of campaign media.

Thus, for each candidate, we have a model of the form

$$(19)\quad \text{Chances}_{ijt} = [(a_j + b_j(\text{Cumulative Vote Share}_{jt}) + c_j(\text{Last Week's Share}_{jt}) + d_j(\text{"Objective" Chances}_{jt})] (1 + p_j(\text{Predisp}_{ij} - .5))\,(1 + m_j(\text{Media Use}_i))$$

where i indexes respondents, j indexes candidates, and t indexes time periods (weeks of the primary season).

Parameter estimates for models of this form are presented in Table A.8. The relative weights attached to the three separate measures of objective campaign circumstances are quite similar in the results for Hart and Mondale. However, the multiplier effects for the two candidates are more distinct, with predispositions playing a more important role in perceptions of Hart's chances and media use playing a more important role in perceptions of Mondale's chances.

The statistical results for perceptions of Hart's chances in Table A.8 were used to generate the individual-level analysis of expectations for survey respondents in Chapter 3. However, a simpler model is needed to translate the role of expectations to the aggregate level in order to analyze actual primary outcomes. For campaigns other than the 1984 Democratic campaign it is possible to generate measures of objective campaign events but not to relate those campaign events directly to public perceptions of each can-

TABLE A.8 Parameter Estimates for Perceived Chances, 1984 (Complete Model)

	"Seemingly Unrelated" Parameter Estimates (Standard Errors)	
	Hart	Mondale
Intercept	−0.062 (0.014)	−0.114 (0.089)
Cumulative primary vote share	0.464 (0.066)	0.397 (0.198)
Last week's vote share	0.142 (0.043)	0.075 (0.118)
"Objective" probabilities of nomination	0.525 (0.066)	0.430 (0.055)
Multiplier effect of predispositions	1.332 (0.462)	−0.322 (0.172)
Multiplier effect of media use	0.077 (0.089)	0.396 (0.083)

Notes: Cross-equation correlation of residuals = −0.33. N = 868. For Hart, standard error of equation = 0.159 and R^2 = 0.31; for Mondale, standard error of equation = 0.215 and R^2 = 0.13.

didate's chances of being nominated since survey data on perceived chances are lacking for other campaigns. In the absence of individual-level data, it is also impossible to take explicit account of the role of subjective factors like predispositions and media use in determining the perceptions of individual prospective voters.

My solution to these problems was to reestimate the relationship between campaign events and perceived chances in the 1984 NES data using a simpler model of perceptions than the one reflected in equation (19) and in the results in Table A.8. The simpler model includes only the three available measures of objective campaign events, and it is based on the assumption that these objective campaign events have similar effects on perceptions of each candidates' chances in every recent nominating campaign. The resulting relationship is

$$(20)\quad \text{Chances}_{ijt} = b\ (\text{Cumulative Vote Share}_{jt}) + c\ (\text{Last Week's Share}_{jt}) + d\ (\text{“Objective” Chances}_{jt})$$

Parameter estimates for this model applied to perceptions about Hart and Mondale in the 1984 NES data are presented in Table A.9.

Not surprisingly, the simpler model does somewhat less well than the more complicated model in equation (19) in accounting

TABLE A.9 Parameter Estimates for Perceived Chances, 1984 (Objective Factors Only)

	Parameter Estimates	Standard Errors
Cumulative primary vote share	0.373	(0.056)
Last week's vote share	0.218	(0.051)
"Objective" probabilities of nomination	0.297	(0.012)

Notes: Parameter estimates identical for Hart and Mondale by assumption. No intercept included in the model. N = 868. For Hart, standard error of equation = 0.162 and R^2 = 0.28; for Mondale, standard error of equation = 0.222 and R^2 = 0.07.

for actual perceptions of Hart's and Mondale's chances. But what is more important for my purposes is that the effects of the three kinds of campaign events included in the model are roughly similar in the two analyses and also similar for the two candidates. As a result, I have used the results in Table A.9 to simulate public perceptions of each major candidate's chances in each of the five nominating campaigns analyzed in this book. In effect, I assume that the process generating public expectations was the same in 1976 and 1980 as in 1984 and the same for Republicans as for Democrats. The resulting simulated expectations, labeled "subjective probabilities of nomination," are presented in graphic form in Figures 8.2, 9.2, 9.6, 10.2, and 10.5.[1]

C.2 FAMILIARITY

I used the threshold model of familiarity described in Appendix B.1 to generate estimates of information levels for major candidates in each campaign on the basis of survey data.[2] All these esti-

[1] A comparison between the average perceptions of Hart's chances shown in Figure 3.4 (based on actual survey responses) and the simulated perceptions in Figure 10.5 (based on the statistical results shown in Table A.9) provides some indication of the magnitude of the errors generated by my procedure for simulating public expectations about the various candidates' chances of being nominated. Although there are some notable differences between the two figures, the major trends in perceptions of Hart's chances in Figure 3.4 are, I think, adequately captured in Figure 10.5.

[2] The survey data employed in these analyses are described in Appendix A.2. Purely as a matter of convenience, the parameters were estimated using a logit model, based on slightly different assumptions about the distributions of the e_{ij} terms than those given in Appendix B.1. The differences are inconsequential.

mates are based on the presumption that information varies with both personal characteristics, such as education and media use, and the amount of campaign coverage at any given point in the primary season.

For the 1984 campaign, the "continuous monitoring" design of the NES survey provides considerable variation across respondents in amounts of cumulative media coverage. In effect, we have dozens of survey respondents for each weekly reading of media coverage in Table A.6. In 1976 and 1980 the available survey data are bunched into three relatively brief and widely spaced time periods: the beginning of the primary season, the middle, and the end. As a result, estimated levels of cumulative media coverage for survey respondents in these campaigns are almost constant within each of three distinct groups, and the effect of media coverage on respondents' information about the candidates at other points in the campaign must be estimated by extrapolation.

The parameter estimates from logit models relating familiarity with each major primary candidate to education, media use, cumulative media coverage, and the interaction between media use and cumulative media coverage are shown in Tables A.10 through A.14.[3] Estimated levels of information about each candidate among the party rank-and-file, generated on the basis of these parameter estimates, appear in Figures 7.7 through 7.11.

C.3 Predispositions

The profiles of predispositions toward the candidates derived from survey respondents' political and social characteristics, shown in Table 5.1, were generated by regressing thermometer ratings for each candidate in the 1984 NES survey data on relevant political and demographic factors. To get a clear picture of the underlying relationship between the candidates' political identities and the

[3] In addition to these standard personal characteristics, the logit models for Carter in 1976 and Hart in 1984 include dummy variables to represent the extraordinary effects of the New Hampshire primary on familiarity with those candidates. The effect of the 1980 Republican caucuses in Iowa on familiarity with Bush cannot be estimated because the first wave of the 1980 NES survey occurred after the Iowa caucuses; similarly, Anderson's emergence later in the 1980 Republican campaign cannot be monitored because he was omitted from the first wave of the 1980 NES survey. The models for familiarity with Udall and Jackson in the 1976 Democratic primary campaign include separate estimates of the effect of cumulative media coverage after the Pennsylvania primary, since both candidates were virtually ignored by the media after that point.

TABLE A.10 Parameter Estimates for Democratic Familiarity, 1976

	Logit Parameter Estimates (Standard Errors)			
	Carter	Jackson	Udall	Wallace
Intercept	−4.918 (0.391)	−4.344 (0.333)	−5.622 (0.371)	−2.395 (0.291)
Education (in years)	0.2136 (0.0238)	0.2199 (0.0221)	0.2928 (0.0241)	0.2637 (0.0222)
Media use (0 to 1)	2.550 (0.392)	2.051 (0.360)	1.842 (0.380)	1.211 (0.382)
Cumulative media coverage (0 to 131.6)	0.0089 (0.0154)	0.0053 (0.0023)	0.0100 (0.0024)	0.0000 (0.0014)
Media use—coverage interaction	−0.0127 (0.0062)	0.0038 (0.0053)	−0.0036 (0.0054)	−0.0014 (0.0041)
New Hampshire primary (dummy variable)	2.460 (1.305)	—	—	—
Late coverage (after Penn.)	0.0004 (0.0046)	−0.0021 (0.0018)	−0.0033 (0.0018)	—
Late interaction (after Penn.)	0.0057 (0.0056)	−0.0059 (0.0043)	0.0021 (0.0042)	—
% correct:	80.9	72.5	74.3	74.4
−2 ln L:	1,485.3	1,868.4	1,785.8	1,729.4

Note: $N = 1{,}667$.

prospective voters' preexisting political tendencies, I limited each analysis to survey respondents interviewed after Super Tuesday whose estimated probability of being familiar with a candidate (based on the analysis described in Appendix C.2) was greater than 0.9. In addition, to control for dynamic factors which might also affect respondents' thermometer ratings of the candidates, I included in the analysis dummy variables for each of the twenty-three weeks of the 1984 primary season. The parameter estimates for those regressions, excluding the weekly dummies, for Hart, Mondale, and John Glenn are shown in Table A.15.

C.4 Issue Perceptions

The model of issue perceptions outlined in Appendix B.2 produces a specification—equation (6)—that is nonlinear in parameters but estimable using nonlinear least squares or nonlinear two-stage least squares techniques.[4] For purposes of empirical analysis,

[4] Two-stage techniques are appropriate if the stochastic components of percep-

TABLE A.11 Parameter Estimates for Republican Familiarity, 1976

	Logit Parameter Estimates (Standard Errors)	
	Ford	Reagan
Intercept	−0.755 (0.521)	−1.500 (0.454)
Education (in years)	0.2381 (1.012)	0.2112 (0.749)
Media Use (0 to 1)	1.552 (1.012)	2.062 (0.749)
Cumulative media coverage (0 to 95.8)	−0.0009 (0.0044)	0.0078 (0.0036)
Media use—coverage interaction	0.0015 (0.0150)	−0.0159 (0.0110)
% correct:	91.5	84.4
−2 ln L:	413.1	602.8

Note: N = 780.

TABLE A.12 Parameter Estimates for Democratic Familiarity, 1980

	Logit Parameter Estimates (Standard Errors)	
	Carter	Kennedy
Intercept	1.354 (0.703)	−0.263 (0.456)
Education (in years)	0.1570 (0.0577)	0.1933 (0.0352)
Media use (0 to 1)	2.315 (1.573)	2.658 (0.925)
Cumulative media coverage (0 to 48.7)	0.0166 (0.0184)	−0.0260 (0.0114)
Media use—coverage interaction	−0.0007 (0.0536)	−0.0435 (0.0281)
% correct:	98.6	95.7
−2 ln L:	190.8	467.7

Note: N = 1,443.

TABLE A.13 Parameter Estimates for Republican Familiarity, 1980

	Logit Parameter Estimates (Standard Errors)		
	Reagan	Bush	Anderson
Intercept	−1.929 (0.624)	−3.811 (0.428)	−7.505 (1.342)
Education (in years)	0.2545 (0.0469)	0.2013 (0.0270)	0.3302 (0.0380)
Media use (0 to 1)	3.723 (1.051)	2.190 (0.464)	3.994 (2.161)
Cumulative media coverage (0 to 63.4)	0.0164 (0.0086)	0.0212 (0.0054)	0.0525 (0.0217)
Media use—coverage interaction	−0.0039 (0.0263)	−0.0067 (0.0103)	−0.0460 (0.0385)
% correct:	94.2	69.8	71.8
−2 ln L:	347.1	1155.8	751.4

Note: N = 985 for Reagan and Bush, 646 for Anderson. Familiarity with Anderson not ascertained in January–February wave of 1980 NES survey.

TABLE A.14 Parameter Estimates for Democratic Familiarity, 1984

	Logit Parameter Estimates (Standard Errors)		
	Glenn	Mondale	Hart
Intercept	−1.573 (0.913)	−1.078 (1.026)	−4.276 (0.695)
Education (in years)	0.2727 (0.0659)	0.2858 (0.0763)	0.2300 (0.0468)
Media use (0 to 1)	3.467 (1.655)	0.882 (1.472)	2.611 (0.723)
Cumulative media coverage (0 to 142.5)	0.0123 (0.0060)	0.0103 (0.0073)	0.0138 (0.0059)
Media use—coverage interaction	−0.0208 (0.0182)	0.0146 (0.0222)	0.0207 (0.0138)
New Hampshire primary (dummy variable)	—	—	1.648 (0.488)
% correct:	96.3	97.2	86.1
−2 ln L:	250.9	185.2	531.4

Note: N = 868.

TABLE A.15 Parameter Estimates for Political Predispositions, 1984

	Parameter Estimates (Standard Errors)		
	Hart	Mondale	Glenn
Liberalism			
Liberal ideology	4.7 (2.9)	—	−2.6 (2.6)
(−) Cut government spending	10.4 (4.0)	7.6 (4.4)	—
Environmental spending	9.4 (3.1)	7.2 (3.2)	—
Government jobs	—	5.4 (2.9)	1.8 (2.5)
Social security	—	—	−4.5 (3.1)
Cooperate with Russia	—	4.3 (3.1)	—
(−) Defense spending	—	3.8 (3.3)	−2.7 (2.8)
(−) Central America	—	—	−6.0 (2.9)
New Deal			
Black	−8.9 (2.7)	4.9 (2.9)	−7.0 (2.4)
Jewish	−6.6 (4.7)	8.7 (5.1)	—
Catholic	−3.1 (2.0)	1.2 (2.1)	—
Union household	−4.9 (2.1)	3.8 (2.1)	1.6 (1.8)
(−) Income (in $1,000s)	—	0.093 (0.068)	0.042 (0.058)
Traditionalism			
(−) Education (in years)	−1.04 (0.47)	—	−0.57 (0.43)
Age (in years)	−0.048 (0.063)	0.115 (0.065)	−0.082 (0.055)
(−) Residential mobility	—	7.6 (3.0)	3.1 (2.6)
Church attendance	—	2.7 (3.1)	3.2 (2.6)
Fight crime	—	4.1 (3.6)	1.1 (3.0)
(−) Science and technology	—	—	−0.1 (2.5)
(−) Worse off financially	−8.8 (3.4)	−1.8 (3.5)	3.2 (3.1)

TABLE A.15 Parameter Estimates for Political Predispositions, 1984 (*cont.*)

	Parameter Estimates (Standard Errors)		
	Hart	Mondale	Glenn
Partisanship			
Strong Democrat	—	8.9 (2.5)	−2.9 (2.2)
Weak Democrat	—	3.3 (2.2)	—
Intercept (Week 23)[a]	50.5 (8.7)	46.6 (9.9)	49.0 (8.6)
R-squared:	0.15	0.15	0.10
N:	463	545	534

Notes: Dependent variables are thermometer ratings. Independent variables range between 0 and 1.0 unless otherwise indicated. Parameter estimates are based only on Democratic respondents interviewed after Super Tuesday whose estimated probability of rating the candidate was greater than 0.9. Omitted independent variables had negligible effects in preliminary analyses.

[a] Dummy variables for each week of the 1984 primary season not shown.

I assume that the parameters of the model in equation (6), other than the "true" candidate positions, are constant across candidates and across issues.[5] The issues included in my analysis are those for which the 1984 NES survey asked respondents to place themselves, Walter Mondale, and Gary Hart: defense spending, government spending and services, and abstract ideology.[6]

tions are correlated with the explanatory variables in equation (6). This would be the case, for example, if issue perceptions had a reciprocal effect on thermometer ratings. Brady and Sniderman (1985: 1070–71) argued that two-stage techniques were unnecessary for their problem. I adopt the same position here, partly because perceived issue positions are likely a priori to include sufficient random measurement error to swamp any systematic error components and partly because the parameter estimates from a two-stage analysis are simply too imprecise to tell us anything of interest.

[5] This simplification can be relaxed, but at the cost of considerable additional imprecision in the resulting parameter estimates.

[6] Two sources of missing data substantially reduce the effective sample size for the empirical analysis of issue perceptions. First, the 1984 NES survey did not include questions about Gary Hart's issue positions until after the New Hampshire primary; as a result, 239 of the 868 respondents in the survey were not asked to place Hart on the issues. Second, as is always the case with these sorts of questions, many of the respondents who *were* asked to place Hart and Mondale on the issues declined to do so. The usual procedures for dealing with these missing data, such as recoding them to the middle of the issue scale, could confound an analysis of

The results of the analysis for these three issues are shown in Table A.16. The key parameter estimates—for Information, Interest, "False consensus," and "Differential projection"—are estimated rather imprecisely, but all the estimated effects are consistent with my a priori expectations. The implications of the results are described in Section 5.3.

The candidates' "true" positions on the three issues, also shown in Table A.16, are estimated much more precisely on the same

TABLE A.16 Parameter Estimates for Issue Perceptions, 1984

	Parameter Estimates	Standard Errors
S (Information)	2.62	(3.92)
R (Interest)	2.34	(2.16)
Q ("False consensus")	0.346	(0.454)
P ("Differential projection")	1.815	(2.391)
Actual Positions		
Mondale: Defense	0.640	(0.012)
Services	0.554	(0.011)
Ideology	0.534	(0.019)
Hart: Defense	0.652	(0.013)
Services	0.506	(0.011)
Ideology	0.523	(0.020)

	Standard Error of Equation	R^2
Mondale: Defense	0.216	0.12
Services	0.200	0.02
Ideology	0.340	0.09
Hart: Defense	0.216	0.21
Services	0.185	0.09
Ideology	0.348	0.07

Note: Estimates based on the model in Equation (6) in Appendix B.2. $N = 499$.

issue perceptions of the sort attempted here. For example, respondents with little interest in the campaign could appear most active in projecting their own positions onto the candidates, when in fact the apparent consistency between their own positions and their perceptions of the candidates' positions merely reflected a higher proportion of missing data for both kinds of questions (and thus artificial agreement between the two) among relatively uninterested respondents. In an attempt to minimize biases of this sort while retaining enough cases to estimate the underlying parameters of interest, I have limited my analysis to respondents who provided candidate placements for at least *four* of the six candidate-issue pairs (three each for Hart and Mondale). This group included 499 (about 80 percent) of the 629 respondents interviewed after the New Hampshire primary.

zero-to-one scale pictured in Figures 5.1 and 5.5, with zero representing the conservative end of the scale and one the liberal end. Thus, the estimated actual positions shown in the table indicate that Mondale and Hart were both slightly to the liberal side of the midpoint on each issue, more notably on defense spending than on services or ideology, and that the only significant, though still minor, difference between the two candidates' positions was that Mondale was somewhat more liberal than Hart on the issue of government spending and services. These results seem consistent with the conclusions drawn by observers of the 1984 Democratic campaign.[7] Table A.16 also shows the standard errors of estimation for each of the six equations on which the parameter estimates are based. None of the six sets of perceived issue stands is accounted for especially precisely. The errors are largest for the abstract liberal–conservative scale—an unsurprising result, given the well-documented unfamiliarity of abstract ideological thinking for typical survey respondents.

C.5 Candidate Evaluations and Choice

The electoral effects of information, political predispositions, and horse race expectations—described in Chapters 4, 5, and 6 respectively—are documented in Tables A.17 and A.18. In keeping with the two-step model of candidate choice introduced in Appendix B.3, Table A.17 focuses on the effect of political predispositions and perceived chances on respondents' thermometer ratings of Gary Hart and Walter Mondale in the 1984 NES survey. The parameter estimates in Table A.17, based on the model for thermometer ratings in equation (7) in Appendix B, were estimated using two-stage least squares.[8]

All the estimated effects in Table A.17 are fairly precise and in the expected directions. The results suggest that political predispositions and perceived chances both affected respondents' thermometer ratings of the candidates, with increasing information

[7] It is possible in principle that the candidates' actual positions on the issues might change during the primary season. There is no evidence of such change in the 1984 NES data.

[8] The two-stage least squares technique was used here to account for the fact that perceptions of the candidates' chances are themselves affected by predispositions and thus by evaluations of the candidates.

TABLE A.17 Parameter Estimates for Candidate Evaluations, 1984

	2SLS Parameter Estimates	Standard Errors
H (Predispositions—Information Interaction)	0.103	(0.007)
K (Expectations—Information Interaction)	0.116	(0.010)
M (Expectations—intercept)	−0.171	(0.027)
N (Expectations—slope)	0.463	(0.081)

Note: Estimates based on the model in Equation (7) in Appendix B.3. $N = 868$. For Hart, standard error of equation = 0.176; $R^2 = 0.17$. For Mondale, standard error of equation = 0.197; $R^2 = 0.13$.

producing substantial increases in the impact of predispositions and substantial decreases in the effect of chances.[9]

The effects of thermometer ratings and dynamic circumstances on actual choices between Mondale and Hart are shown in Table A.18. The statistical results presented in the table are based on the model of candidate choice set out in equations (7) and (13) in Appendix B, except that the probit relationship implied in equation (13) is approximated, as a matter of computational convenience, by a logit relationship. In addition, the analysis is restricted to dichotomous choices between Mondale and Hart by excluding respondents who did not mention either of these two candidates as their first or second choice for the Democratic nomination.

Table A.18 shows two separate sets of parameter estimates; the first is based on a straightforward logit analysis, and the second is derived from a more complicated model using purged values of the explanatory variables.[10] My substantive analysis is based on the first set of estimates; the results from the more complicated model

[9] Information is measured here using the scale shown in Figure 4.9. The range of average information levels for Gary Hart during the 1984 campaign was from about two to seven on this scale. The results in Table A.17 thus imply that changing levels of information produced differences of up to 350 percent in the relative weight assigned to predispositions, and differences of up to 215 percent in the relative weight assigned to perceptions of Hart's chances, over the course of the campaign.

[10] The advantage of the more complicated model is that it produces consistent parameter estimates even if the unmeasured causes of horse race perceptions, evaluations, and actual choices are correlated. The simpler model is based on the assumption that these unmeasured causes are uncorrelated, or at least on the belief that the correlations are not sufficiently strong to seriously distort the results.

TABLE A.18 Parameter Estimates for Candidate Choice, 1984

	Logit Parameter Estimates (Standard Errors)	
	Unpurged	Purged[a]
A (Intercept)	0.378	−0.222
	(0.261)	(0.336)
B (Information)	0.615	0.055
	(0.162)	(0.147)
C (Thermometer)	5.721	13.24[illegible]
	(1.808)	(5.521)
D (Thermometer—Expectations Interaction)	8.070	−8.375
	(2.755)	(9.579)
E (Expectations)	11.728	4.556
	(2.103)	(2.948)
F (Expectations—Information Interaction)	−1.484	−0.173
	(0.303)	(0.456)
% correct:	88.2	73.2
−2 ln L:	378.2	643.0

Note: Estimates based on the model in Equation (8) in Appendix B.3. $N = 628$. Analysis includes only Democratic respondents who mentioned Mondale or Hart as their first or second choice for the 1984 Democratic nomination.

[a] Results in this column based on purged versions of explanatory variables. See text for explanation and discussion.

are roughly similar in their general outlines (in particular, in the overall weight attached to expectations and thermometer ratings), but they are too imprecise to support detailed analysis of the interactions among the various explanatory factors.

As in Table A.17, all estimated effects in the first column of Table A.18 are fairly precise and in the expected directions. The effect of information on choice, represented by the parameter B in the table, is illustrated in Figure 4.10. The internalized effect of political predispositions on choice, the product of the parameter Z in Table A.17 and the parameter C in Table A.18, is illustrated in Figure 6.3. The direct and interactive effects of expectations on choice, represented in Table A.18 by the parameters E and F and D, respectively, are illustrated in Figures 6.4 and 6.5.

C.6 Primary Outcomes

Parameter estimates for the aggregate-level analyses of primary outcomes described in Chapters 8, 9, and 10 are presented in

Tables A.19 through A.22 and A.29 through A.32. All parameter estimates are based on aggregate logit analyses.[11] In this respect the aggregate statistical model parallels the individual-level analysis described in Chapters 4, 5 and 6.

The data used to measure the political predispositions of primary states are described in Appendix A.4. Measures of the dynamic forces shaping each campaign were constructed to parallel as closely as possible the individual-level analysis. In particular, the parameter estimates shown in Tables A.19 through A.22 and A.29 through A.32 for "Relative Momentum" and "Relative Risk Aversion" reflect the impact of expectations and uncertainty, respectively, *relative to* the effects of expectations and uncertainty in the 1984 survey data.

The effect of chances on survey respondents in the 1984 Democratic campaign is taken to be

(21) $(16.16 - 1.467 \text{ Information}) (\text{Chances})^{1/2} + (2.461 - .2166 \text{ Information}) (\text{Chances})$

where "Information" is the estimated level of information about a given candidate in a given week and "Chances" represents the subjective public perception of the candidate's probability of being nominated. This is a close approximation of the combined "direct" and "internalized" effects of expectations estimated from the survey data and described in Chapter 6.

Thus, the parameter estimate of 1.085 for "Relative Momentum" in the analysis of 1984 Democratic primary outcomes in Table A.32 implies that a given difference in chances between Mondale and Hart had an effect on primary voters approximately 8 percent greater than its effect on survey respondents. The parameter estimate of .883 for "Relative Risk Aversion" indicates that uncertainty mattered about 12 percent less to primary voters than it did to survey respondents in the 1984 campaign. The effect of uncertainty on 1984 Democratic survey respondents, from the first column of results in Table A.18, is

(22) $(.615 \text{ Information})$

where "Information" is the estimated level of information about a given candidate in a given week.

Estimated information levels for primary voters in each cam-

[11] That is, the dependent variable in each instance is the log of the ratio of the vote shares of the two major candidates.

paign are shown in Figures 7.7 through 7.11 in Chapter 7. These information levels are estimated from survey data using the familiarity equations in Tables A.10 through A.14 (multiplied by 1.1 for Republicans and by 1.15 for Democrats to reflect compositional differences between survey respondents and primary voters) plus the "Local Information" estimates shown in Tables A.19 through A.22 and A.29 through A.32, which reflect the informational effects of local campaigning in the primary states.

The 1976 Democratic campaign presented some special estimation problems because, unlike the other four campaigns, it did not quickly resolve into a two-candidate race. Instead, Jackson, Udall, and Wallace continued to challenge Carter in some, though not all, states through most of the primary season, and Brown and Church each entered some of the later primaries. To deal with these complexities I have estimated four separate models of the usual sort—one each for Carter versus Jackson, Carter versus Udall, Carter versus Wallace, and Carter versus Brown and Church combined.[12]

In each of the four models, the logit-transformed dependent variable is truncated to have a maximum value of 3. This value implies a Carter share of the two-candidate vote of approximately 95 percent; variations in outcomes beyond this rather lopsided level were deemed politically uninteresting; many reflected the fact that Carter's opponents did not appear on a given state's primary ballot.

Standard errors of estimation and R-squared statistics for the logit-transformed primary outcomes for each of Carter's head-to-head competitions are shown in Tables A.19 through A.22. State-by-state residuals in untransformed (percentage point) terms are shown in Table A.23, along with an estimate of the serial correlation of average weekly residuals for all four analyses.

Another complication in the analysis for the 1976 Democratic campaign arises because each of Carter's challengers chose to concentrate his campaign effort in certain primary states and avoid others. By contrast, Carter ran in every state except West Virginia, where favorite son Robert Byrd won almost 90 percent of the primary vote. To capture both the direct effect of these strategic decisions on primary outcomes and the indirect effect of chances on outcomes through their effect on strategic decisions, I have used

[12] The analysis for Brown and Church takes a slightly different form from that for the other candidates because these late contenders each entered too few primaries to allow a statistical analysis of exactly the same form as for the other candidates.

TABLE A.19 Parameter Estimates for 1976 Democratic Primary Outcomes (Carter versus Jackson)

	Logit Parameter Estimates	Standard Errors
Intercept	1.141	(0.573)
Relative momentum	−0.638[a]	(0.366)
Relative risk aversion	−0.473[a]	(0.636)
Local information	9.36[a]	(1.44)
Campaign effort	0.722[a]	(0.113)
Effort—Information Interaction	−0.1237[a]	(0.0340)
Percentage Manufacturing	0.0370	(0.0364)
Western region	−0.341	(0.322)
Udall campaign effort	−0.1464	(0.0682)
Wallace campaign effort	0.0409	(0.1110)

Note: Standard error of equation = 0.497; R^2 = 0.78; *N* = 26.
[a] Parameters identical in Tables A.19 through A.22 by assumption.

TABLE A.20 Parameter Estimates for 1976 Democratic Primary Outcomes (Carter versus Udall)

	Logit Parameter Estimates	Standard Errors
Intercept	−1.089	(2.342)
Relative momentum	−0.638[a]	(0.366)
Relative risk aversion	−0.473[a]	(0.636)
Local information	9.36[a]	(1.44)
Campaign effort	0.722[a]	(0.113)
Effort—Information Interaction	−0.1237[a]	(0.0340)
Liberalism	0.05144	(0.07382)
Liberalism squared	−0.0005966	(0.0005721)
Percentage Manufacturing	0.0764	(0.0425)
Southern region	−0.772	(0.489)
Jackson campaign effort	−0.1284	(0.1009)

Note: Standard error of equation = 0.616; R^2 = 0.77; *N* = 26.
[a] Parameters identical in Tables A.19 through A.22 by assumption.

Table A.21 Parameter Estimates for 1976 Democratic Primary Outcomes (Carter versus Wallace)

	Logit Parameter Estimates	Standard Errors
Intercept	−0.634	(0.363)
Relative momentum	−0.638[a]	(0.366)
Relative risk aversion	−0.473[a]	(0.636)
Local information	9.36[a]	(1.44)
Campaign effort	0.722[a]	(0.113)
Effort—Information Interaction	−0.1237[a]	(0.0340)
Liberalism	0.02072	(0.00484)
Percentage Black	0.00494	(0.00543)
Home states	1.453	(0.263)
Jackson campaign effort	−0.1345	(0.0640)

Note: Standard error of equation = 0.354; R^2 = 0.90; *N* = 26.
[a] Parameters identical in Tables A.19 through A.22 by assumption.

Table A.22 Parameter Estimates for 1976 Democratic Primary Outcomes (Carter versus Brown and Church)

	Logit Parameter Estimates	Standard Errors
Intercept	−1.020	(0.629)
Relative momentum	−0.638[a]	(0.366)
Relative risk aversion	−0.473[a]	(0.636)
Local information	9.36[a]	(1.44)
Campaign effort	0.722[a]	(0.113)
Effort—Information Interaction	−0.1237[a]	(0.0340)
Western region	−1.609	(0.461)
Home states	1.414	(0.555)

Note: Standard error of equation = 0.847; R^2 = 0.81; *N* = 26.
[a] Parameters identical in Tables A.19 through A.22 by assumption.

TABLE A.23 Differences Between Carter's Actual and Estimated Vote Shares, 1976 Democratic Primaries

		Carter versus Jackson	Carter versus Udall	Carter versus Wallace	Carter versus Brown and Church
24 Feb	New Hampshire	−3.1	4.9	1.7	−1.1
2 Mar	Massachusetts	−1.0	20.2	−13.3	2.5
9 Mar	Florida	−5.9	1.8	10.8	1.8
16 Mar	Illinois	6.5	12.8	−1.1	3.2
23 Mar	North Carolina	0.5	1.7	−1.3	2.8
6 Apr	Wisconsin	−4.7	−4.5	−3.1	0.6
27 Apr	Pennsylvania	−13.9	−9.9	−0.9	0
1 May	Texas	−0.6	5.2	−2.8	1.3
4 May	Alabama	0.4	5.4	−11.6	16.1
	D.C.	−0.3	−6.5	1.1	0.6
	Georgia	2.1	14.6	−4.3	−2.4
	Indiana	−8.6	0.1	2.7	0.6
11 May	Nebraska	3.8	1.8	3.1	22.3
18 May	Maryland	0.5	2.0	0.3	−21.3
	Michigan	3.3	−23.8	−0.1	−0.4
25 May	Arkansas	0.1	4.6	2.8	2.0
	Idaho	0.2	0.9	−1.9	−16.7
	Kentucky	4.7	7.0	1.1	2.0
	Nevada	−3.6	0.3	−1.8	−26.0
	Oregon	−0.6	1.3	0.6	20.1
	Tennessee	−0.4	11.7	7.0	0.8
1 Jun	Montana	−2.8	−6.4	−1.4	−46.0
	Rhode Island	0.4	−5.9	4.5	−1.1
	South Dakota	2.5	−6.5	0.2	14.9
8 Jun	California	−0.4	−0.2	−4.2	5.5
	Ohio	1.6	−4.8	−1.4	−6.2
AVERAGE ERRORS		2.8%	6.3%	3.3%	8.4%

Notes: Differences based on shares of two-candidate vote. Serial correlation of average weekly residuals = −0.032.

Aldrich's (1980a: 232) data on campaign days spent by each candidate in each primary state. I treat the square root of the number of days each candidate spent in each state as an endogenous explanatory variable in the corresponding equations for primary outcomes. Carter's and Jackson's efforts appear in the Carter–Jackson outcome equation in Table A.19, and so on.

The variables used to account for campaign effort and the resulting parameter estimates are shown in Tables A.24 through A.28. The two-stage least squares estimates for the effects of campaign effort in the corresponding primary outcome equations are shown in Tables A.19 through A.22.

TABLE A.24 Parameter Estimates for Carter Campaign Effort, 1976 Democratic Primaries

	Parameter Estimates	Standard Errors
Intercept	−1.688	(1.822)
Liberalism	0.1901	(0.0613)
Liberalism squared	−0.001460	(0.000520)
Home states	−0.600	(0.364)
Percentage urbanized	0.01867	(0.00641)
Carter chances	−7.286	(1.259)

Notes: Dependent variable is square root of Carter "visitation days" in each state. Standard error of equation = 0.680; R^2 = 0.74; N = 26.

TABLE A.25 Parameter Estimates for Jackson Campaign Effort, 1976 Democratic Primaries

	Parameter Estimates	Standard Errors
Intercept	3.500	(3.931)
Liberalism	−0.1491	(0.1338)
Liberalism squared	−0.001378	(0.001122)
Western region	−0.926	(0.727)
Percentage black	−0.0422	(0.0234)
Percentage unionized	0.0494	(0.0366)
Jackson chances	12.719	(6.057)

Notes: Dependent variable is square root of Jackson "visitation days" in each state. Standard error of equation = 1.213; R^2 = 0.48; N = 26.

The parameter estimates for the somewhat simpler analyses of the other four recent nominating campaigns are shown in Tables A.29 through A.32. Substantive discussion of these results is presented in Chapters 9 and 10, as are the state-by-state residuals (in percentage point terms) for each analysis.[13]

[13] The serial correlation coefficients for these campaigns range from −0.271 for the 1980 Republican campaign to 0.156 for the 1980 Democratic campaign and average −0.051. Given these relatively small coefficients, and the very limited number of observations for each campaign, it seemed to me unlikely that any attempt to adjust for the serial correlation would improve the efficiency of the parameter estimates.

TABLE A.26 Parameter Estimates for Udall Campaign Effort, 1976 Democratic Primaries

	Parameter Estimates	Standard Errors
Intercept	−1.057	(1.403)
Liberalism	0.0611	(0.0179)
Western region	−2.660	(0.681)
Percentage black	−0.0444	(0.0225)
Percentage unionized	0.0475	(0.0419)
Percentage urbanized	−0.0208	(0.0152)
Udall chances	7.702	(7.704)

Notes: Dependent variable is square root of Udall "visitation days" in each state. Standard error of equation = 1.259; R^2 = 0.60; N = 26.

TABLE A.27 Parameter Estimates for Wallace Campaign Effort, 1976 Democratic Primaries

	Parameter Estimates	Standard Errors
Intercept	−2.303	(1.349)
Liberalism	0.0305	(0.0186)
Western region	−0.952	(0.582)
Southern region	1.623	(0.688)
Percentage black	−0.0326	(0.0164)
Percentage urbanized	−0.0235	(0.0102)
Wallace chances	7.976	(5.369)

Notes: Dependent variable is square root of Wallace "visitation days" in each state. Standard error of equation = 0.981; R^2 = 0.59; N = 26.

TABLE A.28 Parameter Estimates for Brown and Church Campaign Efforts, 1976 Democratic Primaries

	Parameter Estimates	Standard Errors
Intercept	−8.100	(3.421)
Liberalism	0.1609	(0.1132)
Liberalism squared	−0.001311	(0.000955)
Western region	1.203	(0.745)
Percentage urbanized	−0.0310	(0.0131)
Carter chances	4.597	(2.637)

Notes: Dependent variable is square root of Brown and Church "visitation days" in each state. Standard error of equation = 1.296; R^2 = 0.81; *N* = 26.

TABLE A.29 Parameter Estimates for 1976 Republican Primary Outcomes (Ford versus Reagan)

	Logit Parameter Estimates	Standard Errors
Intercept	1.948	(0.805)
Relative momentum	10.89	(6.53)
Relative risk aversion	19.65	(11.81)
Local information	5.817	(0.028)
Conservatism	−0.0261	(0.0049)
Western region	−0.565	(0.157)
Percentage unionized	0.01751	(0.00796)

Note: Standard error of equation = 0.268; R^2 = 0.75; *N* = 25.

Table A.30 Parameter Estimates for 1980 Democratic Primary Outcomes (Carter versus Kennedy)

	Logit Parameter Estimates	Standard Errors
Intercept	0.010	(1.675)
Relative momentum	4.476	(2.071)
Relative risk aversion	9.396	(4.887)
Local information	3.905	(0.160)
Liberalism	0.0432	(0.0327)
Liberalism squared	−0.000428	(0.000263)
Percentage urban	0.0157	(0.0029)
Percentage unemployed	0.0607	(0.0373)
Southern region	0.407	(0.193)
Northeastern region	−0.644	(0.170)
Home states	0.536	(0.224)

Note: Standard error of equation = 0.251; adjusted R^2 = 0.88; N = 34.

Table A.31 Parameter Estimates for 1980 Republican Primary Outcomes (Reagan versus Bush)

	Logit Parameter Estimates	Standard Errors
Intercept	50.10	(21.60)
Relative momentum	1.418	(0.927)
Relative risk aversion	−23.19	(9.79)
Local information	7.174	(0.693)
Bush withdrawal	1.101	(0.233)
Conservatism	0.0223	(0.0079)
Home states	1.049	(0.286)
Percentage unemployed	0.1682	(0.0510)
Percentage urban	0.01013	(0.00528)
Anderson vote	0.01374	(0.00913)

Note: Standard error of equation = 0.397; adjusted R^2 = 0.83; N = 32.

TABLE A.32 Parameter Estimates for 1984 Democratic Primary Outcomes (Mondale versus Hart)

	Logit Parameter Estimates	Standard Errors
Intercept	2.153	(1.517)
Relative momentum	1.085	(0.749)
Relative risk aversion	0.883	(0.291)
Local information	3.811	(0.452)
Liberalism	0.0389	(0.0404)
Liberalism squared	0.000396	(0.000329)
Anderson support, 1980	0.1372	(0.0301)
Percentage urban	0.00843	(0.00335)
Percentage black	0.0198	(0.0158)
Southern region	−0.684	(0.273)
Western region	−0.282	(0.195)
Jackson vote	0.0105	(0.0173)

Note: Standard error of equation = 0.289; adjusted R^2 = 0.73; N = 28.

REFERENCES

Adams, William C. 1985. "Media Coverage of Campaign '84: A Preliminary Report." In Michael J. Robinson and Austin Ranney, eds., *The Mass Media in Campaign '84: Articles from Public Opinion Magazine.* Washington, D.C.: American Enterprise Institute.

Aldrich, John H. 1980a. *Before the Convention: Strategies and Choices in Presidential Nomination Campaigns.* Chicago: University of Chicago Press.

———. 1980b. "A Dynamic Model of Presidential Nomination Campaigns." *American Political Science Review* 74: 651–69.

Arrow, Kenneth J. 1951, 1963. *Social Choice and Individual Values,* 1st and 2d eds. New Haven: Yale University Press.

Arterton, F. Christopher. 1978a. "Campaign Organizations Confront the Media-Political Environment." In James David Barber, ed., *Race for the Presidency.* Englewood Cliffs, N.J.: Prentice-Hall.

———. 1978b. "The Media Politics of Presidential Campaigns: A Study of the Carter Nomination Drive." In James David Barber, ed., *Race for the Presidency.* Englewood Cliffs, N.J.: Prentice-Hall.

———. 1984. *Media Politics: The News Strategies of Presidential Campaigns.* Lexington, Mass.: Heath.

Bain, Richard C., and Judith H. Parris. 1973. *Convention Decisions and Voting Records,* 2d ed. Washington, D.C.: Brookings Institution.

Barone, Michael, Grant Ujifusa, and Douglas Matthews. 1979. *Almanac of American Politics 1980.* New York: Dutton.

Bartels, Larry M. 1985. "Expectations and Preferences in Presidential Nominating Campaigns." *American Political Science Review* 79: 804–15.

———. 1986. "Issue Voting Under Uncertainty: An Empirical Test." *American Journal of Political Science* 30: 709–28.

———. 1987. "Candidate Choice and the Dynamics of the Presidential Nominating Process." *American Journal of Political Science* 31: 1–30.

Beniger, James R. 1976. "Winning the Presidential Nomination: National Polls and State Primary Elections, 1936–1972." *Public Opinion Quarterly* 40: 22–38.

Berelson, Bernard R., Paul F. Lazarsfeld, and William N. McPhee. 1954. *Voting: A Study of Opinion Formation in a Presidential Campaign.* Chicago: University of Chicago Press.

Bicker, William E. 1978. "Network Television News and the 1976 Presidential Primaries: A Look From the Networks' Side of the Cameras." In James David Barber, *Race for the Presidency.* Englewood Cliffs, N.J.: Prentice-Hall.

Black, Duncan. 1958. *The Theory of Committees and Elections.* Cambridge: Cambridge University Press.

Blackwell, David. 1969. *Basic Statistics.* New York: McGraw-Hill.

Bluhm, William T. 1987. "Liberalism as the Aggregation of Individual Preferences: Problems of Coherence and Rationality in Social Choice." In Kenneth L. Deutsch and Walter Soffer, eds., *The Crisis of Liberal Democracy: A Straussian Perspective.* Albany: State University of New York Press.

Bode, Kenneth A., and Carol F. Casey. 1980. "Party Reform: Revisionism Revisited." In Robert A. Goldwin, ed., *Political Parties in the Eighties.* Washington, D.C.: American Enterprise Institute.

Brady, Henry E. 1984a. "Knowledge, Strategy, and Momentum in Presidential Primaries." Paper presented at the Weingart Conference, California Institute of Technology.

———. 1984b. "Chances, Utilities, and Voting in Presidential Primaries." Paper presented at the Annual Meeting of the Public Choice Society, Phoenix.

———. 1985a. "Media and Momentum." Paper presented at the Annual Meeting of the American Political Science Association, New Orleans.

———. 1985b. "Conventions or Primaries?" Occasional Paper No. 85–89, Center for American Political Studies, Harvard University.

Brady, Henry E., and Larry M. Bartels. 1982. "An Agenda for Studying Presidential Primaries." SRC Working Paper No. 62, Survey Research Center, University of California, Berkeley.

Brady, Henry E., and Richard Johnston. 1985. "Conventions versus Primaries: A Canadian-American Comparison." Paper presented at the World Congress of the International Political Science Association, Paris.

Brady, Henry E., and Paul M. Sniderman. 1985. "Attitude Attribution: A Group Basis for Political Reasoning." *American Political Science Review* 79: 1061–78.

Brams, Steven J. 1978. *The Presidential Election Game.* New Haven: Yale University Press.

Brams, Steven J., and Peter C. Fishburn. 1983. *Approval Voting.* Boston: Birkhauser.

Campbell, Angus, Philip E. Converse, Warren E. Miller, and Donald E. Stokes. 1960. *The American Voter.* New York: Wiley.

Cannon, Lou, and William Peterson. 1980. "GOP." In Richard Harwood, ed., *The Pursuit of the Presidency 1980.* New York: Berkley Books.

Carroll, Lewis. 1865. *Alice's Adventures in Wonderland.* Reprint. Berkeley: University of California Press, 1982.

Ceaser, James W. 1979. *Presidential Selection: Theory and Development.* Princeton: Princeton University Press.

———. 1982. *Reforming the Reforms: A Critical Analysis of the Presidential Selection Process.* Cambridge, Mass.: Ballinger.

Chester, Lewis, Godfrey Hodgson, and Bruce Page. 1969. *An American Melodrama: The Presidential Campaign of 1968.* New York: Viking.

Cohen, Morton N., ed. 1982. *The Selected Letters of Lewis Carroll.* New York: Pantheon.

Conover, Pamela Johnston, and Stanley Feldman. 1984. "Candidate Perception in an Ambiguous World: Campaigns, Cues, and Inference Processes." Rev. version of paper presented at the Annual Meeting of the American Political Science Association, Washington, D. C.

Crotty, William J. 1978. *Decision for the Democrats: Reforming the Party Structure.* Baltimore: Johns Hopkins University Press.

———. 1983. *Party Reform.* New York: Longman.

Crotty, William, and John S. Jackson III. 1985. *Presidential Primaries and Nominations.* Washington, D.C.: Congressional Quarterly Press.

Crouse, Timothy. 1973. *The Boys on the Bus: Riding with the Campaign Press Corps.* New York: Ballantine.

David, Paul T., and James W. Ceaser. 1980. *Proportional Representation in Presidential Nominating Politics.* Charlottesville: University Press of Virginia.

David, Paul T., Ralph M. Goldman, and Richard C. Bain. 1960. *The Politics of National Party Conventions.* Washington, D.C.: Brookings Institution.

Davis, James W. 1967. *Presidential Primaries: Road to the White House.* New York: Crowell.

[Democratic Party] Commission on Party Structure and Delegate Selection. 1970. *Mandate for Reform.* Washington, D. C.: Democratic National Committee.

Edelman, Murray. 1971. *Politics as Symbolic Action: Mass Arousal and Quiescence.* Chicago: Markham.

Enelow, James, and Melvin J. Hinich. 1984. *The Spatial Theory of Voting: An Introduction.* Cambridge: Cambridge University Press.

Feldman, Stanley. 1985. "The Reliability and Stability of Policy Positions: Evidence from a Five-Wave Panel Study." Paper presented at the Annual Meeting of the American Political Science Association, New Orleans.

Flanigan, William H., and Nancy H. Zingale. 1985. "Changing Perceptions of Presidential Candidates during the 1984 Primary Season." Paper presented at the Annual Meeting of the Western Political Science Association, Las Vegas.

Foley, John, Dennis A. Britton, and Eugene B. Everett, Jr., eds. 1980. *Nominating a President: The Process and the Press.* New York: Praeger.

Gardner, Martin. 1960. *The Annotated Alice.* New York: Bramhall House.

Geer, John G. 1986. "Assessing Voters in Presidential Primaries." Arizona State University.

Germond, Jack, and Jules Witcover. 1981. *Blue Smoke and Mirrors.* New York: Viking.

Gopoian, J. David. 1982. "Issue Preferences and Candidate Choice in Presidential Primaries." *American Journal of Political Science* 26: 523–46.

Greenfield, Jeff. 1982. *The Real Campaign: How the Media Missed the Story of the 1980 Campaign.* New York: Summit Books.

Gurian, Paul-Henri. 1986. "Resource Allocation Strategies in Presidential Nomination Campaigns." *American Journal of Political Science* 30: 802–21.

Harwood, Richard, ed. 1980. *The Pursuit of the Presidency 1980.* New York: Berkley Books.

Hess, Stephen. 1978. *The Presidential Campaign.* Rev. ed. Washington, D.C.: Brookings Institution.

Joslyn, Richard. 1976. "The Impact of Decision Rules in Multi-Candidate Campaigns: The Case of the 1972 Democratic Presidential Nomination." *Public Choice* 37: 425–34.

Kamarck, Elaine Ciulla. 1986. *Structure as Strategy: Presidential Nominating Politics Since Reform.* Ph.D. diss., Department of Political Science, University of California, Berkeley.

Keech, William R., and Donald R. Matthews. 1976. *The Party's Choice.* Washington, D.C.: Brookings Institution.

Keeter, Scott, and Cliff Zukin. 1984. *Uninformed Choice.* New York: Praeger.

Key, V. O., Jr. 1956. *American State Politics: An Introduction.* New York: Knopf.

———. 1964. *Politics, Parties, and Pressure Groups.* 5th ed. New York: Crowell.

Knight, Frank H. 1951. "Ethics and the Economic Interpretation." In *The Ethics of Competition and Other Essays.* London: Allen & Unwin.

Lemann, Nicholas. 1980. In Richard Harwood, ed., *The Pursuit of the Presidency 1980.* New York: Berkley Books.

Lengle, James I. 1981. *Representation and Presidential Primaries: The Democratic Party in the Post-Reform Era.* Wesport, Conn.: Greenwood Press.

Lengle, James I., and Byron E. Shafer, eds. 1983. *Presidential Politics: Readings on Nominations and Elections.* 2d ed. New York: St. Martin's Press.

Lindley, D. V. 1985. *Making Decisions.* 2d ed. London: Wiley & Sons.

Markus, Gregory B., and Philip E. Converse. 1979. "A Dynamic Simultaneous Equation Model of Electoral Choice." *American Political Science Review* 73: 1055–70.

Marshall, Thomas R. 1981. *Presidential Nominations in a Reform Age.* New York: Praeger.

Matthews, Donald R. 1978. " 'Winnowing': The News Media and the 1976 Presidential Nominations." In James David Barber, ed., *Race for the Presidency.* Englewood Cliffs, N.J.: Prentice-Hall.

McFadden, Daniel. 1976. "Quantal Choice Analysis: A Survey." *Annals of Economic and Social Measurement* 5: 363–90.

McKelvey, Richard D., and Peter C. Ordeshook. 1982. "Elections With Limited Information: A Fulfilled Expectations Model Using Contemporaneous Poll and Endorsement Data as Information Sources." California Institute of Technology and Carnegie Mellon University.

Moore, David. 1985. "The Death of Politics in New Hampshire." In Michael J. Robinson and Austin Ranney, eds., *The Mass Media in Campaign '84: Articles from Public Opinion Magazine.* Washington, D.C.: American Enterprise Institute.

Moore, Jonathan, ed. 1981. *The Campaign for President: 1980 in Retrospect.* Cambridge, Mass.: Ballinger.

———, ed. 1986. *Campaign for President: The Managers Look at '84.* Dover, Mass.: Auburn House.

Moore, Jonathan, and Janet Fraser, eds. 1977. *Campaign for President: The Managers Look at '76.* Cambridge, Mass.: Ballinger.

Niemi, Richard G., and Larry M. Bartels. 1984. "The Responsiveness of Approval Voting to Political Circumstances." *PS* 17: 571–77.

Niemi, Richard G., and Herbert F. Weisberg, eds. 1972. *Probability Models of Collective Decision Making.* Columbus, Ohio: Charles E. Merrill.

Orren, Gary R. 1985. "The Nomination Process: Vicissitudes of Candidate Selection." In Michael Nelson, ed., *The Elections of 1984.* Washington, D.C.: Congressional Quarterly Press.

Page, Benjamin I. 1976. "The Theory of Political Ambiguity." *American Political Science Review* 70: 742–52.

———. 1978. *Choices and Echoes in Presidential Elections: Rational Man and Electoral Democracy.* Chicago: University of Chicago Press.

Page, Benjamin I., and Calvin C. Jones. 1979. "Reciprocal Effects of Policy Preferences, Party Loyalties and the Vote." *American Political Science Review* 73: 1071–89.

Parent, T. Wayne, Calvin C. Jillson, and Ronald E. Weber. 1987. "Voting Outcomes in the 1984 Democratic Party Primaries and Caucuses." *American Political Science Review* 81: 67–84.

Parsons, Talcott. 1937. *The Structure of Social Action: A Study in Social Theory With Special Reference to a Group of Recent European Writers.* 2 vols. Reprint. New York: Free Press, 1968.

Patterson, Thomas E. 1980. *The Mass Media Election: How Americans Choose Their President.* New York: Praeger.

Plott, Charles R. 1976. "Axiomatic Social Choice Theory: An Overview and Interpretation." *American Journal of Political Science* 20: 511–96.

Polsby, Nelson W. 1980. "The News Media as an Alternative to Party in the Presidential Selection Process." In Robert A. Goldwin, ed., *Political Parties in the Eighties.* Washington, D.C.: American Enterprise Institute.

———. 1983. *Consequences of Party Reform.* Oxford: Oxford University Press.

Polsby, Nelson W., and Aaron Wildavsky. 1964, 1971, 1976, 1980. *Presidential Elections: Strategies of American Electoral Politics.* 1st, 3d, 4th, and 5th eds. New York: Scribner's.

Pomper, Gerald M. 1985. "The Nominations." In Marlene Michels Pomper, ed., *The Election of 1984.* Chatham, N.J.: Chatham House.

Popkin, Samuel L. *Voting and Campaigning in Presidential Elections.* Preliminary results provided by the author in personal communication. Forthcoming.

Rae, Douglas. 1980. "An Altimeter for Mr. Escher's Stairway: A Comment on William H. Riker's 'Implications from the Disequilibrium of Majority Rule for the Study of Institutions.' " *American Political Science Review* 74: 451–55.

Ranney, Austin. 1972. "Turnout and Representation in Presidential Primary Elections." *American Political Science Review* 66: 21–37.

———. 1975. *Curing the Mischiefs of Faction: Party Reform in America.* Berkeley: University of California Press.

———. 1977. *Participation in American Presidential Nominations: 1976.* Washington, D.C.: American Enterprise Institute.

Reeves, Richard. 1977. *Convention.* New York: Harcourt Brace Jovanovich.

Reid, T. R. 1980. "Kennedy." In Richard Harwood, ed., *The Pursuit of the Presidency 1980.* New York: Berkley Books.

Riker, William H. 1980. "Implications from the Disequilibrium of Majority Rule for the Study of Institutions." *American Political Science Review* 74: 432–46.

———. 1982. *Liberalism Against Populism: A Confrontation Between the Theory of Democracy and the Theory of Social Choice.* San Francisco: Freeman.

Robinson, Michael J. 1981. "The Media in 1980." In Austin Ranney, ed., *The American Elections of 1980.* Washington, D.C.: American Enterprise Institute.

Robinson, Michael J., and Maura Clancey. 1985. "Teflon Politics." In Michael J. Robinson and Austin Ranney, eds., *The Mass Media in Campaign '84: Articles from Public Opinion Magazine.* Washington, D.C.: American Enterprise Institute.

Robinson, Michael J., and Margaret A. Sheehan. 1983. *Over the Wire and On TV.* New York: Russell Sage Foundation.

Rosenstone, Steven J. 1983. *Forecasting Presidential Elections.* New Haven: Yale University Press.

Runyon, John H., Jennefer Verdini, and Sally S. Runyon. 1971. *Source Book of American Presidential Campaign and Election Statistics, 1948–1968.* New York: Ungar.

Saloma, John S. III, and Frederick H. Sontag. 1972. *Parties: The Real Opportunity for Effective Citizen Politics.* New York: Knopf.

Schattschneider, E. E. 1942. *Party Government.* New York: Holt, Rinehart and Winston.

Schram, Martin. 1980. "Carter." In Richard Harwood, ed., *The Pursuit of the Presidency 1980.* New York: Berkley Books.

———. 1977. *Running for President 1976: The Carter Campaign.* New York: Stein and Day.

Shafer, Byron. 1984. *Quiet Revolution: The Struggle for the Democratic Party and the Shaping of Post Reform Politics.* New York: Russell Sage Foundation.

Shanks, J. Merrill, Warren E. Miller, Henry E. Brady, and Bradley L. Palmquist. 1985. "Viability, Electability, and Presidential 'Preference': Initial Results from the 1984 NES Continuous Monitoring Design." Paper presented at the Annual Meeting of the Midwest Political Science Association, Chicago.

Shanks, J. Merrill, and Bradley Palmquist. 1981. "Intra-Party Candidate Choice in 1980: An Early Portrait of Pre-Convention Preferences." Paper presented at the Annual Meeting of the Midwest Political Science Association, Cincinnati.

Shepsle, Kenneth A. 1972. "The Strategy of Ambiguity: Uncertainty and Electoral Competition." *American Political Science Review* 66: 555–68.

———. 1979. "Institutional Arrangements and Equilibrium in Multidimensional Voting Models." *American Journal of Political Science* 23: 27–59.

Slovic, Paul, and Sarah Lichtenstein. 1971. "Comparison of Bayesian and Regression Approaches to the Study of Information Processing in Judgment." *Organizational Behavior and Human Performance* 6: 649–744.

Smith, Carolyn, ed. N.d. *The '84 Vote.* New York: ABC News.

Stanley, Harold W., and Charles D. Hadley. 1987. "The Southern Presidential Primary: Regional Intentions With National Implications." *Publius.* Forthcoming.

Stavely, E. S. 1972. *Greek and Roman Voting and Elections.* Ithaca, N.Y.: Cornell University Press.

Straffin, Phillip D., Jr. 1977. "The Bandwagon Curve." *American Journal of Political Science* 21: 695–709.

Sundquist, James L. 1983. *Dynamics of the Party System: Alignment and Realignment of Political Parties in the United States.* Rev. ed. Washington, D.C.: The Brookings Institution.

Wattier, Mark J. 1983. "Ideological Voting in 1980 Republican Presidential Primaries." *Journal of Politics* 45: 1016–26.

WGBH. 1984. *So You Want to Be President* (FRONTLINE transcript No. 216). Boston: WGBH Transcripts.

White, Theodore H. 1969. *The Making of the President 1968.* New York: Atheneum.

Witcover, Jules. 1977. *Marathon: The Pursuit of the Presidency 1972–1976.* New York: New American Library.

Wolfinger, Raymond E., and Steven J. Rosenstone. 1980. *Who Votes?* New Haven: Yale University Press.

Wright, Gerald C., Robert S. Erikson, and John P. McIver. 1985. "Measuring State Partisanship and Ideology with Survey Data." *Journal of Politics* 47: 469–89.

Zaller, John. 1984. "Toward a Theory of the Survey Response." Paper presented at the Annual Meeting of the American Political Science Association, Washington, D.C.

INDEX

Library of Congress Cataloging-in-Publication Data

Bartels, Larry M., 1956–
Presidential primaries and the dynamics of public choice / Larry M. Bartels.
p. cm.
ISBN 0–691–07765–7. ISBN 0–691–02283–6 (pbk.)
1. Presidents—United States—Nomination. 2. Primaries—United States.
I. Title.
JK522.B37 1988 324.5′4—dc19 87–38187 CIP

Larry Bartels is Associate Professor of Political Science at the University of Rochester.